COMMON
# Insects
## OF Texas
### AND SURROUNDING STATES

Number Seventy-one
The Corrie Herring Hooks Series

# COMMON
# Insects
# OF Texas
## AND SURROUNDING STATES
## A FIELD GUIDE

JOHN ABBOTT AND KENDRA ABBOTT

University of Texas Press ✦ Austin

Requests for permission to reproduce material from this work should be sent to:
  Permissions
  University of Texas Press
  P.O. Box 7819
  Austin, TX 78713-7819
  utpress.utexas.edu

♾ The paper used in this book meets the minimum requirements of ANSI/NISO
Z39.48-1992 (R1997) (Permanence of Paper).

Library of Congress Cataloging-in-Publication Data

Names: Abbott, John C., 1972– author. | Abbott, Kendra, author.
Title: Common insects of Texas and surrounding states : a field guide / John Ab-
  bott and Kendra Abbott.
Description: First edition. | Austin, TX : University of Texas Press, 2020. | Series:
  The Corrie Herring Hooks series ; no. 71 | Includes bibliographical references
  and index.
Identifiers: LCCN 2020007556
  ISBN 978-1-4773-1035-9 (paperback)
  ISBN 978-1-4773-2235-2 (ebook)
  ISBN 978-1-4773-2237-6 (ebook other)
Subjects: LCSH: Insects—Texas—Identification.
Classification: LCC QL466 .A23 2020 | DDC 595.709764—dc23
LC record available at https://lccn.loc.gov/2020007556


doi:10.7560/310359

# Contents

# Contents

# Key to Color Groupings

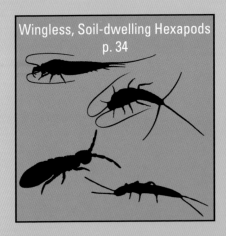

Wingless, Soil-dwelling Hexapods
p. 34

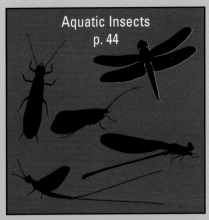

Aquatic Insects
p. 44

Small Insect Orders
p. 70

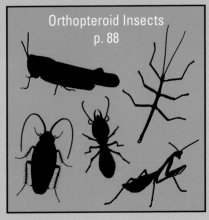

Orthopteroid Insects
p. 88

True Bugs
p. 120

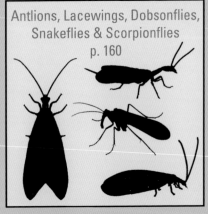

Antlions, Lacewings, Dobsonflies,
Snakeflies & Scorpionflies
p. 160

Beetles
p. 176

Flies
p. 250

Butterflies & Moths
p. 276

Ants, Bees, Wasps & Sawflies
p. 358

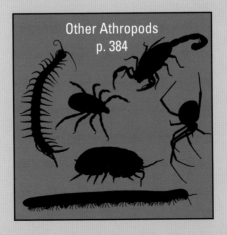

Other Athropods
p. 384

Glowworm Beetle
(*Phengodes* sp.)

# Acknowledgments

We have tried to create a unique guide to a diverse fauna that will hopefully serve a wide audience. It was however not done alone. We have many influences, but would like to recognize particularly Eric Eaton and Ken Kaufman's *Kaufman Field Guide to Insects of North America*, Seabrooke Leckie and David Beadle's Peterson Field Guides to Moths and Richard Bradley's *Common Spiders of North America*. We use them all often and tried to incorporate what we consider to be the best elements of each in this book.

We would like to thank the following people for reviewing various chapters of this book and providing valuable feedback: David Baumgardner, Ernie Bernard, David Bowles, Jerry Cook, Christopher Dietrich, Dan Hardy, Joshua Jones, Boris Kondratieff, Joe Lapp, Katrina Menard, Jack Neff, John Oswald, Ed Riley, Chuck Sexton, John Stidham, Brandon Woo and Diane Young. Valerie Bugh, James Kennedy, and Benjamin Schwartz graciously read over the entire book for us and provided valuable comments and feedback.

We are also thankful to Alysa Joaquin, Maryanne Rodriguez, and Diane Young who provided assistance with the collecting of specimens for us. Charlie Covell and Andy Warren (McGuire Center for Lepidoptera & Biodiversity), Rachel Hawkins (Museum of Comparative Zoology), and Alex Wild (University of Texas Insect Collection) provided access and/or loaned us specimens needed to complete the book.

The BugGuide.net and iNaturalist.org communities are a tremendous resource and collectively provide an amazing wealth of knowledge. Without help from the members of this community, this book would have certainly suffered. Many users on one or both of these sites assisted us in providing locations and identifications of species.

We thank the many individuals that we have spent time with chasing bugs throughout Texas. This book would not have been possible without the many friendships we have forged in Texas over the years. We continue to be grateful for all these friends sharing their tremendous knowledge with us.

Finally, we would like to thank Casey Kittrell, Lynne Ferguson, Linda Ronan, and the entire team at the University of Texas Press for all their help in seeing the book through its final production stages.

# Introduction

Clouded Skipper
(*Lerema accius*)

**CLASSIFICATION & NOMENCLATURE**   More than 90% of all animal species belong to the phylum Arthropoda and the vast majority of arthropods are insects. With such diversity, it can be difficult to categorize groups with specific characteristics; the takeaway being that there are almost always exceptions to generalities. Having said that, the Arthropoda are a group of animals that have a segmented body (head, thorax and or abdomen), exoskeleton, and paired jointed appendages.

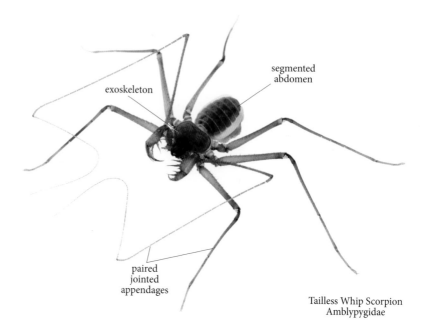

segmented abdomen

exoskeleton

paired jointed appendages

Tailless Whip Scorpion
Amblypygidae

In order to study, communicate, and better understand the relationships within such diversity, we use a binomial system of classification. This system, first established by the eighteenth century Swedish botanist Carl Linnaeus, groups organisms hierarchical by similarity. The fundamental unit in this system is the species, made up of a genus and specific epithet. You can think of these as a first and last name. A species is a group of organisms that, at least theoretically, are reproductively isolated and are similar in appearance, genetics, and ecology. One or more similar species are grouped together in a genus, multiple genera in a family, multiple families in an order and so on. While it can be frustrating, it is important to understand that because the evolutionary process is constant, resulting in continual change, species are not fixed. In addition, our understanding of the relationships of species and the tools that help elucidate these relationships is constantly changing. All of this means that the names themselves are not static. Remember that in the end, the goal is to communicate and to show the relationship among species and groups.

**Domain** Eukarya
**Kingdom** Animalia
**Phylum** Arthropoda
**Class** Hexapoda
**Order** Odonata
**Family** Libellulidae
**Genus** *Plathemis*
**Specific epithet** *lydia*
**Author & Year** (Drury, 1773)

The genus and specific epithet are combined to form the species name that is latinized in its spelling and italicized. Only the first letter of the generic name is capitalized. The original author and year that a species was described also often accompanies the species name. If it is determined that the species belongs in a different genus from the one it was originally placed in, the author and year are placed in parentheses. So in the example above, Drury described *Libellula lydia* in 1773. A subsequent author determined the species was best placed in the genus *Plathemis*, so it is correctly written as *Plathemis lydia* (Drury, 1773).

In addition to the above categories, intermediate groups are often used. Some of these, such as subphylum or superfamily are obvious in their placement. Others, like tribe (a designation between subfamily and genus), are not as obvious. Families always end in the suffix "-idae," pronounced "dē" and subfamilies end in the suffix "-inae" pronounced "nē." The broad groups that most enthusiasts are familiar with when it comes to insects, are orders. There is no set suffix to designate orders, but within insects, most of them end in "-ptera," which means wing.

Common or English names are common for birds, mammals and even reptiles and amphibians. They are often used more frequently than the scientific names in these groups. Most insects do not have common names, though more and more are being coined, in large part to facilitate the interest of enthusiasts. As a result, it is the more common and readily identifiable groups (butterflies and dragonflies, for example) that have been given these names. Even for those groups that have them, they are not very well standardized. In this book, we have tried to use common names wherever possible because we feel it best serves our primary audience. We tried to use the most widely accepted common name, usually represented in BugGuide. net or iNaturalist.org. An additional resource is the Entomological Society of America's Common Names of Insects Database (www.entsoc.org/common-names). We however encourage the use of scientific names because while they do change, they are governed under a set of official rules and show the relationship of the insects they are naming. In this guide, we capitalize common names of species.

Within the Arthropoda, five subphyla are generally recognized:

Subphylum Trilobitomorpha – trilobites (extinct)
Subphylum Chelicerata – spiders, scorpions, horseshoe crabs & sea spiders
Subphylum Myriapoda – centipedes & millipedes
Subphylum Crustacea – shrimp, barnacles, lobsters, crabs & woodlice
Subphylum Hexapoda – insects

**TRILOBITOMORPHA**

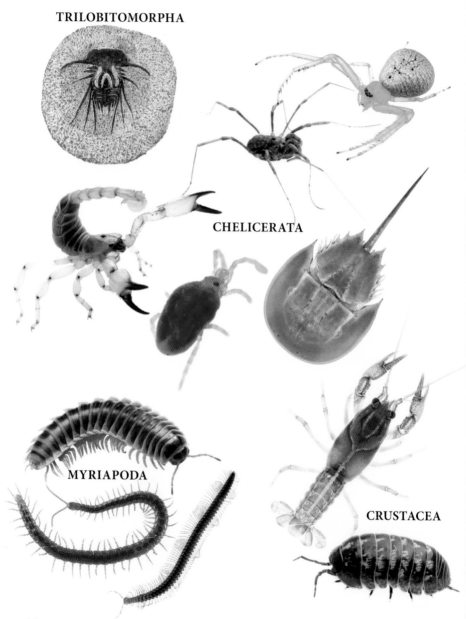

**CHELICERATA**

**MYRIAPODA**

**CRUSTACEA**

**WHAT IS AN INSECT?**  This field guide focuses on the Hexapoda and more specifically, the class Insecta within it.  Insects are the largest group within the phylum Arthropoda and the most diverse group of animals on the planet. In addition to the features mentioned uniting the phylum, they posses a three-part body, three pairs of jointed legs, compound eyes and one pair of antennae. Most also bear a pair of wings.

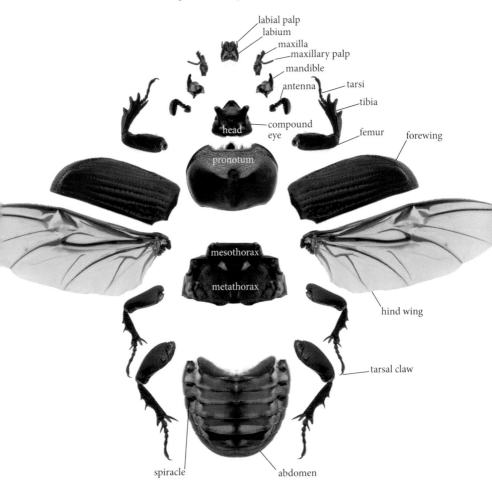

Insects have an open circulatory system, which means hemolymph (blood) flows openly within the body, bathing tissues and organs. They respire through the simple diffusion of gasses across the body membranes and through a series of tubules called trachea that are connected to the outside via spiracles. They exhibit a dazzling array of feeding habits (fluids, solid, plant, animal) and can be found in nearly every habitat imaginable. The single exception being the open ocean where only a few species have managed to invade.

**INSECT DIVERSITY**   It is hard to say how many species of insects are known, much less how many actually exist. Digital databases have made it easier and the numbers more accurate, but for the large groups, they are still just estimates. It is also the case that insect species are still being described on a daily basis. The numbers in the table to the right are taken from various sources and in most cases provide approximations. Insects are most diverse in tropical regions with about 10%, or just under 100,000 species, occurring in North America (N.A.), north of Mexico. As much as 30%, or nearly 30,000 species, of the North American insect fauna occur in Texas making it likely the most diverse state. This is due to its large size and geographic positioning. Like no other state, it has a true mix of eastern and western species and temperate and tropical species.

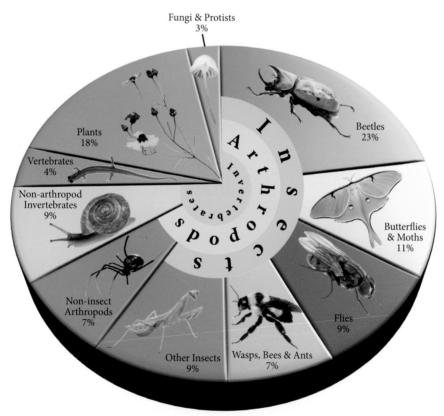

With over 1.7 million species currently described, the above pie graph shows the relative proportions of major groups. Seventy-five percent of described species are invertebrates; it is estimated that this number is probably closer to 95%. Sixty-five percent of all described species are arthropods and nearly 60% are insects. The numbers used above are extracted from The World Conservation Union (IUCN Red List of Threatened Species 2014.3. Summary Statistics for Globally Threatened Species. Table 1: Numbers of threatened species by major groups of organisms, 1996-2018).

| Group | Species in Texas | Species in N.A. | Species in the World |
|-------|-----------------:|----------------:|---------------------:|
| Springtails (Collembola) | 250* | 1,056 | 8,977 |
| Two-pronged Bristletails (Diplura) | 10 | 173 | 800 |
| Bristletails (Archaeognatha) | 2 | 35 | 350 |
| Silverfish (Zygentoma) | 10 | 19 | 120 |
| Mayflies (Ephemeroptera) | 130 | 657 | 3,000 |
| Dragonflies and Damselflies (Odonata) | 246 | 461 | 6,250 |
| Stoneflies (Plecoptera) | 28 | 670 | 3,400 |
| Caddisflies (Trichoptera) | 218 | 1,492 | 13,600 |
| Earwigs (Dermaptera) | 15 | 27 | 2,000 |
| Webspinners (Embiidina) | 4* | 11 | 380 |
| Angel Insects (Zoraptera) | 1 | 2 | 44 |
| Book, Bark and Parasitic Lice (Psocodea) | 754* | 1,220 | 8,000 |
| Thrips (Thysanoptera) | 200* | 700* | 6,000 |
| Fleas (Siphonaptera) | 100* | 325 | 2,500 |
| Twisted-winged Parasites (Strepsiptera) | 19 | 84 | 600 |
| Grasshoppers, Katydids and Crickets (Orthoptera) | 525 | 1,200* | 20,000 |
| Walkingsticks (Phasmatodea) | 16 | 33 | 3,000 |
| Mantids (Mantodea) | 14 | 20 | 2,300 |
| Roaches (Blattodea) | 45 | 50 | 4,400 |
| Termites (Blattodea) | 15 | 44 | 3,106 |
| True Bugs (Hemiptera) | 3,000* | 10,200* | 70,000 |
| Lacewings, Antlions and Allies (Neuroptera) | 195 | 338 | 4,670 |
| Alderflies, Dobsonflies and Fishflies (Megaloptera) | 13 | 45 | 300 |
| Snakeflies (Raphidioptera) | 1 | 21 | 260 |
| Scorpionflies (Mecoptera) | 7 | 85 | 600 |
| Beetles (Coleoptera) | 7,800* | 25,200* | 400,000 |
| Flies (Diptera) | 5,100* | 17,000* | 153,000 |
| Butterflies and Moths (Lepidoptera) | 5,088 | 12,423 | 180,000 |
| Ants, Bees, Wasps and Sawflies (Hymenoptera) | 5,000* | 18,000* | 150,000 |
| **TOTALS** | 28,806 | 91,591 | 1,047,707 |

*Indicates an approximation. All world species numbers are approximate.

**INSECT GROWTH AND DEVELOPMENT**  Insects grow by shedding their exoskeleton through a process called molting. With each molt, they shed their outer body linings as well as the linings of the fore- and hindgut and respiratory tubes. It is a precarious time that may happen nearly instantly or can take hours depending on the species. It is not uncommon to find the shed skins, called exuviae, of insects clinging to vegetation, rocks and man-made structures. Right after molting, the insect is usually soft-bodied, pale or even white in color, and very fragile. Each molt that an insect goes through is called an instar.

**Insect Exuviae**

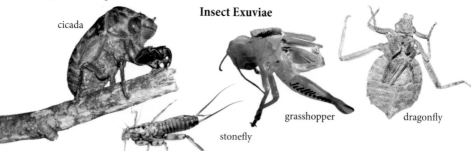

cicada

grasshopper

dragonfly

stonefly

One of the keys to the success of insects is their ability to radically transform themselves, a process called metamorphosis. Insects metamorphosis is either simple (Ametabolous and Hemimetabolous) or complete (Holometabolous). Ametabolous development occurs in primitively wingless Hexapods (springtails, two-pronged bristletails, bristletails and silverfish). Nymphs (the immature stage) hatch from an egg looking like a smaller version of the adult. Unlike all other insects, they continue to molt after reaching sexual maturity. The nymphs and adults are often found living together.

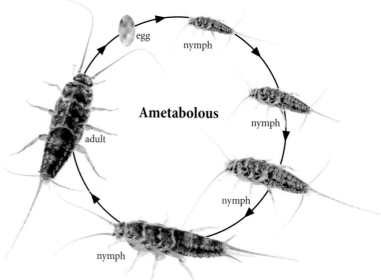

egg

nymph

**Ametabolous**

nymph

nymph

adult

nymph

Insects that develop external wings as nymphs go through Hemimetabolous metamorphosis and include the dragonflies, mayflies, stoneflies, grasshoppers, mantids, walkingsticks, true bugs and a few other related orders. The nymph hatches from an egg and goes through a series of molts (5 to 20 or more, depending upon the species) until reaching a winged, sexually mature adult. With each molt, the external wing pads visible on the nymph get larger and larger. In some groups the nymphs and adults are found in the same habitat (e.g., true bugs and grasshoppers) and in others the nymphs may be aquatic, while the adults are not (e.g., dragonflies and mayflies).

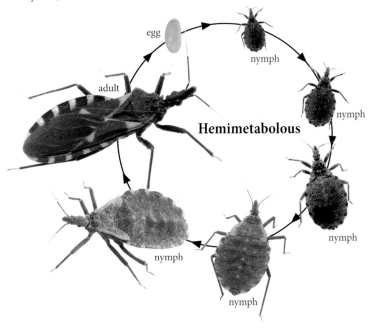

Complete metamorphosis is the type of development most familiar to those just getting interested in insects. It involves an additional stage called the pupa that occurs between the larva (immature) and adult stages. During this stage, the insect undergoes a complete tissue breakdown and rebuilding. This type of development is found in the most familiar of insect groups (butterflies, beetles, wasps and flies). Insect species with complete development have larvae that look remarkably different from the adults. They do not develop external wing pads and often have different mouthparts and feeding habits. They go through fewer (usually three to five) molts than insects with simple metamorphosis. The evolutionary development of the pupa is responsible for a species radiation in insects. This is evident by only one third of insect orders undergoing this type of metamorphosis, yet 90% of all species are holometabolous. There is no doubt that holometaboly has been responsible for much of the success in insects.

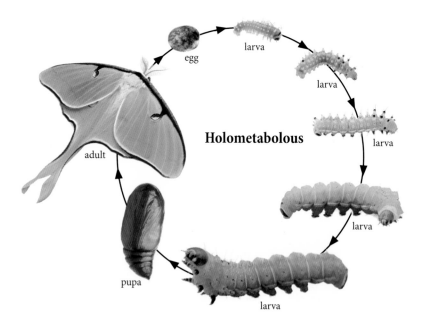

egg
larva
larva
**Holometabolous**
larva
larva
larva
adult
pupa
larva

**STUDYING INSECTS**  One of the best ways to learn about insects is to make a collection. Before the age of digital photography, this is how every insect enthusiast and professional invariably got started. We don't encourage collecting and killing insects just for the sake of killing, but one of the reasons that insects are so popular is their accessibility. They are literally everywhere, in all terrestrial and freshwater habitats that can you imagine. This, along with their reproductive strategy, which typically results in dozens, to hundreds or even thousands of offspring per individual, makes them the perfect subject for every naturalist. Additionally, entomology is a field in which enthusiasts and non-professionals can make serious contributions. There are likely new species waiting to be discovered in your own yard or local park.

Physical collections are critical for the discovery and description of new species. They are also required for genetics studies that have proved so important in understanding the relationships of insects. If you do choose to make an insect collection, we encourage you to take it seriously and consider collecting for a local university or museum collection. A discussion of the proper curatorial techniques is beyond the scope of this field guide, but there are lots of resources online and in print available to guide you through the process.

Not everyone is going to want to physically collect insects and that is fine. As already mentioned, digital photography has resulted in a resurgence of interest in insects. That is because nearly everyone now carries around a great camera with them, on their phone, everywhere they go. If you want to take it to the next level, there are a host of more advanced digital cameras available. More importantly, but as a result of all of the photos of insects that have been generated, there are numerous resources and communities available online to help with

Curated collection of beetles at The University of Alabama.

identification. Social media platforms like FaceBook (FaceBook.com) are home to numerous groups that post and identify photos. Flickr (flickr.com) is a photo sharing site that is also great for finding, posting and discussing, identified photos. The best place to get help with identifying photos of insects from North America is BugGuide.net. This is a community of knowledgable professionals and enthusiasts dedicated to making the most accurate identifications possible.

There are also many citizen science initiatives focused on insects. There are too many to list here, but try searching the internet for a specific group of interest and citizen science (e.g. "bumblebees citizen science" or "Odonata citizen science") and you will likely find opportunities to contribute. Most

The senior author using an aerial net.

citizen science is done through the contribution of photos to a project, but not always; some solicit physical collections of specimens or other data. iNaturalist (iNaturalist.org) is by far the most popular citizen science web site. This is because it has a beautiful, easy to use, platform and doesn't focus on a particular group, but rather is one-stop shopping for submitting your natural history observations. It is a large and growing community of amateurs and professionals. It also uses some very impressive artificial intelligence to suggest possible id's for photos submitted. Some of our other favorite on-line resources are OdonataCentral.

com (for dragonflies and damselflies), Moth Photographers Group (MothPhotographersGroup.msstate.edu) and e-butterfly.org for butterflies. For any of these websites however, please keep in mind that photos, no matter how good they are, can not replace specimens and it simply may not be possible to make a confident identification. Never-the-less, all of these resources provide a fantastic opportunity for the insect collector and non-collector alike, to learn.

Mercury vapor bulb placed near a sheet for attracting insects.

Composite of different insects flying around a mercury vapor light.

Whether you are going to make a physical collection of insects or not, you may enjoy using some basic collecting techniques, as many are applicable to both physical and digital collections. The most standard piece of insect collecting equipment is the aerial or butterfly net. It is useful for collecting all flying insects, not just butterflies. It can be used as a catch-and-release piece of equipment as well.

Another popular and easy way to attract insects for collection or photography is black lighting. Many nocturnal insects use uv wavelengths of light for navigation and as a result, are attracted to lights at night. Simply turning on your porch light (just don't use yellow or red light bulbs) will attract insects. If you want to up your game, try using a mercury vapor bulb (available from your local hardware store) or a "black light," but make sure to get a "bl" vs. "blb" type bulb as the latter puts out a much narrower range of wave lengths . These lights put out a broad spectrum of uv light attracting many different types of insects. You can either put the attracted insects in a collection or photograph them and post them on the aforementioned sites. If you are interested in insect collecting or preservation equipment and supplies as well as a large selection of insect books, check out BioQuip.com.

You don't need fancy equipment, however, to find insects. Simply walking around with a good search image will readily reveal the diversity that is out there. Good places to find insects include in and along cracks and crevices of homes and buildings, meadows and prairies with flowering vegetation, on fungi, carrion and dung, under rocks and logs, and in freshwater ponds and streams. If you are just getting into insects and a particular group has not already grabbed you, we suggest you consider starting with a relatively well-known group like butterflies, moths, and dragonflies and damselflies. This is just a practical recommendation, because there are many more resources available for identifying and learning about these groups. You might also find a pair of close-focusing binoculars to be a valuable piece of field equipment, especially if you are not photographing.

In Texas, you do not need a permit to collect insects in most places, but state parks, national parks, and many municipal parks do require permits before you do any collecting, so be sure to talk with appropriate administrators before making collections. There are also very few insects that are federally or state listed as threatened or endangered (see the next section on *Endangered Arthropods in Texas* for more information). It is unlikely that you would encounter these during the course of normal insect hunting.

We have made a list of *Additional Resources* at the end of this book that should prove useful to anyone interested in insects in Texas. It is not meant to be exhaustive, but comprehensive and largely focused towards the enthusiast. The resources are organized in the same way that we have grouped the orders in the book in hopes of providing an efficient means of locating the additional information, both on-line and in print.

# Endangered Arthropods in Texas

In Texas, there are 22 species of arthropods that are federally listed, all endangered. There are 10 arachnids, all associated with caves, three amphipods, and nine species of insects, all beetles. The status *category* below corresponds to the global (G) and state (S) conservation ranking system established by NatureServe (www.NatureServe.org): G1 - Critically imperiled globally; G2 - imperiled globally; G3 - Very rare and local throughout range; S1 - Critically imperiled in state; S2 - Imperiled in state. List available at tpwd.texas.gov.

| Common Name | Scientific Name | Group | Status |
|---|---|---|---|
| Robber Baron Cave Meshweaver | *Cicurina baronia* | Arachnid | G1S1 |
| Madla Cave Meshweaver | *Cicurina madla* | Arachnid | G1S1 |
| Bracken Bat Cave Meshweaver | *Cicurina venii* | Arachnid | G1S1 |
| Government Canyon Bat Cave Meshweaver | *Cicurina vespera* | Arachnid | G1S1 |
| Tooth Cave Pseudoscorpion | *Tartarocreagris texana* | Arachnid | G1G2S1 |
| Government Canyon Bat Cave Spider | *Tayshaneta microps* | Arachnid | G1S1 |
| Tooth Cave Spider | *Tayshaneta myopica* | Arachnid | G1G2S1 |
| Cokendolpher Cave Harvestman | *Texella cokendolpheri* | Arachnid | G1S1 |
| Reddell Harvestman | *Texella reddelli* | Arachnid | G2G3S2 |
| Bone Cave Harvestman | *Texella reyesi* | Arachnid | G2G3S2 |
| Diminuitive Amphipod | *Gammarus hyalleloides* | Crustacean | G1S1 |
| Pecos Amphipod | *Gammarus pecos* | Crustacean | G1S1 |
| Peck's Cave Amphipod | *Stygobromus pecki* | Crustacean | G1G2S1 |
| Coffin Cave Mold Beetle | *Batrisodes texanus* | Insect | G1G2S1 |
| Helotes Mold Beetle | *Batrisodes venyivi* | Insect | G1S1 |
| Comal Springs Riffle Beetle | *Heterelmis comalensis* | Insect | G1S1 |
| American Burying Beetle | *Nicrophorus americanus* | Insect | G2G3S1 |
| Ground Beetle | *Rhadine exilis* | Insect | G3S1 |
| Ground Beetle | *Rhadine infernalis* | Insect | G2G3S1 |
| Tooth Cave Ground Beetle | *Rhadine persephone* | Insect | G1G2S1 |
| Comal Springs Dryopid Beetle | *Stygoparnus comalensis* | Insect | G1G2S1 |
| Kretschmarr Cave Mold Beetle | *Texamaurops reddelli* | Insect | G1G2S1 |

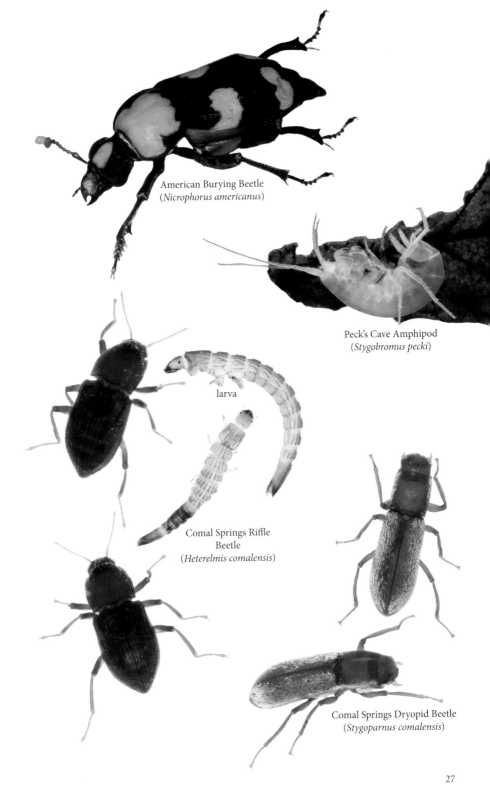

American Burying Beetle
(*Nicrophorus americanus*)

Peck's Cave Amphipod
(*Stygobromus pecki*)

larva

Comal Springs Riffle
Beetle
(*Heterelmis comalensis*)

Comal Springs Dryopid Beetle
(*Stygoparnus comalensis*)

**HOW TO USE THIS GUIDE**   The majority of this book is designed to help you identify common species occurring in the state. There are nearly 1,300 species and more than 2,700 photographs represented in this field guide. As discussed in the previous section on diversity however, that barely scratches the surface of the insect fauna occurring in Texas. Therefore, this guide is not meant to be comprehensive and we encourage caution, especially when starting out, with species level identifications, because many species do look similar or are even indistinguishable from photographs and this book includes fewer than 5% of the insect species known to occur in Texas.

The species accounts are organized by order then family. The smaller orders are sometimes grouped for convenience and we are not implying any phylogenetic relationships with those groupings. We have used 11 different colors across the top and as tabs on the sides of pages for quick reference. These are reflected in the key to color groups on page 8 and are used in the Table of Contents and to organize the Additional Resources at the back of the book. The scientific ordinal name is used at the top of the left page and the common name(s) for the group are used at the top of the right page. Each order is introduced with general natural history information and in most cases, morphological or other characteristics that will be helpful in identifying species in that order. The species pages that follow are laid out with a brief account for each species on the left facing page. There is a map showing the generalized range (east, central, lower Rio Grande Valley, north, panhandle and or west). The ranges of most insect species are poorly known in the state, but it was our goal, based on current information, to reflect the *likely* distribution of each species in the state. These distributions however can be at bit deceiving, because, for example, if there is an eastern species with records that just get into the central part of the state, the map will show it ranging all the way to the Rio Grande. We recognize this has the potential to imply a larger than actual range for some species, but still felt it was an efficient way to display geographical range.

Following the map is a graph showing the basic seasonal distribution in the state ("Sp" for spring, "S" for summer, "F" for fall and "W" for winter). Again, this information is not readily available for most species, but an attempt was made to present the most *likely* occurrence. Both scientific and common names are presented with the common name first and in all caps. In cases where a specific common name has not been established for a species, we used the common name for the genus or family. We used only the common name to identify photos, but occasionally defaulted to scientific name to avoid confusion where more than one species on the page may have the same common name. Most species of insect don't have common names and for those that do, they are rarely standardized. We tried to use the most widely accepted common name, usually represented in BugGuide.net or iNaturalist.org. The scientific family name is presented in all caps and light gray along the right edge of the species accounts. It is only indicated for the first species represented in that family on a given page.

The right side of each spread with species contains one or more images of the species listed on the left. We have tried to maximize their size on the page so the user can glean as much detail as possible. The size of the photos are shown relative to one another, with one individual next to a silhouette that shows its actual size. In some cases we have divided the page by a thin line to separate species of dramatically different sizes and silhouette is given for each section of the page in those cases. We have also used "call outs" or thinly outlined boxes to show more detailed characters, often in preserved specimens; their size is not meant to be relative to the other photos.

Platygastrid Wasp
(*Idris* sp.)

scientific name

order

family

map showing broad
geographical range
(west, central,
panhandle, south, east)

seasonal
range (spring,
summer, fall,
winter)

common name

color tab
corresponding
to order

description
and biological
information on
the species

## ORTHOPTERA

TETTIGONIIDAE

**GREATER ARID-LAND KATYDID** *Neobarrettia spinosa*
Sp **S** F **W** Large, unmistakable species. Bright red eyes and colorful wings that are flared when disturbed. Legs have conspicuous spines. Combined with strong mandibles that can result in a painful bite, this is a species that should be handled carefully.

**BROAD-TIPPED CONEHEAD** *Neoconocephalus triops*
Sp **S** F **W** Distinctive cone protruding between eyes is wider than long. Body can be brown or green. Face somewhat slanted. Hind wings narrow and elongated, extending well beyond abdomen. Males sing earlier in the season than other katydids and are found in a variety of habitats including in suburban areas.

**OBLONG-WINGED KATYDID** *Amblycorypha oblongifolia*
Sp **S** F **W** Head is broadly rounded. Distance between bases of antennae 2 to 3 times width of antenna. Hind wing extends to or beyond tip of forewings. Almost always green, but pink forms are known. Found in the understory of deciduous forests.

**TRUNCATED TRUE KATYDID** *Paracyrtophyllus robustus*
Sp **S** F **W** Comes in both green and red forms. Wings leaf-like, inflated, and with veins darkened making them readily visible. Antennae long and stiff compared to other katydids. Calls from trees in the summer and can be so numerous to constitute as an outbreak.

**COMMON TRUE KATYDID** *Pterophylla camellifolia*
Sp **S** F **W** Green with rounded, inflated wings; veins not outlined in black, but still conspicuous. Pronotum has two shallow grooves. Sings from high in deciduous trees, so seldom seen until the fall when they come down lower. Eggs inserted into loose bark of soft stems.

**FORK-TAILED BUSH KATYDID** *Scudderia furcata*
Sp **S** F **W** Green katydid with long, thin hind legs. Forewings largely uniform in width throughout their length. Yellow stripe extending from thorax over wings. Species are distinguished by Y-shaped male supra-anal plate. Widely distributed and found in weedy fields, meadows, and the edge of woodlands.

RHAPHIDOPHORIDAE

**CAMEL CRICKET** *Ceuthophilus* sp.
Sp **S** F **W** Tan or brown with variable dark markings and usually a distinct hump-backed appearance. Antennae touch or nearly so at their base. Tarsi are laterally compressed and lack ventral pads. Hind femurs extend beyond tip of abdomen.

STENOPELMATIDAE

**JERUSALEM CRICKET** *Stenopelmatus* sp.
Sp **S** F **W** Large, distinctive crickets with orange-brown heads and legs and a white abdomen with black bands. Antennae are widely separated at base on large head. Tibia on all legs are stout with strong spines for digging and hind femora don't extend beyond abdomen.

102

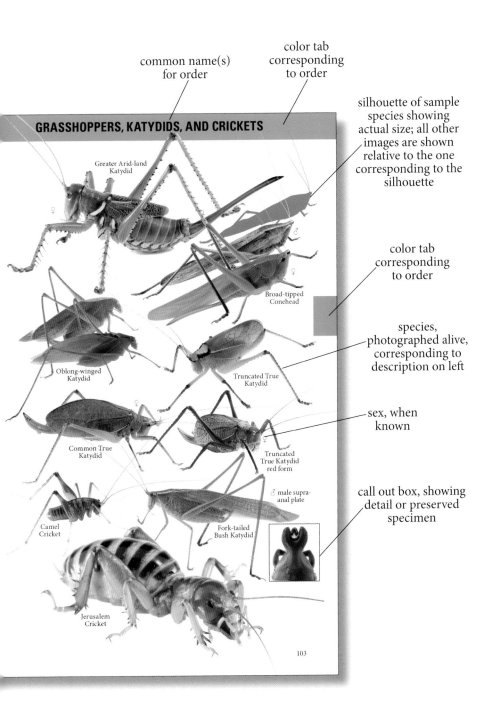

common name(s)
for order

color tab
corresponding
to order

## GRASSHOPPERS, KATYDIDS, AND CRICKETS

silhouette of sample
species showing
actual size; all other
images are shown
relative to the one
corresponding to the
silhouette

Greater Arid-land
Katydid

♀

♂

♀

Broad-tipped
Conehead

color tab
corresponding
to order

Oblong-winged
Katydid

Truncated True
Katydid

species,
photographed alive,
corresponding to
description on left

Common True
Katydid

Truncated
True Katydid
red form

sex, when
known

♂ male supra-
anal plate

Camel
Cricket

Fork-tailed
Bush Katydid

call out box, showing
detail or preserved
specimen

Jerusalem
Cricket

# Insects of
# Texas

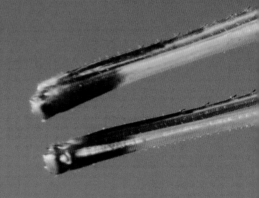

# Springtails
# Class Collembola

Slender Springtail
*Entomobrya* sp.

**NATURAL HISTORY**  Springtails get their name because many of them have a furcula, a forked elongated structure on the underside of the abdomen, that they use to propel or spring themselves through the air. The group is currently treated as their own class (historically placed as an order of insects) and is named for a tube-like structure on the underside of the abdomen, the collophore. The primary functions of this structure are water uptake, excretion, and grooming, but at least in some, it is used for adhesion as well. They are an abundant and diverse group of small, typically 1–3 mm, wingless hexapods found in a variety of habitats.

Their biology is just as bizarre as their morphology. Mating is indirect, with the male depositing a sperm packet or spermatophore on the ground. The female must then pick up the spermatophore with her genital opening. Sometimes a male will encircle a female with a number of stalked spermatophores in order to facilitate her picking up the sperm packet. A number of species perform elaborate courtship rituals to facilitate the transfer of sperm. Some grab the female with their antennae and guide her over the sperm packet while transferring the sperm to her with the third pair of legs. In others the much smaller male may attach himself to the female's antennae and guide her to the spermatophore.

Some estimates are that a square meter of soil can contain tens of thousands of Collembola. They disperse soil microorganisms and are important in the functions of soil respiration and decomposition leading to healthy soils. They feed on plants, fungi, and detritus, and some are carnivorous.

# Identifying Characters

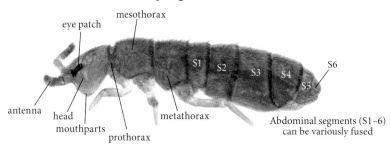

eye patch

mesothorax

S1 S2 S3 S4 S5 S6

antenna

head

mouthparts

prothorax

metathorax

Abdominal segments (S1–6)
can be variously fused

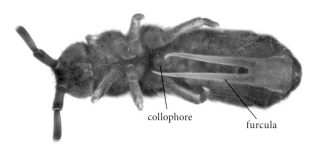

collophore

furcula

# Body Types

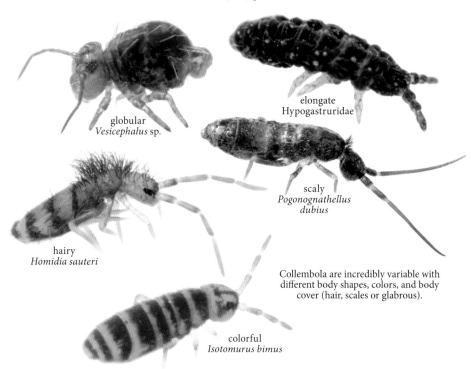

globular
*Vesicephalus* sp.

elongate
Hypogastruridae

scaly
*Pogonognathellus
dubius*

hairy
*Homidia sauteri*

colorful
*Isotomurus bimus*

Collembola are incredibly variable with
different body shapes, colors, and body
cover (hair, scales or glabrous).

# COLLEMBOLA

### ELONGATE-BODIED SPRINGTAIL *Folsomia candida*
ISOTOMIDAE

**Sp S F W** A common and widespread species. It is parthenogenetic. All white with an elongated body with antennae only slightly longer than head. Fourth through sixth abdominal segments fused. Widely used as a laboratory test animal, it is found in soils throughout the world.

### ELONGATE-BODIED SPRINGTAIL *Isotoma viridis*

**Sp S F W** Variable in color, though most commonly greenish; can be yellow, brownish, reddish, or black and generally lacking a pattern. Winter populations are darker than those found in summer. Body is elongate with antennae longer than head. Found in soils.

### SLENDER SPRINGTAIL *Entomobrya clitellaria*
ENTOMOBRYIDAE

**Sp S F W** Color and pattern varied, but usually yellowish or otherwise pale and usually with some degree of dark marking on the thorax (sometimes a complete band). Antennae long, extending backward beyond thorax. Long hairs often present, especially on thorax. Eyes prominent. Fourth abdominal segment at middle, more than three times as long as third.

### SLENDER SPRINGTAIL *Coecobrya tenebricosa*

**Sp S F W** Pale, elongated species. Body covered with hairs. Lacks eyes. Fourth abdominal segment at middle, more than three times as long as third. Common, widespread species, likely introduced. Found in soils.

### GLOBULAR SPRINGTAIL *Sminthurus packardi*
SMINTHURIDAE

**Sp S F W** Globular with fourth antennal segment as long as third and annulated or ringed. Variable in color, but generally with some patterning. Often found associated with vegetation, but occasionally under stones, rock, and loose bark as well.

### GLOBULAR SPRINGTAIL *Ptenothrix renateae*
DICYRTOMIDAE

**Sp S F W** Globular and variably colored, but usually densely patterned with dark markings. The antennae and tibiotarsi are distinctly ringed. The third and fourth antennal segments are subdivided with the fourth segment less than half as long as third.

### SPRINGTAIL *Hypogastrura* sp.
HYPOGASTRURIDAE

**Sp S F W** Generally bluish in color and often gather in mass aggregations. Somewhat dorsoventrally compressed with short furcula and stout, short antennae.

### SPRINGTAIL *Schaefferia duodecimocellata*

**Sp S F W** Small and dorsoventrally compressed. Eyes reduced to 6 facets (vs. normal 8) on each side. Body typically pale yellow with bluish head and antennae.

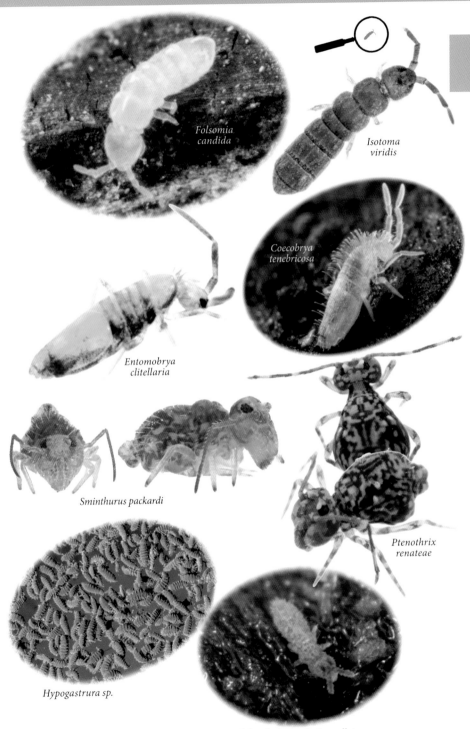

Folsomia
candida

Isotoma
viridis

Coecobrya
tenebricosa

Entomobrya
clitellaria

Sminthurus packardi

Ptenothrix
renateae

Hypogastrura sp.

Schaefferia duodecimocellata

# Two-pronged Bristletails
# Class Diplura

forcepstail

**NATURAL HISTORY**   This is a group of non-insect hexapods, closely related to insects, but now put in their own class. The name Diplura means two tail and refers to the long filamentous cerci that can also be modified into forceps like pincers. The common name refers to the same structures, but also alludes to the numerous setae present on them. The entire class lacks eyes as well as wings. They are unpigmented soil insects with mouthparts similar to those of Collembola, and help to break down and recycle organic matter. They range in size from 2–50 mm, but are generally around 8 mm.

While this group is likely rarely encountered by the casual observer, they can be common in certain situations. They are typically found in leaf litter, under rocks, and in rotting logs within moist, wooded situations. Those with long, thin filamentous cerci are typically herbivorous, while those with cerci modified into forceps like structures are predators, using them for grabbing prey. Some species will bury themselves head-down in the soil with the claspers visible for grabbing small invertebrate prey passing by.

Fertilization is indirect or external. Some males will deposit spermatophores at random. Females deposit eggs in clumps within the soil, cracks in wood, or on vegetation. Some species will lay eggs on stalks suspended from the ceiling of a soil chamber. Some females also show some maternal care by guarding eggs and even early instars. As with most non-insect hexapods, they continue to molt after reaching sexual maturity.

### FORCEPSTAIL

JAPYGIDAE

`Sp` **S** `F` **W**    Generally larger than campodeids and with
1-segmented cerci modified into forceps like structures for grabbing
prey. The cerci, last few abdominal segments, and head are often
darker than the middle abdominal segments.

### SLENDER DIPLURAN

CAMPODEIDAE

`Sp` **S** `F` **W**    Pale, blind, with elongated body. Filamentous
antennae and cerci about the same length and somewhat similar in
appearance with numerous setae. This is the most diverse family
in the group, but species identification is difficult and requires
microscopic examination. They are herbivorous and found under
rocks and rotting wood in damp forests.

# Bristletails
# Order Archaeognatha

Rock Bristletail

**NATURAL HISTORY**   The ordinal name for this group means old jaw, which refers to the primitive means in which the mandibles move and connect. The name Microcoryphia is also often used when referring to this order and means small head. These insects are scaly, elongated, and wingless with a cylindrical, arched body. They can be variously patterned, but have large compound eyes that meet on the top of the head, three ocelli, and two long filamentous antennae. The abdomen has short styli laterally on segments 2–9 and one long median filament flanked by two shorter lateral cerci. They also have paired eversible membranous vesicles in which they absorb water.

They are found along rocky shores and in grassy or wooded areas, including among leaf litter, in rock crevices, and under rocks and fallen logs. They are usually more active at night and feed on algae, lichen, moss, and detritus. They jump when disturbed. They molt continuously throughout their life, in many cases using their feces to anchor themselves down during the process. Mating occurs when the male deposits a sperm packet (spermatophore) on the ground and directs the female over it via silken guides. In some species there is elaborate courtship, while others are parthenogenetic, lacking males. A batch of around 30 eggs is laid with each being glued to a rock or other suitable surface. They desiccate easily and thus are generally found in humid microenvironments.

Rock Bristletail

Rock Bristletail

## JUMPING BRISTLETAILS AND ROCK BRISTLETAILS

Sp **S** F **W** Two families occur in Texas, the Jumping Bristletails (Machilidae) and the Rock Bristletails (Meinertellidae). They are difficult to even determine to family from photos. The Jumping Bristletails have the two basal antennal segments heavily scaled and the Rock Bristletails lack these scales. While species of both families can be found throughout the state, the Jumping Bristletails are more often found among rocks along seashores.

Rock Bristletail

# Silverfish
# Order Zygentoma

Firebrat
(*Thermobia domestica*)

**NATURAL HISTORY**   The ordinal name for this group of insects means "bridge insects" and refers to the idea once held that they represented a link between the flightless and winged groups of insects. They have been given a number of common names including bristletails, fishmoths, silverfish, and firebrats that generally refer to the silvery scales of many species and their fishlike movements. They are wingless with three long caudal or tail filaments and more dorsoventrally compressed compared to the similar jumping bristletails. The compound eyes are smaller and widely separated. Their antennae are long and filamentous and many species have short leg-like appendages laterally on the abdominal segments.

Species are found both in moist humid environments and dry arid habitats. Some are associated with ants and termites, while others are commonly found in domestic situations where they feed on starches in paper, cereals, paste, clothes, and similar items. Many species have an elaborate courtship ritual. Fertilization is external with the male depositing a spermatophore (sperm packet) underneath a silk thread typically placed between the substrate and a vertical object. He then must entice the female to walk under the thread. When her cerci contact the silk, the spermatophore is picked up by her genital opening. The sperm enter her system and then she eats the remaining empty spermatophore for a nutritional supplement. They grow slowly and can live up to four years.

Gray Silverfish

Common Silverfish

Firebrat

*Battigrassiella wheeleri*

### GRAY SILVERFISH *Ctenolepisma longicaudata*     LEPISMATIDAE
**Sp S F W**  Light to dark gray scales covering body. Head with numerous pale to yellowish hairs protruding anteriorly. Thoracic segments with checkered pattern laterally. Last abdominal segment truncated. Commonly found in cracks and crevices within homes.

### COMMON SILVERFISH *Lepisma saccharina*
**Sp S F W**  Silvery gray scales covering body. Femora broad and flat. Thoracic segments lacking checkered pattern laterally. Last abdominal segment rounded. Commonly found indoors.

### FIREBRAT *Thermobia domestica*
**Sp S F W**  Yellow or tan with dark brown bands and mottled spots over entire dorsal surface. Robust or chunky in appearance with abdomen not much longer, or even shorter than thorax. Generally found in warm places like near furnaces and fireplaces.

### *Battigrassiella wheeleri*     NICOLETIIDAE
**Sp S F W**  Small, pale, blind and associated with ant colonies, in particular fire ants. Body tapering with thorax broader than abdomen. Antennae and cerci shorter than body.

# Mayflies
# Order Ephemeroptera

Emergent Mayfly
(*Hexagenia bilineata*)

**NATURAL HISTORY**   This is a group of aquatic insects that get their name from the Greek roots *ephemeros* (ephemeral) and *ptera* (wings) referring to the short-lived adult or winged stage. The aquatic immature or nymph stage remains in the water for a much longer period of time; in some species three or more years. The nymph emerges out of the water and molts into a subadult (subimago) that has milky wings, but otherwise looks like an adult. They are unusual amongst all other insects with wings in that most species then molt one more time into a clear-winged sexually mature adult. Both winged stages may last for no more than a day. Despite this additional stage, they are considered to have simple, hemimetabolous development.

Mayflies are fairly uniform in overall appearance, but can vary widely in color and size. Some have two long tails while others have three, and while all have much smaller hind wings, some groups nearly lack them altogether. Some species, particularly males, have greatly enlarged eyes that are used for finding females in mating swarms. Because this group lives for such a short period of time as adults, they have large synchronized emergences to bring the sexes together. There is also no need to feed as adults, so mouthparts are reduced and non-functional. After mating, females will almost immediately begin laying eggs in the water and some groups, like the Caenidae, actually explode on contact with the water as a mechanism to release eggs. The nymphs vary somewhat in size and shape, but most have variously shaped gills along the abdomen and have either two or three tails.

# Identifying Characters

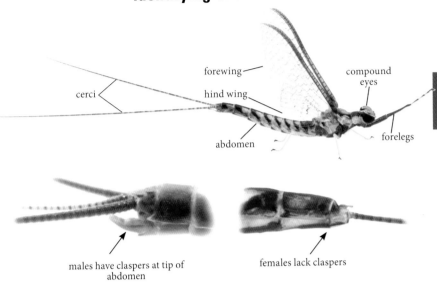

cerci

forewing

hind wing

abdomen

compound eyes

forelegs

males have claspers at tip of abdomen

females lack claspers

# Immature Stages

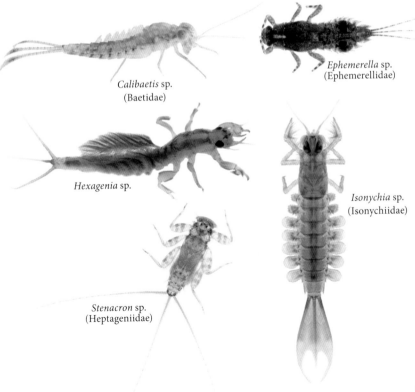

*Calibaetis* sp.
(Baetidae)

*Ephemerella* sp.
(Ephemerellidae)

*Hexagenia* sp.

*Isonychia* sp.
(Isonychiidae)

*Stenacron* sp.
(Heptageniidae)

### SMALL MINNOW MAYFLY *Callibaetis pretiosus*  BAETIDAE

**Sp S F W** Wings with checkered pattern. Upper portion of eyes in males large and expanded on a short stalk. Both sexes with reddish-brown spots in small depressions over body, but spots more intense in females. Nymphs found in ponds, pools, lakes, and ditches.

### SMALL SQUAREGILLED MAYFLY *Caenis sp.*  CAENIDAE

**Sp S F W** Small pale mayflies with relatively large broad forewings, no hind wings, and three terminal filaments. Pedicel of antennae twice as long as scape. They perch with their wings outspread. Nymphs inhabit stagnant or still waters and adults typically live for only a few hours. Attracted to lights.

### EMERGENT MAYFLY *Hexagenia bilineata*  EPHEMERIDAE

**Sp S F W** Large brownish species. Subimago lemon yellow. Adults with abdomen dark above interrupted by pale triangles on each segment. Forelegs very long. Nymphs found in streams and lakes burrowed in substrate. Attracted to lights in large numbers.

### GIANT MAYFLY *Hexagenia limbata*

**Sp S F W** Even larger than emergent mayfly and paler in overall color. Subimago lemon yellow. Adults with pale abdomen crossmarked by dark diagonal stripe coming to middle on each abdominal segment. Forelegs very long. Nymphs found in streams and lakes burrowed in substrate. Attracted to lights.

### RIVERBED BURROWER MAYFLY *Pentagenia vittigera*

**Sp S F W** Large, pale yellowish, with broad dark stripe running on top from head to tip of abdomen. Head appears flattened. Three yellow terminal filaments; shorter than body in female. Pronotum of male reduced to 3x as wide as long. Restricted to large rivers where nymphs burrow in the substrate.

### FLATHEADED MAYFLY *Stenacron sp.*  HEPTAGENIIDAE

**Sp S F W** Yellowish orange with green eyes and usually dark bands on at least forelegs. Eyes in male relatively large and widely separated (usually much greater than width of median ocellus). Nymphs found in rocky, moderately rapid to swift rivers and streams.

### BRUSHLEGGED MAYFLY *Isonychia sp.*  ISONYCHIIDAE

**Sp S F W** Reddish or purplish body. Forefemur and tibia reddish, while foretarsi, middle and hind legs, and cerci are all pale. Male eyes are large and contiguous dorsally. Nymphs found in rapidly flowing streams and rivers.

### BLACK QUILL *Leptophlebia intermedia*  LEPTOPHLEBIIDAE

**Sp S F W** Dark yellowish-brown body. Eyes large and red. Forelegs dark, middle and hind legs paler. Abdomen ringed with pale bands. Three terminal filaments with the middle one shorter. Nymphs are found in ponds, lakes, and quiet eddies of streams.

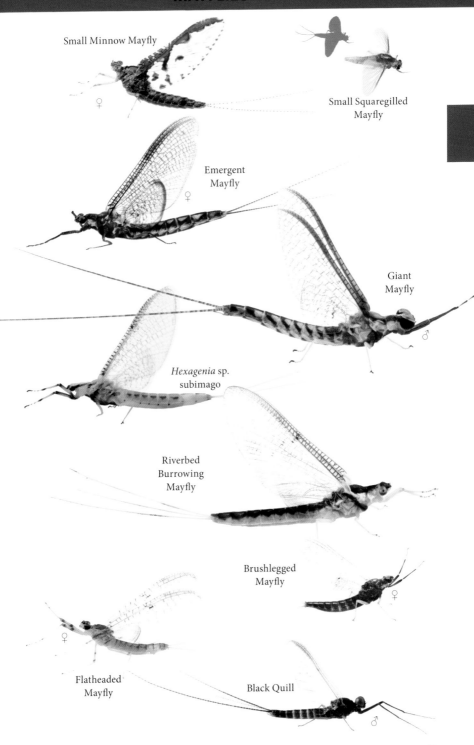

Small Minnow Mayfly ♀

Small Squaregilled Mayfly

Emergent Mayfly ♀

Giant Mayfly ♂

*Hexagenia* sp. subimago

Riverbed Burrowing Mayfly

Brushlegged Mayfly ♀

Flatheaded Mayfly ♀

Black Quill ♂

# Dragonflies and Damselflies Order Odonata

Ebony Jewelwing
(*Calopteryx maculata*)

**NATURAL HISTORY** Dragonflies and damselflies belong to the order Odonata, which is derived from the Greek root *odontos* referring to their large mandibles. They are strong fliers with four large membranous wings and elongate bodies. All four wings in damselflies are the same size and shape, while the hind wings of dragonflies are noticeably broader basally. They have incomplete metamorphosis with aquatic nymphs. In Texas species, the wingspan ranges from 2.5–14 cm.

This group has become very popular among naturalists and Texas is a great place to learn about them as over half (245) of the North American species occur here. They are beneficial insects, feeding on mosquitos and other biting flies as both adults and nymphs. Adults are regularly seen flying around ponds, streams, and seeps. Many are brightly colored and have distinctive patterns on the thorax and abdomen useful in identifying species. Male odonates have a secondary set of genitalia located ventrally on S2–3. Pairs are often seen in tandem (males guarding females) or in copula (wheel position). Immature stages of Odonata, nymphs, are aquatic. They are easily observed by dragging a net along the bottom of ponds or streams. Dragonflies are known to travel long distances and at least 16 species in North America are migratory. The Wandering Glider has the widest distribution of any odonate and migrates nearly 18,000 km round trip from India to Africa.

# Wings

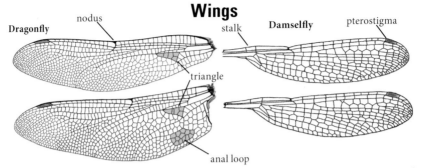

**Dragonfly** nodus stalk **Damselfly** pterostigma

triangle

anal loop

Differences in the dense venation of odonate wings are useful when identifying families, genera, and species. Key landmarks are indicated.

# Immature Stage

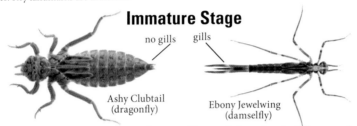

no gills gills

Ashy Clubtail (dragonfly)

Ebony Jewelwing (damselfly)

Dragonfly nymphs have internal rectal gills. Damselfly nymphs have three leaf-like external gills.

# Thorax and Abdomen

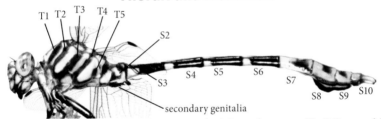

T1 T2 T3 T4 T5

S2

S3 S4 S5 S6 S7 S8 S9 S10

secondary genitalia

Dark stripes on the thorax (T1–T5) and patterns on the abdominal segments (S1–S10) are useful for species identification.

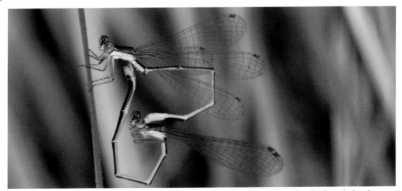

Pair of Sphagnum Sprites (*Nehalennia gracilis*) in copula. The male grabs the female by the prothorax; the female then curls her abdomen up to connect with the male's secondary genitalia where sperm is transferred, ultimately forming a heart shape.

### EBONY JEWELWING *Calopteryx maculata*

**Sp S F W** Large, uniformly dark, broad wings lacking stalk. Head, thorax, and abdomen iridescent green or blue. Male lacks pterostigma, female has white pterostigma made up of many cells. Underside of S8–10 white in males, brown in females.

### AMERICAN RUBYSPOT *Hetaerina americana*

**Sp S F W** Wings narrow, but lacking basal stalk, with large red patch traversed by white veins at base. Red patches become larger with age. Thorax metallic red. Abdomen metallic green with pale underside and pale rings around each segment.

### SMOKY RUBYSPOT *Hetaerina titia*

**Sp S F W** Wings narrow, but lacking basal stalk. Forewings with variable amount of red basally, washed with brown. Base of hind wing dark with red veins. Remainder of wing coloration variable, including solid dark. Thorax and abdomen dark, the former often with metallic green stripes visible.

### GREAT SPREADWING *Archilestes grandis*

**Sp S F W** Perches with wings spread, often with smoky, dark tips. Blue eyes. Thorax with distinctive yellow stripe along sides and metallic green stripes above and below the shoulder line. Dark abdomen; S9–10 with bluish pruinosity. Largest damselfly in US.

### PLATEAU SPREADWING *Lestes alacer*

**Sp S F W** Perches with wings spread. Eyes blue when mature. Thorax bronze or black with pale blue or yellow shoulder stripe. Bottom of thorax becomes pruinose with age. Ventrolateral spots scarce on S3–5. S1–2 and S8–10 become pruinose with age.

### SOUTHERN SPREADWING *Lestes australis*

**Sp S F W** Perches with wings spread. Eyes blue when mature. Thorax with blue or yellow shoulder stripe. Top of abdomen dark, sides blue with dark distal spot on S3–5. S9 pruinose and S10 partially pruinose. More robust than Plateau Spreadwing.

### AMELIA'S THREADTAIL *Neoneura amelia*

**Sp S F W** Males with bright red-orange face, head, and thorax. Legs and underside of thorax and abdomen pale. Long, thin abdomen and relatively short wings. Top of S1–3 red-orange; rest of abdomen pale with narrow dark rings on S3–9.

### BLUE-FRONTED DANCER *Argia apicalis*

**Sp S F W** Eyes and face blue. Thorax mostly blue except for hairline black shoulder and middorsal stripe. Abdomen black except for blue S8–10 and pale rings on S3–7. Black stripe on lower side of S8–10. Pale colors in male become much darker, almost gray when cooled or in tandem with female.

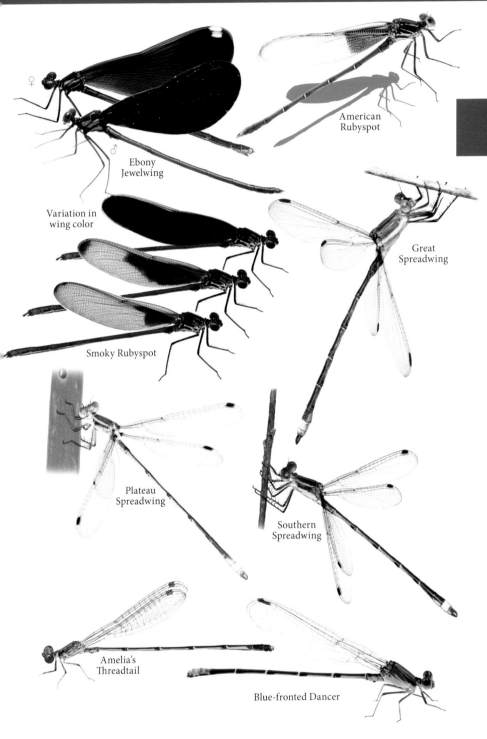

♀

American
Rubyspot

Ebony
Jewelwing

♂

Variation in
wing color

Great
Spreadwing

Smoky Rubyspot

Plateau
Spreadwing

Southern
Spreadwing

Amelia's
Threadtail

Blue-fronted Dancer

51

### VARIABLE DANCER *Argia fumipennis*

COENAGRIONIDAE

**Sp S F W** Most common purple dancer in Texas. Body is purple with black stripe down top of thorax and black shoulder stripe is forked. Abdomen with black stripe on S3–6. S7 largely black above. S8 purple, S9–10 blue with black ventrolateral stripe on S8–10.

### KIOWA DANCER *Argia immunda*

**Sp S F W** Dark purple or blue. Thorax purple and gray with dark middorsal stripe and forked shoulder stripe. Abdomen with violet or blue bands alternating with black when viewed from above. S8–10 blue with continuous black ventrolateral stripe.

### POWDERED DANCER *Argia moesta*

**Sp S F W** Most widespread and variable dancer in Texas. Thorax tan with black middorsal stripe and black shoulder stripe that can be forked in young males. Abdomen is black with pale rings on S3–7. Mature males develop powdered gray or white pruinescence that envelops entire body obscuring markings.

### AZTEC DANCER *Argia nahuana*

**Sp S F W** Blue thorax with black middorsal stripe. Strongly forked shoulder stripe. Abdomen blue with black rings on S3–6. S7 with more black above. S8–10 blue with black ventrolateral stripe.

### SPRINGWATER DANCER *Argia plana*

**Sp S F W** Thorax blue with black middorsal and unforked shoulder stripe. Abdomen blue with black distal rings and black lateral stripe on S3–6. S7 mostly black with blue ring. S8–10 are blue. Wings often with hint of amber.

### BLUE-RINGED DANCER *Argia sedula*

**Sp S F W** Dark blue thorax with broad black middorsal stripe. Wide, black shoulder stripe with small pale triangle at base of wings. Thorax darker blue than abdomen. Abdomen largely black with blue apical rings on S3–7 and partial pale ventrolateral stripe on S3–6. S8–10 with black ventrolateral stripe.

### DUSKY DANCER *Argia translata*

**Sp S F W** Dark purple eyes and black head. Thorax bluish gray with a black shoulder stripe divided by yellow. Yellow stripe becomes obscured in older males. Abdomen black with blue apical rings on S3–6 and sometimes S7. S8–10 black with distinctive pattern of blue.

### BLUE-TIPPED DANCER *Argia tibialis*

**Sp S F W** Face and thorax dark blue or purple. Thorax with thin black middorsal and unforked shoulder stripe. Bottom half of thorax distinctly paler. Abdomen black with pale apical rings on S4–7. S8 all black and S9–10 black with blue above.

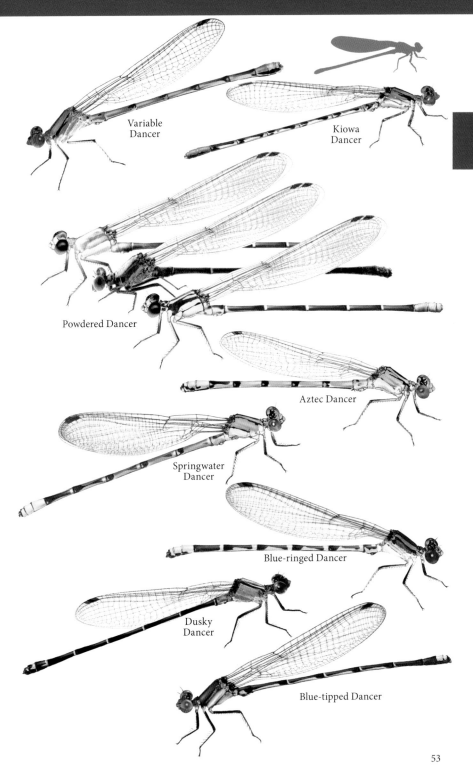

Variable
Dancer

Kiowa
Dancer

Powdered Dancer

Aztec Dancer

Springwater
Dancer

Blue-ringed Dancer

Dusky
Dancer

Blue-tipped Dancer

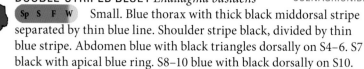

### DOUBLE-STRIPED BLUET *Enallagma basidens*  COENAGRIONIDAE
**Sp S F W**  Small. Blue thorax with thick black middorsal stripe separated by thin blue line. Shoulder stripe black, divided by thin blue stripe. Abdomen blue with black triangles dorsally on S4–6. S7 black with apical blue ring. S8–10 blue with black dorsally on S10.

### FAMILIAR BLUET *Enallagma civile*
**Sp S F W**  Most common blue damselfly around ponds. Thorax blue with black shoulder stripe. Abdomen blue with black spot on top of S2 and large spots on S3–5. S6–7 with distal black bands. S8–10 blue with black dorsally on S10.

### ORANGE BLUET *Enallagma signatum*
**Sp S F W**  Eyes and head orange. Thorax orange with black middorsal stripe and unforked black shoulder stripe. Abdomen orange laterally and black dorsally on S2–8. S9–10 orange with black dorsally on S10. Young males and females are blue.

### STREAM BLUET *Enallagma exsulans*
**Sp S F W**  Blue eyespots distinctly teardrop shaped and connected by blue bar. Blue thorax with black middorsal stripe and wide unforked shoulder stripe. Abdomen black with blue apical rings on S3–7. S8–10 blue with black dorsally on S8 and S10.

### CITRINE FORKTAIL *Ischnura hastata*
**Sp S F W**  Small, dainty yellow damselfly. Forewing pterostigma orange and detached from edge of wing. Head and eyes mostly green. Thorax green with thick black middorsal and shoulder stripes. Abdomen yellow. Distinct divided appendage off S10.

### FRAGILE FORKTAIL *Ischnura posita*
**Sp S F W**  Small, with yellowish-green eyes and head. Thorax yellowish green on sides and black above. Pale shoulder stripe interrupted appearing as an exclamation mark. Rest of body metallic black with yellow rings. S8–10 solid black.

### RAMBUR'S FORKTAIL *Ischnura ramburii*
**Sp S F W**  Dark head with blue eyespots and green eyes. Thorax green with broad black middorsal and shoulder stripe. Forewing pterostigma edged in blue. Abdomen black above. S8–9 blue with black dorsally on S9. Female can be orange, green, or like male.

### DESERT FIRETAIL *Telebasis salva*
**Sp S F W**  Small red damselfly. Top of head black. Thorax red with black stripe, divided by thin red stripe, on top forming arrow pointing toward abdomen. Abdomen uniformly red.

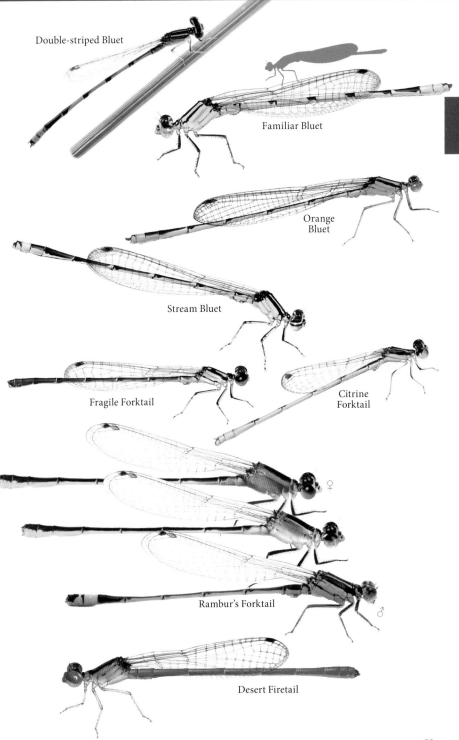

Double-striped Bluet

Familiar Bluet

Orange
Bluet

Stream Bluet

Fragile Forktail

Citrine
Forktail

♀

Rambur's Forktail

♂

Desert Firetail

55

### GRAY PETALTAIL *Tachopteryx thoreyi*

**Sp** **S** **F** **W** Large gray dragonfly with widely separated eyes. Thorax with black shoulder stripe and one black diagonal stripe. Wings clear with long dark pterostigma. Abdomen with S2–7 half black and S8–10 all black. Often lands vertically on tree trunks and even on people.

### COMMON GREEN DARNER *Anax junius*

**Sp** **S** **F** **W** Green eyes and dark "bulls eye" on top of face, in front of eyes. Thorax green. Wings can be clear but can turn amber color with age, especially in females. S1 green and S2–6 blue on sides and brown on top; S7–10 gradually becoming more brown.

### SWAMP DARNER *Epiaeschna heros*

**Sp** **S** **F** **W** Green and brown darner with blue eyes; thorax is brown with green stripe on top and two stripes on the side. Wings have amber color to them especially when older. Abdomen dark with S2–3 thin green rings per segment.

### BROAD-STRIPED FORCEPTAIL *Aphylla angustifolia*

**Sp** **S** **F** **W** Eyes of male blue green. Thorax brown with yellow stripes; T1 and T2 nearly fused, other thoracic stripes uneven. Abdomen yellow-brown, with narrow flange on S8–10 that is uniformly reddish with yellow on edges.

### COMMON SANDDRAGON *Progomphus obscurus*

**Sp** **S** **F** **W** Eyes blue or green. Thorax yellow in front. T1–2 fused at the top and bottom leaving thin yellow line in middle. Wings have dark brown patches where they attach to the body. Abdomen brown with yellow spear points on top and yellow appendages at tip of abdomen.

### FLAG-TAILED SPINYLEG *Dromogomphus spoliatus*

**Sp** **S** **F** **W** Blue eyes and thorax green with dark T1–4 stripes; T3 sometimes interrupted. Abdomen whitish with dark markings. S7–9 forming prominent yellowish-brown club that is darker on top. S10 largely yellow.

### EASTERN RINGTAIL *Erpetogomphus designatus*

**Sp** **S** **F** **W** Blue eyes with green thorax. Thoracic stripes dark with T1 an incomplete stripe and T3 poorly developed. Wings have a small amber patch at base. Abdomen is white with club, S7–10, orange-brown.

### PLAINS CLUBTAIL *Gomphurus externus*

**Sp** **S** **F** **W** Turquoise eyes and yellow face. Thorax yellow with dark stripes T1–2 and T3–4 wide and almost fused. Abdomen yellow with broad dark stripe on S3–7. Club, S8–10, dark with extensive yellow on edges.

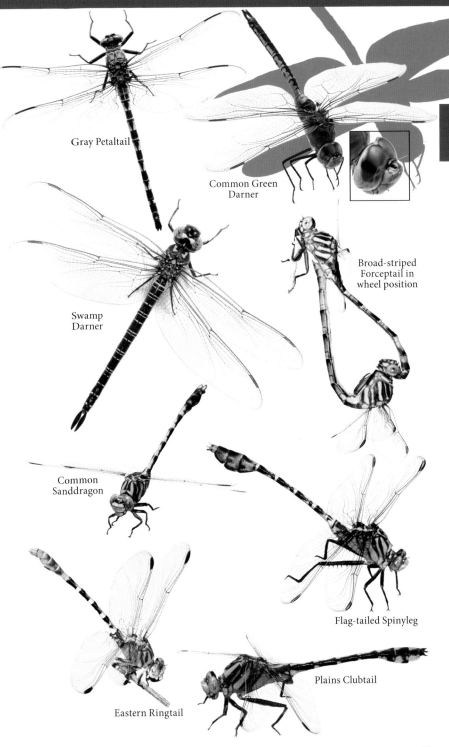

Gray Petaltail

Common Green Darner

Swamp Darner

Broad-striped Forceptail in wheel position

Common Sanddragon

Flag-tailed Spinyleg

Eastern Ringtail

Plains Clubtail

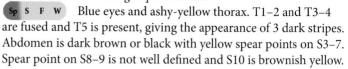

### ASHY CLUBTAIL *Phanogomphus lividus*

**Sp** S F W    Blue eyes and ashy-yellow thorax. T1–2 and T3–4 are fused and T5 is present, giving the appearance of 3 dark stripes. Abdomen is dark brown or black with yellow spear points on S3–7. Spear point on S8–9 is not well defined and S10 is brownish yellow.

### SULPHUR-TIPPED CLUBTAIL *Phanogomphus militaris*
**Sp** S F W    Blue eyes and green thorax with T1–2 barely separated leaving a thin green stripe. T3–4 very narrow and broadly separated. Hind femur relatively short bearing yellow stripe. Abdomen black with yellow spear points on S3–8; S9 yellow above.

### FIVE-STRIPED LEAFTAIL *Phyllogomphoides albrighti*
**Sp** S **F** W    Blue eyes with pale face. Thorax pale yellowish green with black T2–3 and T4–5 each connected at lower end, forming a "U." S3–6 with pale rings narrowly interrupted by black laterally. S7 pale with broad dark ventro-lateral mark. S8–10 orange with dark markings on top and black edge on prominent flange.

### RUSSET-TIPPED CLUBTAIL *Stylurus plagiatus*
**Sp** S F **W**    Blue eyes with greenish-blue thorax. T1–2 twice as wide as T3–4. Abdomen is brown with greenish-blue spear points dorsally. S7–10 with uniformly rusty-orange club with wide flange and black on margins.

### ARROWHEAD SPIKETAIL *Cordulegaster obliqua*
**Sp** S F W    Blue eyes above and brown below. Thorax brown with three yellow stripes on each side. Abdomen black with yellow arrowhead-shaped markings on top of S2–7. S8 with a round spot extending laterally to form a ring. S9 with smaller elongated spot.

### STREAM CRUISER *Didymops transversa*
**Sp** S F W    Turquoise-brown eyes with pale spots on top of face. Thorax brown with single pale lateral stripe. Wings with small brown, narrow patch at base. Abdomen brown with yellow elongated dots on S3–8; S7–9 somewhat clubbed in males.

### SWIFT RIVER CRUISER *Macromia illinoiensis*
**Sp** S F W    Turquoise eyes and yellow face. Two yellow spots on top of face. Thorax metallic-green with anterior yellow stripe that only extends up 3/5 of thorax; 2 yellow stripes laterally. Abdomen dark with complete yellow stripe dorsally on S2; S3–6 with pair of yellow triangles. Male abdomen somewhat clubbed.

### PRINCE BASKETTAIL *Epitheca princeps*
**Sp** S **F** W    Eyes are grayish blue to green; face tan. Thorax is brown with darker patches anteriorly. Wings have dark irregular patches at base, middle, and tips. Abdomen brown; S4–10 outlined in black and top is darker than sides.

Ashy Clubtail

Five-striped
Leaftail

Sulphur-tipped
Clubtail

Russet-tipped
Clubtail

Arrowhead
Spiketail

Stream
Cruiser

Swift River
Cruiser

Prince
Baskettail

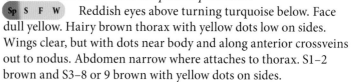

### DOT-WINGED BASKETTAIL *Epitheca petechialis*
CORDULIIDAE

**Sp** S F W  Reddish eyes above turning turquoise below. Face dull yellow. Hairy brown thorax with yellow dots low on sides. Wings clear, but with dots near body and along anterior crossveins out to nodus. Abdomen narrow where attaches to thorax. S1–2 brown and S3–8 or 9 brown with yellow dots on sides.

### FOUR-SPOTTED PENNANT *Brachymesia gravida*
LIBELLULIDAE

**Sp** S F W  Dark eyes, face and frons metallic purplish black with white spots on sides that fade with age. Thorax is bluish gray and abdomen is black or dark brown. Wings have dark patch between nodus and pterostigma. Pterostigmas white.

### HALLOWEEN PENNANT *Celithemis eponina*

**Sp** S F W  Eyes red-brown above and gray below, face red. Thorax is orange-brown. Wings orange with black bands and red pterostigma. Abdomen black with orange where it attaches to the thorax, orange stripe on top of S3–7.

### SWIFT SETWING *Dythemis velox*

**Sp** S F W  Male with reddish-brown-over-gray eyes. Thorax pale with dark stripes creating a YIY pattern. Wings with dark spot at base and tips. Abdomen with pale markings on S1–3, S4–6, and S7.

### CHECKERED SETWING *Dythemis fugax*

**Sp** S F W  Bright red eyes and face in male (female with tan face). Thorax is reddish brown with dark stripes, large brown patch of color at base of wings. Abdomen black with 2 pairs of pale streaks on each segment, S7 has larger elongated streaks.

### EASTERN PONDHAWK *Erythemis simplicicollis*

**Sp** S F W  Green eyes and face, thorax and abdomen are powder blue, S9–10 with black, tip of abdomen pale (on right). Young males (on right) have a green thorax with sutures outlined in black, abdomen green with black bands. Female similar to young male.

### BAND-WINGED DRAGONLET *Erythrodiplax umbrata*

**Sp** S F W  Dark eyes and face, thorax and abdomen have dark pruinescence, but light tan or white tip of abdomen. Juveniles are light blue to brown. Wings have wide dark band between nodus and pterostigma.

### COMMON WHITETAIL *Plathemis lydia*

**Sp** S F W  Dark brown eyes and face. Thorax is dark brown with a pair of pale stripes ending in yellow. Abdomen is solid white, wing with narrow band of black at base and large black bands between nodus and pterostigma. Female abdomen brown with discontinuous lateral stripe and three large dark spots on each wing.

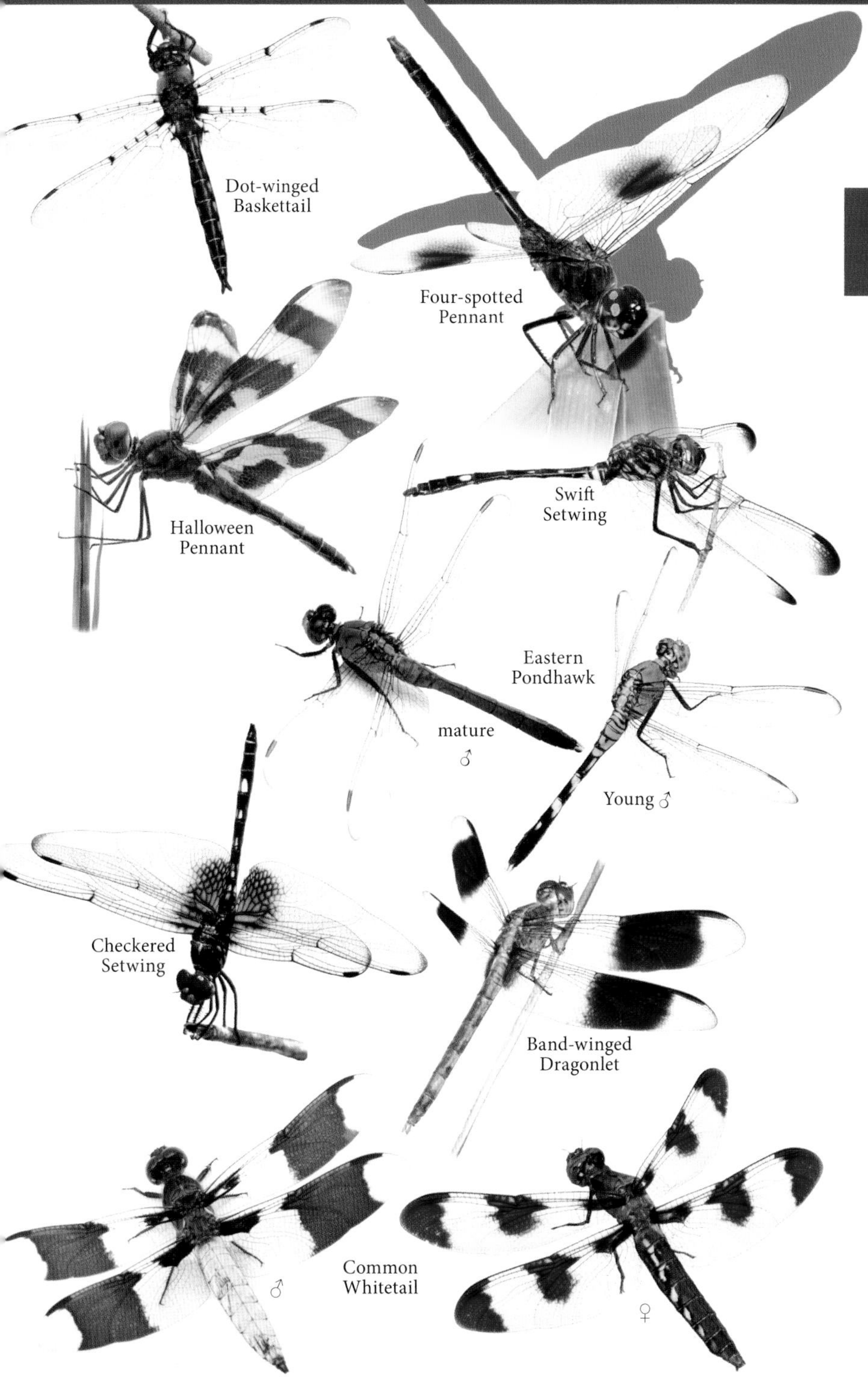

Dot-winged
Baskettail

Four-spotted
Pennant

Halloween
Pennant

Swift
Setwing

Eastern
Pondhawk

mature
♂

Young ♂

Checkered
Setwing

Band-winged
Dragonlet

Common
Whitetail

♂

♀

### SLATY SKIMMER *Libellula incesta*

Sp **S F** W    Dark eyes and metallic-blue or violet face. Thorax and abdomen with slaty-blue pruinescence; tip of abdomen is darkest. Wings typically clear but can have dark tips. Juveniles and females have pale yellow thorax with dark stripe and dark abdomen with yellow on sides.

### WIDOW SKIMMER *Libellula luctuosa*

Sp **S F** W    Dark eyes and face. Thorax dark with white pruinosity on top. Wings black out to nodus, then white pruinosity out to pterostigma. Abdomen white pruinosity with black tip.

### TWELVE-SPOTTED SKIMMER *Libellula pulchella*

Sp **S F** W    Dark eyes and face. Thorax brown with 2 pale stripes ending with yellow. Wings with dark patch at base, nodus, and tip, white pruinescent spot between each; there are a total of 12 dark spots giving the species its common name. Abdomen in young individuals is dark with yellow stripes, becoming pruinose white.

### GREAT BLUE SKIMMER *Libellula vibrans*

Sp **S F W**    Aqua-blue eyes. Thorax covered in bluish-white pruinescence. Wings with short dark streaks at base, dark spot at nodus, dark pterostigma, and dark tips. Abdomen initially black with broad yellow stripes, turning to blue pruinescence at maturity.

### THORNBUSH DASHER *Micrathyria hagenii*

Sp **S F** W    Iridescent green eyes and white face. Thorax greenish with several dark brown stripes forming a YI pattern with the Y and I joined at the top. White pruinosity often visible between wings. S1–6 black with pale squarish spots; S7 with large pale paired spots.

### BLUE DASHER *Pachydiplax longipennis*

Sp **S F** W    Green eyes at maturity with white face. Thorax dark brown with yellow stripes on front and sides. Wings clear with amber patch, crossed by pair of dark stripes at base. Abdomen is pruinose blue on S1–7 and black on S8–10.

### COMANCHE SKIMMER *Libellula comanche*

Sp **S F** W    Aqua-blue eyes and white face. Female and juvenile with reddish-brown eyes. Thorax and abdomen with uniformly blue pruinescence. Wings are clear with bicolored white and dark pterostigmas. Abdomen in young individuals black with lateral yellow stripe.

### ROSEATE SKIMMER *Orthemis ferruginea*

Sp **S F** W    Dark purplish-red eyes and violet face. Thorax and abdomen purplish pink with thin white coating of pruinescence. Wings are clear with reddish-pink veins. Abdomen can be more red than purple in some individuals.

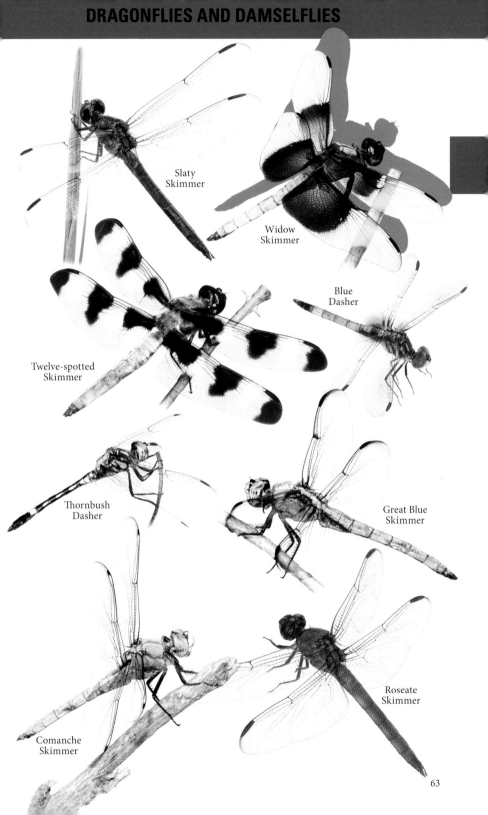

Slaty
Skimmer

Widow
Skimmer

Blue
Dasher

Twelve-spotted
Skimmer

Thornbush
Dasher

Great Blue
Skimmer

Comanche
Skimmer

Roseate
Skimmer

### NEON SKIMMER *Libellula croceipennis*
LIBELLULIDAE

**Sp S F W** Orangish-brown eyes and orange face. Top of thorax red with light colored stripe down the middle; sides orange. Wings reddish orange out to nodus. Abdomen bright orange-red and noticeably broad. Found along streams, ponds, and ditches.

### WANDERING GLIDER *Pantala flavescens*
**Sp S F W** Red eyes and yellow face. Thorax pale brownish-yellow. Wings clear, large, and broad. Abdomen yellow, becoming orange on top with black middorsal stripe. Associated with temporary ponds, man-made ponds, and ditches as well as long distances from water.

### SPOT-WINGED GLIDER *Pantala hymenaea*
**Sp S F W** Brownish-red eyes and dull red face. Thorax brown with 2 pale stripes in front and one pale stripe on each side. Wings large and broad. Hind wing has spot at base of wing. Abdomen brown to yellow with fine dark stripes at each segment and dark stripe running middorsally.

### EASTERN AMBERWING *Perithemis tenera*
**Sp S F W** Small, with red-brown eyes and brown face. Thorax pale yellow with irregular brown stripes on shoulder and sides. Male with amber wings and small dark spots near base with red pterostigma. Female wings clear with orange-brown patch at nodus and halfway between nodus and body; pterostigmas brown. Abdomen yellow orange with pair of chevrons middorsally on S4–9.

### AUTUMN MEADOWHAWK *Sympetrum vicinum*
**Sp S F W** Reddish-brown eyes and brown face. Thorax dark brown or red; legs brown. Wing clear with pterostigma reddish brown. Abdomen red with dark mark dorsally on S9.

### VARIEGATED MEADOWHAWK *Sympetrum corruptum*
**Sp S F W** Reddish-brown eyes and red face. Thorax brown with lateral white stripes ending in yellow dots. Wings clear with red veins and pterostigma darkest at middle. Each abdominal segment outlined in red with brown inside.

### BLACK SADDLEBAGS *Tramea lacerata*
**Sp S F W** Dark eyes and face. Thorax black with metallic reflections. Wings large; hind wing with black saddle at base and often pale veins in this area. Dark pruinosity on thorax and abdomen.

### RED SADDLEBAGS *Tramea onusta*
**Sp S F W** Reddish-brown eyes and dark red face. Thorax brown. Hind wings marked with red saddle with clear window in middle. Veins at base of wings are red. Abdomen red with black spots dorsally on S8–9. Females and young males more brown than red.

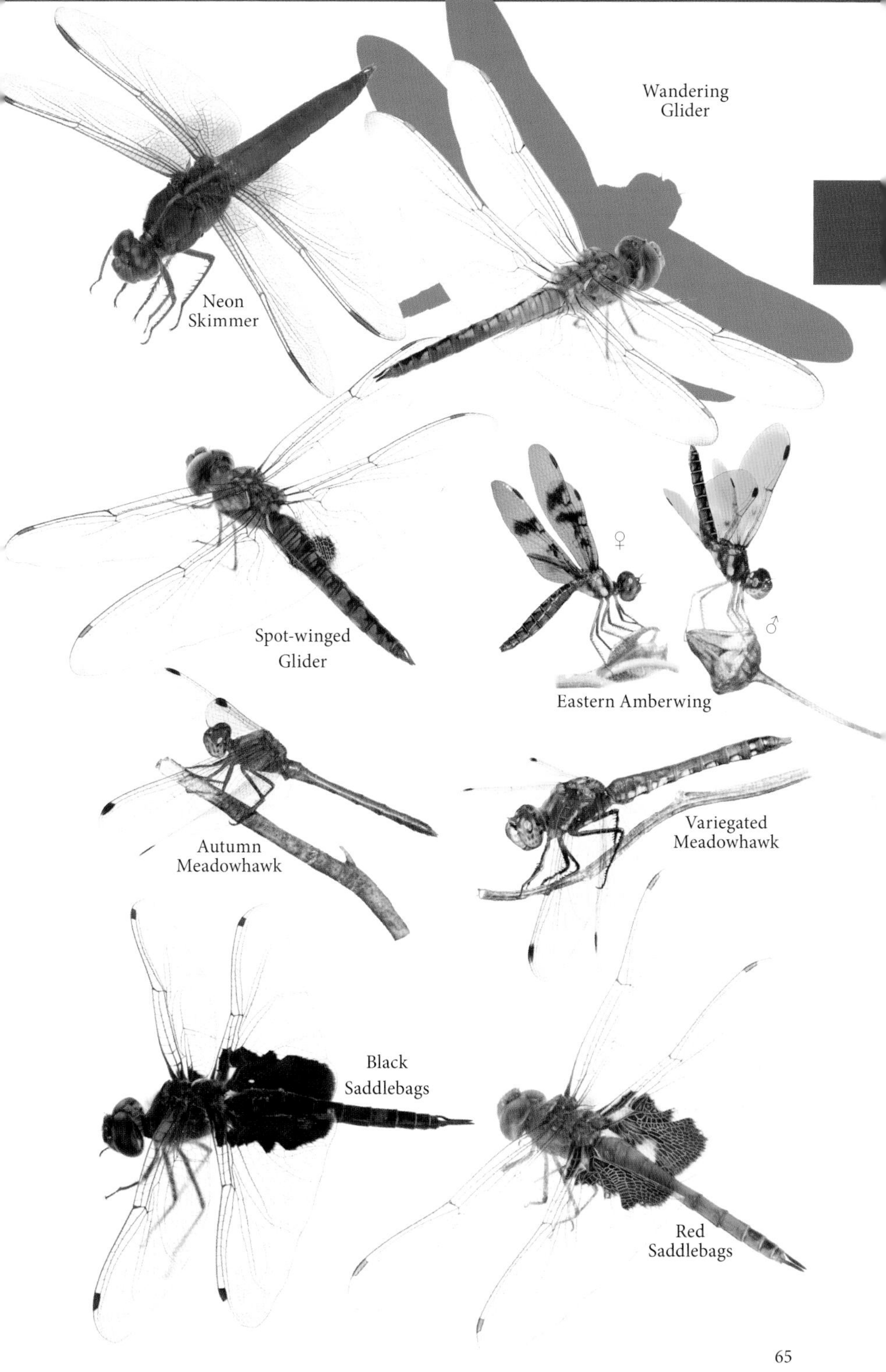

Wandering
Glider

Neon
Skimmer

Spot-winged
Glider

Eastern Amberwing

Autumn
Meadowhawk

Variegated
Meadowhawk

Black
Saddlebags

Red
Saddlebags

# Stoneflies
# Order Plecoptera

Gravid Common Stonefly
(*Perlesta* sp.)

**NATURAL HISTORY** This is a small group of aquatic insects that get
their name because they are often seen running around streamside on rocks,
stones, and vegetation. The ordinal name means pleated (*plecos*) wing (*ptera*)
and refers to the large hind wing that is folded under the forewing when
at rest. This group of insects is most diverse in the fast flowing streams of
higher latitudes, and is not well represented in Texas. They undergo simple
metamorphosis.

As a group, they are sensitive to pollutants and thus their presence is an
indicator of good water quality. The layman is most familiar with them as
models for tying flies for fishing, with patterns such as the "salmonflies"
and "golden stones." While capable of flight, they generally don't venture far
from the water in which the nymphs reside. Most species are fully winged
(macropterous), but some have reduced wings (brachypterous) either in
one or both sexes. They have long filamentous antennae and cerci that often
project past the wings.

The nymphs look remarkably like the adults with only wing pads instead
of full wings. Once the adult emerges, in many species, males and females
engage in a form of vibrational communication. They will either tap their
abdomen against the substrate (percussion) or do pushups (tremulation) on
vegetation in a species-specific pattern. Males will call and virgin females
will answer. Once a female calls, she stops moving and the male must
triangulate on her position by a back and forth call-answer interchange.

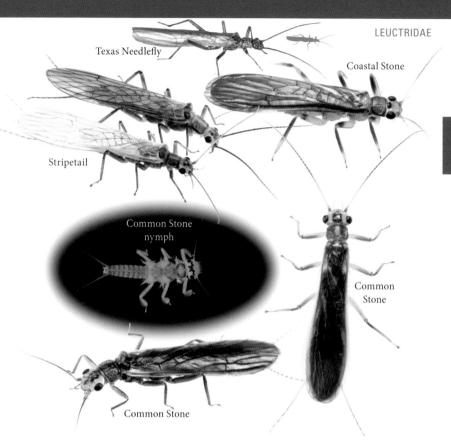

Texas Needlefly

Coastal Stone

Stripetail

Common Stone
nymph

Common
Stone

Common Stone

### TEXAS NEEDLEFLY *Zealeuctra hitei*
LEUCTRIDAE

**Sp S F W** Small, dark, needle-like stonefly with wings rolled around the body when at rest. Cerci are 1-segmented. Found in intermittent streams of the blackland prairie and Edward's Plateau.

### STRIPETAIL *Isoperla* sp.
PERLODIDAE

**Sp S F W** Medium-sized yellowish or greenish to dark stoneflies. Head and pronotum often yellow with dark pattern. Antennae dark. Wings yellowish green often with black veins. Cerci long, extending well beyond wing tip. Nymphs occur in permanently flowing streams.

### COASTAL STONE *Neoperla clymene*
PERLIDAE

**Sp S F W** Medium-sized yellowish stonefly with darker wings and pronotum. Antennae pale basally and distally with middle segments dark. Two ocelli. Legs with dark banding. Cerci just extend beyond wings. Nymphs in permanent flowing streams.

### COMMON STONE *Perlesta* sp.

**Sp S F W** Medium-sized yellowish stonefly with darker wings and pronotum. Head yellow with large dark spot dorsally. Three ocelli. Cerci long, extending well beyond wings. Nymphs in streams.

# Caddisflies
# Order Trichoptera

Northern Caddisfly
(*Pycnopsyche* sp.)

**NATURAL HISTORY** Caddisfly adults superficially look like moths, but they have hairs (sometimes also scales) on their wings and have chewing mouthparts (not a coiled proboscis). The ordinal name in fact means hairy (*trichos*) wing (*ptera*). The wings are usually held roof-like over the abdomen and they have long filamentous antennae. Most adults are drab, but some species are colorful and/or conspicuously patterned.

They have complete metamorphosis with aquatic larvae. Arguably, the larvae are more interesting than the adults. They are caterpillar-like and may have filamentous gills along the abdomen. They lack abdominal prolegs, but do have a pair of anal prolegs, each with a hook at the end. They live in a variety of habitats including ponds, lakes, streams, and rivers. A number of groups make cases out of plants, sand, or gravel. The cases are often diagnostic and may be easier to recognize as a genus than the adult or larvae itself. The larvae build these cases using silk produced from modified salivary glands. Other species build silk retreats, while still others are free-living. The retreats and cases are often seen attached to the sides of submerged rocks, logs, and other substrates. Most larvae feed on phytoplankton and various organic materials in the water, but a few are predatory on black fly larvae and other small insects. The larvae pupate underwater and then swim to the surface when they are ready to emerge as adults. Adults are not strong fliers, but are very common at lights, especially near water.

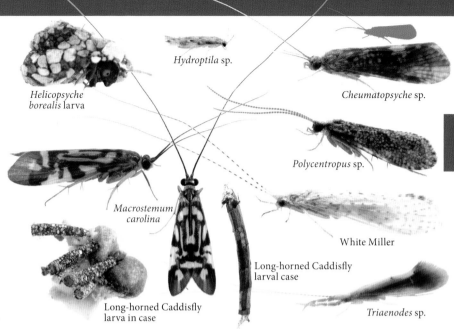

Helicopsyche
borealis larva

Hydroptila sp.

Cheumatopsyche sp.

Polycentropus sp.

Macrostemum
carolina

White Miller

Long-horned Caddisfly
larval case

Long-horned Caddisfly
larva in case

Triaenodes sp.

**SNAIL-CASE CADDISFLY** *Helicopsyche borealis*   HELICOPSYCHIDAE
[ Sp  **S**  **F**  **W** ]   Larvae in flowing water and littoral zones of lakes where they make coiled case. Adults (not shown) small, grayish brown with heavily fringed wings and antennae half length of body.

**MICROCADDISFLY** *Hydroptila sp.*   HYDROPTILIDAE
[ Sp  **S**  **F**  **W** ]   Variably colored, very tiny, often quick moving. Larvae feed on filamentous green algae. Larvae free-living until final instar.

**NETSPINNING CADDISFLY** *Cheumatopsyche sp.*   HYDROPSYCHIDAE
[ Sp  **S**  **F**  **W** ]   Grayish brown with variously mottled wings. Thorax sometimes with greenish cast. Wings not much longer than body. Larvae make net retreats in creeks, streams, and rivers.

**NETSPINNING CADDISFLY** *Macrostemum carolina*
[ Sp  **S**  **F**  **W** ]   Distinctively patterned orange-brown and black wings, dark antennae and orange-brown legs. Eyes large. Antennae long.

**TUBE MAKING CADDISFLY** *Polycentropus sp.*   POLYCENTROPODIDAE
[ Sp  **S**  **F**  **W** ]   Usually brownish with speckled wings and dark spots at veins along distal margin. Antennae somewhat thickened.

**WHITE MILLER** *Nectopsyche sp.*   LEPTOCERIDAE
[ Sp  **S**  **F**  **W** ]   Elongated, white speckled wings with green body. Antennae twice as long as body and banded. Larvae found in lakes and slow rivers; make a long case out of plant and mineral fragments.

**LONG-HORNED CADDISFLY** *Triaenodes sp.*
[ Sp  **S**  **F**  **W** ]   Tan to dark brown. Wings swept up posteriorly; pale stripe running down middorsally. Antennae twice as long as body.

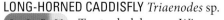

# Earwigs
# Order Dermaptera

European Earwig
(*Forficula auricularia*)

**NATURAL HISTORY** This is a small, largely tropical group. The ordinal name means skin (*derma*) wing (*ptera*) and refers to the hardened forewings called tegmina or elytra. The hind wings, when present, are folded up under these covers. The common name results from an old wives' tale that these insects would crawl into your ears. They are harmless, though some will emit foul smelling odors when disturbed.

The most noticeable feature of this group is the paired pincers (cerci) at the tip of the abdomen. They are usually larger in males and are used for defense, grabbing and holding prey when feeding, and even folding and unfolding wings. They have well-developed compound eyes, but lack ocelli. The mouthparts are chewing and most species feed on detritus, but some are predaceous on other insects. They are largely nocturnal, hiding under bark, fallen logs, leaf litter, and rocks.

Eggs are laid in clusters within burrows in the soil. The female will guard the eggs and groom the young, protecting them from invasive fungi. Nymphs have fewer antennal segments than the adults, adding a segment with each molt. Males have a 10-segmented abdomen, while females have 8 segments and usually the pincers are straight.

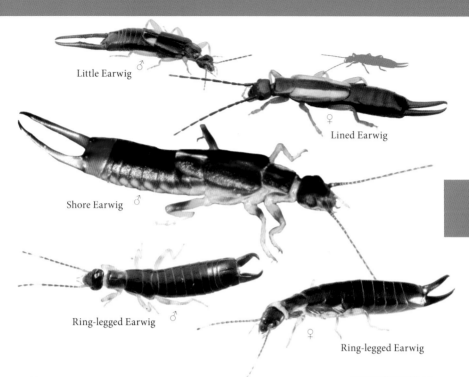

Little Earwig ♂

Lined Earwig ♀

Shore Earwig ♂

Ring-legged Earwig ♂

Ring-legged Earwig ♀

**LITTLE EARWIG** *Vostox brunneipennis*          SPONGIPHORIDAE

**Sp S F W**   Small colorful earwig with yellow legs. Head, pronotum, and tegmina dark brown. Distance behind eyes shorter than head length. Tip of hind wing protruding from under tegmina dark with yellow spot. Abdomen and cerci reddish brown. Male with longer cerci. Found under bark of dead trees.

**LINED EARWIG** *Doru taeniatum*          FORFICULIDAE

**Sp S F W**   Reddish head and pronotum. Distance behind eyes longer than eye length. Tegmina and tips of hind wings yellow with broad, black middorsal stripe. Antennae dark. Legs yellowish brown. Abdomen dark brown. Found on grasses and readily attracted to lights.

**SHORE EARWIG** *Labidura riparia*          LABIDURIDAE

**Sp S F W**   Large, variable species with dark head and pronotum. Tegmina dark with reddish middorsal stripe. Protruding hind wings tan with large black diffuse spot. Legs yellowish-brown. Abdomen dark. Found in leaf litter, especially along beaches and rivers.

**RING-LEGGED EARWIG** *Euborellia annulipes*          ANISOLABIDIDAE

**Sp S F W**   Dark brown wingless species. Antennae dark, usually with penultimate segments pale. Legs tan and usually with dark rings. Male's right cerci curved in more than left. Common under debris, logs, and rocks and indoors in plants and soil mixes.

# Webspinners
# Order Embiidina

Black Webspinner
(*Oligotoma nigra*)

**NATURAL HISTORY** This is a small group of slender, largely tropical species found under rocks, on and under the bark of trees and within leaf litter, where they create silken galleries. The ordinal name is derived from *embio,* meaning "lively," and presumably refers to their active behavior within their galleries. They have simple metamorphosis with usually one generation per year. Females and young are generally more cylindrical in cross-section, while males are somewhat dorsoventrally flattened. Antennae are filiform, usually about two-thirds the length of the body. They have well-developed compound eyes, but lack ocelli. Adult males do not feed, but use their mandibles to chew through silk gaining entrance to a gallery and for grasping the female's head prior to mating. The basal segment of the front tarsus is enlarged and contains silk-producing glands. The hind femur is also enlarged. Most males are winged, while females and young are wingless. The tip of the abdomen bears a pair of two-segmented cerci, but in adult males of some species, the terminal segment of the left cercus is absorbed, resulting in asymmetrical cerci. Females always have symmetrical cerci.

   Most species spend their lives within the silken galleries they create. These can be in leaf litter, crevices in the soil, under rocks, on trees and even on epiphytic plants. Webspinners are unusual in that they produce silk from glands in their front tarsi as opposed to salivary or rectal glands. Most colonies are made up of a mother and her offspring. They may feign death, but most often run backward quickly when disturbed. They feed on detritus, lichens, and mosses.

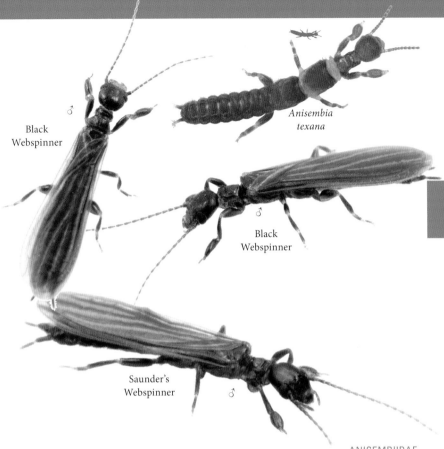

Black
Webspinner ♂

Anisembia
texana

Black
Webspinner ♂

Saunder's
Webspinner ♂

### WEBSPINNER *Anisembia texana*
ANISEMBIIDAE

Sp **S F W**  Slender, reddish-orange, with or without wings. Mandibles of adult males not dentate. Left cercus 1-segmented. Intersegmental membranes of thorax obvious, remaining light as the rest of the body darkens. Found under rocks and on and under loose bark in silken galleries.

### BLACK WEBSPINNER *Oligotoma nigra*
OLIGOTOMIDAE

Sp **S F W**  Slender, uniformly black, including wings. Males winged; females wingless. Males with mandibles apically dentate and left cercus 2-segmented. Males with broad, slender left tergal process and talon-like ventrally directed hook on left side of apex of 9th abdominal sternum. Males attracted to lights. Native to India.

### SAUNDER'S WEBSPINNER *Oligotoma saundersii*

Sp **S F W**  Slender, uniformly black, including wings. Males winged; females wingless. Males with mandibles apically dentate and left cercus 2-segmented. Males with broad, spatulate left tergal process and sickle-shaped horizontal hook beneath apex of 9th abdominal sternum. Males are attracted to lights. Native to Asia.

# Angel Insects
# Order Zoraptera

*Zorotypus hubbardi*

**NATURAL HISTORY** *Zor* in Zoraptera is derived from the word "Zoroastrian," an ancient Persian religion where the pure will end in an angelic state. It, along with *aptera*, meaning "wingless," was meant to describe the "purely wingless" group as no winged individuals were known when the group was initially discovered. The common name Angel Insects is also a reference to the Zoroastrian religion.

A single family, Zorotypidae, and genus, *Zorotypus,* are known worldwide. Thirty-nine species have been described and two occur in the United States, one in Texas. Species identification is very difficult and primarily done by examining genitalic differences. They have simple metamorphosis and are 2–3 mm long.

Angel insects can be very hard to find in the wild. They prefer a very specific stage of rotting log. But if you find the perfect log, you will likely find a whole colony (~30 individuals). There is usually one dominant male, the oldest, per colony. During reproduction, males produce only one sperm that is 2 mm long, their entire body length! When a rotting log is no longer a suitable habitat, a winged female will be born and she will fly off to discover another appropriate rotten log to start a new colony. She will then lose her wings and begin laying eggs. It takes several months for the eggs to go from nymph to adult. Winged individuals have compound eyes while the wingless individuals lack them. They eat fungus spores and other small soft bodied invertebrates like springtails and termites.

*Zorotypus hubbardi*

### *Zorotypus hubbardi*                    ZOROTYPIDAE

**Sp  S  F  W**   Long, soft, cylindrical body, tan, white, or nearly clear in color. Antennae are long with 9 bead-like segments (moniliform) and chewing mouthparts. Compound eyes and ocelli are only found in winged forms. Males have a distinctive "mating hook" off the tip of the abdomen. Colonies are found in rotting logs or sawdust eating fungal spores and small insects. They exhibit unique grooming behaviors.

*Zorotypus hubbardi*

Individuals are often overlooked because of their small size. They are easily confused with ants, termites, and springtails that are often found running along with them.

# Barklice, Booklice, and True Lice
# Order Psocodea

Common Bark Louse
(*Ptycta polluta*)

**NATURAL HISTORY** The Psocodea contain both free-living (book and bark lice) and parasitic (true lice) groups. The ordinal name is derived from the Greek root *psokos*, meaning rubbed small or gnawed, referring to the manner in which barklice feed. They are all small, ranging from 1–10 mm and have simple metamorphosis.

Barklice and booklice are a small and easily overlooked, understudied group of insects. They can be winged or wingless and have an enlarged clypeus. Barklice are considered beneficial because they clean up debris. They are found on bark, shrubs, and foliage, under rocks, and on dead leaves. Booklice, however, can become a nuisance, living indoors feeding on books and paper. The most frequently encountered species in Texas is also one of the largest, *Cerastipsocus venosus*. They will form aggregations on the side of trees. Other barklice will envelop a tree trunk in webbing.

True lice are parasitic. They were historically placed in two separate orders: sucking lice (Anoplura) and chewing lice (Mallophaga). They are pests and can be vectors for a number of diseases. Animals with large infestations can become run down and emaciated. They generally have species-specific hosts and many are found on specific parts of the body. Two species of lice infect humans: the head louse and crab louse.

# Identifying Characters

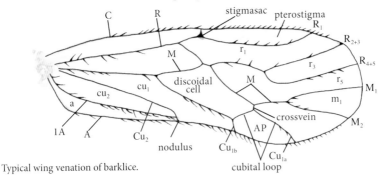

Typical wing venation of barklice.

The enlarged clypeus looks like a swollen structure on the front of the head.

Some individuals and groups can be identified by location and amount of hair on the wings.

Nymph of *Cerastipsocus venosus*; note short wing pads.

## Immature Stages

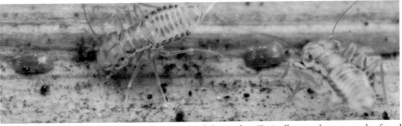

Iridescent barklice eggs from *Lachesilla* sp. with adult wingless *Tapinella maculata* on a palm frond.

## Behavior

Webbing of ancient barklice on hackberry tree. This species lives under the protective webbing.

*Cerastipsocus venosus* in feeding aggregation on tree trunk.

**BARKLOUSE** *Cerobasis guestfalica*                    TROGIIDAE

**Sp** S F W   Wings small, just reaching middle of thorax. Area below swollen clypeus dark. Dark lateral line on head, extending from below eye back through thorax and anchor-shaped mark on frons. Abdomen with distinctive checkered pattern. Found on trees, shrubs, and stone outcroppings.

**RETICULATE-WINGED TROGIID** *Lepinotus reticulatus*

**Sp** S F W   Body light brown. Wing pads small, normally not reaching past first third of abdomen and with a reticulated pattern. Found in granaries, leaf litter, and bird and mammal nests. Species is an obligate parthenogen, with only females known.

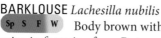

**BARKLOUSE** *Lachesilla nubilis*                    LACHESILLIDAE

**Sp** S **F** W   Body brown with blotches of color along terminal veins in forewing from $R_1$ to nodulus. Found in dead grasses and other decaying vegetation.

**LARGE-WINGED PSOCID** *Ectopsocopsis cryptomeriae*     ECTOPSOCIDAE

**Sp** S F W   Light brown in color. Forewing pterostigma rectangular. Found on dead leaves, including crop species, but rarely a pest in agriculture. Can survive where other psocids cannot.

**BARKLOUSE** *Peripsocus madidus*                    PERIPSOCIDAE

**Sp** S F W   Males have much larger eyes than females. Some females with wings only extending to tip of abdomen. Very little pigment at the base of cell $r_s$. Abdomen with reddish brown rings. Found on branches of broad-leaved trees and conifers.

**BOOKLOUSE** *Liposcelis bostrychophila*              LIPOSCELIDIDAE

**Sp** S F W   Very small, uniformly light brown. Found in bird nests, on bark, and in domestic areas like chicken coops, grain stores, and in books. Only females known from this species.

**ANCIENT BARKLOUSE** *Archipsocus* sp.              ARCHIPSOCIDAE

**Sp** S F W   Typically found under webbing on trunks of trees. Body is brown or orange-brown in color. Long hairs found on thorax point backward. Females give live birth. Common along the Gulf coast, but reaches far inland as well.

**BARKLOUSE** *Blaste garciorum*                    PSOCIDAE

**Sp** S **F** W   Females with dark patch on either side of $Cu_{1a}$, lacking in males. Both sexes with dark patches on pterostigma. Found in west Texas and the Rio Grande valley up to central Texas on branches of small trees and shrubs.

**BARKLOUSE** *Cerastipsocus venosus*

**Sp** S F W   Large with wings uniformly dark. Pterostigma usually white in females, dark in males. Yellow and brown stripes on abdomen particularly obvious on nymphs. Found in aggregations on trunks and branches of broad-leaved trees.

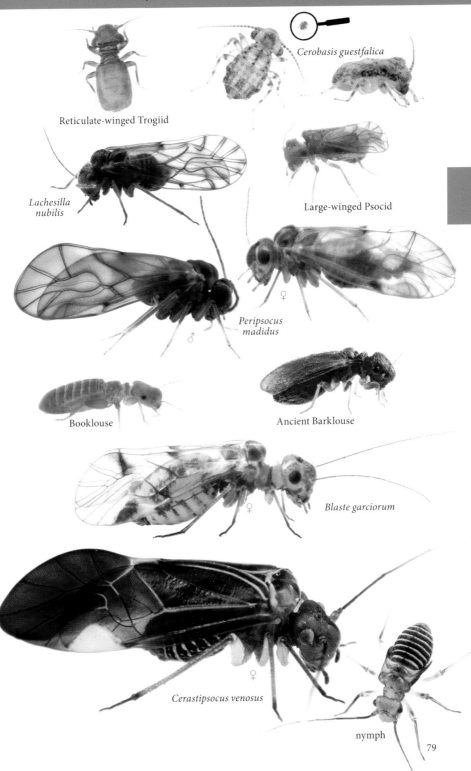

Reticulate-winged Trogiid

*Cerobasis guestfalica*

*Lachesilla nubilis*

Large-winged Psocid

*Peripsocus madidus* ♂ ♀

Booklouse

Ancient Barklouse

*Blaste garciorum* ♀

*Cerastipsocus venosus* ♀

nymph

79

### BARKLOUSE *Trichopsocus dalii* — AMPHIENTOMIDAE
**Sp S F W** Pale body. Brown on either side of Cu$_1$ vein in hind wing becoming broader distally. Found on bay and citrus leaves; not known to be a pest. Introduced to the United States from North Africa and Europe.

### BARKLOUSE *Lithoseopsis hellmani* — TRICHOPSOCIDAE
**Sp S F W** Head uniformly brown with long scales covering wings. Only females are known. Found on limestone outcroppings under leaf litter.

### DEER LOUSE *Tricholipeurus parallelus* — TRICHODECTIDAE
**Sp S F W** Found on deer. Have elongated abdomen and head less triangular than in poultry lice. Tarsi have 1 claw and antennae is 3-segmented. Some studies have found them to be more abundant in winter months.

### DOG LOUSE *Trichodectes canis*
**Sp S F W** Found on dogs and wild canids. Round abdomen. Tarsi with 1 claw and antennae 3-segmented. Can be a vector for dog tapeworms, but dogs generally show little irritation unless there is a large infestation.

### CHICKEN BODY LOUSE *Menacanthus stramineus* — MENOPONIDAE
**Sp S F W** Yellow elongated body with triangular head. Antennae hidden below head. Each leg with 2 tarsal claws and 2 or more rows of hairs on each abdominal segment. Most common louse found on chickens. Can cause reddening and irritation of the skin.

### SPINY RAT LOUSE *Polyplax spinulosa* — POLYPLACIDAE
**Sp S F W** Found on various species of rats. Has elongated body with 5-segmented antennae. Triangular sternal plate followed by series of plates running down sides of abdomen.

### HEAD LOUSE *Pediculus humanus* — PEDICULIDAE
**Sp S F W** Only found on human head and body. Elongated and white or grayish tan color. One tarsal claw on each leg. Adults live up to 30 days and need to feed on blood several times a day. Can lay up to 8 eggs a day and go from egg to adult in 2 weeks.

### HAWK LOUSE *Laemobothrion* sp. — LAEMOBOTHRIIDAE
**Sp S F W** One of the largest species of lice, reaching up to 11 mm. Found on waterfowl and birds of prey. Similar to poultry lice but head is less triangular and with prominent swelling at base of antennae.

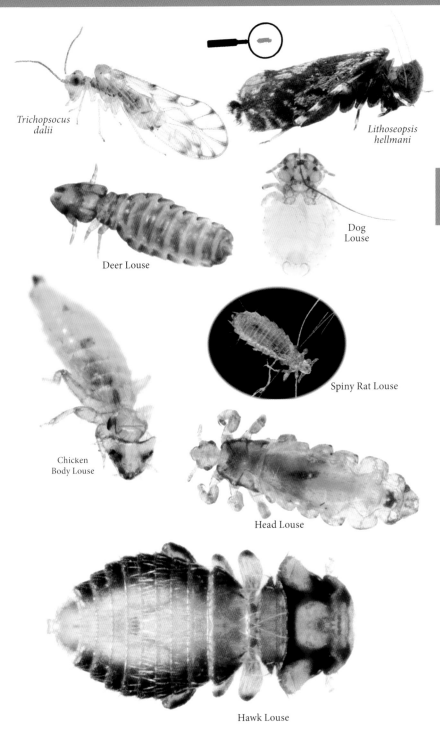

*Trichopsocus dalii*

*Lithoseopsis hellmani*

Deer Louse

Dog Louse

Spiny Rat Louse

Chicken Body Louse

Head Louse

Hawk Louse

# Thrips
# Order Thysanoptera

Thrips on a flower

**NATURAL HISTORY**   This is a common, but often unnoticed, group of minute insects. The name thrips means "wood louse." While wings may be present or absent, the ordinal name means fringe (*thysanos*) wing (*ptera*) and refers to the distinctive wings that characterize the group. They have few or no veins and long hairs creating a fringe. They have piercing-sucking mouthparts and are largely plant feeders, with some species predaceous. The antennae are relatively short and four to nine segmented. Some species possess an ovipositor and others have the abdomen elongated into a tube.

Metamorphosis in this group is unusual and somewhat intermediate between simple and complete. They have four to five instars. The first two are called larvae and lack external wings. In some groups the next two instars are inactive, don't feed, and have external wings. The third instar is referred to as a prepupa and the fourth a pupa, in these groups. The latter is sometimes enclosed in a silken cocoon. In the Phlaeothripidae, the third instar, called a propupa, lacks external wings and is followed by two pupal instars for a total of five instars. In both cases, the adult then follows the pupa. Parthenogenesis is known in many species. They are common, attacking the various parts of plants, and can be a pest. Some are even known to bite people.

Fringed wings, showing numerous hairs.

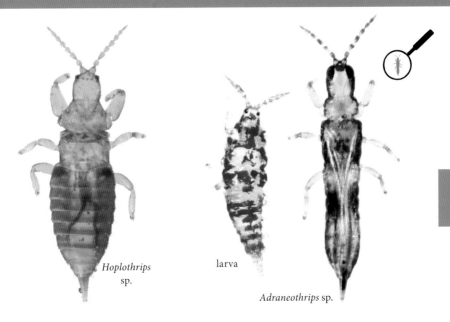

Hoplothrips
sp.

larva

Adraneothrips sp.

Aggregation of young and adult thrips (Phlaeothripinae) on log.

**TUBE-TAILED THRIP** (*Adraneothrips* sp.)          PHLAEOTHRIPIDAE

Sp S F W    Narrow, banded body with flecks of red. Prominent eyes. Antennae with dark diffuse banding. Abdomen extended into tube distally. Feed on fungus.

**TUBE-TAILED THRIP** (*Hoplothrips* sp.)

Sp S F W    Comparatively robust body with abdomen extended into short tube distally. Forewings, when present, are constricted medially. Front femora enlarged. Found in the flowers of composites and grasses.

83

# Fleas
# Order Siphonaptera

Cat Flea
(*Ctenocephalides felis*)

**NATURAL HISTORY**   Fleas are small to minute, wingless, laterally compressed, brownish ectoparasites found on a variety of vertebrates. The ordinal name means siphoning without wings; a good description! Adults have numerous rearward-directed spines and setae that make it more difficult for the flea to be removed as it moves through the hair or feathers of the host. They can be yellowish, brown, or nearly black. Eyes are small, but can be vestigial or absent in some species. Antennae are small and usually hidden within grooves. The legs are similar in shape with the hind legs being larger. Most species are capable of walking or jumping considerable distances relative to their size. Some species will attach themselves to the host permanently and may have reduced legs.

The mouthparts are designed to rip a hole in tissue and then excrete saliva to keep the blood from clotting. Blood from the host is then sucked up via a tube. Fleas have complete metamorphosis with a free-living legless larva that feeds on organic debris, especially the bloody frass of the adult, within the host's nest before pupating in a silken cocoon. A single cat flea can lay hundreds of eggs over its month-long life span as an adult.

Because fleas are blood-feeding ectoparasites, some species are capable of transmitting disease. Cat Scratch Disease or Cat Scratch Fever is a bacteria carried by cat fleas that infects numerous humans every year. The most well-known disease transmitted by fleas, however, is Bubonic Plague, responsible for millions for deaths. Historically, it was transmitted from rats to humans by the rat flea. Microscopic examination of detailed characters is needed to identify most species.

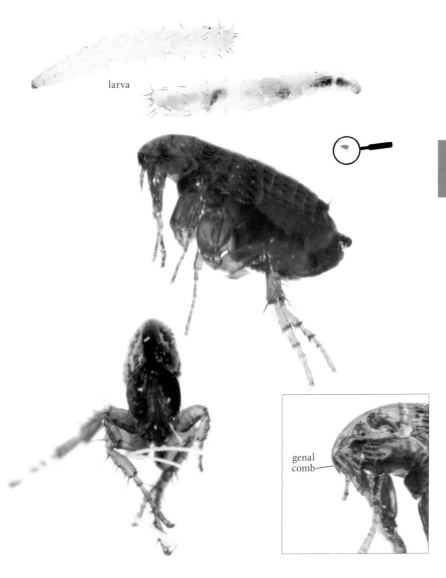

larva

genal comb

## CAT FLEA *Ctenocephalides felis*

PULICIDAE

(Sp S F W)   Small, brown, laterally compressed with low, sloping forehead. Genal comb with 7–8 sharp teeth. Adults feed on blood of host; larvae on various organic debris in the host nest. The most common domestic flea. Found on both cats and dogs as well as coyotes, foxes, rabbits, rats, and humans. A vector for murine typhus in humans in south Texas. They also are a host for tapeworms that commonly occur in infected hosts.

# Twisted-winged Parasites
# Order Strepsiptera

Twisted-wing Parasite (*Xenos pecki*) infecting a paper wasp (*Polistes metricus*) abdomen

**NATURAL HISTORY**   The Strepsiptera are minute, peculiar parasitic insects. The name twisted (*strepsi*) wing (*ptera*) refers to the relatively large hind wings and reduced forewings in males. They parasitize other insects including bees, wasps, grasshoppers, leafhoppers, silverfish, cockroaches, and even caddisflies. This order is a sister group to the beetles and was once even considered a family within the Coleoptera.

The sexes are quite different. The males are winged and free living. The females are wingless and do not leave their host except in the primitive family Mengenillidae, which does not occur in Texas. Males are superficially similar to beetles. They have large raspberry-like eyes with antennae that usually have elongated processes off some segments. The forewings are reduced to club-like structures similar to halteres in the Diptera. The hind wings are large and fan-like with reduced venation having only longitudinal veins and no crossveins. Females usually lack eyes, antennae, and legs and the body segments are somewhat fused.

The group has complete metamorphosis, but a complicated life history involving hypermetamorphosis. Males will emerge from the host and seek out a female still in the host. She produces sometimes up to thousands of small larvae that have well-developed eyes and legs. These active larvae then seek out and enter the body of a potential host. At this point, the larvae molt into a legless form that feeds on the host. Following several molts, they then pupate, usually between abdominal sclerites of the host. The female remains, the male flies off, and the cycle continues. Usually the host is killed, but not always.

forewing

Triozocera sp.
♂

Paraxenos westwoodi
in abdomen of *Sphex
ichneumoneus*

Xenos peckii ♂ pupa *in
Polistes metricus*

**TWISTED-WINGED PARASITE** *Triozocera* sp.     CORIOXENIDAE
Sp **S F W**   Parasitizes burrowing bugs (Cydnidae). Males with
finger-like 3-lobed antennae. Mandibles absent.

**TWISTED-WINGED PARASITE** *Paraxenos westwoodi*     STYLOPIDAE
Sp **S F W**   Parasitizes thread-wasted wasps (Sphecidae).

**TWISTED-WINGED PARASITE** *Xenos peckii*
Sp **S F W**   Parasitizes *Polistes* paper wasps (Vespidae).

# Grasshoppers, Katydids, and Crickets
## Order Orthoptera

Clip-wing Grasshopper
(*Metaleptea brevicornis*)

**NATURAL HISTORY** The ordinal name Orthoptera means "straight wing" and refers to the elongated forewings or tegmina, though a number of species have reduced wings. This group is fairly easy to recognize with enlarged hind legs modified for jumping. Most feed on plants, but some katydid species are predatory. There are distinctive groups, the grasshoppers and relatives (Suborder Caelifera) that have antennae shorter than their body and the katydids and crickets (Suborder Ensifera) that have antennae longer than the body.

Another very distinctive characteristic of Orthoptera is their ability to "sing." Many males will sing to attract and find females. Females can make sounds as well, but males are usually the dominant caller. The sound can be made by rubbing the two wings together or rubbing a leg and wing together. Calls are species-specific. Some species call at such a high level that we can not hear them. They hear with a pair of tympana either on the front leg or on the abdomen. When males and females find each other they will mate and lay eggs either on or in the ground or vegetation. The sex lives of many species of Orthoptera is very interesting with some male katydids and crickets plugging the female's genital opening with a spermatophore that not only provides sperm to fertilize eggs, but also a nutritional supplement for the female to eat, all while preventing other males from mating with her.

# Identifying Characters

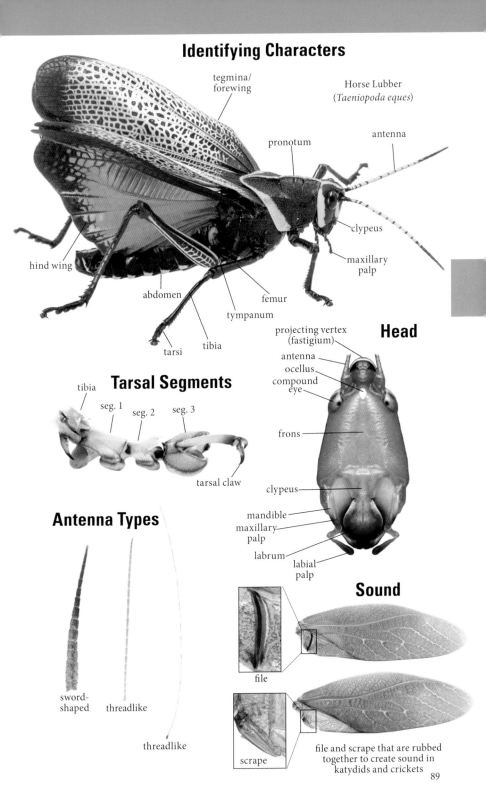

tegmina/
forewing

Horse Lubber
(*Taeniopoda eques*)

pronotum

antenna

clypeus

maxillary
palp

hind wing

abdomen

femur

tympanum

tarsi

tibia

## Tarsal Segments

tibia

seg. 1

seg. 2

seg. 3

tarsal claw

## Head

projecting vertex
(fastigium)

antenna

ocellus

compound
eye

frons

clypeus

mandible

maxillary
palp

labrum

labial
palp

## Antenna Types

sword-
shaped

threadlike

threadlike

## Sound

file

scrape

file and scrape that are rubbed
together to create sound in
katydids and crickets

89

### GREEN-STRIPED GRASSHOPPER *Chortophaga viridifasciata*

ACRIDIDAE

**Sp S F W** Both green and brown forms exist along with intermediates. Elevated median ridge visible on pronotum. Wings unmarked and abdomen reddish brown. Found in wet areas with short grass where it feeds.

### AMERICAN BIRD GRASSHOPPER *Schistocerca americana*

**Sp S F W** Large, strong-flying species. Several color forms exist from yellow to brown. Dorsal cream stripe present from tip of head through middle of wings. When conditions are good, can become abundant and swarm. Feeds on grass, shrubs, and trees.

### OBSCURE BIRD GRASSHOPPER *Schistocerca obscura*

**Sp S F W** Large and green, gray or reddish brown. Has bright yellow spot on "knee" and side of thorax. Occasionally females lack this spot. Tibia are blackish purple with yellow spines. Found in fields and open woodlands, occasionally feeds on flowers.

### MISCHIEVOUS BIRD GRASSHOPPER *Schistocerca damnifica*

**Sp S F W** Reddish brown in color with an elevated ridge on pronotum and sometimes a pale yellow line on top of head, otherwise lacking a prominent dorsal stripe down the body. Found in old grasslands or open woodlands.

### SPOTTED BIRD GRASSHOPPER *Schistocerca lineata*

**Sp S F W** Large and yellow, brown, or green with distinctive pits and yellow dots on the top of the pronotum. Dorsal coloring usually darker than lateral coloring. Yellow line from top of head to middle of forewing. Front and middle femora distinctly swollen. Often abundant in sandy areas near shrubs; rarely forested habitats.

### WRINKLED GRASSHOPPER *Hippiscus ocelote*

**Sp S F W** Large and heavy bodied. Top of pronotum is rough or wrinkled with a light-colored "X" on pronotum to head. Wings are panther spotted with a light-colored line down the top of the abdomen on forewings. Found in pastures and feeds on low grass.

### TEXAS MERMIRIA *Mermiria texana*

**Sp S F W** Face somewhat slanted. Contrasting brown and pale yellow stripes on head and pronotum. Dark stripe runs from top of head along midline to halfway down wings. Two pale streaks near costal margin of forewing. Eats grass in areas of rocky slopes.

### CLIP-WING GRASSHOPPER *Metaleptea brevicornis*

**Sp S F W** Slant-faced species with forewings angled at tip. Hind wings not pigmented. May be green or brown. Antennae sword-shaped. Prefers tall grasses around ponds and marshes. Strong flyer that may be attracted to lights unlike most species.

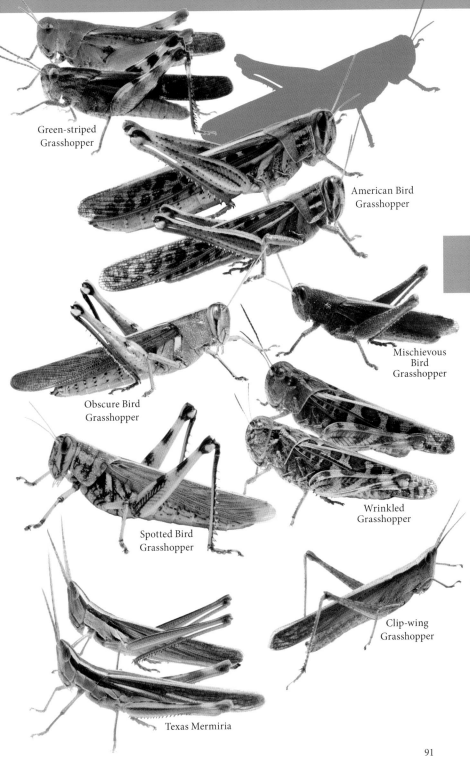

Green-striped Grasshopper

American Bird Grasshopper

Mischievous Bird Grasshopper

Obscure Bird Grasshopper

Wrinkled Grasshopper

Spotted Bird Grasshopper

Clip-wing Grasshopper

Texas Mermiria

91

## MONTEZUMA'S GRASSHOPPER *Syrbula montezuma*

**Sp S F W** Slanted face and antennae thin with expanded tips in males. Hind legs long and slender. Forewings more uniform in pattern; hind wings black. May be green or black. Both sexes with black stripe on sides of pronotum; female with it interrupted in middle forming two dark triangles. Found on taller grass in arid grasslands.

## ADMIRABLE GRASSHOPPER *Syrbula admirabilis*

**Sp S F W** Face more slanted than in Montezuma's Grasshopper. Antennae thin and thicker at tip in males. Pronotum with lateral ridges marked by white and continuous black stripe in female. Hind legs long and slender. Leading edge of wing green or gray; trailing edge is dark. Overall color brown to green.

## PINE TREE SPUR-THROAT GRASSHOPPER *Melanoplus punctulatus*

**Sp S F W** Gray, brown, tan, or yellow mottled color. Hind legs with light and dark bands. Hind tibiae reddish or gray. Body and forewings with numerous dark brown or black spots. Often found associated with pines, found on trunks of trees.

## ARID LANDS SPUR-THROAT GRASSHOPPER *Melanoplus aridus*

**Sp S F W** Small with short, oval tegmina widely separated. Brown, gray, or green. Black bar behind eyes wide, often with included white spot. Usually has thin black stripe down middle of pronotum. Hind femur brown with pale stripes; tibia blue.

## RED-LEGGED GRASSHOPPER *Melanoplus femurrubrum*

**Sp S F W** One of the most common grasshoppers in the US. Black stripe extending from back of eye along side of pronotum. Hind tibia red or blue, sometimes with black bands. Found in thick vegetation, disturbed areas, and near water in arid areas.

## TWO-STRIPED GRASSHOPPER *Melanoplus bivittatus*

**Sp S F W** Yellow stripe starting at eyes and extending back to middle of forewings, forming "V" when seen from above. Body olive or greenish-yellow above and yellow below. Hind femur yellow with dark longitudinal stripe. Often found in meadows.

## PLEBEIAN SHORT-WING GRASSHOPPER *Melanoplus plebejus*

**Sp S F W** Both fully winged and reduced-winged individuals. Forewings longer than pronotum and pointed in reduced-winged individuals. Overall color tan or brown. Hind tibia bluish. Found in areas with short grass and weeds, also found on flowers.

## DIFFERENTIAL GRASSHOPPER *Melanoplus differentialis*

**Sp S F W** Very common species; variable in color. Body olive green with dark contrasting markings. Pronotum and forewings uniform in color lacking distinguishing characters. Hind femur with black chevron markings on the outer side even obvious in dark morphs.

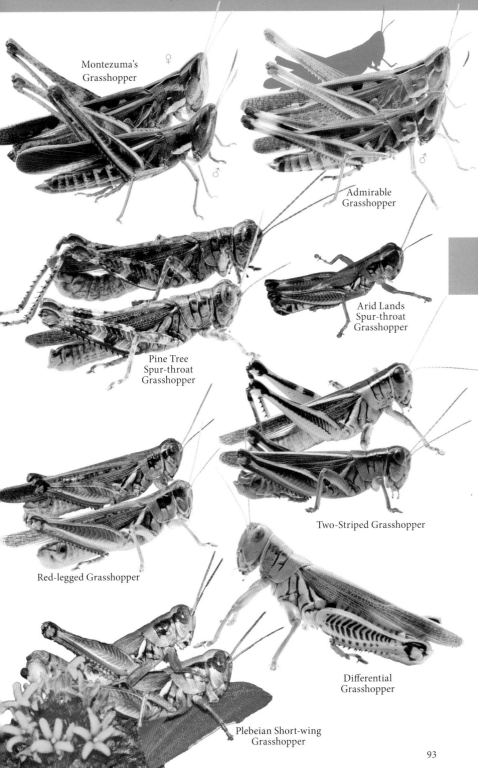

Montezuma's Grasshopper ♀

♂

Admirable Grasshopper ♂

Pine Tree Spur-throat Grasshopper

Arid Lands Spur-throat Grasshopper

Two-Striped Grasshopper

Red-legged Grasshopper

Differential Grasshopper

Plebeian Short-wing Grasshopper

### SLENDER RANGE GRASSHOPPER *Acantherus piperatus* ACRIDIDAE

**Sp S F W** Face somewhat slanted. Eyes distinctly peppered. Body, including tegmina, reddish gray and mottled. Antennae long and thin. Hind femur long and slender with white band distally.

### RAINBOW GRASSHOPPER *Dactylotum bicolor*

**Sp S F W** Distinctive color with reddish orange, yellow, or white on blue or black. Forewings are reduced and black with yellow veins. Hind tibia yellow and green. Found in areas with low vegetation, feeding on broad-leaved plants.

### PRAIRIE BOOPIE *Boopedon gracile*

**Sp S F W** Large grasshopper with unusually large rounded head. Hind tibia red, black and cream. Three broad bands cross the hind femur. In males the wings usually reach the end of the abdomen and in females the wings are shorter than the abdomen. Feeds on medium tall grass in prairies and rangelands.

### CREOSOTE BUSH GRASSHOPPER *Bootettix argentatus*

**Sp S F W** Green grasshopper with pointed head marked with white and black thorax and legs. Forewings spotted. Hind tibia green. Exclusively feeds on creosote bush.

### SOUTHWESTERN DUSKY GRASSHOPPER *Encoptolophus subgracilis*

**Sp S F W** Grayish brown with dark bands on forewings. Females can be green. Median ridge of pronotum raised, but not significantly so. Light-colored "X" visible on pronotum when viewed from above. Hind femur with dark bands and tibia bright blue. Found in grasslands, including within deserts.

### PALLID-WINGED GRASSHOPPER *Trimerotropis pallidipennis*

**Sp S F W** Variable species with two dark bands on forewing. Hind wing is clear to light yellow with dark band in middle. Hind tibia can be yellow, orange, or brown. Found in grasslands and deserts but not found at high elevations.

### APACHE GRASSHOPPER *Hippopedon capito*

**Sp S F W** Gray or tan with black markings. Wide black band may be present below the eye with a wider pale stripe below that. Median ridge on pronotum elevated, but reduced posteriorly. Wings long; forewings with large black spots or bands. Hind wings yellow basally with black band medially. Inhabits hilly prairies.

### MODEST GRASSHOPPER *Agroecotettix modestus*

**Sp S F W** Brown or gray and generally mottled. Forewings reduced, widely separated, and oval. Thin, dark parallel lines on top of pronotum. Hind tibia and inner surface of femur red. Found on Chihuahuan Desert scrub.

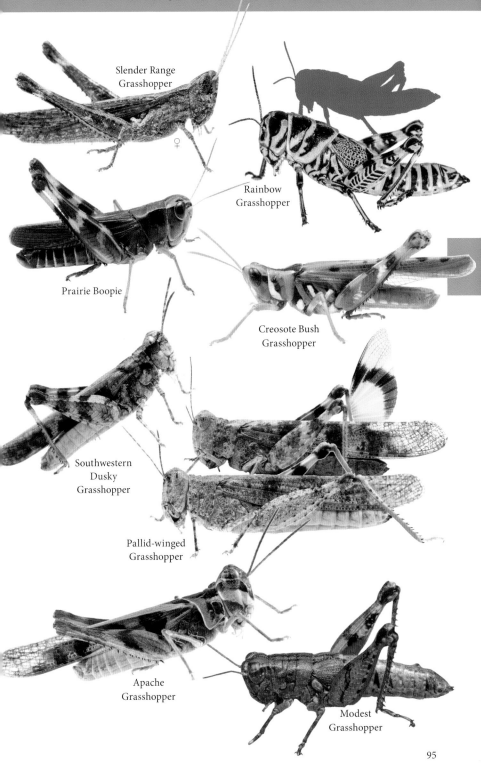

Slender Range Grasshopper

♀

Rainbow Grasshopper

Prairie Boopie

Creosote Bush Grasshopper

Southwestern Dusky Grasshopper

Pallid-winged Grasshopper

Apache Grasshopper

Modest Grasshopper

ACRIDIDAE

### SAUSSURE'S BLUE-WINGED GRASSHOPPER *Leprus intermedius*

**Sp S F W** Highly variable in color; gray, brown, black, or red. Forewings with 3 broad, dark bands or spots separated by paler areas with pale stripe along leading edge. When it flies blue hind wings and abdomen are visible. Found in arid, barren areas where it can be locally abundant but generally uncommon.

### WHEELER'S BLUE-WINGED GRASSHOPPER *Leprus wheeleri*

**Sp S F W** Gray or brown. Wings with 3 broad, dark bands. Hind wings yellow east of the Pecos, blue or green further west, with a medial black band. Pale stripes running along leading edge of each wing. Generally on exposed gravelly slopes in hilly terrain.

### PLAINS YELLOW-WINGED GRASSHOPPER *Arphia simplex*

**Sp S F W** Light to dark brown, sometimes with speckles. Wings long. Hind wings can be yellow to dark orange with a black band near the tip. Hind tibia is dark, sometimes blue. Found in bunchgrass prairies, open fields, and edge of wooded areas.

### RED-WINGED GRASSHOPPER *Arphia pseudonietana*

**Sp S F W** Color pattern can vary from mottled to solid black. Hind wings red to red-orange with a black margin. Hind tibia and femur with light-colored band near knee. Found in western grasslands and feeds on grasses and broad-leaved plants.

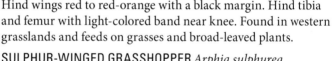

### SULPHUR-WINGED GRASSHOPPER *Arphia sulphurea*

**Sp S F W** Body reddish to dark brown. Raised ridge on pronotum continuous; sometimes shallowly notched. Hind wing deep yellow, sometimes more orange, with broad marginal black band and narrow spur extending basally. Found in prairies and on roadsides.

### AZTEC GRASSHOPPER *Lactista azteca*

**Sp S F W** Smallish, light gray, cream, brown, or red-brown with a dark stripe on forewing. Pronotum narrows sharply rearward. Hind wing yellow with dark band. Found in arid environments, however infrequently found aggregating in grasslands.

### EASTERN LUBBER GRASSHOPPER *Romalea microptera*

**Sp S F W** Large and colorful, but variable from black to mostly yellow with red and black markings. Reduced forewings about two-thirds length of abdomen. Nymphs usually black with yellow to red markings. Found in various habitats but prefers wooded habitats.

### PLAINS LUBBER GRASSHOPPER *Brachystola magna*

**Sp S F W** Large, heavy-bodied. Either reddish brown marked with green or green marked with brown. Forewings reduced and pink with black spots. Pronotum rough and edged in white. Hind tibia with large spines. Generally abundant in areas with poor soil.

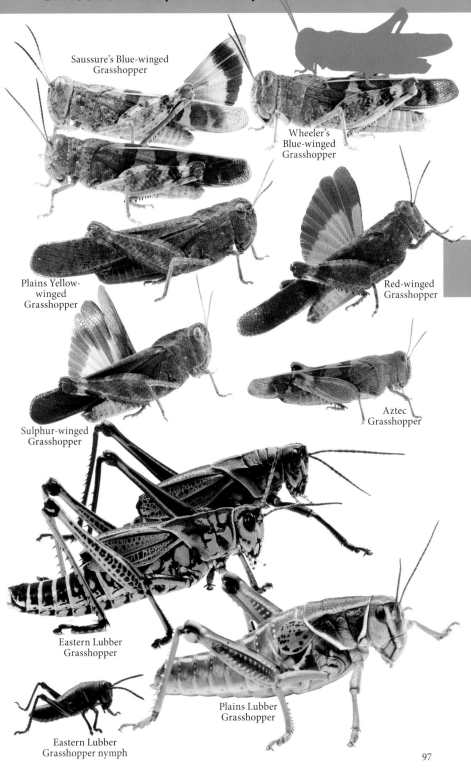

Saussure's Blue-winged Grasshopper

Wheeler's Blue-winged Grasshopper

Plains Yellow-winged Grasshopper

Red-winged Grasshopper

Sulphur-winged Grasshopper

Aztec Grasshopper

Eastern Lubber Grasshopper

Plains Lubber Grasshopper

Eastern Lubber Grasshopper nymph

97

### HOODED GROUSE LOCUST *Paratettix cucullatus*

( Sp S F W ) Gray, brown, or reddish brown. Robust with strongly lobed middle femur. Legs banded and hind femur with some mottling. Area between the eyes narrow and not protruding forward. Pronotum truncate near head, narrowing to a tip past the abdomen and with raised lateral ridges.

### AZTEC PYGMY GRASSHOPPER *Paratettix aztecus*

( Sp S F W ) Red, brown, or grayish brown. Head and thorax white below. Front and mid legs pale and banded. Pronotum with lateral ridges weak anteriorly. Common on gravelly margins of streams.

### LARGER PYGMY MOLE CRICKET *Neotridactylus apicialis*

( Sp S F W ) Small, blackish or dark brown with pale markings along side and back margins of pronotum, forewings, and legs. Forewings short, covering about half abdomen length. Hind wings reach tip of abdomen or beyond. Front tarsi broad, thin, modified for digging. May be gregarious; found in sandy habitats near water.

### HOUSE CRICKET *Acheta domesticus*

( Sp S F W ) Head light brown with three dark transverse bands. Pronotum light brown with dark markings laterally and above. Wings brown coming to a tip and extending beyond abdomen. Hind tibia with two rows of several spines. Female with straight ovipositor.

### BROWN TRIG *Anaxipha* sp.

( Sp S F W ) Small, pale straw or brown colored. Relatively large, bulging eyes. First tarsal segment longer than remaining two. Females with short, upturned, sword-like ovipositors. Actively moving around feeding on vegetation.

### FIELD CRICKET *Gryllus* sp.

( Sp S F W ) Head, pronotum, and body black. Wings usually brown and extending beyond abdomen. Large eyes with ocelli in a triangular pattern. Easiest to identify this group by their calls, a series of clear, loud chirps.

### TWO-SPOTTED TREE CRICKET *Neoxabea bipunctata*

( Sp S F W ) Head and thorax reddish brown, fading to yellow posteriorly. Basal segment of antenna with blunt tooth laterally. Legs yellow. Female with two elongated dark spots on tegmina. Hind tibia lack spines. Found in deciduous woodlands and edges.

### NARROW-WINGED TREE CRICKET *Oecanthus niveus*

( Sp S F W ) Elongated green cricket with dark markings on head. First antennal segment with a dark "J" mark, second with an elongated spot. Wings narrow extending beyond abdomen. Often found on shrubs and trees around dwellings.

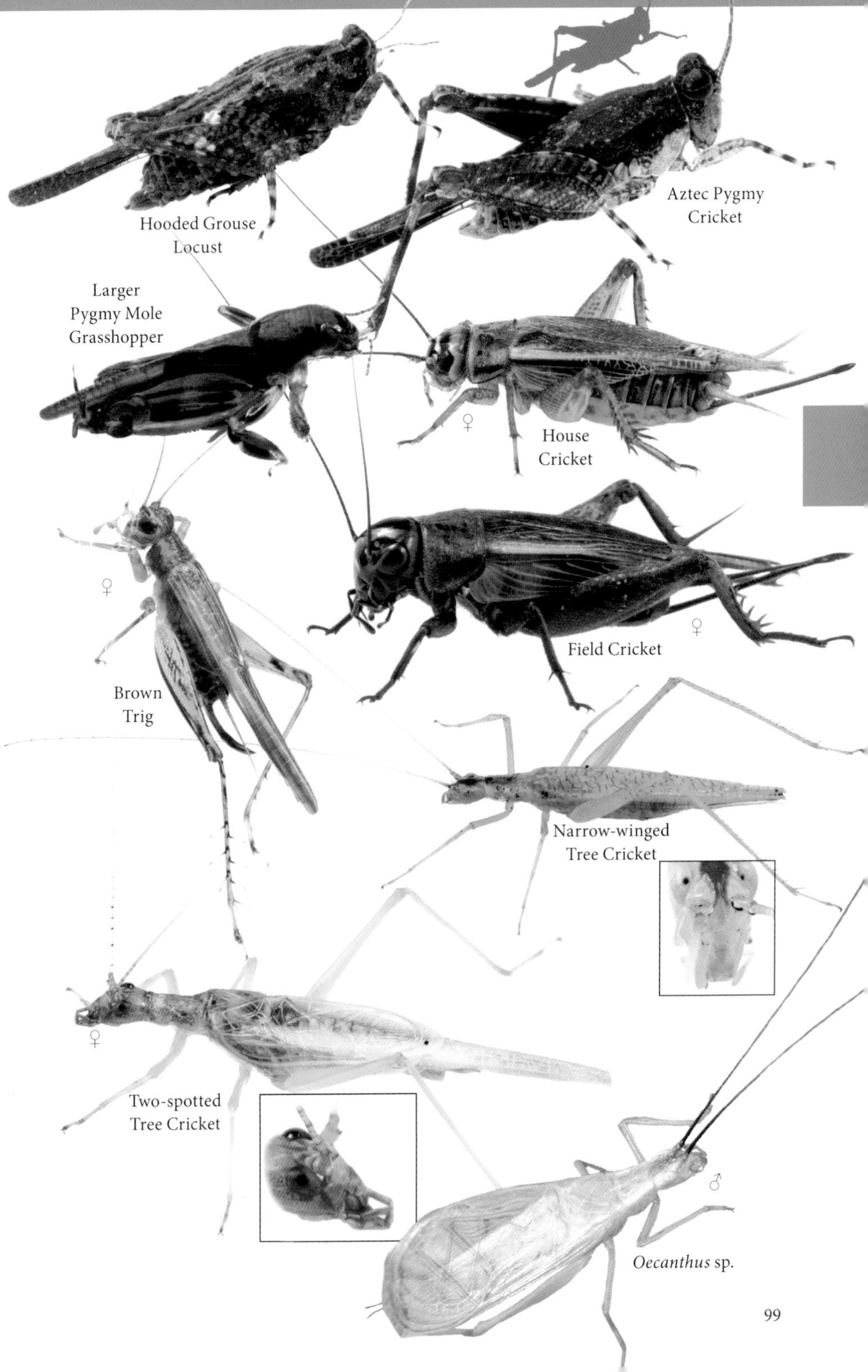

Hooded Grouse
Locust

Aztec Pygmy
Cricket

Larger
Pygmy Mole
Grasshopper

♀

House
Cricket

♀

Field Cricket ♀

Brown
Trig

Narrow-winged
Tree Cricket

♀

Two-spotted
Tree Cricket

♂

*Oecanthus* sp.

**NORTHERN MOLE CRICKET** *Neocurtilla hexadactyla*

**Sp S F W** Pronotum brownish. Six digging claws on each foreleg (4 on tibia and 2 more on the first and second tarsal segments). Front femur lacks a blade-like projection. Tegmina only slightly longer than pronotum.

**SOUTHERN MOLE CRICKET** *Neoscapteriscus borellii*

**Sp S F W** Pronotum gray, usually with 4 pale spots. Four digging claws on each foreleg (2 on tibia and 2 more on the first and second tarsal segments). Front femur armed with a blade-like projection. The hind femur does not reach the tip of the abdomen. Females lack an ovipositor.

**THIN-FOOTED THREAD-LEG KATYDID** *Arethaea* sp.

**Sp S F W** Legs, wings, and antennae all elongated. Femora twice as long as abdomen and forewing 8 times as long as wide. Eyes elliptical and pronotum saddle-like with rounded edges. Found on grasses, weeds, and brush out in the open and in woodlands.

**SOUTHERN PROTEAN SHIELDBACK** *Atlanticus pachymerus*

**Sp S F W** Brown, stout bodied with reduced wings. Antennae twice or more the length of the body. Hind femurs thin and longer than body length. Female with sword-like ovipositor the length of the body.

**SLENDER MEADOW KATYDID** *Conocephalus fasciatus*

**Sp S F W** Slender green katydid with brownish forewings longer than abdomen. Reddish eyes and antennae more than three times the body length. Ovipositor is straight and 2/3 the length of the abdomen. Found in grassy and weedy vegetation.

**CHESTNUT SHORT-WING KATYDID** *Dichopetala castanea*

**Sp S F W** Green body; brown on top of head, thorax, and abdomen. Female with wings reduced to small scales, males with forewings extending to 1/3 of the abdomen. Hind femurs long, thin and green basally, becoming orange then black distally.

**LESSER ANGLE-WING KATYDID** *Microcentrum retinerve*

**Sp S F W** Large broad-winged katydid. Forewings curved more sharply along top than bottom. Tegmina rounded distally and hind wings pointed, extending beyond forewings. Area in front of male stridulatory organ brown. Front margin of pronotum lacks tooth.

**MODEST KATYDID** *Montezumina modesta*

**Sp S F W** Green with long, but moderately narrow wings. Eyes are oblong and oval. Two pale stripes originate at pronotum and extend rearward along leading edge of wing. Tegmina rounded and hind wings pointed. Found in a variety of habitats, but often more common in bottomland forests.

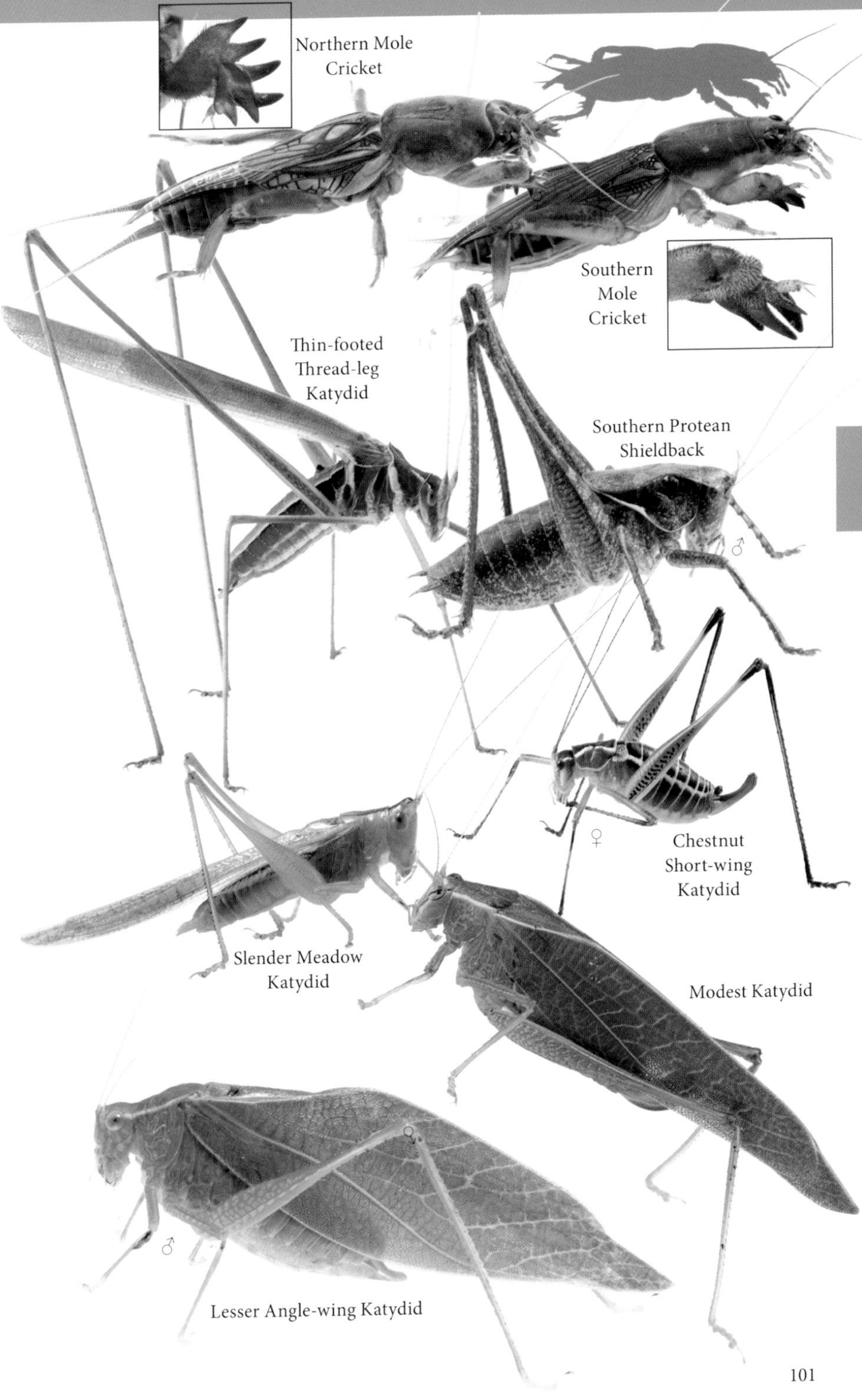

Northern Mole
Cricket

Southern
Mole
Cricket

Thin-footed
Thread-leg
Katydid

Southern Protean
Shieldback

♂

Chestnut
Short-wing
Katydid

♀

Slender Meadow
Katydid

Modest Katydid

♂

Lesser Angle-wing Katydid

## GREATER ARID-LAND KATYDID *Neobarrettia spinosa* TETTIGONIIDAE

Sp **S** F **W** Large, unmistakable species. Bright red eyes and colorful wings that are flared when disturbed. Legs have conspicuous spines. Combined with strong mandibles that can result in a painful bite, this is a species that should be handled carefully.

## BROAD-TIPPED CONEHEAD *Neoconocephalus triops*

Sp **S** F **W** Distinctive cone protruding between eyes is wider than long. Body can be brown or green. Face somewhat slanted. Hind wings narrow and elongated, extending well beyond abdomen. Males sing earlier in the season than other katydids and are found in a variety of habitats including in suburban areas.

## OBLONG-WINGED KATYDID *Amblycorypha oblongifolia*

Sp **S** F **W** Head is broadly rounded. Distance between bases of antennae 2 to 3 times width of antenna. Hind wing extends to or beyond tip of forewings. Almost always green, but pink forms are known. Found in the understory of deciduous forests.

## TRUNCATED TRUE KATYDID *Paracyrtophyllus robustus*

Sp **S** F **W** Comes in both green and red forms. Wings leaf-like, inflated, and with veins darkened making them readily visible. Antennae long and stiff compared to other katydids. Calls from trees in the summer and can be so numerous to constitute as an outbreak.

## COMMON TRUE KATYDID *Pterophylla camellifolia*

Sp **S** F **W** Green with rounded, inflated wings; veins not outlined in black, but still conspicuous. Pronotum has two shallow grooves. Sings from high in deciduous trees, so seldom seen until the fall when they come down lower. Eggs inserted into loose bark of soft stems.

## FORK-TAILED BUSH KATYDID *Scudderia furcata*

Sp **S** F **W** Green katydid with long, thin hind legs. Forewings largely uniform in width throughout their length. Yellow stripe extending from thorax over wings. Species are distinguished by Y-shaped male supra-anal plate. Widely distributed and found in weedy fields, meadows, and the edge of woodlands.

## CAMEL CRICKET *Ceuthophilus* sp. RHAPHIDOPHORIDAE

Sp **S** F **W** Tan or brown with variable dark markings and usually a distinct hump-backed appearance. Antennae touch or nearly so at their base. Tarsi are laterally compressed and lack ventral pads. Hind femurs extend beyond tip of abdomen.

## JERUSALEM CRICKET *Stenopelmatus* sp. STENOPELMATIDAE

Sp **S** F **W** Large, distinctive crickets with orange-brown heads and legs and a white abdomen with black bands. Antennae are widely separated at base on large head. Tibia on all legs are stout with strong spines for digging and hind femora don't extend beyond abdomen.

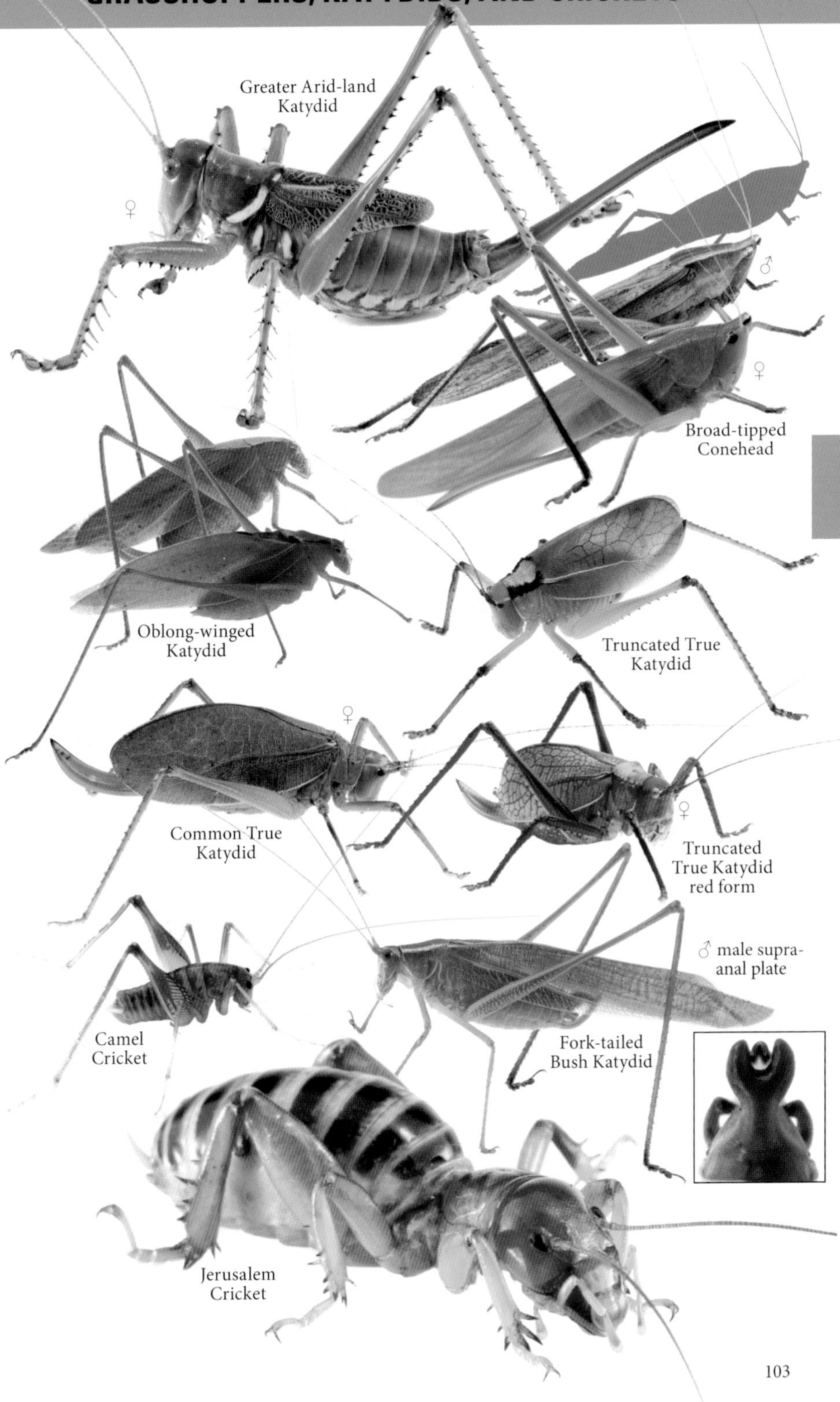

# GRASSHOPPERS, KATYDIDS, AND CRICKETS

Greater Arid-land
Katydid

♀

♂

♀

Broad-tipped
Conehead

Oblong-winged
Katydid

Truncated True
Katydid

♀

Common True
Katydid

♀

Truncated
True Katydid
red form

♂ male supra-
anal plate

Camel
Cricket

Fork-tailed
Bush Katydid

Jerusalem
Cricket

# Walkingsticks
# Order Phasmida

Prairie Walkingstick
(*Diapheromera velii*)

**NATURAL HISTORY** Walkingsticks are thin with an elongated stick-like body making it difficult to spot them in trees and grass. The ordinal name is derived from the Greek *phasma*, referring to their apparitional or phantom-like (seeming to appear or disappear readily) behavior. Many species will sway back and forth like a ghost or wave in the wind when disturbed. None of the species in Texas have wings. The cerci are short and ovipositors are small and concealed. They have incomplete metamorphosis and can be as long as 10 cm.

Some species are parthenogeneic, meaning they do not need a male to reproduce. Females will fertilize the eggs on their own and drop them randomly on the ground. There is evidence to suggest some species are more abundant every two years, with eggs requiring two years to develop. They can become very abundant, found on trees, shrubs, and grass, however they rarely cause enough damage to be considered a pest. Their body shape means they can easily blend in with vegetation and can be very difficult to find. Some species like the two-striped walkingstick can also excrete an obnoxious foul-smelling chemical that may even cause temporary blindness. This group has gained popularity in the pet trade because they are low maintenance, but do require a steady supply of vegetation to eat.

# Identifying Characters

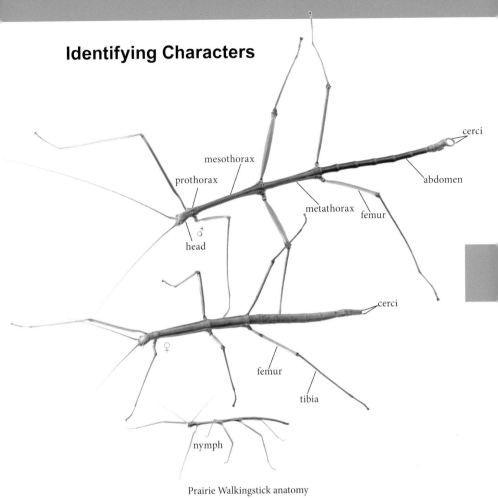

Prairie Walkingstick anatomy

# Eggs

*Diapheromera* sp.          Giant Walkingstick          Southern Two-Striped
                                                        Walkingstick

## NORTHERN WALKINGSTICK *Diapheromera femorata*

DIAPHEROMERIDAE

Sp **S** **F** **W** Can be brown, gray or green in color. Head is slightly longer than wide giving a square appearance. Hind femur has a single spine and middle femur of male is swollen and usually appears banded. It is often found associated with several species of oak trees with softer leaves, like red oak (*Quercus texana*).

## GRAY WALKINGSTICK *Pseudosermyle stramineus*

Sp **S** **F** **W** Mesothorax at least four times longer than prothorax. Antennae longer than front leg femurs in both sexes. Middle leg femora lack spines or swelling. Female cerci 2.5–3 times longer than broad. Often associated with sagebrush, grass, burroweed, *Haplopappus,* and rabbit-weed.

## GIANT WALKINGSTICK *Megaphasma denticrus*

Sp **S** **F** **W** This is the longest American insect (up to 15 cm). They can be found on juniper and oak trees. The color of this species can vary from reddish to green and gray. Both sexes have long antennae and numerous teeth on the underside of middle femur. Both sexes have a large spine on middle and hind femur.

## MEXICAN WALKINGSTICK *Sermyle mexicana*

Sp **S** **F** **W** Brownish gray and mottled with white. Only females are known in the species. Middle femur and 5th abdominal segment are lobed helping to give an overall appearance of a stick. Feeds on huisache vines.

## SOUTHERN TWO-STRIPED WALKINGSTICK

PSEUDOPHASMATIDAE

Sp **S** **F** **W**                     *Anisomorpha buprestoides*
Three black stripes usually pronounced down the back of this walkingstick; less obvious in juveniles. Males are smaller and more slender than females which can grow up to 8 cm. Males are often seen riding on females. Color can vary from yellow to red. They have a defensive chemical that is expelled by glands on the thorax when disturbed. Found on grasses and brush or under loose bark.

Creosote Bush Walkingstick
(*Diapheromera covilleae*) with horns
on head of both ♂ and ♀

Tamaulipan Walkingstick
(*Diapheromera tamaulipensis*) with
horns on head of ♀ only

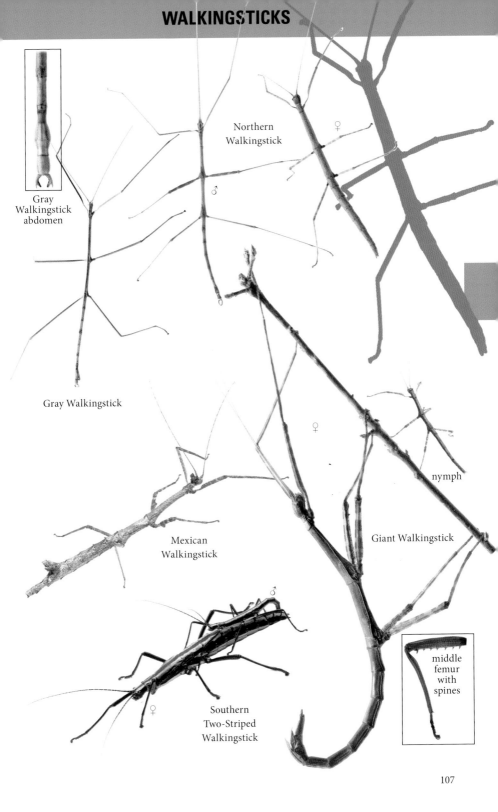

Gray
Walkingstick
abdomen

Northern
Walkingstick

♀

♂

Gray Walkingstick

♀

nymph

Mexican
Walkingstick

Giant Walkingstick

♂

middle
femur
with
spines

♀

Southern
Two-Striped
Walkingstick

107

# ♀ *Diapheromera* Abdomen Comparison

**Creosote Bush Walkingstick** (*D. covilleae*), ♂ and ♀ with spine on head; middle tibia with numerous spines; found on creosote bush in extreme west Texas

7—
8—
9—
cerci—

**Northern Walkingstick** (*D. femorata*), cerci stout and half as long as 8th abdominal segment; found throughout Texas

7—
8—
9—
cerci —

**Similar Walkingstick** (*D. persimilis*), hind femur often missing spine; cerci as long as the 8th abdominal segment; central and south Texas

—7
—8
—9
— cerci

**Tamaulipan Walkingstick** (*D. tamaulipensis*), ♀ has spine on head; middle tibia without numerous spines on middle tibia; found in central and south Texas

—7
—8
—9
—cerci

*D. torquata* (not pictured), 7th abdominal segment longer than 9th; 8th segment slightly longer than broad; found in Chisos Mountains

**Prairie Walkingstick** (*D. velii*), cerci slender almost as long as 9th abdominal segment; found throughout Texas

7—
8—
9—
cerci—

108

# ♂ *Diapheromera* Abdomen Comparison

**Creosote Bush Walkingstick (D. covilleae),** ♂ and ♀ with spine on head; middle tibia with numerous spines; found on creosote bush in extreme west Texas

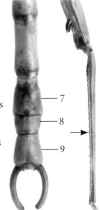

— 7

— 8

— 9

**Northern Walkingstick (D. femorata),** hind femur spined; middle leg swollen and striped; 7th abdominal segment longer than 9th; found throughout Texas

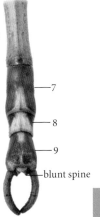

— 7

— 8

— 9

— blunt spine

7 —

8 —

9 —

fine — spine

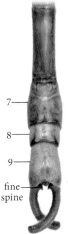

**Similar Walkingstick (D. persimilis),** 9th abdominal segment longer than wide; cerci with fine spine although can look blunt like *D. femorata;* head longer than *D. velii;* underside of hind femur with minute serrations; found in central and south Texas

**Tamaulipan Walkingstick (D. tamaulipensis),** 9th abdominal segment longer than wide; ♂ no horn ♀ with horn; found in south and central Texas

7 —

8 —

9 —

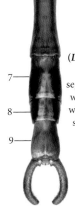

**D. torquata,** poculum is twisted to one side; found in Chisos Mountains

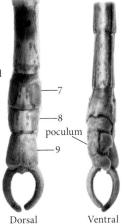

— 7

— 8

poculum

— 9

Dorsal          Ventral

**Prairie Walkingstick (D. velii),** cerci with fine spine; hind femur with spine; 7th abdominal segment narrows where it attaches to 6th; 9th segment slightly longer than wide; found throughout Texas

— 7

— 8

— 9

— fine spine

# Mantids
# Order Mantodea

male Carolina Mantis
(*Stagmomantis carolina*)

**NATURAL HISTORY** The name mantid comes from the Greek meaning soothsayer or prophet and refers to the prayer-like stance they often adopt. Most mantids are long-bodied, large insects with the front legs modified for capturing prey. Some are winged, most often the males, and capable of flight. The forewings are generally a leathery covering over the membranous hind wings and the head is triangular in shape. They have incomplete metamorphosis and in Texas range in size from 33–90 mm.

They have excellent eyesight and can turn their head to look behind them. They are often seen around flowers sitting and waiting for visiting insects. Mantids are formidable predators that can even capture and eat small hummingbirds. A number of species have become popular in the pet trade. They are very charismatic, watching your movements, and will take food from your hand. It is estimated that around 15 percent of the time, female mantids will eat the male after mating. When well fed, male and female frequently survive mating events.

Oothecas (egg sacs) are sometimes sold as biological control within gardens; however, mantids are generalists and do not distinguish between beneficial and pest insects. Oothecas are often species specific in appearance. Features to note when identifying adults are the shape of facial shield, antennae length and thickness, femur thickness and number of spines, as well as hind wing shape and color.

# Legs & Head

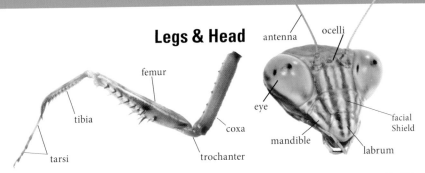

antenna · ocelli · eye · facial Shield · mandible · labrum · femur · tibia · tarsi · coxa · trochanter

The coxa is elongated in mantid forelegs making them raptorial and efficient at capturing and holding prey. Check shape of facial shield which can be distinctive for certain species.

# Ootheca (egg case)

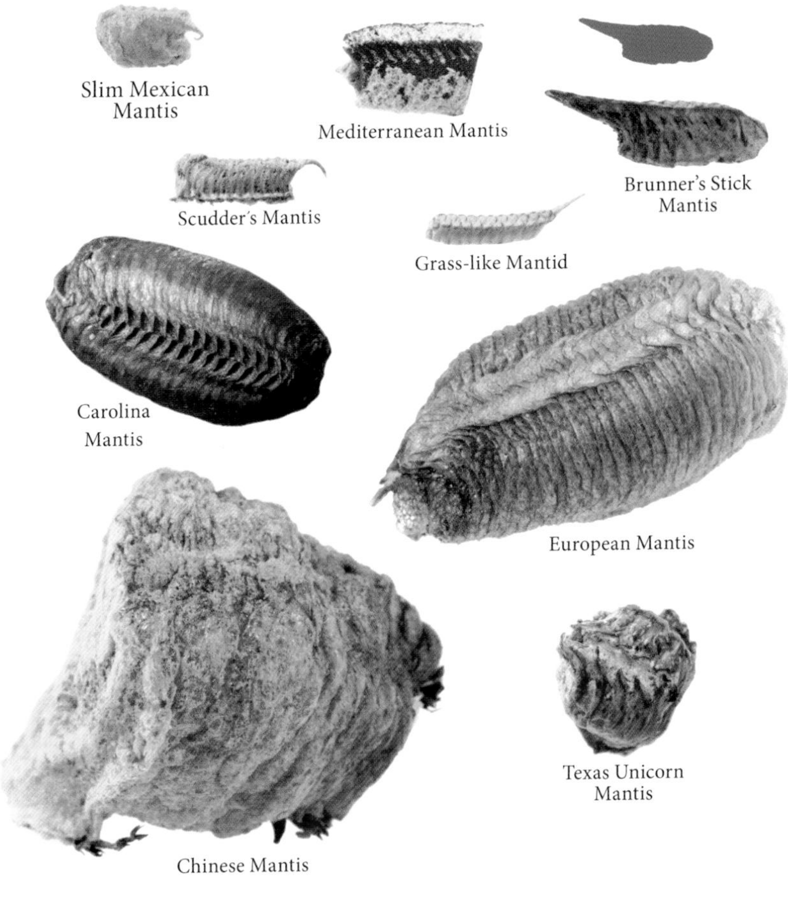

Slim Mexican Mantis

Mediterranean Mantis

Brunner's Stick Mantis

Scudder's Mantis

Grass-like Mantid

Carolina Mantis

European Mantis

Chinese Mantis

Texas Unicorn Mantis

Ootheca of mantids can be identified to species. Above are several oothecas from Texas.

### BRUNNER'S STICK MANTIS *Brunneria borealis*

**Sp S F W** Large elongated stick-like mantid; green to tan in color. Antennae short and thick, especially at base. Pronotum serrated on sides. Wings reduced. Species is parthenogenetic with only females known. Found in meadows with tall grass.

### CAROLINA MANTIS *Stagmomantis carolina*

**Sp S F W** Can be green, brown, or gray. Facial shield more than twice as wide as long. First pair of wings in female longer than pronotum, but don't extend past last third of abdomen. Female abdomen widened in middle. Male with well-developed wings.

### AGILE GROUND MANTIS *Litaneutria minor*

**Sp S F W** Small, reddish or brown. Front tibia without dorsal teeth; femur usually with 4 spines. Males usually have brown spot on base of first pair of wings. Female with rough pronotum. Can be found on ground or sometimes vegetation.

### TEXAS UNICORN MANTIS *Phyllovates chlorophaea*

**Sp S F W** Brown to green with greenish-yellow wings. Central horn on top of head resembling a unicorn, bifurcated at tip. Males and females look similar. Usually prefer prey items smaller than themselves, differing from many other mantids.

### CHINESE MANTIS *Tenodera sinensis*

**Sp S F W** Larger, tan or green with green color on front edge of forewing. Facial shield slight bit wider than high. Yellow spot between front coxae. Hind wing is broad from front to back and marbled in color. Introduced to the US in 1896, where it has spread widely since. Ootheca are sold in Texas.

### SLIM MEXICAN MANTIS *Bactromantis mexicana*

**Sp S F W** Brownish and slender. Antennae long and uniform throughout length in males; females have short antennae. Pronotum behind legs twice as long as front portion. Front femur very slender. Females wingless; males with fully developed wings. Found on flowers, but will come to lights.

### SCUDDER'S MANTIS *Oligonicella scudderi*

**Sp S F W** Small, slender, brownish or tan. Pronotum behind legs not much longer than the front portion. Females with reduced wings; males with fully developed wings. Found on ground, grass, and low vegetation. Will come to lights. Most common in fall.

### GRASS-LIKE MANTID *Thesprotia graminis*

**Sp S F W** Small, tan colored, resembling grass or pine needles. Pronotum behind forelegs 3-4 times longer than front portion. Females wingless; males with fully developed wings. Found on grass or shrubs. Easily mistaken for a walkingstick.

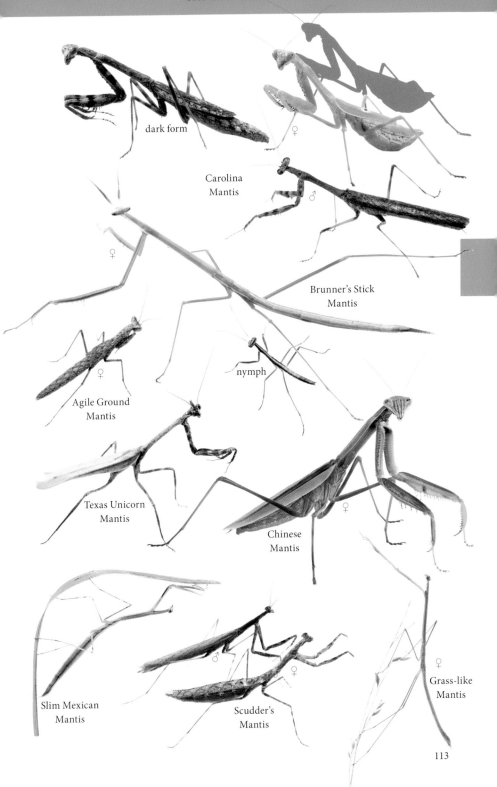

dark form

Carolina
Mantis

♀

♂

Brunner's Stick
Mantis

♀

Agile Ground
Mantis

nymph

Texas Unicorn
Mantis

Chinese
Mantis

♀

Slim Mexican
Mantis

Scudder's
Mantis

♂

♀

Grass-like
Mantis

♀

113

# Cockroaches
# Order Blattodea

Surinam Cockroach
(*Pycnoscelus surinamensis*)

**NATURAL HISTORY** Cockroaches usually have two pairs of leathery wings that cover most of the abdomen. In some species males and females are wingless while in other species just females are wingless. The body shape is oval and flat to the ground. Antennae are long and thin; total adult length is usually between 8 mm to 36 mm. They have simple metamorphosis and the name root *Blatta* is Latin for cockroach.

Most cockroach species live outdoors and do not invade homes. Generally cockroaches eat dead leaves, bark, and even dung. Some species like the Cuban cockroach are very colorful and kept as pets while other species resemble beetles. Cockroaches can have eggs in an ootheca or egg capsule. Some species will keep the ootheca inside and give birth to live offspring, while other species will just drop the ootheca to let it hatch, or will carry the ootheca off the tip of the abdomen. There are some species like the Surinam cockroach that are parthenogenic and do not need a male to reproduce. The offspring from parthenogenesis are all female.

Cockroaches are closely related to mantids, in fact some ancestral cockroaches even have predatory forelegs and were thought to be predators. Termites are now considered to be in the same order Blattodea and are considered to be social cockroaches. One family of cockroaches, cryptocercids, are social with nymphs staying with adults for 3 years and feeding on the excretions of adults for up to a year.

# Cockroach Anatomy

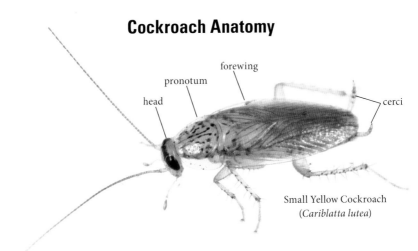

Small Yellow Cockroach
(*Cariblatta lutea*)

# Wings, Ootheca (egg case), and Nymphs

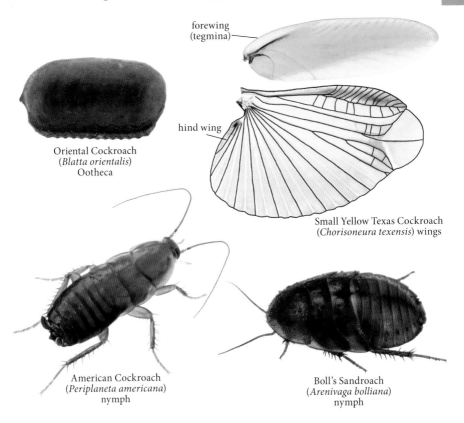

Oriental Cockroach
(*Blatta orientalis*)
Ootheca

Small Yellow Texas Cockroach
(*Chorisoneura texensis*) wings

American Cockroach
(*Periplaneta americana*)
nymph

Boll's Sandroach
(*Arenivaga bolliana*)
nymph

### SURINAM COCKROACH *Pycnoscelus surinamensis*
BLABERIDAE

**Sp S F W** Pronotum is dark brown, almost black, with a light line on front edge. Wings are brown with round pits on first fourth. Nymphs have a rough area on last half of abdomen. Can be found on leaf litter, parthenogenic and give birth to live young.

### GREEN BANANA COCKROACH *Panchlora nivea*

**Sp S F W** Adults are bright green with yellow on sides. Head is white with brown band across eyes. Can be found in plants and leaf litter. Rarely found indoors, presumed to be found on bananas in its native Cuba.

### GERMAN COCKROACH *Blattella germanica*
ECTOBIIDAE

**Sp S F W** Small, brownish yellow, with two dark stripes on pronotum. Distance between eyes is 3/4 as long as the distance between antennae. Household pest usually found in bathrooms and kitchens. Originally from northeast Africa.

### PALE BORDERED FIELD COCKROACH *Pseudomops septentrionalis*

**Sp S F W** Small cockroach that is brightly colored. Head reddish orange with black eyes. Pronotum dark or red with cream-colored border. Can be found on low vegetation, flowers, and leaf litter where it is active during the day.

### AMERICAN COCKROACH *Periplaneta americana*
BLATTIDAE

**Sp S F W** Reddish brown glossy color that is pale toward tips of abdomen and thorax. Cerci are long, thin, and tapered at end. Male's last abdominal segment notched and translucent. This is an important pest species and not native to the United States.

### SMOKY BROWN COCKROACH *Periplaneta fuliginosa*

**Sp S F W** Glossy blackish brown in color all over, no pattern on the pronotum. Cerci shorter and stockier compared to American Cockroach. Found outside under logs and other material. Not native to the United States, likely from East Asia.

### ORIENTAL COCKROACH *Blatta orientalis*

**Sp S F W** Blackish-brown cockroach that is usually found in numbers. Males with wings covering only 3/4 of abdomen; females have very reduced wings. Can be found inside in cool damp places but moves outside in warm weather. Originally from area around the Crimean Peninsula, now with a cosmopolitan distribution.

### BOLL'S SANDROACH *Arenivaga bolliana*
CORYDIIDAE

**Sp S F W** Females are black except for tan on front edge of pronotum. Male brown with wings that cover the abdomen; it is twice as long as its widest width. Found in wood rat nests and *Atta texana* ant nests and feeds on refuse.

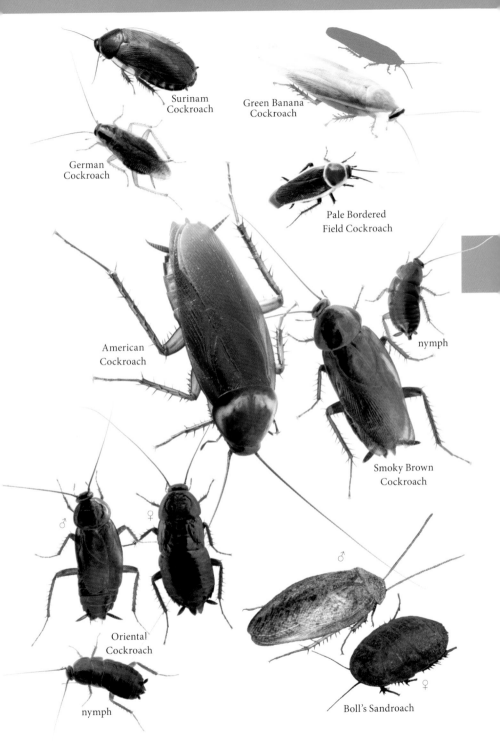

Surinam Cockroach

Green Banana Cockroach

German Cockroach

Pale Bordered Field Cockroach

American Cockroach

nymph

Smoky Brown Cockroach

♂ ♀

Oriental Cockroach

♂

nymph

♀

Boll's Sandroach

# Termites
# Order Blattodea

Subterranean Termite reproductives
(Reticulitermes flavipes)

**NATURAL HISTORY**  Termites are often confused with ants and
sometimes even called white ants, but termites are actually more closely
related to cockroaches and mantids. They have a soft, light-colored body
where ants have a hard, usually dark body. The antennae of termites are
straight and moniliform while ants have geniculate or elbowed antennae. The
wings in reproductive termites are equal in size and in ants the hind wing is
much smaller. The abdomen of termites is also joined broadly to the thorax,
while in ants the abdomen is constricted where it joins the thorax creating a
waist.

    Termites are social, with workers and soldiers comprised of both males
and females. The only individuals that reproduce in the colony are the king
and queen. The queen can be quite large, up to 4 in. because of all the egg
laying, and the king is only about 0.5 in. Once a year, large numbers of kings
and queens are produced and they fly from the nest. Once they find a mate
and a new nest site they create a new colony. In the early stages of the colony,
the king and queen will take care of the nest and feed the young. If a king
or queen dies a new one is created from the nymphs. Workers are the most
numerous caste in the colony. They are small with chewing mouth parts and
charged with the general care of the nest and feeding others. The soldiers
have a darker, more elongated head and enlarged mandibles to help in
defending the nest. In some species, the soldiers are called nasutiforms and
the head is prolonged into a beak for squirting a chemical defense.

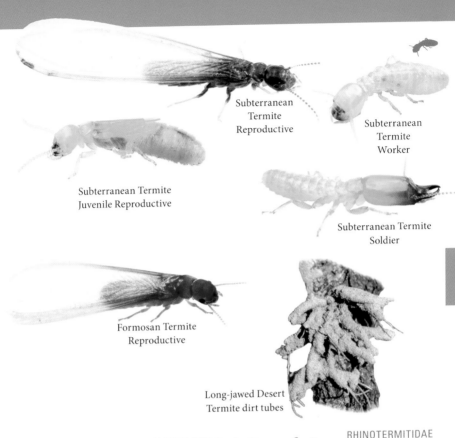

Subterranean
Termite
Reproductive

Subterranean
Termite
Worker

Subterranean Termite
Juvenile Reproductive

Subterranean Termite
Soldier

Formosan Termite
Reproductive

Long-jawed Desert
Termite dirt tubes

## SUBTERRANEAN TERMITE *Reticulitermes flavipes*

**Sp S F W** Reproductives can be dark, wings clear with gray tint. Winged forms have ocellus separated from eye by more than the diameter of the ocellus. Soldiers are yellow with yellow-orange rectangular head. Can be very destructive to buildings, posts, flowers,. and even living trees.

## FORMOSAN TERMITE *Coptotermes formosanus*

**Sp S F W** Yellowish-brown body, winged individuals have hairs on the margins. Soldiers have an orange, oval shaped head with curved black mandibles, body is whitish. Reproductives and soldiers are most easily identified. These can be pests in homes and make large subterranean colonies.

TERMITIDAE

## LONG-JAWED DESERT TERMITE *Gnathamitermes* sp.

**Sp S F W** Can be common in rangelands where mud tubes are formed around plant stems, leaf litter, dung, fence posts, and other wooden structures. They feed on living or dead vegetation, including grasses, by encasing them with mud and then consuming the weathered surface. Often more active following rains. Workers are white, soft-bodied, and have dark heads.

119

# True Bugs
# Order Hemiptera

Giant Strong-nosed Stink Bug
(*Alcaeorrhynchus grandis*)

**NATURAL HISTORY** The Hemiptera make up the most diverse order of non-holometabolous insects, probably coinciding with angiosperm radiations, and are the only appropriate insects to be called "bugs." It is made up of four to five suborders worldwide depending upon the classification followed. Here, we recognize three suborders found in Texas and North America: (1) Heteroptera, the "true" bugs; (2) Auchenorrhyncha, cicadas and hoppers, and (3) Sternorrhyncha, the aphids, scale insects, and white flies. The latter two have historically received ordinal status as the Homoptera. The ordinal name means half (*hemi*) wing (*ptera*) and refers to the half membranous, half leathery forewings (hemelytra) of the Heteroptera.

Their mouthparts are highly modified for piercing-sucking. Virtually all the Auchenorrhyncha and Sternorrhyncha feed on plants and while a number of basal Heteroptera families are predators, most are phytophagous. A number of heteropteran families are aquatic and across the Hemiptera many are wingless. Within the aquatic groups, most are capable of flight and thus of leaving the water and dispersing to different habitats. A number of species are vectors of disease. Phytophagous feeders can be destructive to crops both through mechanical damage and the viruses they transmit. *Triatoma* spp. can transmit Chagas to humans and dogs. Many species have scent glands and can excrete noxious chemicals as a defense against predation.

# Identifying Characters

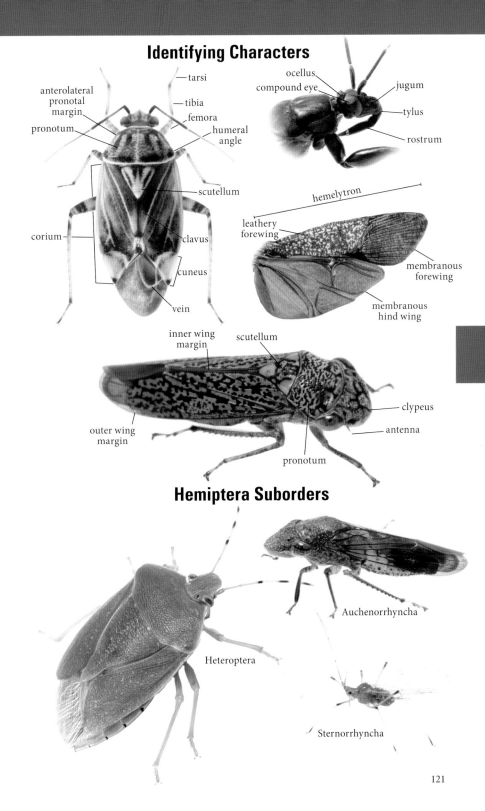

- tarsi
- anterolateral pronotal margin
- pronotum
- tibia
- femora
- humeral angle
- scutellum
- corium
- clavus
- cuneus
- vein
- ocellus
- compound eye
- jugum
- tylus
- rostrum
- hemelytron
- leathery forewing
- membranous forewing
- membranous hind wing
- inner wing margin
- scutellum
- clypeus
- antenna
- outer wing margin
- pronotum

# Hemiptera Suborders

- Auchenorrhyncha
- Heteroptera
- Sternorrhyncha

### WATER MEASURER *Hydrometra* sp.

**Sp S F W**  Resemble small walkingsticks. Head distinctly prolonged with small eye laterally on basal third. Usually wingless; sometimes winged. Thin legs, antennae, and body. Found in and on the water along margins of ponds or amongst the overhanging vegetation.

### WATER STRIDER *Limnoporus* sp.

**Sp S F W**  Inner margin of eyes S-shaped or C-shaped. Body long and narrow, often wingless. Pronotum not shiny. Antennal segment 1 not more than eight-tenths combined lengths of segments 2 and 3. Tarsi with preapical claws.

### WATER STRIDER *Trepobates* sp.

**Sp S F W**  Wings generally absent. Eyes C-shaped. First antenna segment shorter than or equal to three others combined. Abdomen shorter than head and thorax combined. Body with pattern of pale spots and lines. Fore- and middle femurs longer than abdomen. Tarsi with preapical claws. Found on water surface of ponds.

### SMALL WATER STRIDER *Microvelia* sp.

**Sp S F W**  Pronotum broader than abdomen. Often wingless. Hind femur not longer than abdomen. Middle tarsi not deeply cleft. Often found swimming in groups on surface of ponds and slow moving streams and rivers.

### SMALL WATER STRIDER *Rhagovelia* sp.

**Sp S F W**  Pronotum broader than abdomen. Usually wingless. Hind femur not longer than abdomen. Middle tarsi deeply cleft, usually with plumose hairs arising from base. Often found swimming in groups on water surface of fast moving streams and rivers.

### WATER BOATMAN various species

**Sp S F W**  Family is distinctive and diverse, but species are difficult to recognize. Somewhat dorso-ventrally flattened with dark crosslines on upper surface. Front legs short with 1-segmented scoop-shaped tarsi. Generally found in pools and ponds.

### CREEPING WATER BUG *Ambrysus circumcinctus*

**Sp S F W**  Oval, but somewhat elongated body, with greenish head, pronotum, and forelegs and relatively uniformly brownish colored hemelytra. Posterior portion of prosternum fused. Hind wings are vestigial. Restricted to permanently flowing streams.

### CREEPING WATER BUG *Ambrysus lunatus*

**Sp S F W**  Oval body with contrasting pattern of brown and yellowish mottling. Hemelytra with distinctive crescent markings. Hind wings fully developed. Found along edges in shallow waters of various sized clear streams.

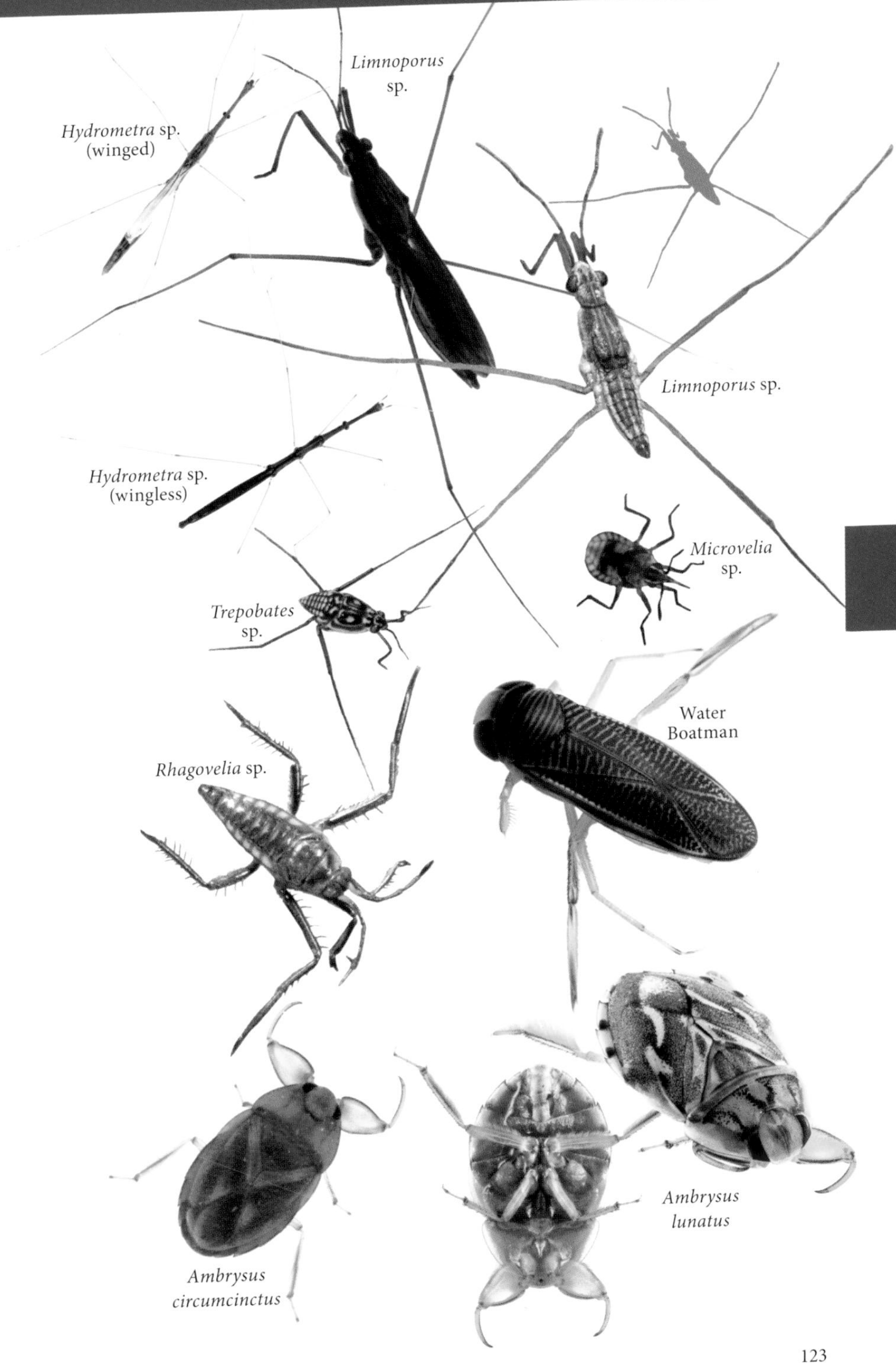

*Hydrometra* sp.
(winged)

*Limnoporus*
sp.

*Limnoporus* sp.

*Hydrometra* sp.
(wingless)

*Microvelia*
sp.

*Trepobates*
sp.

Water
Boatman

*Rhagovelia* sp.

*Ambrysus
lunatus*

*Ambrysus
circumcinctus*

### GIANT WATER BUG *Belastoma* sp.     BELASTOMATIDAE

**Sp S F W**   Body is oblong and pointed at both ends. Forelegs are raptorial and hind legs are modified for swimming. Smaller than *Lethocerus*, they are predacious on other invertebrates and small vertebrates. Females cement eggs on the backs of males. Often hang in the water with head pointed downward.

### UHLER'S WATER BUG *Lethocerus uhleri*

**Sp S F W**   Large, with distinctly pointed abdomen; breathing tubes may be visible protruding from tip. Middle and hind legs are distinctly banded. Space between eyes no more than 3/4 width of eye. Short, stout beak capable of inflicting painful bite. Feed on invertebrates and vertebrates such as fish.

### WATER SCORPION *Ranatra* sp.     NEPIDAE

**Sp S F W**   Very elongated body with distal breathing tube nearly as long as body itself. Raptorial forelegs often held at 90-degree angles from body. Commonly seen suspended downward in water with breathing tube piercing water surface. Found in ponds and lakes and along edges of streams and rivers.

### BACKSWIMMER *Notonecta* sp.     NOTONECTIDAE

**Sp S F W**   Swims with keeled back facing down. Eyes widely separated. Hind legs modified for swimming with long hairs; middle femur with pointed spine before distal end. Often rests with head pointed downward. Common in ponds and slow streams.

### BIG-EYED TOAD BUG *Gelastocoris oculatus*     GELASTOCORIDAE

**Sp S F W**   Large prominent eyes. Sits and jumps like a small toad. Humeral angles of pronotum are pronounced and sharper than in *G. rotundatus*. Color and patterning quite variable. Found along muddy shores of ponds, lakes, and rivers.

### TOAD BUG *Gelastocoris rotundatus*

**Sp S F W**   Sits and jumps like a small toad. Humeral angles of pronotum less pronounced and more rounded than in *G. oculatus*. Found along muddy shores of ponds, lakes, and rivers in the west.

### SHORE BUG *Pentacora* sp.     SALDIDAE

**Sp S F W**   Body usually mottled, oval, and flattened. Antennae long, 4-segmented, and uniformly slender. Forewing membrane with four or five long closed cells. Found scurrying about along sandy or rocky lake, stream, and river shorelines.

### BED BUG *Cimex lectularius*     CIMICIDAE

**Sp S F W**   Body is oval, flattened, and reddish brown, with greatly reduced wings. Sides of pronotum covered with short stiff hairs. Found in cracks and crevices associated with human dwellings. Nymphs and adults feed on blood of humans; not known to transmit any diseases.

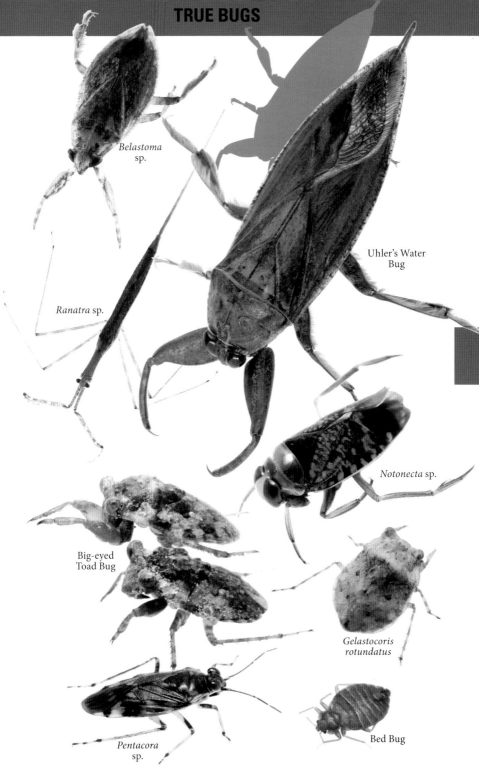

*Belastoma* sp.

Uhler's Water Bug

*Ranatra* sp.

*Notonecta* sp.

Big-eyed Toad Bug

*Gelastocoris rotundatus*

*Pentacora* sp.

Bed Bug

**BROKEN-BACKED BUG** *Taylorilygus apicalis*

`Sp` `S` `F` `W`   Greenish with membranous area of forewings brown and angled downward. Head nearly width of pronotum. Legs green basally, tan distally. 3rd antennal segment longer than head length.

**PLANT BUG** *Collaria oculata*

`Sp` `S` `F` `W`   Elongated body with antennae longer than body. Eyes set forward, at least dorsal width of eye, from anterior margin of pronotum. Yellowish-brown body and legs. Pronotum brownish with pair of dark spots posteriorly. Found in meadows.

**PLANT BUG** *Deraeocoris sayi*

`Sp` `S` `F` `W`   Variable in color, but often black with red scutellum and banded legs. Head, including eyes, half as wide as posterior margin of pronotum. 2nd antennal segment straight and moderately enlarged distally. Membranous area of forewing dark.

**PLANT BUG** *Hesperolabops gelastops*

`Sp` `S` `F` `W`   Moderately elongated with red head and anterior portion of pronotum. Posterior portion of pronotum and wings largely dark; sometimes scutellum often appearing reddish. Costal margin of wings white. Eyes stalked for at least as long as width of eye. Adults and nymphs found feeding on *Opuntia*.

**PLANT BUG** *Oncerometopus nigriclavus*

`Sp` `S` `F` `W`   Red with black band behind eyes, paired spots anteriorly on pronotum, "V" pattern with red scutellum on anterior forewing and dark membranous area. Legs black.

**PLANT BUG** *Paraxenetus guttulatus*

`Sp` `S` `F` `W`   Grayish brown with elongated body and antennae nearly twice as long as body. Often marked with red on veins and legs. Often pulls its hind legs forward in a distinct orientation. Feeds primarily on grape.

**PLANT BUG** *Phytocoris* spp.

`Sp` `S` `F` `W`   Color variable, but usually dark gray to light brown, mottled with yellow, white, greenish, or dark brown spots. Antennae long, extending beyond abdomen. Hind legs long with hind femora and tibiae about twice as long as mid and front femora and tibiae. Hind femurs extending beyond end of abdomen and tapering.

**PLANT BUG** *Prepops insitivus*

`Sp` `S` `F` `W`   Black except for sharply contrasting, bright yellow pronotum and scutellum. Head small, shorter than wide. Body elliptical with antennae long, length of body, and tapered. Pronotum sloped strongly downward from posterior lobe. Found along woodland edges.

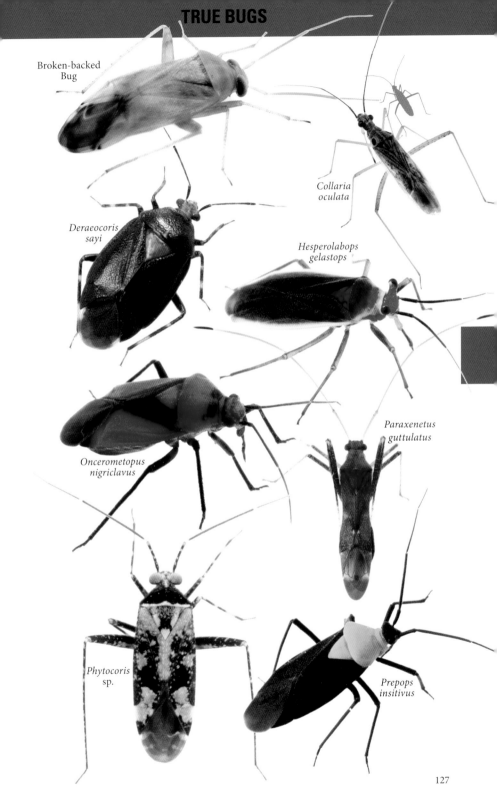

Broken-backed
Bug

Collaria
oculata

Deraeocoris
sayi

Hesperolabops
gelastops

Oncerometopus
nigriclavus

Paraxenetus
guttulatus

Phytocoris
sp.

Prepops
insitivus

### TARNISHED PLANT BUG *Lygus lineolaris*
MIRIDAE

**Sp S F W** Greenish-brown body with pale yellow "Y" on scutellum. Pronotum usually with several dark elongated bands. Hemelytra vary from light to dark brown with a yellowish, strongly deflexed cuneus and small black spot apically. Overwinter as adults.

### LACE BUG *Corythuca* sp.
TINGIDAE

**Sp S F W** Sculptured body and wings with dense, distinct veins giving a lacelike appearance. Often patterned with dark blotches. Scutellum reduced. Antennae usually pale and uniformly colored; moderately clubbed. Feeds on leaves of trees and shrubs.

### LACE BUG *Gargaphia iridescens*

**Sp S F W** Sculptured body with well-defined veins giving them a lace-like appearance, but no patches of color. Relatively elongated compared to other lace bugs. Light gray with three ridge lines across pronotum. Base of antennae black, middle pale, and tips dark. Legs pale.

### JAGGED AMBUSH BUGS *Phymata* sp.
REDUVIIDAE

**Sp S F W** Pronotum and middle of hemelytra wider than rest of body appearing hourglass-shaped. Forelegs raptorial with small but distinct protarsi. Scutellum triangular and shorter than pronotum. Cryptically colored and found on flowers in open fields.

### ASSASSIN BUG *Ctenotrachelus shermani*

**Sp S F W** Distinctive elongated teardrop-shaped body with truncate or split abdomen tip. Brownish with banded middle and hind legs and foretibia. Front femora swollen with dark spots.

### ASSASSIN BUG *Diaditus tejanus*

**Sp S F W** Dark brown with banded lateral margin of abdomen. With wings at rest, middle of body showing two or three dark triangular or crescent-shaped marks. Femora largely dark (pale at base); tibia paler, often with some banding. Readily comes to lights.

### ASSASSIN BUG *Pnirontis infirma*

**Sp S F W** Elongated body, light or yellowish brown. Tip of first antennal segment is a blunt spine (easiest seen when antennae are elbowed). Forelegs with prominent spines. Each abdominal segment with a dark spot distolaterally.

### ASSASSIN BUG *Pygolampis pectoralis*

**Sp S F W** Dark reddish-brown, elongated body clothed in fine silvery pubescence. First antennal segment nearly twice as long as area in front of eyes. Apex of head lacks spines, but one or more split spines present on each side below and behind eye. Front femora not appreciably swollen and lacks spines. Readily comes to lights.

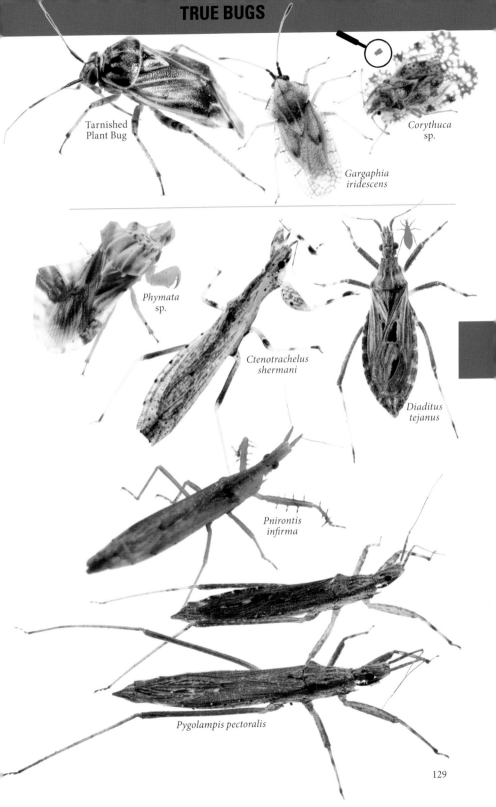

Tarnished
Plant Bug

*Gargaphia
iridescens*

*Corythuca*
sp.

*Phymata*
sp.

*Ctenotrachelus
shermani*

*Diaditus
tejanus*

*Pnirontis
infirma*

*Pygolampis pectoralis*

129

### ASSASSIN BUG *Pselliopus cinctus*
REDUVIIDAE

**Sp S F W** Dull orangish-yellow body with black-banded legs and face. Edge of abdomen with black bands. Pronotum smooth throughout, but with pronotum in front of scutellum straight and black lateral spine projecting beyond side of thorax and backward.

### ASSASSIN BUG *Rasahus hamatus*
**Sp S F W** Elongated black body with two prominent orangish spots on hemelytra. Legs pale orangish yellow. Front femora and tibia slightly swollen. Often found under loose bark or stones on the ground, but is commonly attracted to lights.

### ASSASSIN BUG *Rocconota annulicornis*
**Sp S F W** Elongated reddish-brown body covered with fine yellow hairs. Pronotum with four prominent spines. Hemelytra uniformly colored. Margins of abdomen banded. Legs pale, but often with distal bands on some segments.

### ASSASSIN BUG *Zelus luridus*
**Sp S F W** Narrow, elongated pale to bright green body with dorsal color ranging from very dark to pale. Pair of delicate spines on posterior corners of pronotum. Femora often with dark reddish bands distally. Arboreal species typically found on shrubs and trees.

### BLACK CORSAIR *Melanolestes picipes*
**Sp S F W** Elongated black body, with black or red abdomen. Males always winged; females often with reduced wings. Front tibia with thick patch of yellow hairs distally. Found under wood, logs, and rocks feeding on other insects including beetle larvae.

### CORSAIR *Sirthenea carinata*
**Sp S F W** Large, elongated body with relatively short antennae, reaching just to posterior edge of pronotum. Hemelytra with large prominent orange mark laterally and anteriorly. Legs pale orange to brown. Will come to lights.

### THREAD-LEGGED BUG *Barce* sp.
**Sp S F W** Dark brown and very thin, walkingstick-like, but small with raptorial forelegs held out in front. Tarsal claws of middle and hind legs simple, lacking a medial tooth. Often found around cellars, old buildings, and beneath loose bark.

### THREAD-LEGGED BUG *Emesaya brevipennis*
**Sp S F W** Thin, very elongated, brown body covered with silvery pubescence. Legs pale with dark bands distally. Front femur with basalmost spine conspicuously larger than others in front of it. Scutellum and metanotum lack spines. Often found in barns.

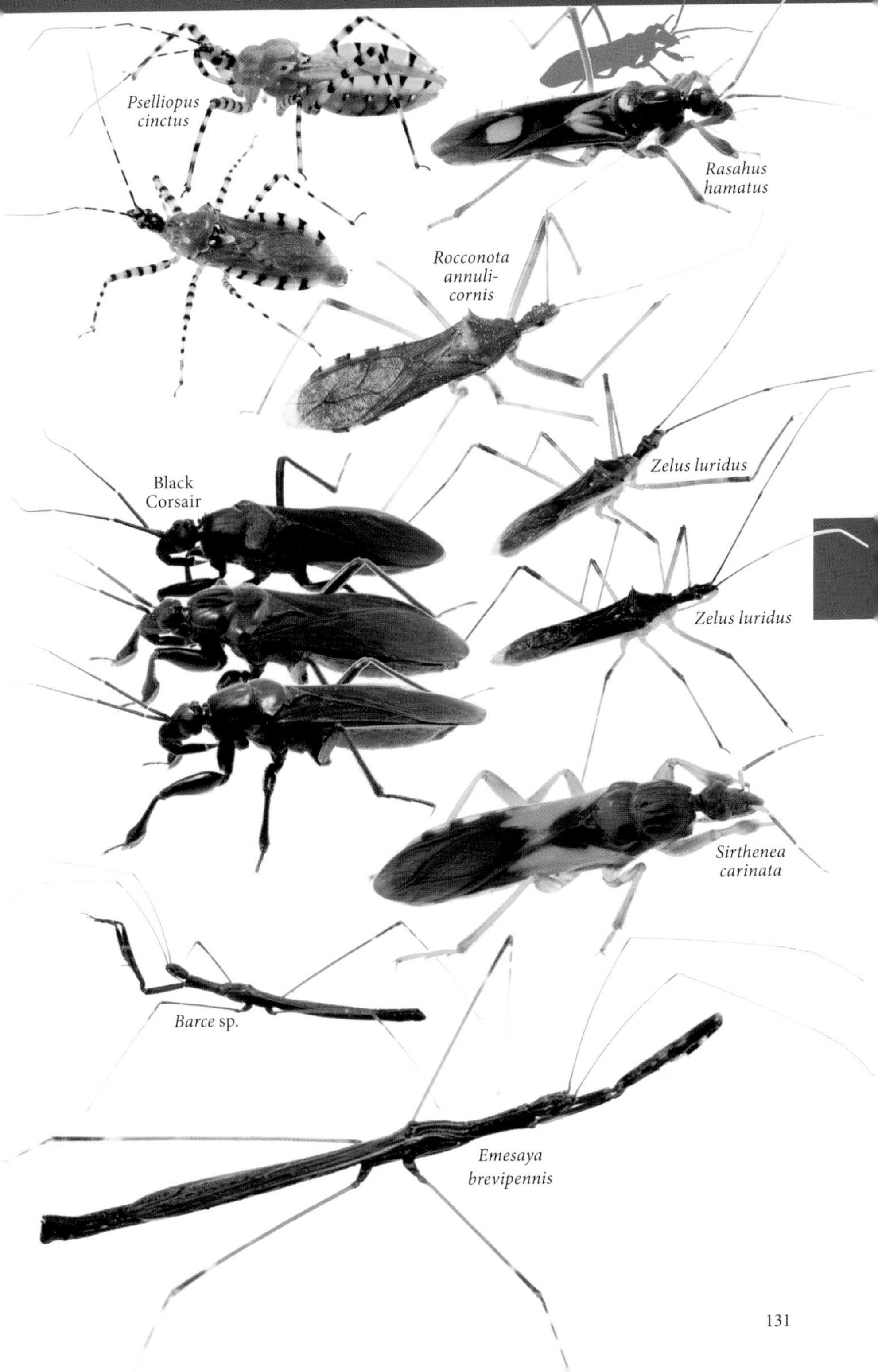

*Pselliopus cinctus*

*Rasahus hamatus*

*Rocconota annuli-cornis*

Black Corsair

*Zelus luridus*

*Zelus luridus*

*Sirthenea carinata*

*Barce* sp.

*Emesaya brevipennis*

**BLOOD-SUCKING CONENOSE** *Triatoma gerstaeckeri* REDUVIIDAE
Sp **S** F W Medium-sized, boldly patterned black and orange. *T. gerstaeckeri* has a solid black pronotum and narrower orange bands on the abdomen than *T. sanguisuga*, which also had red posteriorly on the pronotum. Feeds on mammalian blood and can bite humans causing painful swelling. Will come to lights.

 **WESTERN BLOODSUCKING CONENOSE** *Triatoma protracta*
Sp **S** F W More or less uniformly dark brown or black. Thin lines of colored banding may be visible laterally on the abdomen and a pale "X" may be visible above where the wings come together.

 **ASSASSIN BUG** *Microtomus purcis*
Sp **S** F W Large, with head, pronotum, and scutellum black. Anterior portion of hemelytra white, distal portion black. Sides of abdomen red and black banded. Legs black except basal hind femora, which are red. Found under bark and comes to lights.

 **MILKWEED ASSASSIN BUG** *Zelus longipes*
Sp **S** F W Orange, with large black area on pronotum as well as middle and distal hemelytra. Prominent black stripe usually running from the eye posteriorly to the pronotum. Pronotum rounded laterally and lacking spines. Can be somewhat variable in color. Found hunting on plants and shrubs with legs held in the air.

 **RED BULL ASSASSIN** *Repipta taurus*
Sp **S** F W Orange body with largely black hemelytra. Pronotum orange with four black stripes, generally connected anteriorly on both sides. Pronotum bears a pair of prominent spines on each side. Scutellum orange and legs black.

 **SCARLET-BORDERED ASSASSIN BUG** *Rhiginia cruciata*
Sp **S** F W Somewhat teardrop shaped. Orange body with central area of pronotum, scutellum, and hemelytra black. Lateral edges of abdomen largely orange with black spots not reaching margin. Found under logs, but males come to lights.

 **BEE ASSASSIN** *Apiomerus crassipes*
Sp **S** F W Mostly black with pronotum, scutellum, and abdomen edged in orange. Prominent upright hairs on broad, oval body. Hangs out on flowers where it hunts bees and similar insects.

 **BEE ASSASSIN** *Apiomerus spissipes*
Sp **S** F W Variously colored, broad, oblong body. General pattern is usually a reddish-brown body with pronotum, scutellum, posterior margin of corium, and margin of abdomen pale yellow. Legs reddish brown. Like other members of the genus, found on flowers in meadows and fields where it primarily feeds on bees.

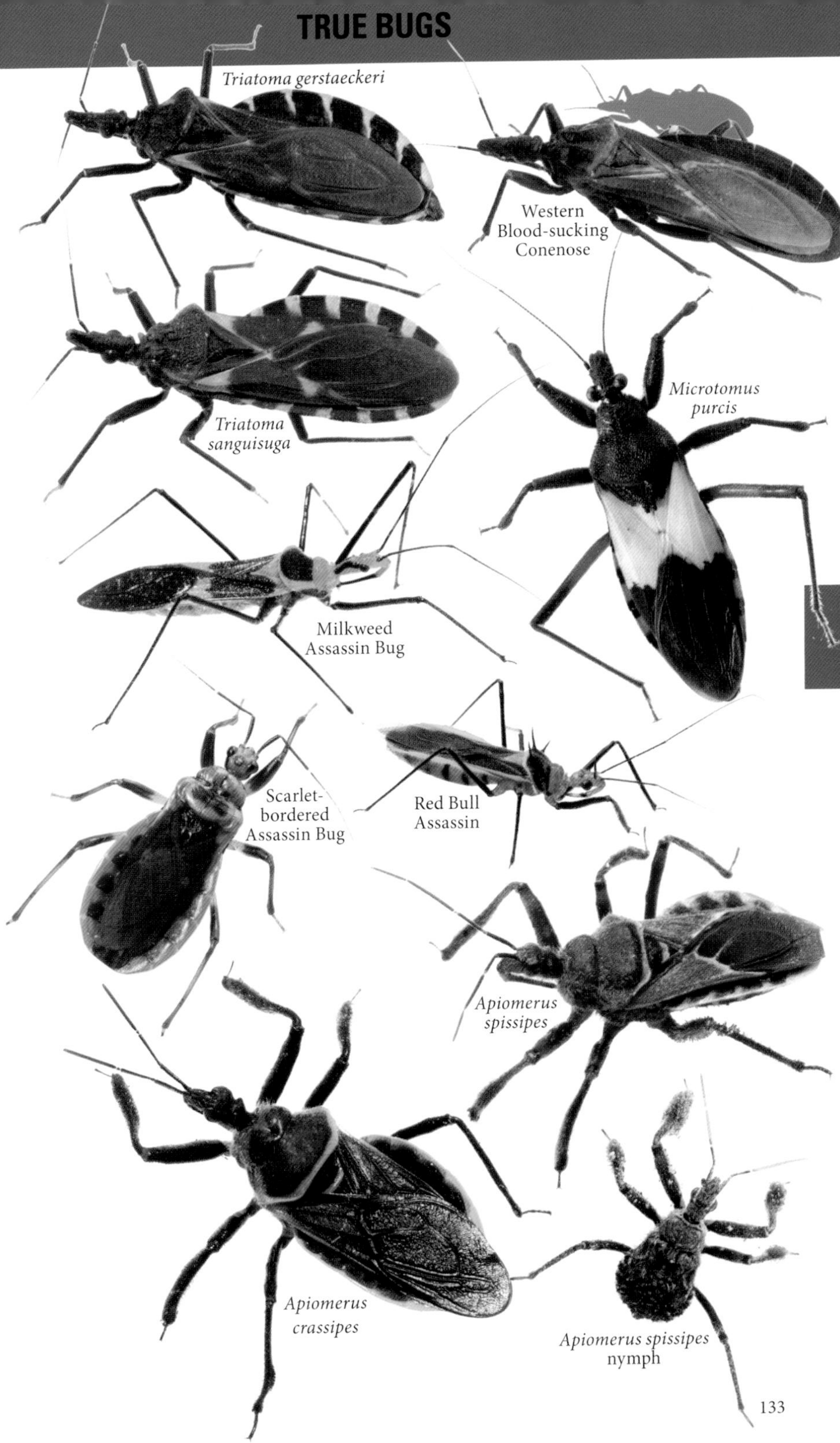

*Triatoma gerstaeckeri*

Western Blood-sucking Conenose

*Triatoma sanguisuga*

*Microtomus purcis*

Milkweed Assassin Bug

Scarlet-bordered Assassin Bug

Red Bull Assassin

*Apiomerus spissipes*

*Apiomerus crassipes*

*Apiomerus spissipes* nymph

133

### WHEEL BUG *Arilus cristatus*
REDUVIIDAE

**Sp S F W** Adult, largest of our assassin bugs and unmistakable with cog-shaped wheel on pronotum. Body is brown, covered with gray pubescence. Antennae, proboscis, and distal part of legs reddish. Nymphs are reddish or gray. Feeds on other insects and can administer a painful bite.

### FLAT BUG *Aradus* sp.
ARADIDAE

**Sp S F W** Dorso-ventrally flattened bug with wings variously developed. Tylus, forward projection between eyes at anterior of head, with lateral projections. Bucculae usually not extending beyond tylus. Antennae often flattened or variously modified. Found under loose bark of dead trees feeding on fungi.

### FLAT BUG *Mezira* sp.

**Sp S F W** Dorso-ventrally flattened bug with wings usually rather short. Bucculae large and elongated, usually extending forward beyond tip of tylus. First antennal segment noticeably swollen. Found under loose bark of dead trees.

### STILT BUG *Jalysus* sp.
BERYTIDAE

**Sp S F W** Long slender brown bug with very long thin legs. No tylus projecting forward. Fourth antennal segment longer than head. Stout spine projecting from thoracic scent gland. Found in fields on shrubs, but also comes to lights and feeds on moth eggs.

### CHARCOAL SEED BUG *Melacoryphus lateralis*
LYGAEIDAE

**Sp S F W** Dark gray, marked with orange stripe anteriorly on pronotum, three spots posteriorly on pronotum and laterally on hemelytra. Membranous area of wing outlined in white. Can be attracted to lights in large numbers.

### LARGE MILKWEED BUG *Oncopeltus fasciatus*

**Sp S F W** Orange or yellow with black on the pronotum and scutellum, and two black bands on the wings (middle and distal). Legs black. Orange color becomes darker with age. Feeds on seeds of milkweed plants where they can be numerous.

### SEED BUG *Neortholomus* sp.

**Sp S F W** Dull grayish-brown body covered with silvery hairs with transparent membranous area of hemelytra. Tylus extends beyond first antennal segment.

### WHITECROSSED SEED BUG *Neacoryphus bicrucis*

**Sp S F W** Bright red with black head, anterior portion of pronotum, scutellum, and membranous area of wings. Anterior portion of pronotum with white stripe. Medial edge of corium outlined in white. Can be attracted to lights in large numbers.

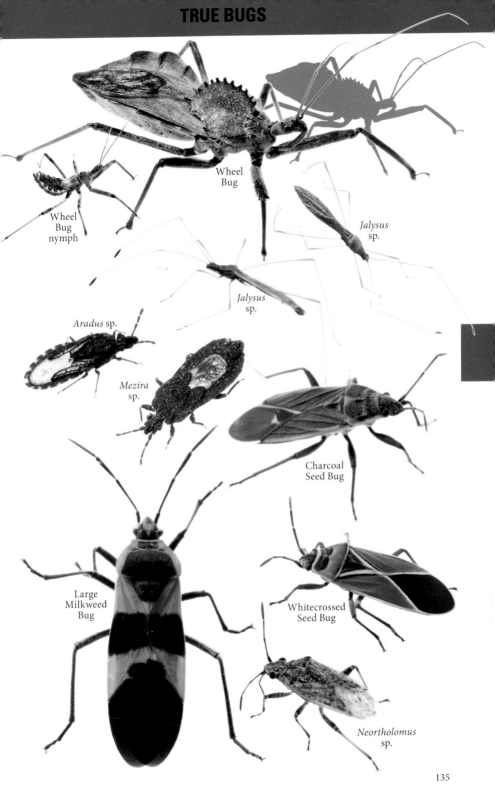

Wheel
Bug

Wheel
Bug
nymph

*Jalysus*
sp.

*Jalysus*
sp.

*Aradus* sp.

*Mezira*
sp.

Charcoal
Seed Bug

Large
Milkweed
Bug

Whitecrossed
Seed Bug

*Neortholomus*
sp.

### SIX-SPOTTED MILKWEED BUG *Oncopeltus sexmaculatus* LYGAEIDAE
**Sp S F W** Orange with a red head and black banding including 3 longitudinal black stripes on pronotum. One or more white patches in black wing membrane. Nymphs largely orangish-red with black wing pads. Feeds on milkweed.

### SMALL MILKWEED BUG *Lygaeus kalmii*
**Sp S F W** Dark gray to black with orangish-red band forming an "X" in the forewing. Head with red spot in middle on top; pronotum with reddish transverse band at middle that is usually interrupted by two small black spots. Two additional pairs of black spots in corium of forewing. Black membranous area of wing can be all black or have white spots. Feeds on milkweed.

### DIRT-COLORED SEED BUG *Ozophora picturata* RHYPAROCHROMIDAE
**Sp S F W** Small mottled brown bug with pale yellowish legs. Basal portion of antennal segment 4 white. Found on forest floors in areas with shaded leaf litter.

### DIRT-COLORED SEED BUG *Paromius longulus*
**Sp S F W** Small, elongated, yellowish-brown bug. Femora reddish with front femur swollen, rest of leg is yellowish with black at apices. Antennae yellowish with last segment noticeably darker. Found on the ground as well as on plants and can be very numerous.

### DIRT-COLORED SEED BUGS *Eremocoris depressus*
**Sp S F W** Reddish-brown species with darker head, pronotum, scutellum, and membranous wings. Front femora swollen. Is attracted to lights and may be more abundant in coastal areas.

### LONG-NECKED SEED BUG *Myodocha serripes*
**Sp S F W** Small distinctively shaped bug with long narrow neck. Head and pronotum black, wings brown and mottled. Legs pale white with dark band distally on femur, especially on foreleg. Antennae pale with terminal segment darker. Nymph with yellower legs and antennae. Abdomen longitudinally striped. Feeds on seeds of strawberry and St. John's wort. Adults will come to lights.

### BROAD-HEADED BUG *Alydus eurinus* ALYDIDAE
**Sp S F W** Dark gray with head as wide or wider than pronotum and both head and pronotum covered in dense hairs. Pronotum with hind angles rounded and uniformly colored. Wing membrane uniformly dark. Hind femur slightly swollen with ventral spines; all femora black. Tibia and tarsi pale with dark distal band.

### TEXAS BOW-LEGGED BUG *Hyalymenus tarsatus*
**Sp S F W** Brown with broad head. Hind femur swollen with short, stout, dark spines and dark band distally. Hind tibia distinctly bowed and lightest in middle. Nymphs mimic ants.

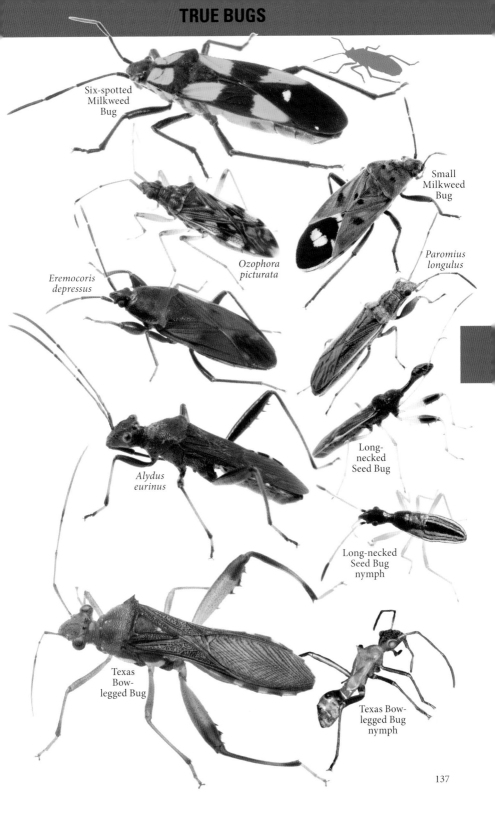

Six-spotted
Milkweed
Bug

Small
Milkweed
Bug

*Ozophora
picturata*

*Paromius
longulus*

*Eremocoris
depressus*

*Alydus
eurinus*

Long-
necked
Seed Bug

Long-necked
Seed Bug
nymph

Texas
Bow-
legged Bug

Texas Bow-
legged Bug
nymph

### CACTUS COREID *Chelinidea vittiger*
COREIDAE

Sp S F W    Dark head with a yellow stripe. Pronotum and lateral edges of abdomen yellow. Veins in corium conspicuously pale. Legs dark with reddish tarsi. Body lacks hairs throughout. Found on *Opuntia* in large groups including different stages of nymphs.

### GIANT AGAVE BUG *Acanthocephala thomasi*

Sp S F W    Large brown leaf-footed bug of west Texas. Dark antennae with last segment bright orange. Humeral angles of pronotum not greatly expanded. Front and mid tibia and tarsi and hind tarsi orange. Can aggregate in large numbers on Agave.

### HELMETED SQUASH BUG *Euthochtha galeator*

Sp S F W    Large dull uniformly brown body. Tan antennae with terminal segment darker. Humeral angles of pronotum rounded. Femora brown, remainder of legs pale. Hind tibia lacks a flange. Found along wooded margins and in weedy fields.

### LEAF-FOOTED BUG *Acanthocephala declivis*

Sp S F W    Large, gray body with membranous wing area dark. Antennae gray with terminal segment orange. Humeral angles of pronotum greatly expanded laterally. Prominent flanges on metatibia, curved sharply inward at about half its length.

### LEAF-FOOTED BUG *Acanthocephala femorata*

Sp S F W    Large and more robust than our other leaf-footed bugs. Grayish-brown in color with uniformly colored antennae. Male hind femur greatly swollen with several ventral spines and one large spike; female hind femur more slender with only small spines. Flange on hind tibia relatively straight and tapering distally.

### LEAF-FOOTED BUG *Acanthocephala terminalis*

Sp S F W    Uniformly colored brown. Antennae brown with terminal segment orange or yellow. Pronotum covered with fine golden hairs and small tubercles. Hind femur moderately swollen with row of uniform spines. Metatibial flange relatively narrow and wavy. Found on shrubs and trees at wooded edges and meadows.

### LEAF-FOOTED BUG *Catorhintha guttula*

Sp S F W    Relatively small leaf-footed bug that is uniformly brown in color. Legs are pale with black bands. Hind femur is not swollen and there is no metatibial flange.

### SQUASH BUG *Anasa tristis*

Sp S F W    Uniformly brown or dark gray. Pronotum and basal half of forewings speckled with brown. Pronotum edged in yellow. Hind femur not swollen and metatibia lacks a flange. Lateral edge of abdomen with pale banding. Can be very destructive to crops.

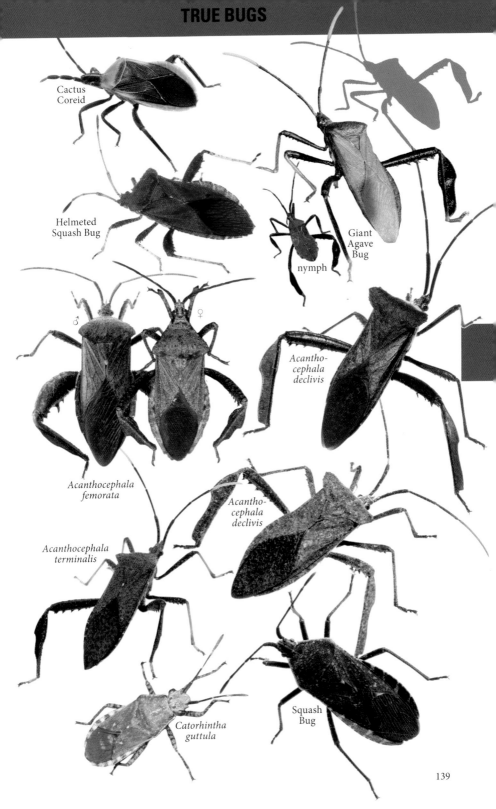

Cactus
Coreid

Helmeted
Squash Bug

Giant
Agave
Bug

nymph

♂

♀

Acantho-
cephala
declivis

Acanthocephala
femorata

Acantho-
cephala
declivis

Acanthocephala
terminalis

Catorhintha
guttula

Squash
Bug

## EASTERN LEAF-FOOTED BUG *Leptoglossus phyllopus*
COREIDAE

**Sp S F W** Brown with prominent metatibial flanges and straight white or pale stripe crossing the wings midway. Femora brown, hind tibia brown, the rest of the legs paler. Antennal segment 1 dark, 2–3 paler, 4 darker, but not as dark as 1. Can be numerous causing damage to crops and ornamentals.

## LEAF-FOOTED BUG *Leptoglossus zonatus*

**Sp S F W** Brown body with two poorly defined pale spots on anterior portion of pronotum and zigzag stripe across middle of wings. Metatibial flanges large and jagged. Femora brown, hind tibia brown, the rest of the legs paler. Antennal segment 1 dark, 2–4 pale.

## LEAF-FOOTED BUG *Leptoglossus oppositus*

**Sp S F W** More uniformly brown than other similar species. Pale stripe on wings reduced to a couple of spots. Metatibial flanges prominent and scalloped. Antennae and legs much like *L. zonatus*.

## LEAF-FOOTED BUG *Mozena lunata*

**Sp S F W** Brownish gray with humeral angles of pronotum expanded laterally, elevated and projecting forward to sharp points. Hind femur moderately swollen; lacking metatibial flange. Hind legs darker than middle and front pair. Last antennal segment orange.

## LEAF-FOOTED BUG *Mozena obtusa*

**Sp S F W** Uniformly reddish brown. Humeral angles of pronotum with sharp points, but not as elevated as in *M. lunata*. Antennal segments 1 and 4 dark, 2–3 orange. Scutellum with a pale ill-defined stripe on each side.

## LEAF-FOOTED BUG *Narnia* sp.

**Sp S F W** Brownish-gray body. Antennal segment 1 shorter than length of head. Hind femora moderately swollen with short spines. Metatibial flange not scalloped. Adults and nymphs often found on *Opuntia* in small aggregations. No transverse band on wings.

## SPOT-SIDED COREID *Hypselonotus punctiventris*

**Sp S F W** Distinctively patterned. Pale with black striping or bands over body, including legs. Posterior half of corium pinkish. Membranous area of wings black. Posterior margin of pronotum scalloped, coming to a point on each side. Common in gardens.

## EASTERN BOXELDER BUG *Boisea trivittata*
RHOPALIDAE

**Sp S F W** Black or gray with reddish-orange stripes laterally and medially on pronotum and outer edges of corium. Membranous area of forewing black. Legs and antennae uniformly black. Found in deciduous forests and meadows. Can be a nuisance in houses.

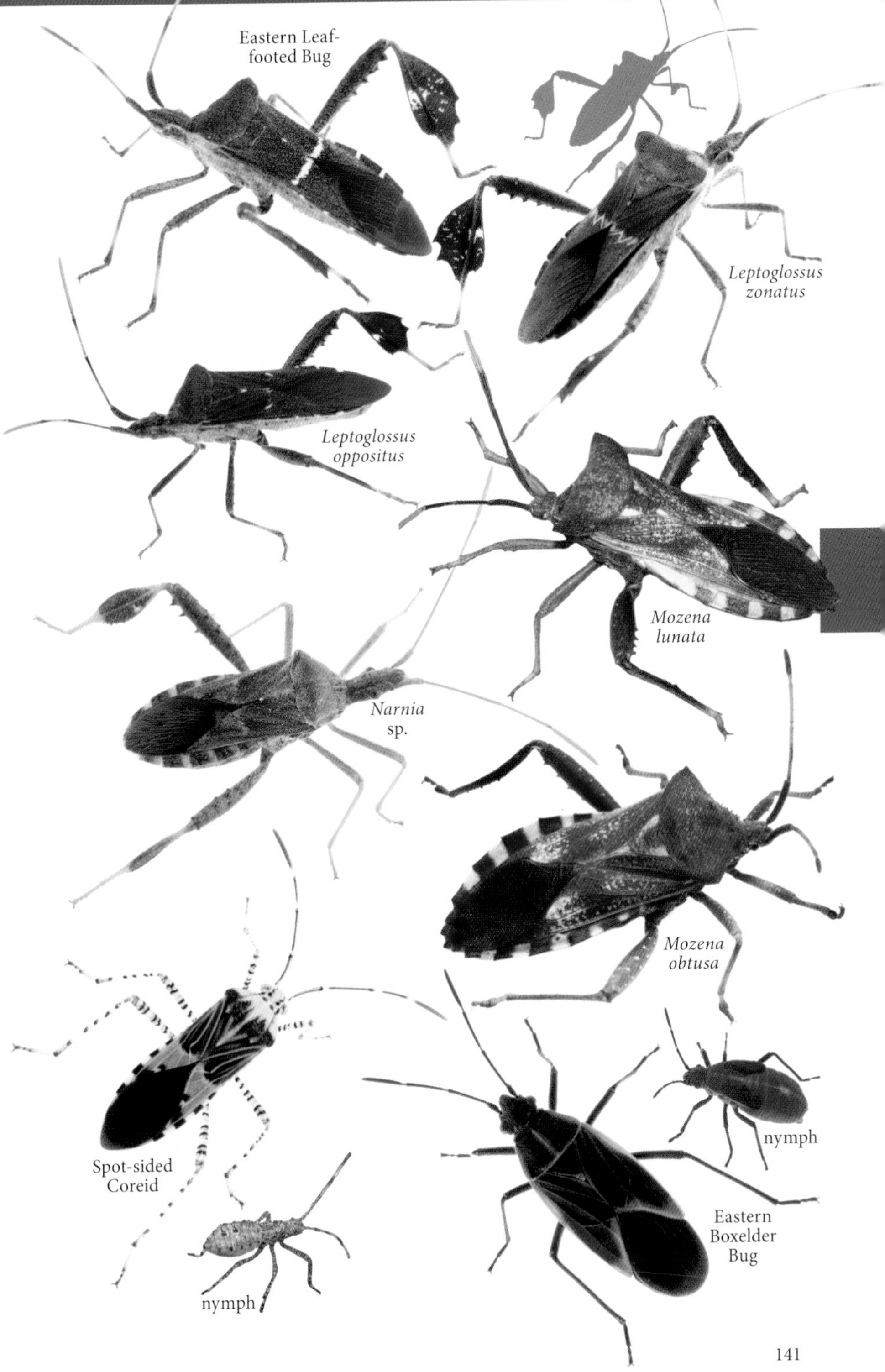

Eastern Leaf-footed Bug

*Leptoglossus zonatus*

*Leptoglossus oppositus*

*Mozena lunata*

*Narnia sp.*

*Mozena obtusa*

Spot-sided Coreid

nymph

nymph

Eastern Boxelder Bug

141

### SCENTLESS PLANT BUG *Arhyssus* sp.
RHOPALIDAE

**Sp S F W**   Variably colored. The wider fourth antennal segment is 1.5 times as long as the third. The membranous area of the forewing extends slightly beyond the tip of the abdomen. Found in fields, weedy areas, savannas, and similar habitats.

### SCENTLESS PLANT BUG *Niesthrea louisianica*

**Sp S F W**   Variable color; either reddish to orange or gray to yellow, or combinations of these. Corium and head may or may not contrast with other areas. The body, including legs, is sprinkled with dark spots. Forewing projects beyond abdomen. Found on *Hibiscus*.

### LARGUS BUG *Largus succinctus*
LARGIDAE

**Sp S F W**   Grayish black with orange-red striping around pronotum, along margins of corium and base of legs. They are commonly seen walking about on the ground in woodlands and their margins. Nymphs are metallic blue with a large orange spot in middle of abdomen and legs largely orange.

### BAGRADA BUG *Bagrada hilaris*
PENTATOMIDAE

**Sp S F W**   Smallish, distinctively colored stink bug having orange spots within white areas all on a dark background. Can be invasive feeding on many families including cruciferous crops.

### CONCHUELA BUG *Chlorochroa ligata*

**Sp S F W**   Grayish brown or black with pronotum and abdomen margined with red. Tip of scutellum also red. Legs and antennae dark and uniformly colored. Feeds on the fleshy fruits from a variety of plants including agarita, mesquite, yucca, and *Opuntia*.

### DUSKY STINK BUG *Euschistus tristigmus*

**Sp S F W**   Variable species, but generally brown in overall color. Humeral angles of pronotum can be rounded or pronounced into sharp lateral spines. Legs generally pale with lots of black dots. Identification is best done by usual presence of 1–4 black spots running ventrally down midline of abdomen.

### FOUR-HUMPED STINK BUG *Brochymena quadripustulata*

**Sp S F W**   Reddish brown or gray, mottled, and bark-like. Front of head extending forward a considerable distance. Humeral angles of pronotum bluntly pointed. Four protuberances or humps on pronotum. Legs often distinctly banded. Often found on bark.

### STINK BUG *Brochymena carolinensis*

**Sp S F W**   Gray mottled color resembling bark. Humeral angles of pronotum typically not as blunt as in *B. quadripustulata*. Legs usually uniformly gray-brown except for pale band on tibia.

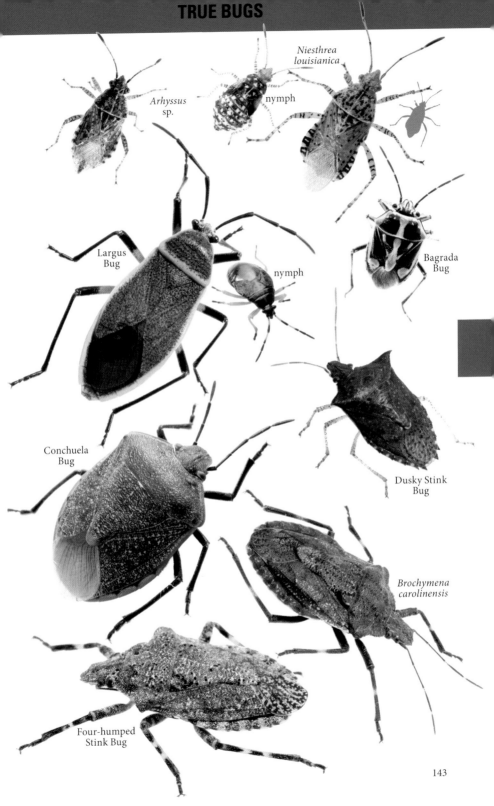

*Arhyssus* sp.

*Niesthrea louisianica*

nymph

Largus Bug

nymph

Bagrada Bug

Conchuela Bug

Dusky Stink Bug

*Brochymena carolinensis*

Four-humped Stink Bug

143

### GREEN STINK BUG *Chinavia hilaris*

PENTATOMIDAE

**Sp S F W** Large, bright green stink bug. Uniformly green, sometimes head and pronotum with narrow orange or yellow lateral margin. Membranous area of forewings clear. Last three antennal segments paler with dark distal band. Found in woodland areas.

### JUNIPER STINK BUG *Banasa euchlora*

**Sp S F W** Jade-like mottling over a paler base. Scutellum with each corner bearing a yellow spot. Membranous area of forewings clear. Antennae and legs uniform in color. Feeds on *Juniperus*.

### HARLEQUIN BUG *Murgantia histrionica*

**Sp S F W** Distinctly patterned orange and black stink bug. Pattern, however, can vary from predominately orange to predominately black. Migrates north in the spring and summer. Feeds primarily on mustards, cabbage, and relatives.

### PREDATORY STINK BUG *Perillus splendidus*

**Sp S F W** Reddish-orange and black stink bug. Variably patterned, sometimes nearly all black above, but usually with orange pronotum bearing two large back spots and scutellum and hemelytra black except for lateral margins of scutellum. Front femur with small downward projecting spine on distal third. Abdomen orange below.

### RED-SHOULDERED STINK BUG *Thyanta custator*

**Sp S F W** Highly variable, smallish species, appearing from green to brown. Anterolateral margins of pronotum with narrow dark margin. Sometimes with reddish stripe across middle of pronotum. Ventral side of abdomen with small black spot laterally on each segment larger than spiracle. Considered minor pest of crops.

### STINK BUG *Holcostethus limbolarius*

**Sp S F W** Compact, somewhat oval dark brown body, peppered with black dots. Humeral angles rounded. Tip of scutellum distinctly pale. Pronotum and hemelytra margins cream colored. Found in weedy fields, gardens, and a variety of other habitats.

### SPINED SOLDIER BUG *Podisus maculiventris*

**Sp S F W** Tan or brown with sharply spined, laterally projecting, humeral angles of pronotum. Wing membrane extends beyond abdomen and usually marked with a medial black spot. Predacious on small arthropods including caterpillars and beetle larvae.

### STINK BUG *Banasa calva*

**Sp S F W** Variable, with green to brown color forms. Green forms sometimes with posterior portion of scutellum yellow. Some individuals with pronotum green anteriorly and brown posteriorly. Legs can be pale or green.

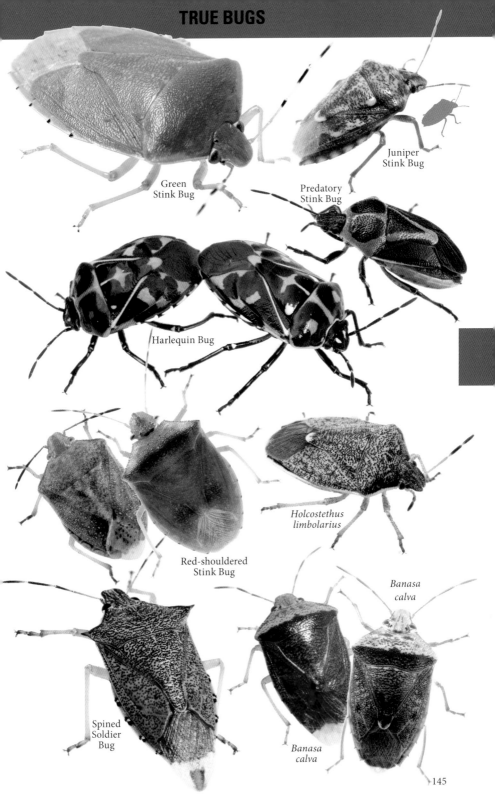

Green
Stink Bug

Juniper
Stink Bug

Predatory
Stink Bug

Harlequin Bug

*Holcostethus
limbolarius*

Red-shouldered
Stink Bug

*Banasa
calva*

Spined
Soldier
Bug

*Banasa
calva*

PENTATOMIDAE

### GIANT STRONG-NOSED STINK BUG *Alcaeorrhynchus grandis*
**Sp S F W** Large, speckled brown with smatterings of orange throughout, especially on head and lateral margins of abdomen. Bifurcated humeral spines are stout and prominent. Nymph is more round and metallic blue with red margins to pronotum. Commonly found on shrubs near streams. Attracted to lights.

### NARROW STINK BUG *Mecidea* sp.
**Sp S F W** Noticeably elongated (four times as long as wide) compared to other stink bugs. Generally pale yellow. Feed on various grasses and will come to lights.

### STINK BUG *Menecles insertus*
**Sp S F W** More rounded and somewhat flattened compared to other stink bugs. Tan to brown with pronotum projecting anteriorly around head on the sides, seeming to envelop it. Membranous area of forewings dark. Primarily nocturnal feeding in trees.

### RICE STINK BUG *Oebalus pugnax*
**Sp S F W** Narrowly elongated and tan to yellow with prominent spines projecting forward from pronotal humeral angles. Body and legs with fine dark spots. Feeds on grasses including rice, wheat, and corn where it can achieve pest status.

### STINKBUG *Proxys punctulatus*
**Sp S F W** Somewhat elongated, black with white speckling. Antennae and legs banded. Posterior tip of scutellum white. Feeds on many crops including cotton, soybean, and citrus, but can also be predaceous.

### TOMATO STINK BUG *Arvelius albopunctatus*
**Sp S F W** Yellowish green, generally getting darker rearward. Head with longitudinal black stripes. Humeral angles of pronotum with sharp, pronounced spines projecting forward. Pronotum and scutellum with black speckling. Corium with raised yellow bumps. Feeds on tomato, potato, beans, sunflowers, and other related crops.

THYREOCORIDAE

### EBONY BUG *Galgupha* sp.
**Sp S F W** Small, strongly convex body with scutellum extended over abdomen to give it a beetle-like appearance. Shiny and black, the basal antennal segments and tarsi are contrastingly pale yellow. Found on weedy plants in open fields.

CYDNIDAE

### WHITE-MARGINED BURROWER BUG *Sehirus cinctus*
**Sp S F W** Shiny black oval body. Pronotum and forewing with distinct white stripe at their margin. Membranous area of forewing deflected downward. Found in fields and meadows where it will readily climb vegetation.

nymph

Narrow Stink Bug

Giant Strong-nosed Stink Bug

Rice Stink Bug

*Menecles insertus*

Tomato Stink Bug

White-margined Burrower Bug

*Galgupha* sp.

*Proxys punctulatus*

## COTTON STAINER *Dysdercus mimulus* PYRRHOCORIDAE

**Sp S F W** Brightly colored red, white, orange, and black. Head and pronotum red, the latter with a narrow white anterior band and a black semicircle posteriorly. The outer edge of each corium is orange, with the middle, including membranous area, black. Sometimes inner margin of corium outlined by thin white stripe.

## PALE RED BUG *Dysdercus concinnus*

**Sp S F W** This brightly colored bug is striking with a mix of red, yellow, white, and black. The red pronotum has a narrow white anterior band and a broad black posterior band. The cuneus bordering the scutellum is yellow, the rest is white with a large black semicircular spot at the middle edge. Feeds on Turk's Cap.

## HILL-PRAIRIE SPITTLEBUG *Lepyronia gibbosa* APHROPHORIDAE

**Sp S F W** Gray or tan with dark speckling over body. Triangular-shaped head projects anteriorly. Forewings broadly rounded, extending laterally to almost envelop the body. Legs black. Found in well-drained soils, gravel plains, and sometimes pastures.

## SUNFLOWER SPITTLEBUG *Clastoptera xanthocephala* CLASTOPTERIDAE

**Sp S F W** Variously colored from brown to black. Short and stubby body with hind legs extending beyond abdomen when at rest. Scutellum usually darker than wings. Can be numerous on ragweed.

## TWO-LINED SPITTLEBUG *Prosapia bicincta* CERCOPIDAE

**Sp S F W** Black with reddish head and legs. Red stripe across middle of pronotum and typically two orange stripes across forewings. Nymphs are usually concealed in frothy spittle they produce while feeding on plants.

## BESPECKLED LEAFHOPPER *Paraphlepsius irroratus* CICADELLIDAE

**Sp S F W** Slender, grayish brown to green and speckled throughout. Usually uniform in color, but vertex and scutellum sometimes paler than forewings and pronotum.

## BROAD-HEADED SHARPSHOOTER *Oncometopia orbona*

**Sp S F W** Pronotum and wings various shades of blue, green, and purple. Rest of body usually yellowish orange. Head, pronotum, and wings with black speckled pattern. Female forms white patches of brochosomes on wings from anal secretions that is then used to cover eggs protecting them against parasitoids.

## GLASSY-WINGED SHARPSHOOTER *Homalodisca vitripennis*

**Sp S F W** Elongated body with pointed head. Wings dark with clear patches. Head and pronotum dark with speckling. This species is a major vector of Pierce's disease on grape.

Pale Red
Bug

*Dysdercus
mimulus*

Spittlebug
nymph

Hill-prairie
Spittlebug

Two-lined
Spittlebug

Sunflower
Spittlebug

Bespeckled
Leafhopper

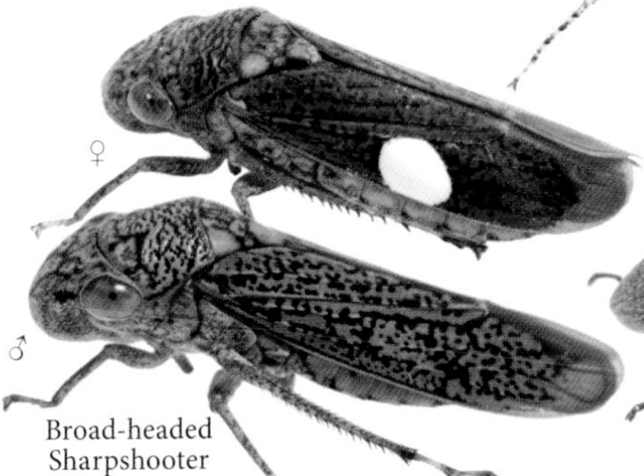

♀

♂

Broad-headed
Sharpshooter

Glassy-winged
Sharpshooter

### LEAFHOPPER *Excultanus excultus)*

CICADELLIDAE

**Sp S F W** Grayish or brown wings with head distinctly paler than rest of body. Head somewhat triangular shaped. Three white diamond-shaped spots running down the midline. Numerous spines along tibia. Found on vegetation in meadows. Attracted to lights.

### LEAFHOPPER *Gyponana angulata*

**Sp S F W** Lime green in front becoming paler rearward. Rounded, forward projecting head with red eyes. Relatively few veins in wings. Attracted to lights.

### LEAFHOPPER *Ponana* sp.

**Sp S F W** Members of this genus are variously colored from gray to green to pink. Some with finely speckled pronotum and larger spots on wings. Widespread throughout the state. Found on various types of vegetation in meadows.

### RED-BANDED LEAFHOPPER *Graphocephala coccinea*

**Sp S F W** Colorful, streamlined species. Head yellowish green. Pronotum and wings vary from mostly red with bluish-green stripes, to mostly green with red stripes. Found in meadows.

### SHARPSHOOTER *Draeculacephala* sp.

**Sp S F W** Narrow, elongated, green leafhopper with a very pointed head. Body various shades of green with veins a lighter green to blue. Numerous similar-looking species that are difficult to tell apart. Can become a pest on some crop species.

### SPECKLED SHARPSHOOTER *Paraulacizes irrorata*

**Sp S F W** Dark, elongated leafhopper with pale speckling over head, pronotum, and wings. Margins of wings often with yellow speckling. Feeds on various asters including thistle and sorghum. Can be common in meadows.

### HIEROGLYPHIC CICADA *Neocicada hieroglyphica*

CICADIDAE

**Sp S F W** Head and pronotum green with black patterning. Pronotum widened to a point posterolaterally. Abdomen tan. Wings with veins, particularly distally, broadly outlined with brown. Prefers oaks and will call morning until dusk. Readily attracted to lights.

### LITTLE MESQUITE CICADA *Pacarina puella*

**Sp S F W** Small cicada with a proportionately large head. Reddish-brown body with black markings on head and pronotum. Wings with some veins outlined in brown. As name implies, feeds primarily on mesquite.

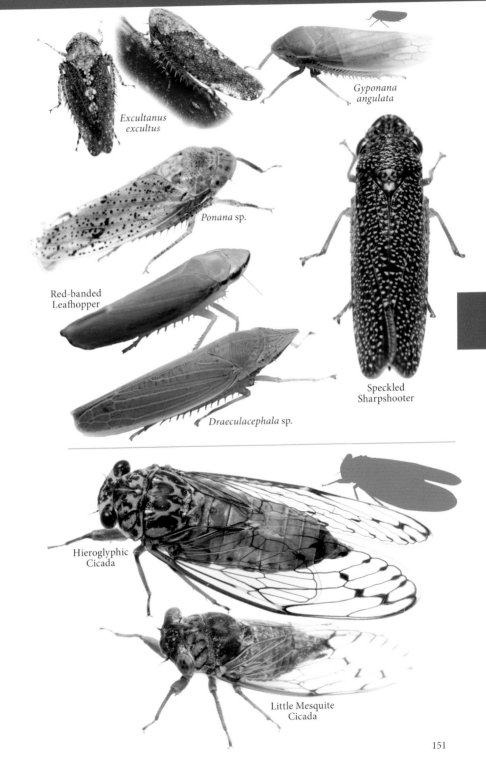

*Excultanus excultus*

*Gyponana angulata*

*Ponana* sp.

Red-banded Leafhopper

Speckled Sharpshooter

*Draeculacephala* sp.

Hieroglyphic Cicada

Little Mesquite Cicada

### WESTERN DUSK SINGING CICADA *Megatibicen resh*

CICADIDAE

**Sp S F W** Large cicada with largely green, tan, or rust-colored head and brown or black thorax and abdomen. Green mark on thorax looks like an upside down pair of the Hebrew letter resh. Western individuals develop more white pruinosity. One of our loudest cicadas. Found associated with oaks.

### SWAMP CICADA *Neotibicen tibicen*

**Sp S F W** Large dark cicada, often nearly all black. Pronotum often marked with dark green. A small thin brown line often visible on each side of mesonotal midline. Base of wings extensively dark green. A large prominent white spot basally on each side of abdomen. Common in many habitats, but especially deciduous forests.

### BLACK TREEHOPPER *Acutalis tartarea*

MEMBRACIDAE

**Sp S F W** Has multiple forms, from all black, to black anteriorly and either tan or green posteriorly. The tips of the wings, however, are always clear with the veins heavily outlined. Overall shape is rounded above without pronotal ornamentation.

### BUFFALO TREEHOPPER *Stictocephala* sp.

**Sp S F W** Can be green or brown or a mix of the two. Somewhat truncated appearance in front. Pronotum rounded and extending laterally, sometimes into a sharp point well beyond the thorax width. Wings are clear, but veins may be green or tan.

### OAK TREEHOPPER *Platycotis vittata*

**Sp S F W** Highly variable species appearing gray, green, or turquoise. Eyes often red and a horn may or may not be present, but if present can be varying lengths projecting upward and forward. Despite the variation, it can be recognized from most other species by the short hind tarsi. Found in oak forest edges.

### TREEHOPPER *Archasia auriculata*

**Sp S F W** Pronotum tall and rounded, appearing almost like a semicircle. Pronotum usually green, but can be brown; always edged in brown with small spots. Found on oaks.

### TREEHOPPER *Cyrtolobus tuberosus*

**Sp S F W** Tan or brownish with a variably raised pronotum that is distinctively notched just before tip and shows a distinctive brown and white banding pattern.

### TREEHOPPER *Entylia carinata*

**Sp S F W** Various shades of tan and brown. Pronotum with two truncate-shaped humps and white longitudinal veins. Pronotum usually has a somewhat banded appearance. Feeds on asters.

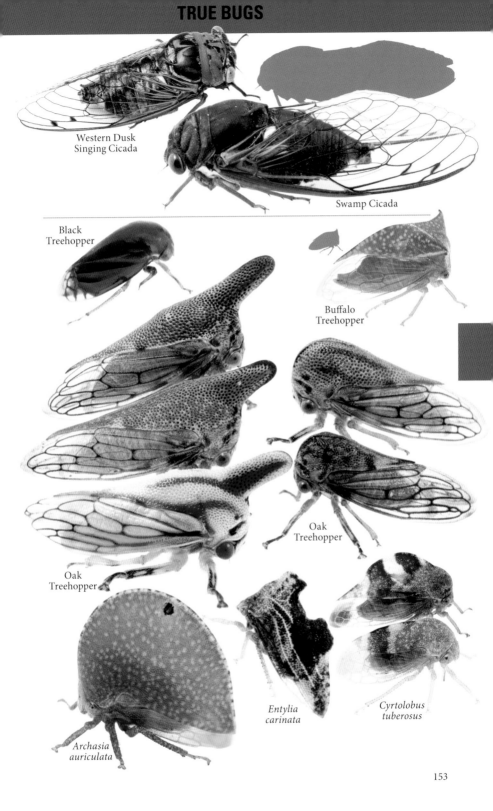

Western Dusk
Singing Cicada

Swamp Cicada

Black
Treehopper

Buffalo
Treehopper

Oak
Treehopper

Oak
Treehopper

*Archasia
auriculata*

*Entylia
carinata*

*Cyrtolobus
tuberosus*

153

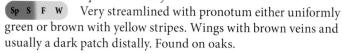

**TREEHOPPER** *Ophiderma evelyna* MEMBRACIDAE

Sp S F W   Very streamlined with pronotum either uniformly green or brown with yellow stripes. Wings with brown veins and usually a dark patch distally. Found on oaks.

**TREEHOPPER** *Smilia fasciata*

Sp S F W   Brown or black raised, rounded pronotum that sharply angles backward near its tip. Broad white stripe running from top of pronotum through wings; in some individuals, this stripe is green. Eyes are red and individuals are attracted to lights. Feeds on oaks.

**TREEHOPPER** *Telamona concava*

Sp S F W   Relatively large variable species with a pronounced, broad pronotal crest. Crest can be variably shaped, but the leading edge is always vertical and it is rounded at the top. Variously mottled with browns and greens. Will come to lights.

**ACANALONIID PLANTHOPPER** *Acanalonia servillei* ACANALONIIDAE

Sp S F W   Lime green with leaf-like venation. Three long veins running parallel to one another are visible in the forewing. With wings together, a dorsal yellow stripe is visible. Eyes are red. Feeds on caper and is attracted to lights.

**ACHILID PLANTHOPPER** *Catonia nava* ACHILIIDAE

Sp S F W   Small, dark bug with body angled upward when sitting. Front of head rounded. Eyes are pale turquoise with antennae inserted below. Wings are heavily reticulated with white veins and dark spots within cells. Legs pale. Readily comes to lights.

**ACHILID PLANTHOPPER** *Cixidia opaca*

Sp S F W   Dark brown with head somewhat pointed, projecting forward between eyes and slanted rearward below. Wings with pale orangish speckling and a larger spot of orange on scutellum and two thirds of the way down the wing margin. Attracted to lights.

**CIXIID PLANTHOPPER** *Melanoliarus* sp. CIXIIDAE

Sp S F W   Large, diverse genus. Head in profile is straight above, then angled rearward below. The mesonotum bears five raised ridges. Most with clear wings spotted with various degrees of dark markings and a pronounced pterostigma. Hind tibia with numerous spines and hind tarsomere with 10 or fewer teeth. Attracted to lights.

**CIXIID PLANTHOPPERS** *Pintalia vibex*

Sp S F W   Tan or brown and distinctively laterally compressed with wing tips rounded and angled slightly upward. Wings often mottled with pale spots and margin of wings sometimes outlined in white. Attracted to lights.

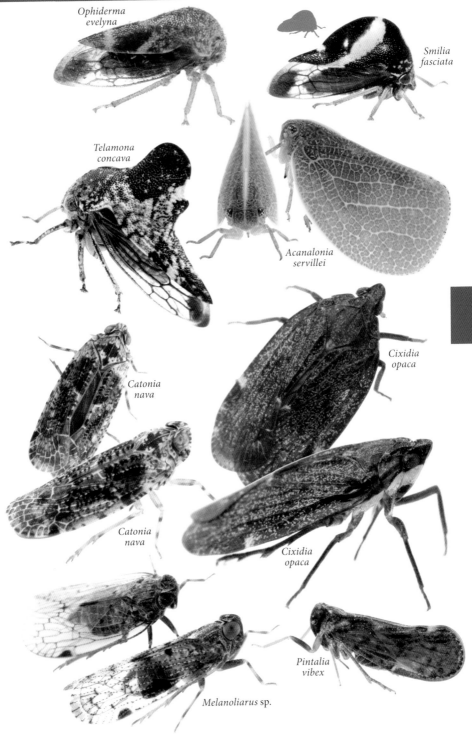

*Ophiderma evelyna*

*Smilia fasciata*

*Telamona concava*

*Acanalonia servillei*

*Cixidia opaca*

*Catonia nava*

*Catonia nava*

*Cixidia opaca*

*Pintalia vibex*

*Melanoliarus* sp.

### DELPHACID PLANTHOPPER *Liburniella ornata* — DELPHACIDAE

Sp **S** **F** W   This is a dainty, ornate, distinctive hopper. The eyes are green and antennae project laterally from head with the basal segments greatly enlarged. There is a white stripe with dark margins running down the middle of the head and thorax dorsally. The wing pattern is diagnostic. Feeds on sedges and possibly grasses.

### DELPHACID PLANTHOPPER *Penepissonotus bicolor*

Sp **S** **F** W   Pinkish body and legs with dark head and pronotum. Antennae project laterally from head with basal segment dark, next three segments pale, then a long filamentous segment. Body is angled upward when at rest.

### DELPHACID PLANTHOPPER *Stenocranus* sp.

Sp **S** **F** W   A number of similar-looking species in this genus. They are somewhat laterally compressed and usually tan in color with a prominent white stripe going down the midline. Eyes may be reddish. Antennae held laterally out from head with long filamentous terminal segment. Attracted to lights.

### DERBID PLANTHOPPER *Cedusa* sp. — DERBIDAE

Sp **S** **F** **W**   A large and variable genus. Many are uniformly gray, others with gray wings and thorax and pale face. Wings are broadly rounded distally. Nymphs known to feed on fungi in leaf litter.

### DERBID PLANTHOPPER *Paramysidia mississippiensis*

Sp **S** **F** W   Sits with wings outspread appearing mothlike. Peach to gray body and pale wings with veins heavily traced in shades of brown. Multiple individuals often seen together feeding on sabal palm, irises, and maples.

### DICTYOPHARID PLANTHOPPERS *Nersia florida* — DICTYOPHARIDAE

Sp **S** F W   Lime-green body with pointed head and often reddish eyes. White stripe on side of head that runs through eye and continues on to wing's leading edge. Sits with body angled upward.

### CITRUS FLATID PLANTHOPPER *Metcalfa pruinosa* — FLATIDAE

Sp **S** **F** W   Pale white or gray anteriorly with dark spots transitioning to darker wings with smaller white spots. Color varies due to extent of pruinescent or waxy covering. Overall shape is rectangular with wings truncated, but rounded on edges. Despite its name, feeds on numerous plants other than citrus.

### NORTHERN FLATID PLANTHOPPER *Flatormenis proxima*

Sp **S** **F** W   White to pale green and rectangular in profile with wings less rounded than in other species. Combined with overall appearance, a double line of apical cells in the wing is diagnostic, but may require in-hand examination. Attracted to lights.

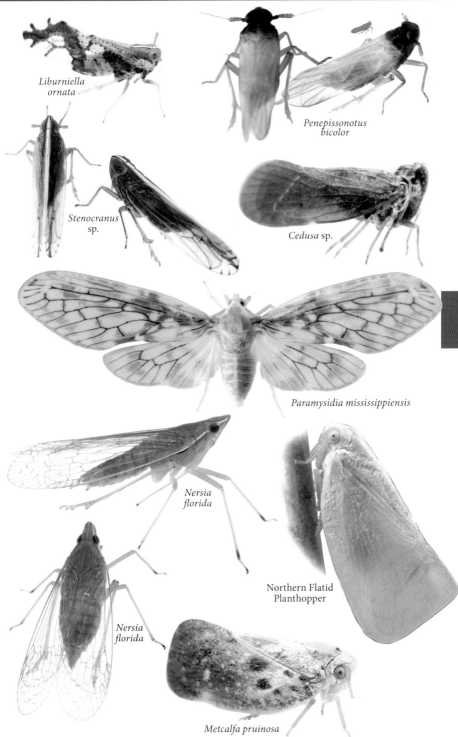

Liburniella
ornata

Penepissonotus
bicolor

Stenocranus
sp.

Cedusa sp.

Paramysidia mississippiensis

Nersia
florida

Northern Flatid
Planthopper

Nersia
florida

Metcalfa pruinosa

157

### FLATID PLANTHOPPER *Flataloides scabrosa*

**Sp S F W** Greenish, gray, white, or brown and dorsoventrally flattened. When viewed laterally, wings are undulated. Tip of wings broadly rounded. Uncommon on vegetation, but attracted to lights where it is irregularly seen.

### FULGORID PLANTHOPPER *Cyrpoptus belfragei*

**Sp S F W** Dark to light brown with darker streaks in wings. Head is broadly rounded when viewed from above. Anterior half of hind wings bright red with large black patch in middle. Feeds on various grasses and pines. Attracted to lights.

### ISSID PLANTHOPPER *Thionia bullata*

**Sp S F W** Short, stout-bodied hopper. Varies from light tan to darker brown with darker mottling throughout. Eyes reddish. Feeds on various pine species.

### HACKBERRY PSYLLID *Pachypsylla* sp.

**Sp S F W** Dark brown with rounded wings. Wings with dark speckling and brownish veins. Many species similar looking, but can often be identified from galls produced by the hackberry trees they infect. Antennae often with dark tips.

### GIANT BARK APHID *Longistigma caryae*

**Sp S F W** Largest aphid in North America (up to 6 mm in length). Grayish body with relatively long legs. Femora, especially on mid and hind legs, reddish orange. Males and some females winged, most females are wingless. Abdomen with series of dark spots laterally. Feeds on a number of trees including elm, oak, hickory, sycamore, and golden rain tree.

### MILKWEED APHID *Aphis nerii*

**Sp S F W** Bright yellow with black legs, antennae, and cornicles. Winged individuals have a pigmented thorax. Can be numerous on milkweed and oleander. This species ingests cardiac glycosides from the host plants making them noxious to predators.

### RED APHID *Uroleucon* sp.

**Sp S F W** Many species red. Can be winged or wingless. Two taxonomic lineages are recognized by those with dark cornicles and those with light cornicles. Most feed on composites including goldenrod.

### COCHINEAL *Dactylopius* sp.

**Sp S F W** Feeds on the pads of *Opuntia*. Nymphs produce a cottony waxy covering over their bodies for protection from dessication. The adults and nymphs produce a red pigment that is used as a dye in food, clothing, and artwork.

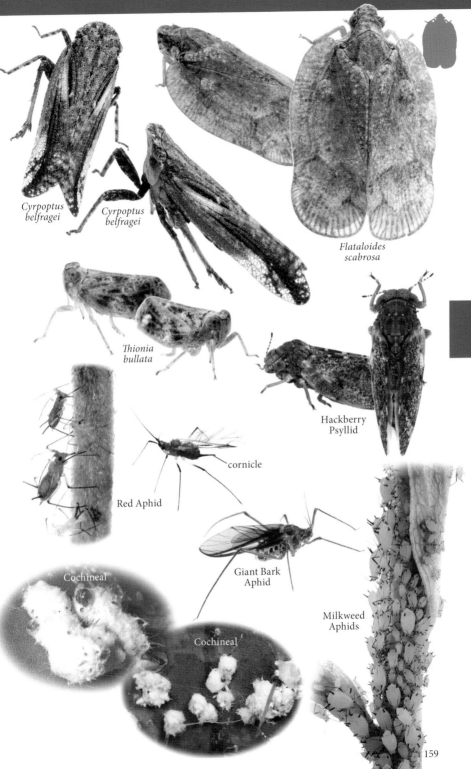

*Cyrpoptus belfragei*

*Cyrpoptus belfragei*

*Flataloides scabrosa*

*Thionia bullata*

Hackberry Psyllid

cornicle

Red Aphid

Giant Bark Aphid

Cochineal

Cochineal

Milkweed Aphids

159

# Lacewings, Antlions, and Allies
# Order Neuroptera

Green Lacewing
(*Abachrysa eureka*)

**NATURAL HISTORY**    This is a relatively small, but morphologically diverse group of soft-bodied insects with four subequal membranous wings (in our species), which are generally held roof-like over abdomen at rest. The name Neuroptera means "nerve wing" and refers to the characteristically intricate network of wing veins. This group has complete metamorphosis and most species are predaceous as both larvae and adults. The larvae are unusual in having sucking mouthparts. Most adults are weak fliers and many feed on small insects, like aphids and mealybugs, which they find on plants. In some groups, like the green lacewings, the eggs are laid on long stalks, which may help to reduce predation on their eggs.

The larvae of many green lacewing species also camouflage their bodies with the dead carcasses of their prey or other bits of debris, such as small pieces of lichen, but the larvae of other green lacewing species are bare. Most adult green lacewings have an "ear" at the base of each forewing, which allows them to detect the cries of bats and helps them avoid being eaten when flying at night. Brown lacewing larvae are always bare, and do not lay their eggs on stalks. Antlions get their name from their larvae, which feed on ants and other small arthropods. Most people are familiar with the cone-shaped pits made in sand by the larvae of some species, but most species don't make pits and are sit-and-wait predators that live on, or just under, the surface of sand or soil. Mantidfly larvae are predators or parasites on a variety of arthropods, particularly the eggs of spiders. Spongillafly larvae are aquatic and feed mostly on freshwater sponges. All Neuroptera species pupate in a silken cocoon spun by the mature larva.

# Identifying Characters

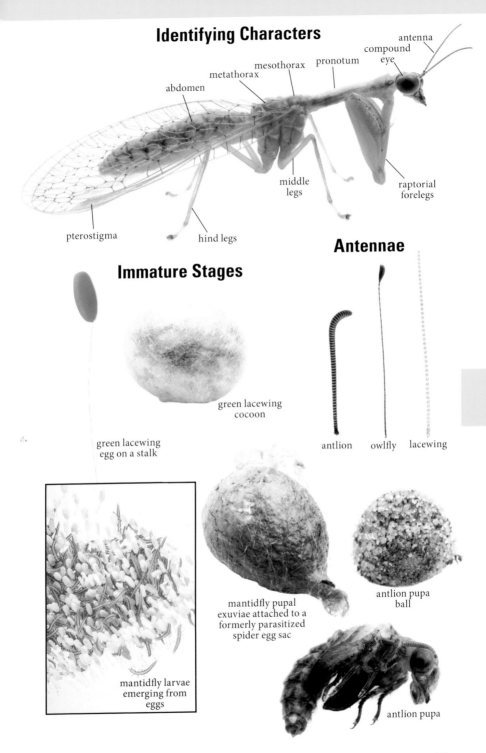

antenna

compound eye

pronotum

mesothorax

metathorax

abdomen

middle legs

raptorial forelegs

pterostigma

hind legs

## Antennae

antlion

owlfly

lacewing

## Immature Stages

green lacewing egg on a stalk

green lacewing cocoon

mantidfly larvae emerging from eggs

mantidfly pupal exuviae attached to a formerly parasitized spider egg sac

antlion pupa ball

antlion pupa

161

### BEADED LACEWING *Lomamyia* sp. BEROTHIDAE

**Sp S F W** Forewings conspicuously upturned at tip. Antennae often yellowish with no club, but thickened at base. Overall color tan to dark brown. Eggs are stalked and laid on wood. Larvae are predaceous on termites physically injecting them with an immobilizing venom from the tip of their mandibles. Adults are readily attracted to lights.

### GREEN LACEWING *Abachrysa eureka* CHRYSOPIDAE

**Sp S F W** White with dark spots over body. Yellow on head, meso- and metathorax, and abdominal tip. Legs white with black spots. Wings clear with black veins. Attracted to lights.

### GREEN LACEWING *Nodita pavida*

**Sp S F W** Pale green body with long antennae. Face and head paler than pronotum. "Smudge" of red laterally in front of eyes. Basal antennal segment with red stripe. Thin dark stripe behind eye.

### GREEN LACEWING *Chrysoperla rufilabris*

**Sp S F W** Green with red genae (cheeks) and reddish stripe behind eye. Wings with dark crossveins. Found throughout the year and in the winter often present in a red form. Attracted to lights.

### SHADOW LACEWING *Eremochrysa* sp.

**Sp S F W** Pale with heavy brown to black mottling over head, thorax, and abdomen. Wings rather rounded, often with streaks of brown along most crossveins. Attracted to lights.

### DUSTYWING *Coniopteryx* sp. CONIOPTERYGIDAE

**Sp S F W** Covered with white or gray waxy pruinesence over entire body, including wings. Antennae long and slender. Mouthparts, especially palps, noticeably long. Hind legs also proportionately longer than front and middle legs. Adults and larvae feed on aphids, spider mites, various scale insects, and other small arthropods. Adults fly slowly between plants and are attracted to lights.

### BROWN LACEWING *Megalomus fidelis* HEMEROBIIDAE

**Sp S F W** Short and stout with very rounded wings. Head with pale antennae and relatively large eyes. Light brown wings with two diagonal tan streaks. Crossveins in middle of forewing dark brown. Typically found in woodland habitats. Adults attracted to lights.

### BROWN LACEWING *Hemerobius stigma*

**Sp S F W** Dark brown with heavily mottled wings (most crossveins with dark suffusion of color). Antennae same color as body. Associated with woodland habitats, especially conifers. Attracted to lights.

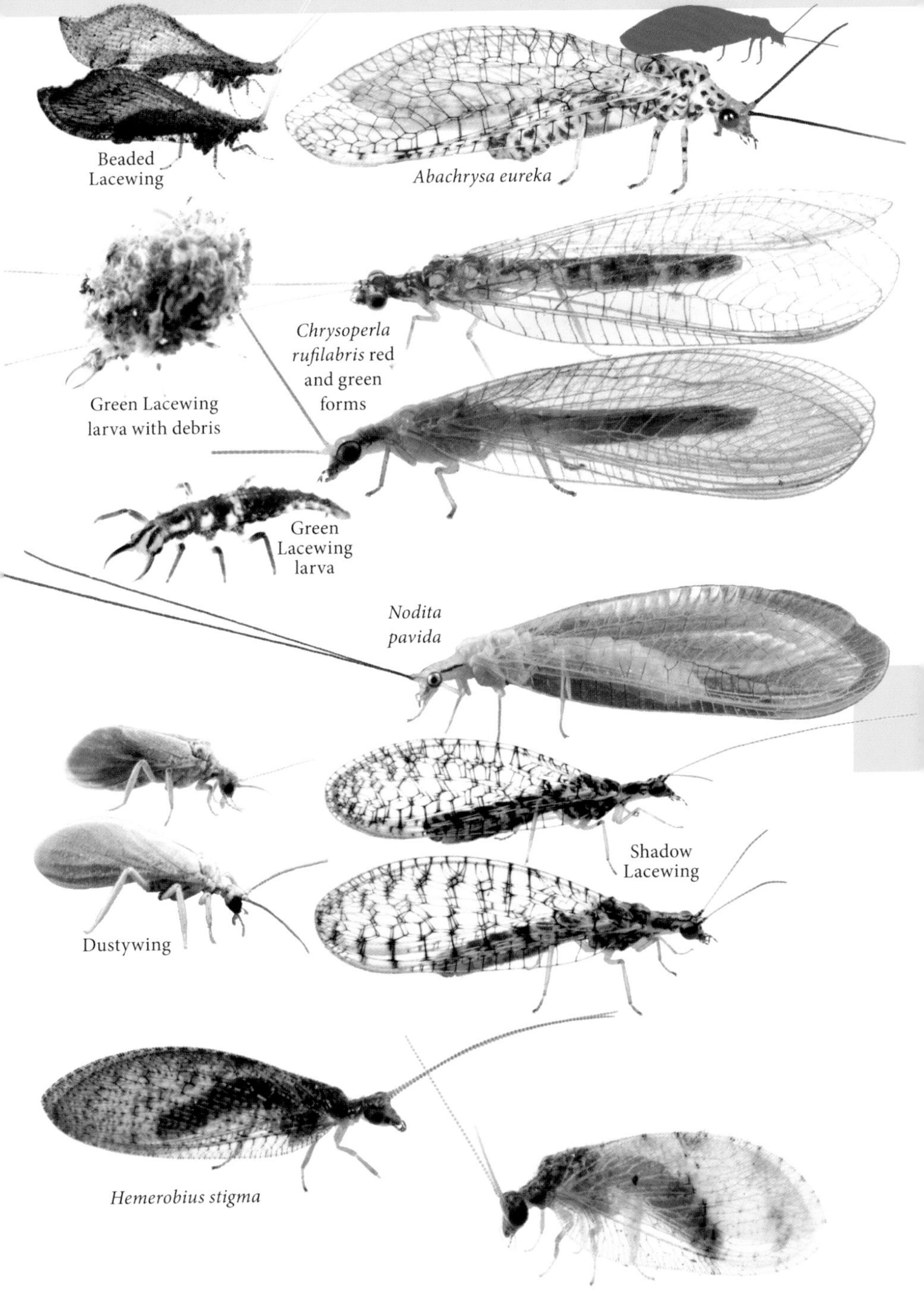

Beaded
Lacewing

*Abachrysa eureka*

Green Lacewing
larva with debris

*Chrysoperla
rufilabris* red
and green
forms

Green
Lacewing
larva

*Nodita
pavida*

Dustywing

Shadow
Lacewing

*Hemerobius stigma*

*Megalomus fidelis*

163

# NEUROPTERA

**BROWN LACEWING** *Micromus subanticus*  HEMEROBIIDAE

Sp **S F W**   Reddish-brown to tan with narrow wings (relative to other brown lacewings). Eyes small. Wings with very dark speckling throughout and series of diagonal crossveins forming a dark irregular line distally in forewing. Larvae and adults feed on aphids. Adults are attracted to lights.

**BARBER'S BROWN LACEWING** *Sympherobius barberi*

Sp **S F W**   Rounded wings with tan color diffuse. Eyes large, head and thorax dark. Antennae pale except for basal third which is dark. Forewing may have a dark diagonal band. Found in woodland areas, especially with oaks and pines. Larvae and adults feed on mealybugs and aphids. Adults attracted to lights.

**MANTIDFLY** *Dicromantispa interrupta*  MANTISPIDAE

Sp **S F** W   Brown with greenish-bronze eyes. Pronotum with transverse ridges. Antennae uniformly colored. Otherwise clear wings with brownish pterostigma and dark spot at apex. Like many mantidflies, larvae feed on spider eggs. Attracted to lights.

**MANTIDFLY** *Dicromantispa sayi*

Sp **S F** W   Brown with greenish-bronze eyes. Pronotum with transverse ridges throughout length. Antennae brown with basal segments yellow or tricolored (mostly brown, pale towards tip, with dark tips). Variably colored with dark pronotum and mostly yellow thorax and abdomen or more uniformly brown. Wings clear with brown pterostigma. Attracted to lights.

**WASP MANTIDFLY** *Climaciella brunnea*

Sp **S F** W   Colored like paper wasps, which it mimics. Variably colored from mostly red to a combination of yellows, reds, and blacks. Wings heavily pigmented along anterior edge. Long pronotum and raptorial forelegs. Feeds on small insects at flowers.

**MANTIDFLY** *Leptomantispa pulchella*

Sp **S F** W   Yellowish to reddish brown. Pronotum smooth, no transverse ridges. Wings clear with tan pterostigma; distal angle sometimes broader than in *Dichromantispa sayi*. Attracted to lights.

**GREEN MANTIDFLY** *Zeugomantispa minuta*

Sp **S F** W   Bright green with yellow stripe running middorsally. Antennae reddish brown. Elongated pronotum with streaks of red laterally. Abdomen with dark reddish-brown dorsal markings. Pterostigma green. Attracted to lights.

**MANTIDFLY** *Plega dactylota*

Sp **S F** W   Mottled brown and more robust than other mantidflies. Antennae longer than pronotum. Wings diffuse brown throughout. Pterostigma dark, elongated with median pale spot. Female with long ovipositor. Larvae feed on small arthropods.

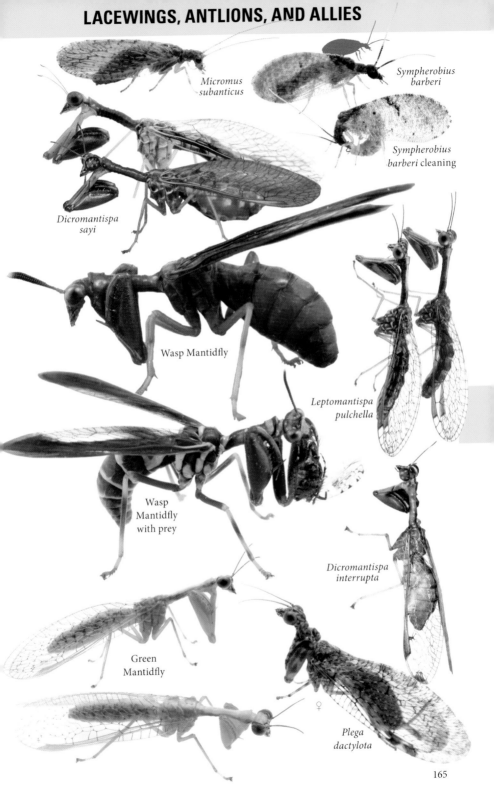

*Micromus subanticus*

*Sympherobius barberi*

*Sympherobius barberi* cleaning

*Dicromantispa sayi*

Wasp Mantidfly

*Leptomantispa pulchella*

Wasp Mantidfly with prey

*Dicromantispa interrupta*

Green Mantidfly

♀

*Plega dactylota*

**SPONGILLAFLY** *Climacia areolaris*  SISYRIDAE

Sp **S** **F** **W**  Costal crossveins not forked (unlike in brown lacewings). Eyes purple. Wings elongated and dark with broad, pale irregular diagonal band and pale spot along leading edge of wing more basally. Antennae dark. Head with reddish brown above, pronotum dark. Legs yellow or tan. Larvae feed on sponges.

**OWLFLY** *Ascaloptynx appendiculata*  MYRMELEONTIDAE

Sp **S** **F** **W**  Large, with four equal-sized stalked wings. Antennae long and clubbed. Eyes large and not divided. Wings with dark streak along leading edge. Hairy thorax with yellow stripe middorsally. Perches with abdomen directed away from body.

**OWLFLY** *Ululodes* sp.

Sp **S** **F** **W**  Large eyes that are divided. Four wings, usually lacking any color. Antennae long and clubbed. Hairy thorax. Often perches with abdomen directed away from body. Larvae sit and wait on ground for small insect prey to walk by. Attracted to lights.

**ANTLION** *Scotoleon* sp.

Sp **S** **F** **W**  Gray body. Males with abdomens longer than wings as in *Brachynemurus*. Antennae with hook on end. Wings with crossveins often darkly marked. Attracted to lights.

**ANTLION** *Brachynemurus sackeni*

Sp **S** **F** **W**  Male with very long abdomen and large claspers and banded yellow or reddish and black. Female abdomen no longer than wings. Head and much of thorax pale yellow with dark markings. Antennae hooked at tip. Crossveins in wings with dark markings.

**ANTLION** *Glenurus gratus*

Sp **S** **F** **W**  Large antlion with distinctively pink and brown marked wings. Antennae hooked at tip. Body fairly dark with pale stripe dorsally on thorax. Larvae are found in tree holes, usually associated with wood dust. Adults attracted to lights.

**ANTLION** *Myrmeleon* sp.

Sp **S** **F** **W**  Tan to dark gray body. Antennae hooked at tip. Wings either clear or with crossveins marked by brown. Only genus of antlion in the state whose larvae make pits in the sand. Adults attracted to lights.

**ANTLION** *Vella fallax*

Sp **S** **F** **W**  Large, gray, hairy antlion. Wings heavily marked with darkened veins and darker dashes along leading edge. Antennae hooked at tip. Larvae live in deep sand. Adults can be common at lights.

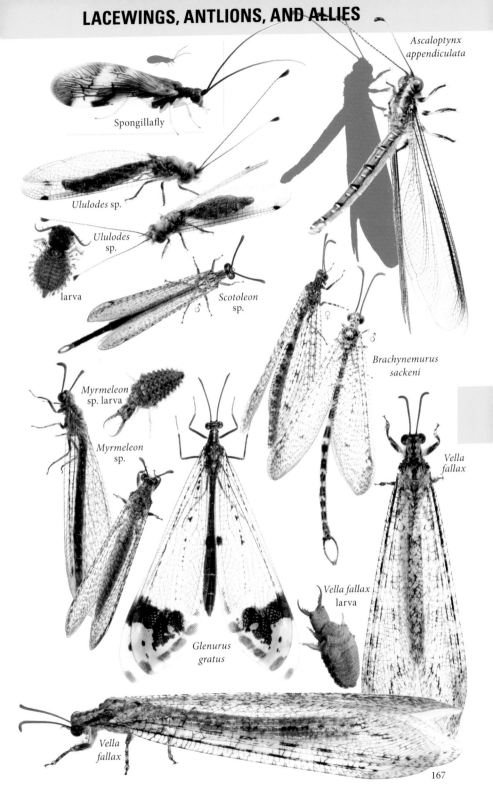

*Ascaloptynx
appendiculata*

Spongillafly

*Ululodes* sp.

*Ululodes*
sp.

larva

*Scotoleon*
sp.
♂

♀

♂

*Brachynemurus
sackeni*

*Myrmeleon*
sp. larva

*Myrmeleon*
sp.

*Vella
fallax*

*Glenurus
gratus*

*Vella fallax*
larva

*Vella
fallax*

167

# Alderflies, Dobsonflies, and Fishflies
# Order Megaloptera

Spring Fishfly
(*Chauliodes rastricornis*)

**NATURAL HISTORY** This small group of insects is a sister order to the Neuroptera and Rhaphidioptera. They differ in having the anal (basal) region of the hind wing broader than the forewing. It is folded when at rest. The ordinal name means big (*megalo*) wing (*ptera*). They undergo complete metamorphosis.

The group contains two families that have predaceous aquatic larvae with chewing mandibles, as opposed to the sickle-shaped mandibles of the Neuroptera larvae, and lateral gills on the abdomen. The larvae are often referred to as hellgrammites and commonly used as fishing bait. Alderfly larvae have a terminal filament but lack anal prolegs, while dobsonfly and fishfly larvae lack the terminal filament but have a pair of anal prolegs. Dobsonfly larvae also have tufts of gills on each segment that are lacking in fishfly and alderfly larvae.

Larvae pupate under rocks and logs in earthen chambers near the shoreline of the larval habitat. The pupae look similar to the adults with poorly developed wings, but they have functional mandibles and legs. Female dobsonflies lay clusters of eggs on the undersides of bridges and on rocks and leaves overhanging the water. The larvae emerge and fall into the water, pupate, and become adults all in one year. Alderflies lay eggs in a row on emergent vegetation. Adult dobsonflies and fishflies are generally nocturnal, while alderflies are diurnal. Both have large compound eyes, with or without ocelli. The adults are rather short-lived and may actively feed on fruit as is known in tropical species.

# Immature Stages

Alderfly larva

Fishfly larva

Dobsonfly eggs

eggs on bridge

Dobsonfly Larva

underside showing fluffy gills

Dobsonfly Pupa

Fishfly larva in earthen burrow preparing to pupate.

### ALDERFLY *Sialis* sp.
SIALIDAE

**Sp S F W** Small for the group, dark brown to black with heavily-veined wings held roof-like over abdomen. Large compound eyes, but no ocelli. Antennae about half the length of the body. Fourth tarsal segment widened, bearing two lobes. Adults found on riparian vegetation surrounding larval habitat. Larvae generally found in mucky, detritus-rich ponds and slow reaches of streams.

### SPRING FISHFLY *Chauliodes rastricornis*
CORYDALIDAE

**Sp S F W** Large, brownish wings with dark speckled veins. Dark markings on otherwise pale head and pronotum. Antennae of male pectinate; female with serrate antennae. Larvae found in standing bodies of water and are somewhat omnivorous, feeding on small insects as well as detritus. Adults likely don't feed.

### SUMMER FISHFLY *Chauliodes pectinicornis*

**Sp S F W** Large, brownish wings with dark speckled veins. Pale markings on otherwise dark head and pronotum. Antennae of male and female pectinate. Larvae found in standing bodies of water.

### DOBSONFLY *Corydalus luteus*

**Sp S F W** Very large with brownish wings and white spots within cells. Males have large sickle-shaped mandibles. Females with shorter, reddish mandibles contrasting with head color. Head and pronotum lacking a pattern, uniformly brown.

### EASTERN DOBSONFLY *Corydalus cornutus*

**Sp S F W** Very large with brownish wings and white spots within cells. Males have large sickle-shaped mandibles used to hold females during mating. Females with shorter, but robust, brown mandibles the same color as head. Head and pronotum moderately to extensively patterned.

Alderfly
(*Sialis* sp.)

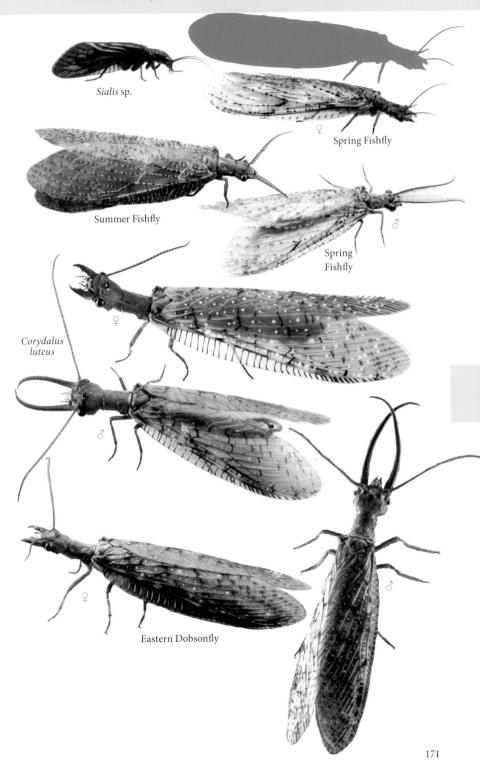

*Sialis* sp.

Spring Fishfly ♀

Summer Fishfly

Spring Fishfly ♂

*Corydalus luteus* ♀

♂

Eastern Dobsonfly ♀

♂

# Snakeflies
# Order Raphidioptera

Snakefly
(*Agulla bicolor*)

**NATURAL HISTORY**   Snakeflies are an unusual looking group of insects with an elongated pronotum and head that together resemble a snake. The ordinal name is derived from the Greek roots *raphio*, meaning needle and *ptera*, meaning wing. The long, needle-like ovipositor of the females looks like a stinger. Only one species occurs in Texas, *Agulla bicolor*. They are found in central and west Texas from April through May, and are predaceous on other insects including aphids, bark lice, and scales. They have complete metamorphosis, and are about 13 mm long as adults.

Eggs are likely laid on the bark of juniper (*Juniperus* spp.) and larvae generally hatch in about eight days. The larvae typically go through ten instars in a year (many more than in the closely related Neuroptera), but can take up to several years depending on conditions. The pupa stage lasts about fourteen days before the adult emerges and adults live two to three months.

Adults exhibit courtship behavior. When a male and female encounter one another, the male vibrates his abdomen. When he stops, the female responds with short bursts of vibrations. This sometimes elicits another burst of vibrations from the male. The pair will simultaneously arch their abdomens and move their wings. At this point, the male may walk a distance from the female and then return to face her. The antennae become intertwined, mouth parts touch, and they graze each other's cheeks. The male then moves under the female when she arches her abdomen to mate.

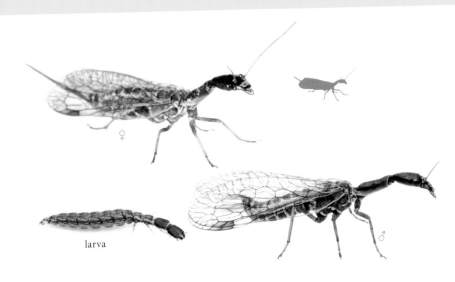

♀

larva

### SNAKEFLY *Agulla bicolor*

RAPHIDIIDAE

**Sp S F W** Have an elongated prothorax and triangular-shaped head that resembles a snake. Clear wings except for a bicolored dark and pale amber pterostigma that is divided by a single veinlet. Females with an elongated ovipositor used to deposit eggs in bark. Larvae with an elongated head and prothorax, short legs, and an elongated abdomen. They can be found under bark and rocks, where they are capable of moving rapidly both forward and backward. Adults and larvae are predaceous feeding on small insects including some pest species.

Snakefly
(*Agulla bicolor*)

Female snakefly (*A. bicolor*). Note the long ovipositor at the tip of her abdomen extending past the wings. Snakeflies have been associated with 15 different species of plants, but this species seems most closely associated with juniper (*Juniperus* spp.).

# Scorpionflies & Hangingflies
## Order Mecoptera

*Panorpa nuptialis*

**NATURAL HISTORY**   Scorpionflies and hangingflies are a fascinating group of insects with an elongated face forming a proboscis and typically, a long, slender abdomen. The ordinal name is derived from *meco*, meaning long, and *ptera*, meaning wing. The tip of the abdomen in many male scorpionflies resembles the stinger of a scorpion, but it is actually used for holding on to females when mating; they are harmless to humans. Scorpionflies and hangingflies have complete metamorphosis. In Texas they range in length from 20–32mm. Scorpionflies can be found in wooded areas among dense understory, usually near water. The most frequently encountered scorpionfly in Texas, *Panorpa nuptialis*, is only found in the fall, when it can be abundant. The less common *Panorpa vernalis*, conversely, only occurs in spring.

Hangingflies get their name from their hanging behavior, which is facilitated by their modified tarsi. They suspend themselves in vegetation from their foreleg tarsi, and use their highly specialized raptorial hind tarsi to grasp and pull in a prey item against the elongated and sharp tibial spines. Grasping is additionally enabled by the folding of the 5th tarsal segment onto the 4th, which functions as an additional clamp. They are found hanging from grass or leaves in fields and forests. When mating, males will capture prey, then release a pheromone to attract a female. The prey is then offered as a nuptial gift. As the female eats, the male mates with her. Some males sense the pheromone of other males, approach them and grab the prey, only to fly off and offer it to a female they attract. Studies have shown that males stealing prey are less likely to be killed by predators. They also have a higher chance of mating, while expending less time and energy looking for food. Hangingflies occur in many of the same habitats as scorpionflies, but *Bittacus occidentis* may occur in dry arroyos in the west desert. Some species are attracted to lights.

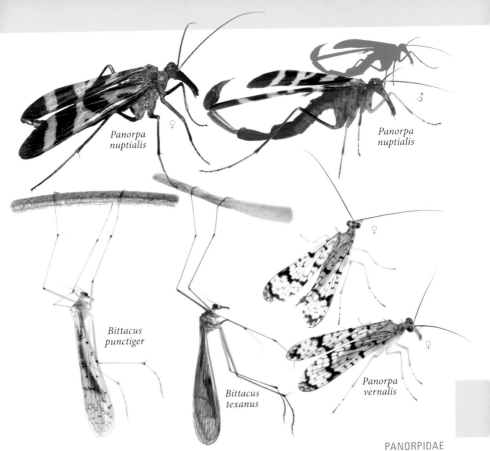

Panorpa nuptialis ♀

Panorpa nuptialis ♂

Bittacus punctiger

Bittacus texanus

Panorpa vernalis ♀

♀

PANORPIDAE

### COMMON SCORPIONFLY *Panorpa nuptialis*

**Sp S F W** Black wings with orange bands. Body is red with an elongated face. Males have a bulbous abdomen that resembles a scorpion. Found in the fall feeding on dead insects.

### COMMON SCORPIONFLY *Panorpa vernalis*

**Sp S F W** Wings translucent amber with veins darkly outlined. Usually a basal, medial, and apical band of black is recognizable. Body pale orange.

BITTACIDAE

### HANGINGFLY *Bittacus punctiger*

**Sp S F W** Body pale yellow to brown with dark brown abdomen. Raptorial legs with 5-segmented tarsi and 1 claw. Hind femur has dark spots. Dark pigments at crossveins in wings. More common throughout the state than *B. texanus*.

### HANGINGFLY *Bittacus texanus*

**Sp S F W** Orangish-brown body, 9th tergum has several black spines. Legs reddish brown with hind femurs slightly swollen. Raptorial legs with 5-segmented tarsi and 1 claw. Wings amber, lacking dark pigments at crossveins. Found throughout much of the state; most frequently seen in lower Rio Grande valley.

175

# Beetles
# Order Coleoptera

Blind Click Beetle
(*Alaus myops*)

**NATURAL HISTORY**   This is a large diverse group of insects characterized by their hardened forewings called elytra. The ordinal name, sheath (*coleos*) wing (*ptera*), refers to these protective structures that are lifted out of the way in those species that fly. They have complete metamorphosis and are the most diverse group of animals on Earth comprising over 40% of all insect species. There are over 400,000 described species and it is estimated that this represents only a quarter of the species. You can find beetles everywhere except the open ocean and the polar regions. Some live in fresh water, while others are found underground. They can be associated with nests of social insects and others are parasites. Still others will feed on fungi, carrion, leaves, flowers, bark, and dung. This diversity in numbers and habitat has also lead to incredible variation in form and function and many species perform important functions within the ecosystem as decomposers. Some species have been introduced as biological control agents, while others are considered pests.

The general anatomy of beetles is uniform, but there is tremendous variation in the antennae, leg types, the number of tarsi on each leg and their shape, and wings that are all helpful in recognizing the different families. In North America, beetles range in size from less than 1 mm to over 7.5 cm.

# Identifying Characters

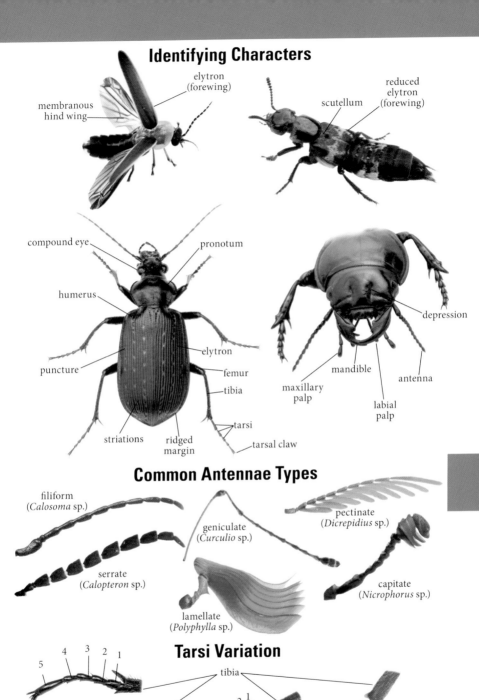

elytron (forewing)

membranous hind wing

reduced elytron (forewing)

scutellum

compound eye

pronotum

humerus

puncture

elytron

femur

tibia

striations

ridged margin

tarsi

tarsal claw

depression

mandible

antenna

maxillary palp

labial palp

## Common Antennae Types

filiform (*Calosoma* sp.)

geniculate (*Curculio* sp.)

pectinate (*Dicrepidius* sp.)

serrate (*Calopteron* sp.)

capitate (*Nicrophorus* sp.)

lamellate (*Polyphylla* sp.)

## Tarsi Variation

tibia

claw

### RETICULATED BEETLE *Tenomerga cinerea*

CUPEDIDAE

Sp **S** F **W**  Tan, brown, or gray with darker elongated patches on elytra. Antennae as long or nearly so, as the abdomen and usually projected anteriorly. Legs pale and often concealed under body when it at rest. Larvae feed on wooden poles, rotting oak, and pines. Adults are attracted to lights.

### GROUND BEETLE *Stenomorphus californicus*

CARABIDAE

Sp **S** F **W**  Reddish brown. Head with prominent mandibles. Pronotum broadly rounded anteriorly, tapering posteriorly; sharply defined crevice down midline. Elytra with numerous grooves. Legs reddish brown. Attracted to lights.

### CATERPILLAR HUNTER *Calosoma macrum*

Sp **S** F **W**  Large, stocky, black beetle with prominent mandibles. Elytra with shallow striations. Those nearest midline with small punctures. Numerous irregular punctures on elytra anteriorly. Elytra margin often with hints of violet. Adults attracted to lights.

### SAY'S CATERPILLAR HUNTER *Calosoma sayi*

Sp **S** F **W**  Large, black or bronzy ground beetle. Pronotum margin red or gold. Each elytra has pronounced grooves and 3 rows of metallic red or gold spots and blue or green margins.

### FIERY SEARCHER *Calosoma scrutator*

Sp **S** F **W**  Large, brilliantly colored ground beetle. Head dark, pronotum dark blue or violet with red or gold edges. Elytra shiny green with reddish-gold edges. Legs dark, but femora with blue metallic luster. Adults and larvae prey on caterpillars.

### VIVID METALLIC GROUND BEETLE *Chlaenius erythropus*

Sp **S** F **W**  Dark blue to black body with orangish legs and antennae. Antennae with third segment elongated. Pronotum broad posteriorly with small punctures over entire surface and pair of indentions basally. Elytra grooved with fine punctures.

### GROUND BEETLE *Clivina* sp.

Sp **S** F **W**  Reddish-brown to black elongated beetle. Pronotum somewhat truncated anteriorly and rounded posteriorly, narrowing to a "neck" between it and the abdomen. Elytra with prominent grooves. Antennae and legs slightly lighter than rest of body.

### GROUND BEETLE *Pasimachus* sp.

Sp **S** F **W**  Large, black beetle with prominent mandibles. Pronotum smooth and usually with violet margin. Elytra of male is shiny; female dull and lacking grooves or punctures. Flightless and found under rocks, logs, and leaf litter where it feeds on caterpillars and other insect larvae.

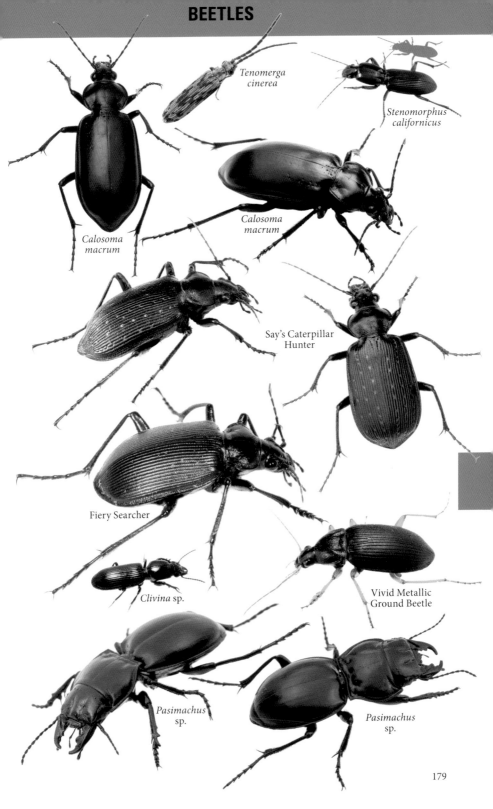

Tenomerga
cinerea

Stenomorphus
californicus

Calosoma
macrum

Calosoma
macrum

Say's Caterpillar
Hunter

Fiery Searcher

Clivina sp.

Vivid Metallic
Ground Beetle

Pasimachus
sp.

Pasimachus
sp.

## BRONZED TIGER BEETLE *Cicindela repanda*

CARABIDAE

Sp **S F** W   Copper-brown body with three white markings on elytra. White mandibles. Pronotum bronze and hairy. Anterior-most marking on abdomen nearly touches middle marking laterally. Found on sand, gravel, and clay soil, usually with sparse vegetation. Feeds on small insects.

## SPLENDID TIGER BEETLE *Cicindela splendida*

Sp **S F** W   Greenish-blue body contrasting with red elytra. Head and pronotum green or blue. Elytra coppery red with green margins and one or two pale crescent-shaped spots laterally and basally. Typically found on open red clay soils.

## PUNCTURED TIGER BEETLE *Cicindelidia punctulata*

Sp **S F** W   Dark, bronzy brown, slender species with or without white markings on elytra. Elytra with row of bronzy or green longitudinal pits. Common in a wide variety of open habitats, including sparsely vegetated and disturbed paths and roads.

## SIX-SPOTTED TIGER BEETLE *Cicindela sexguttata*

Sp **S F** W   Brilliant green species, usually with six white markings on elytra. Common along dirt paths in grassy areas, near forest edges. Also found hunting on sidewalks and asphalt roads.

## WHITE-STRIPED TIGER BEETLE *Cylindera lemniscata*

Sp **S F** W   Small, slender, red species. Elytra with broad, pale, irregular stripe along each side. Common along Rio Grande where it is attracted to lights.

## WHITE-CLOAKED TIGER BEETLE *Eunota togata*

Sp **S F** W   Bronze head and thorax. Elytra with sinuate, broad pale stripe laterally. Locally abundant, but generally uncommon. Well adapted to hunting on hot roads and sand substrates.

## CAROLINA METALLIC TIGER BEETLE *Tetracha carolina*

Sp **S F** W   Metallic red, green, and purple. Head relatively large and broad with prominent eyes. Legs and antennae pale. Elytra generally green laterally and red medially with cream-colored spot at apex. Common in a variety of habitats including along sandbanks of rivers, pastures, and disturbed areas near water. Will hide under rocks, logs, and boards. Nocturnal, coming to lights, but also active during the day.

## VIRGINIA METALLIC TIGER BEETLE *Tetracha virginica*

Sp **S F** W   Dark, metallic green head and pronotum. Head relatively large and broad with prominent eyes. Elytra usually darker purplish medially and green laterally. Legs and antennae pale. Nocturnal, coming to lights, but also active during the day.

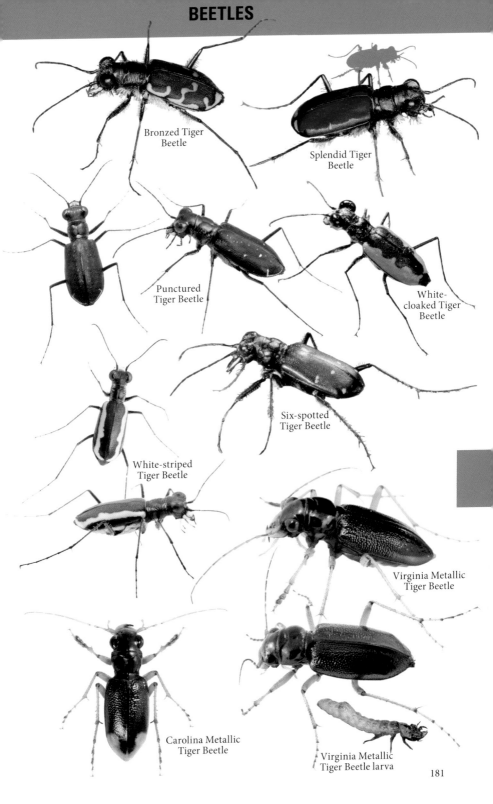

Bronzed Tiger Beetle

Splendid Tiger Beetle

Punctured Tiger Beetle

White-cloaked Tiger Beetle

Six-spotted Tiger Beetle

White-striped Tiger Beetle

Virginia Metallic Tiger Beetle

Carolina Metallic Tiger Beetle

Virginia Metallic Tiger Beetle larva

181

### FALSE BOMBARDIER BEETLE *Galerita bicolor* CARABIDAE

**Sp S F W**  Black head and abdomen with reddish-orange pronotum and legs. Elongated head with diffuse reddish spot medially. Antennae orange basally, then with a few dark segments before becoming orange again distally. Pronotum with broadly convex lateral margins. Elytra with short setae over basal third.

### BOMBARDIER BEETLE *Brachinus* spp.

**Sp S F W**  Medium-sized, fast-moving ground beetles. Head and pronotum orange. Eyes dark, contrasting with head color. Elytra bluish black. Legs and antennae orange. Found under loose bark and stones and actively running at night. When disturbed, will emit a foul-smelling gas from abdomen with a popping sound.

### BEAUTIFUL BANDED LEBIA *Lebia pulchella*

**Sp S F W**  Small, variably colored beetle. Dark, metallic blue head. Antennae orange with dark segments in middle. Pronotum and legs orangish red. Elytra orangish red with metallic blue band anteriorly and broad band just prior to tip.

### COLORFUL FOLIAGE GROUND BEETLE *Lebia viridis*

**Sp S F W**  Uniformly metallic green to purple. Antennae dark. Head with fine grooves above eyes. Elytra with fine grooves. Adults largely diurnal; found on flowers, but also common at lights.

### WOODLAND GROUND BEETLE *Poecilus chalcites*

**Sp S F W**  Variably colored green, red, or bronze. First three antennal segments orange, others dark. Legs dark. Pronotum somewhat rectangular and slightly wider than long. Found under rocks, logs, and debris, often in disturbed habitats.

### WOODLAND GROUND BEETLE *Pterostichus* sp.

**Sp S F W**  Shiny dark brown or black. Antennae pubescent starting with fourth segment. Pronotum with either one or two laterobasal depressions and two lateral setae.

### GROUND BEETLE *Scarites* sp.

**Sp S F W**  Shiny, black, elongated beetles with prominent mandibles. Head with two large depressions. Distinct waist between pronotum and abdomen. Elytra with numerous grooves. Commonly found under rocks and logs. Adults active during the day, but also attracted to lights.

### BURROWING WATER BEETLE *Hydrocanthus atripennis* NOTERIDAE

**Sp S F W**  Small, smooth, usually bicolored aquatic beetle. Head and pronotum orange with dark eyes and pale antennae. Elytra bluish black. Found in temporary and permanent ponds often with weedy or decaying vegetation. Adults attracted to lights.

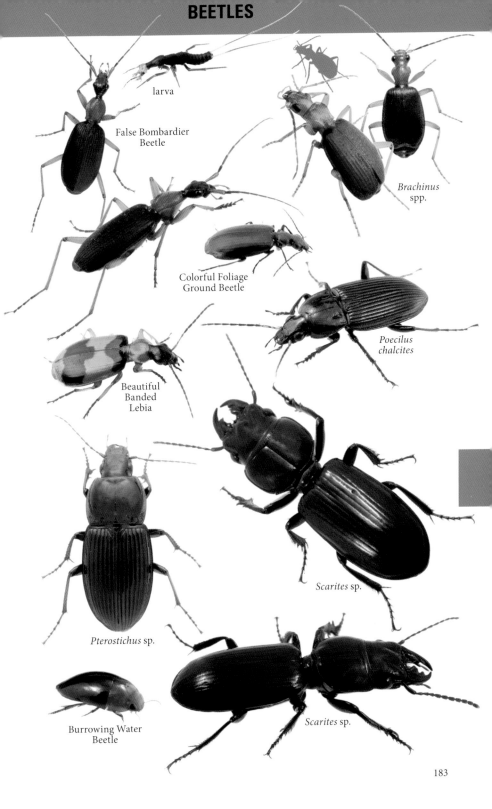

# BEETLES

larva

False Bombardier
Beetle

*Brachinus*
spp.

Colorful Foliage
Ground Beetle

*Poecilus
chalcites*

Beautiful
Banded
Lebia

*Scarites* sp.

*Pterostichus* sp.

Burrowing Water
Beetle

*Scarites* sp.

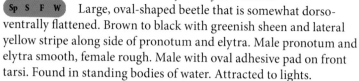

### PREDACEOUS DIVING BEETLE *Cybister fimbriolatus*
DYTISCIDAE

Sp **S F W** Large, oval-shaped beetle that is somewhat dorso-ventrally flattened. Brown to black with greenish sheen and lateral yellow stripe along side of pronotum and elytra. Male pronotum and elytra smooth, female rough. Male with oval adhesive pad on front tarsi. Found in standing bodies of water. Attracted to lights.

### PREDACEOUS DIVING BEETLE *Thermonectus basillaris*

Sp **S F W** Dark, oval, flattened body. Head dark with yellow in front and a posterior stripe. Pronotum dark with yellow across middle and along the sides. Elytra dark with irregular yellow stripe across top and along the sides. Male with expanded adhesive pad on tarsi. Found in ponds and ditches. Attracted to lights.

### SUNBURST DIVING BEETLE *Thermonectus marmoratus*

Sp **S F W** Boldly patterned diving beetle. Black head with yellow anteriorly and posteriorly. Pronotum with interrupted yellow stripe and yellow sides. Elytra with multiple yellow spots. Found in pools and intermittent streams where it feeds on dead organisms.

### WHIRLIGIG BEETLE *Dineutus* sp.
GYRINIDAE

Sp **S F W** Black or bronzy and broadly oval and flattened. Front legs dark, mid and hind legs lighter. Found swimming on water surface of pools, ponds, lakes, and slow reaches of streams. Eyes elongated to see above and below the water.

### WHIRLIGIG BEETLE *Gyrinus* sp.

Sp **S F W** Black, shiny, narrowly oval beetle with long forelegs. Elytra with punctured striations. Found swimming on water surface of pools, ponds, lakes and slow reaches of streams. Eyes elongated to see above and below the water.

### CRAWLING WATER BEETLE *Peltodytes sexmaculatus*
HALIPLIDAE

Sp **S F W** Tiny yellowish oval beetle. Large black eyes. Pronotum with dark spots posteriorly. Elytra with six dark spots. Hind coxae enlarged, covering much of the abdomen. Found in lakes, rivers, slow reaches of streams, and mud flats. Found at lights.

### CLOWN BEETLE *Hololepta yucateca*
HISTERIDAE

Sp **S F W** Shiny, black, flat, and somewhat rectangular with large anteriorly projecting mandible. Elytral striations reduced or absent. Found under bark or in rotting vegetation such as cacti and yuccas.

### CLOWN BEETLE *Hister* sp.

Sp **S F W** Small, shiny round beetle. Head and legs can be retracted close to body giving it a tank-like appearance. Elytra usually with numerous striations and punctures. Generally found in woodlands on carrion or in mammal burrows.

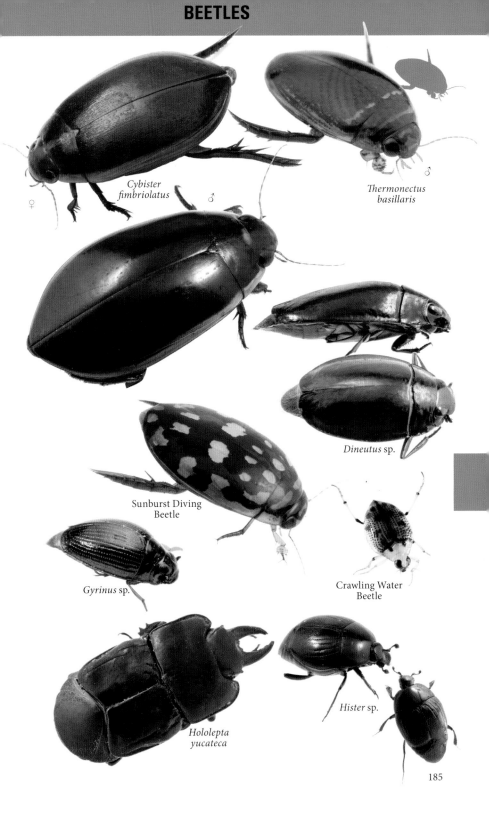

*Cybister*
*fimbriolatus*
♀ ♂

*Thermonectus*
*basillaris*
♂

*Dineutus* sp.

Sunburst Diving
Beetle

*Gyrinus* sp.

Crawling Water
Beetle

*Hister* sp.

*Hololepta*
*yucateca*

185

### WATER SCAVENGER BEETLE *Hydrochara soror*

**Sp S F W** Broadly oval, shiny beetle with a convex dorsum and relatively flat ventrally. Maxillary palps prominent. Head with punctures. Elytra with shallow punctured striations. Keel on underside short, not projecting past hind coxa and not spinelike. Found in ponds, ditches, and streams.

### WATER SCAVENGER BEETLE *Hydrochus* sp.

**Sp S F W** Small, elongated, with head as wide as pronotum. Body dark with metallic reflections and numerous punctures. Antennae and legs pale. Pronotum elongated. Elytra with numerous punctures along fine grooves. Found along edges of lakes, ponds, and swamps.

### GIANT WATER SCAVENGER BEETLE *Hydrophilus ovatus*

**Sp S F W** Large, shiny black beetle, often with a coppery or greenish shimmer. Body more oval than *Hydrophilus triangularis*. Ventral keel long and spinelike. Prosternum is divided. Found in vegetated ponds and lakes. Attracted to lights.

### GIANT BLACK WATER BEETLE *Hydrophilus triangularis*

**Sp S F W** Large, shiny black beetle, often with a coppery or greenish shimmer. Body elongated, compared to *Hydrophilus ovatus*. Ventral keel long and spinelike. Prosternum is undivided. Found in vegetated ponds and lakes. Attracted to lights.

### WATER SCAVENGER BEETLE *Tropisternus collaris*

**Sp S F W** Tan to dark brown or olive with dark longitudinal stripes on elytra. Found in shallow ephemeral or permanent ponds usually with algae and vegetation.

### WATER SCAVENGER BEETLE *Tropisternus lateralis*

**Sp S F W** Shiny with metallic luster and narrowly oval. Head, pronotum, and elytra with pale yellow stripe laterally. Found in temporary and permanent ponds and lakes as well as brackish water. Attracted to lights.

### RED-LINED CARRION BEETLE *Necrodes surinamensis*

**Sp S F W** Dark body with raised ridges on elytra. Large eyes, antennae uniformly colored. Pronotum smooth and rounded. Elytra generally with variable reddish or yellow markings, but sometimes with none. Male hind legs with curved tibia and enlarged femur. Feeds on carrion and maggots. Attracted to lights.

### AMERICAN CARRION BEETLE *Necrophila americana*

**Sp S F W** Round, flattened, dark body with yellow pronotum bearing a large central dark spot. Each elytron with three ridges and surface otherwise sculptured. Adults mimic bumblebees in flight. Found on carrion where they feed on maggots and carrion itself.

# BEETLES

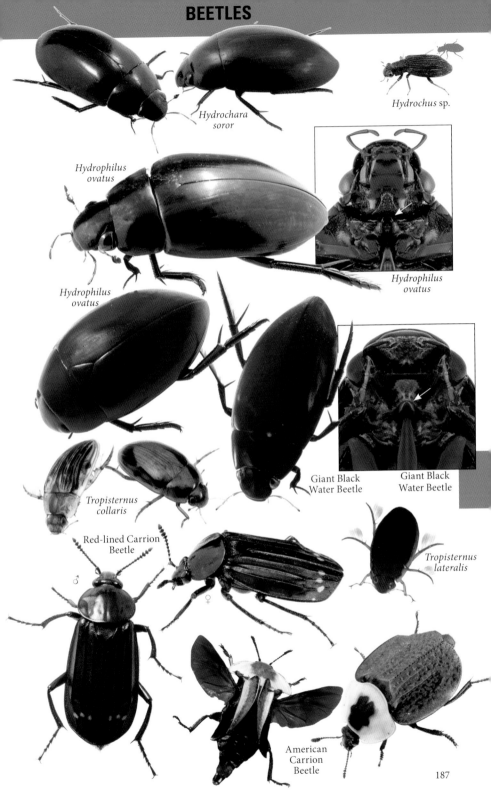

*Hydrochara soror*

*Hydrochus* sp.

*Hydrophilus ovatus*

*Hydrophilus ovatus*

*Hydrophilus ovatus*

*Tropisternus collaris*

Giant Black Water Beetle

Giant Black Water Beetle

Red-lined Carrion Beetle

♂

♀

*Tropisternus lateralis*

American Carrion Beetle

187

### SEXTON BEETLE *Nicrophorus carolinus*
SILPHIDAE

**Sp S F W** Large black beetle with orange patterned elytra. Last four segments of antennae club orange. Pronotum smoothly rounded, decidedly convex, with no texture. Elytra reduced with terminal abdominal segments exposed. Elytra each with three smaller orange spots anteriorly and one elongated spot posteriorly. Found on carrion and attracted to lights.

### ROUNDNECK SEXTON BEETLE *Nicrophorus orbicollis*

**Sp S F W** Large black beetle with orange patterned elytra. Last three segments of antennae club orange. Pronotum rounded in middle with broad flange encircling it. Elytra reduced, with terminal abdominal segments exposed, and four large orange spots. Found on carrion and attracted to lights.

### SEXTON BEETLE *Nicrophorus pustulatus*

**Sp S F W** Large black beetle. Last three segments of antennae club orange. Pronotum rounded with sculpturing. Elytra reduced with terminal abdominal segments exposed. Three small orange spots on each elytron. Found on carrion and attracted to lights.

### CARRION BEETLE *Thanatophilus truncatus*

**Sp S F W** Medium-sized dull black beetle with truncated elytra. Antennae all black. Pronotum somewhat rounded and convex medially. Found on carrion.

### HAIRY ROVE BEETLE *Creophilus maxillosus*
STAPHYLINIDAE

**Sp S F W** Large, elongated, shiny black beetle with gray hairs on sides of pronotum and scattered across reduced elytra and basal abdominal segments. Feeds on maggots, often associated with carrion. Secretes irritating defensive chemical from tip of abdomen.

### ROVE BEETLE *Homaeotarsus* sp.

**Sp S F W** Species in this genus are reddish brown, black, or bicolored. The head and basal abdominal segments are usually black. Mandibles prominent, each with three teeth on inner margin. Basal antennal segment elongated. Legs pale and elytra reduced.

### ROVE BEETLE *Pinophilus* sp.

**Sp S F W** Elongated, shiny black beetle with reduced elytra. Prominent mandibles usually reddish brown. Legs and antennae light brown. Found in leaf littler, but also comes to lights.

### RED-SPOTTED ROVE BEETLE *Platydracus fossator*

**Sp S F W** Elongated dark beetle with large patch of orange or golden hair on each reduced elytra. Head and pronotum densely punctate. Found on decaying fungi and carrion where they feed on maggots and other small insect larvae.

*Nicrophorus carolinus*

Roundneck Sexton Beetle

*Nicrophorus carolinus* larva

*Nicrophorus pustulatus*

*Thanatophilus truncatus*

Hairy Rove Beetle

*Homaeotarsus* sp.

*Pinophilus* sp.

Red-spotted Rove Beetle

### CRAB-LIKE ROVE BEETLE *Coproporus* sp.          STAPHYLINIDAE

`Sp` `S` `F` `W`   Minute, elongated, strongly convex beetle with reduced elytra and tapering abdomen. Head with mouthparts pointed down. Found under bark and logs, in rotting plants and on fungi.

### ANT-LIKE STONE BEETLE *Euconnus* sp.

`Sp` `S` `F` `W`   Minute ant-like beetle. Shiny with somewhat oval abdomen. Tan, reddish brown, or black. Pronotum narrowed anteriorly forming a distinctive neck. Last four segments of antennae forming a club. Femora enlarged. Found in moist leaf litter and under rotting logs. Attracted to lights.

### HORNED PASSALUS *Odontotaenius disjunctus*          PASSALIDAE

`Sp` `S` `F` `W`   Large, shiny black beetle with curved horn projecting anteriorly. Large mandibles. Pronotum smooth, elytra strongly grooved. Body somewhat flattened. All stages found in and under rotting hardwoods. Adults of both sexes care for larvae.

### EARTH-BORING SCARAB BEETLE *Bolbocerosoma* sp.          GEOTRUPIDAE

`Sp` `S` `F` `W`   Medium-sized, somewhat rounded, orangish-brown beetle marked with black. Antennae orangish brown. Head black. Pronotum orange with black spot laterally, thin stripe anteriorly and with posterior margin black. Elytra with deeply punctate grooves and diffuse pattern of black posteriorly as well as up the sides and middle. Found in burrows and attracted to lights.

### EARTH-BORING SCARAB BEETLE *Eucanthus impressus*

`Sp` `S` `F` `W`   Reddish-brown to dark brown, oval body. Antennae orangish brown. Median row of punctures on pronotum, extends down nearly to head. Elytra with deeply punctate grooves. Found in sandy or clay soil habitat. Attracted to lights.

### BLACKBURN'S EARTH-BORING BEETLE *Geotrupes blackburnii*

`Sp` `S` `F` `W`   Rounded, shiny black beetle with copper luster. Pronotum smooth without punctures. Elytra with moderately punctured grooves. Found on dung, rotting fungi, and carrion.

### OPAQUE EARTH-BORING BEETLE *Geotrupes opacus*

`Sp` `S` `F` `W`   Rounded, dull black beetle without elytral striations. Antennae dark. Elytra with rows of fine punctures. Found on dung and carrion in sandy areas.

### EARTH-BORING SCARAB BEETLE *Odonteus thoracicornis*

`Sp` `S` `F` `W`   Reddish brown and oval. Antennae and legs reddish brown. Eyes completely divided by sclerite on head. Males with deep depressions in pronotum, lateral flattened hornlike projections and usually large backward-pointing curved horn on head. Elytra with striations and punctures. Adults burrow, but are attracted to lights.

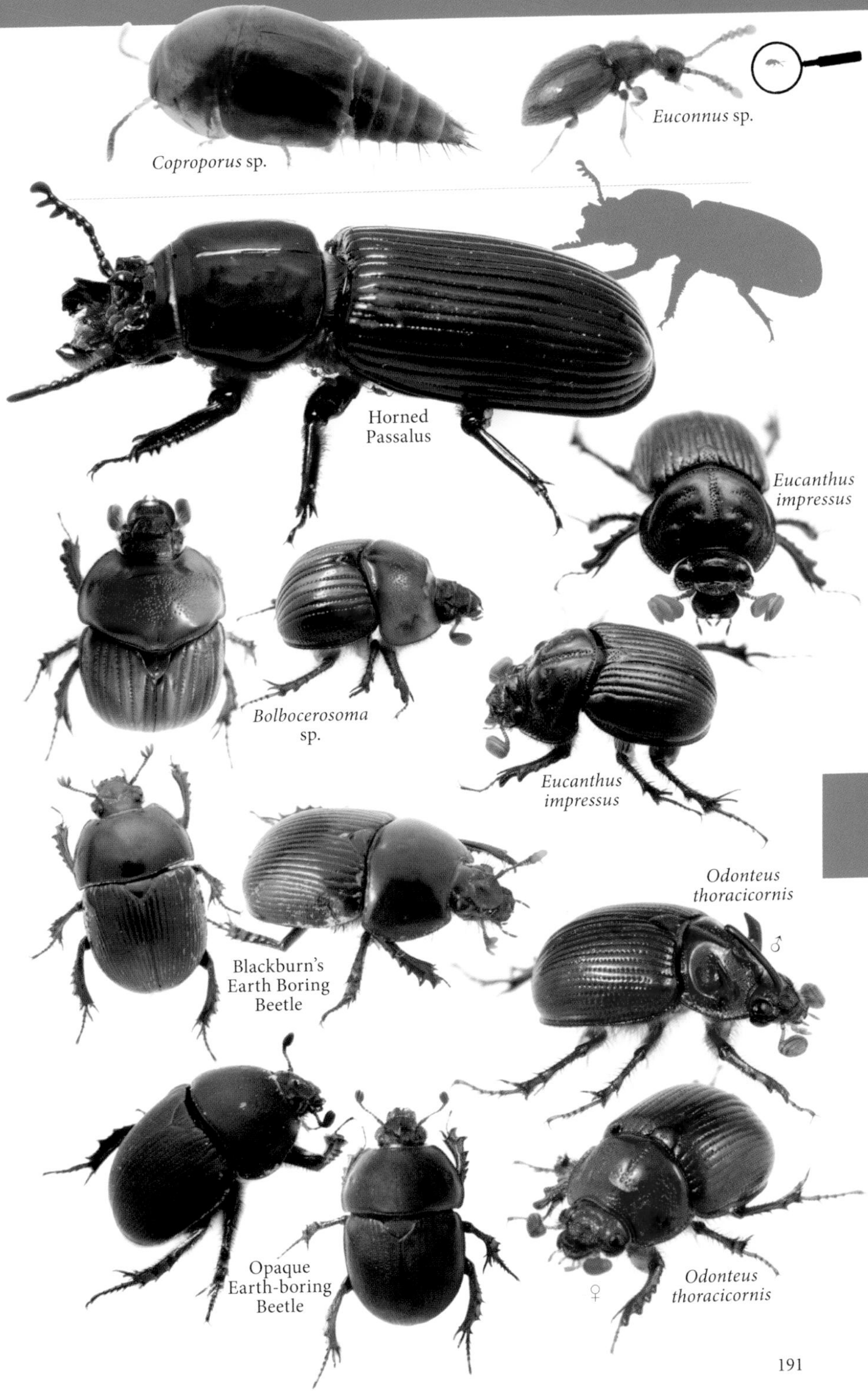

*Coproporus* sp.

*Euconnus* sp.

Horned
Passalus

*Eucanthus
impressus*

*Bolbocerosoma*
sp.

*Eucanthus
impressus*

*Odonteus
thoracicornis*

Blackburn's
Earth Boring
Beetle

♂

Opaque
Earth-boring
Beetle

♀

*Odonteus
thoracicornis*

191

### GIANT STAG BEETLE *Lucanus elaphus*
LUCANIDAE

Sp **S** F W    Large, reddish brown. Males with huge elongated forked mandibles and head wider than prothorax. Females similar, but with shorter mandibles. Larvae feed in moist decaying wood. Adults active at dusk and come to lights.

### REDDISH-BROWN STAG BEETLE *Lucanus capreolus*

Sp **S** F W    Reddish-brown, shiny body. Males with C-shaped mandibles and only a single internal tooth. Female with much shorter mandibles. Femora reddish brown with dark apex. Found in rotting hardwood. Adults attracted to lights.

### HASTATE HIDE BEETLE *Omorgus* sp.
TROGIDAE

Sp **S** F W    Grayish brown to dark brown with head, pronotum, and elytra all roughly sculptured and often with clumps of stiff bristles. Larger than the similar *Trox*. Scutellum somewhat spear-shaped. Adults found on carrion during late stages of decomposition and on owl pellets. Attracted to lights.

### HIDE BEETLE *Trox* sp.

Sp **S** F W    Light brown to grayish brown with head, pronotum, and elytra all roughly sculptured and often with clumps of stiff bristles. Smaller than the similar *Omorgus*. Scutellum rounded. Adults found on carrion during the late stages of decomposition and on owl pellets. Attracted to lights.

### SCARAB BEETLE *Diplotaxis* sp.
SCARABAEIDAE

Sp **S** F W    Medium-sized, shiny black to red beetle lacking hairs dorsally. Antennae, palps, and tarsi typically lighter than rest of beetle. Larvae feed on roots and adults on foliage of a variety of plants. Most species nocturnal and attracted to lights.

### SCARAB BEETLE *Serica* sp.

Sp **S** F W    Reddish brown to dark brown and somewhat oval. Sometimes with evidence of iridescent sheen. Pronotum wider than long and roundly convex. Adults are nocturnal and feed on deciduous foliage, but readily come to lights.

### MAY BEETLE *Phyllophaga* spp.

Sp **S** F W    Common yellow, red, brown, or gray beetles. Some with noticeable hair on thorax and/or abdomen. Numerous species, best identified by male genitalia. Larvae feed on roots and decaying vegetation; adults feed on deciduous foliage. Attracted to lights.

### SAND DUNE JUNE BEETLE *Polyphylla pottsorum*

Sp **S** F W    Brownish oval body with numerous hairs ventrally. Males with large lamellate antennae. Pronotum gray and, along with elytra, covered in small white scales. Found on sand dunes.

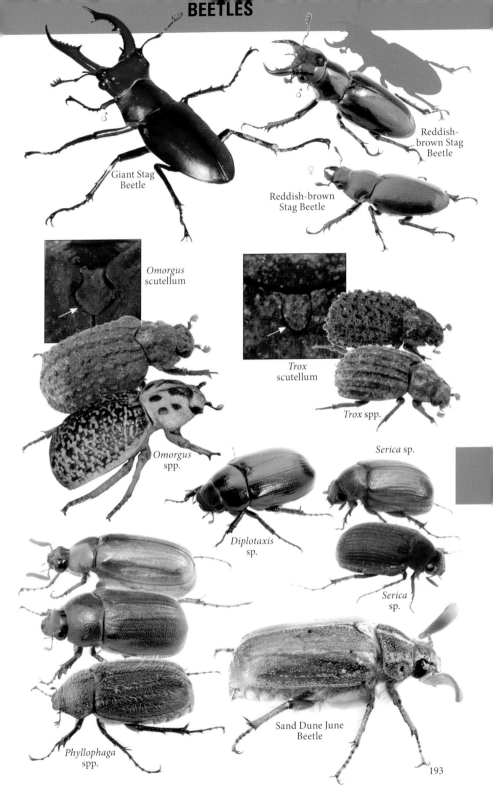

Giant Stag
Beetle

Reddish-
brown Stag
Beetle

Reddish-brown
Stag Beetle

*Omorgus*
scutellum

*Omorgus*
spp.

*Trox*
scutellum

*Trox* spp.

*Serica* sp.

*Diplotaxis*
sp.

*Serica*
sp.

*Phyllophaga*
spp.

Sand Dune June
Beetle

193

**APHODIINE DUNG BEETLE** *Aphodius pseudolividus*

`Sp S F W`   Tiny, dark, elongated beetle with scoop-shaped head. Variable coloration, but generally with dark head with anterior margin reddish. Pronotum dark with pale sides and numerous punctures. Elytra tan with diffuse elongated dark washes and noticeable punctured striations. Found in dung and at lights.

**APHODIINE DUNG BEETLE** *Ataenius* sp.

`Sp S F W`   Tiny, dark, brown, black, or gray with broad scoop-shaped head. Pronotum often heavily punctured and elytra with deep punctured striations. Many species requiring genitalic dissection to ID. Feeds on detritus and dung. Attracted to lights.

**APHODIINE DUNG BEETLE** *Platytomus longulus*

`Sp S F W`   Tiny, elongated reddish-brown beetle. Head with pale, lateral flanges. Pronotum densely punctured. Elytra with deeply punctured striations. Legs and antennae lighter than body. Feeds on dung and detritus. Attracted to lights.

**SHINING LEAF CHAFER** *Callistethus marginatus*

`Sp S F W`   Oblong, light-brown to reddish-brown body with green tint. Sides of pronotum with pale lateral margins. Pronotum and abdomen broadly convex. Can be found resting on vegetation during the day and commonly attracted to lights at night.

**GLORIOUS SCARAB** *Chrysina gloriosa*

`Sp S F W`   Unmistakable lime-green beetle with reflective silver elytral striations and brown antennae. Rare red form has green replaced with reddish brown. Adults feed on juniper; larvae on decaying sycamore logs. Attracted to lights.

**WOOD'S JEWEL BEETLE** *Chrysina woodii*

`Sp S F W`   Large, lime-green head, thorax, elytra, body, and legs. Antennae brown and tarsi purple. Adults are diurnal, feeding on walnut, but are occasionally attracted to lights.

**GOLDSMITH BEETLE** *Cotalpa lanigera*

`Sp S F W`   Large, yellowish brown, with green reflections on head and pronotum. Head, pronotum, and scutellum more yellow than elytra. Legs tan with green luster. Elytra with irregular rows of punctures. Adults feed on a variety of deciduous foliage including oaks, sweetgum, poplar, and hickory. Attracted to lights.

**GRAPEVINE BEETLE** *Pelidnota punctata*

`Sp S F W`   Large tan to yellowish beetle with one dark spot on each side of pronotum and three spots laterally on each elytra. Found in wooded areas where adults feed on foliage and fruit of grape. Larvae feed on dead trees. Attracted to lights.

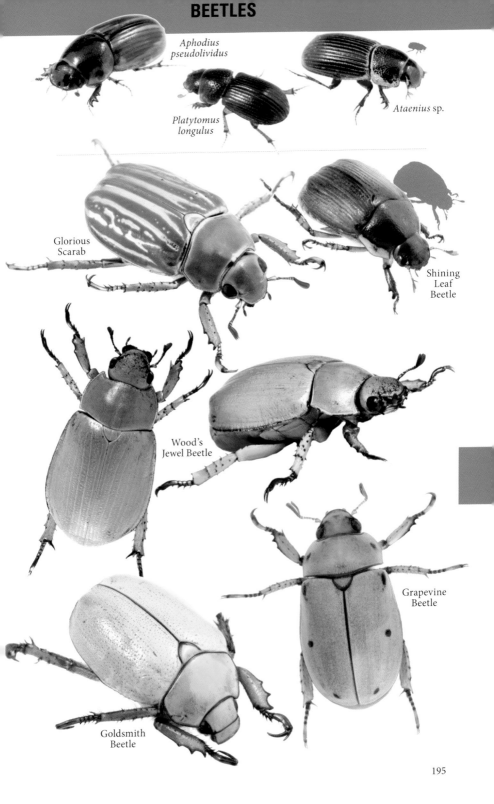

*Aphodius pseudolividus*

*Platytomus longulus*

*Ataenius* sp.

Glorious Scarab

Shining Leaf Beetle

Wood's Jewel Beetle

Grapevine Beetle

Goldsmith Beetle

**GREEN FIG BEETLE** *Cotinis mutabilis*

SCARABAEIDAE

Sp S F W   Large velvety green beetle with variable amount of tan on elytra and pronotum. Front of head with hornlike process apically. Brown can cover most of pronotum. Scutellum concealed. Legs metallic green. Femora metallic green. Adults feed on sap and ripe fruit. Larvae develop in detritus, dung, and compost.

**GREEN JUNE BEETLE** *Cotinis nitida*

Sp S F W   Large velvety green beetle with brown stripe laterally on elytra and pronotum. Front of head with hornlike process apically. Elytra and pronotum can vary from all green to all brown. Scutellum concealed. Legs metallic green. Femora brown with green luster. Adults feed on ripe fruit. Larvae develop in compost.

**EMERALD EUPHORIA** *Euphoria fulgida*

Sp S F W   Colorful green or blue beetle with dark brown on pronotal and elytral margins. Scutellum large. Elytra often with scattered white spots. Legs reddish brown tinged with green. Common visitor to flowers in summer, flying from one to another.

**BUMBLE FLOWER BEETLE** *Euphoria inda*

Sp S F W   Yellowish brown, dull or shiny, elytra marked with black spots. Thorax and underside of body covered in yellow hairs. Flies readily and is likely a mimic of bumblebees. Adults feed on flowers, rotting fruit, and sap. Larvae in decaying wood and dung.

**KERN'S FLOWER SCARAB** *Euphoria kernii*

Sp S F W   Variably colored flower beetle. Can be orange or yellow with large black spot on pronotum and numerous spots on elytra to all black, but without white spots on elytra. Common on various flowers including prickly pear, thistle, and prickly poppy.

**DARK FLOWER CHAFER** *Euphoria sepulcralis*

Sp S F W   Dark reddish-brown to black with bronze-green luster. Elytra variably marked with thin white lines and spots. Adults feed on flowers, pollen, and nectar. Larvae feed on detritus.

**DELTA FLOWER SCARAB** *Trigonopeltastes delta*

Sp S F W   Yellow-orange to brown with orange elytra and yellow delta-shaped mark on pronotum. Head with yellow as well as margins or pronotum. Elytra can be all orange or with four dark spots. Legs orange except dark hind tibia and tarsi. Found on various flowers including coneflower and goldenrod.

**SOUTHERN MASKED CHAFER** *Cyclocephala lurida*

Sp S F W   Oblong, light reddish brown, with a black head and pale antennae. Dark spot usually present on either side of pronotum. Larvae feed on grass roots. Adults attracted to lights.

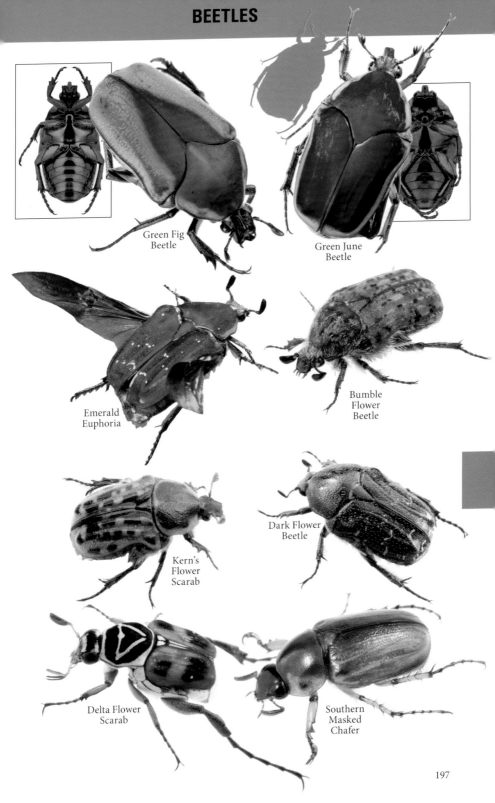

Green Fig
Beetle

Green June
Beetle

Emerald
Euphoria

Bumble
Flower
Beetle

Kern's
Flower
Scarab

Dark Flower
Beetle

Delta Flower
Scarab

Southern
Masked
Chafer

197

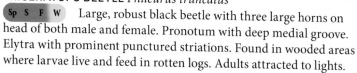

## TRICERATOPS BEETLE *Phileurus truncatus*

**Sp S F W**  Large, robust black beetle with three large horns on head of both male and female. Pronotum with deep medial groove. Elytra with prominent punctured striations. Found in wooded areas where larvae live and feed in rotten logs. Adults attracted to lights.

## RHINOCEROS BEETLE *Phileurus valgus*

**Sp S F W**  Medium-sized, shiny black beetle with single small horn at apex of head. Head triangular with pair of sharp bumps anterior to each eye. Pronotum with medial pitted groove. Elytra with punctured striations. Adults and larvae found in rotting logs. Adults readily attracted to lights.

## OX BEETLE *Strategus aloeus*

**Sp S F W**  Large reddish-brown to black beetle with three horns and smooth elytra. Front of head slightly upturned. Males armed with three blunt to sharp horns on pronotum; females without horns. Elytra in both sexes with deep groove along midline. Larvae and adults in rotting logs. Adults attracted to lights.

## OX BEETLE *Strategus antaeus*

**Sp S F W**  Large reddish-brown shiny beetle. Male varies having three slender horns or just bumps on pronotum. Female without horns. Both sexes lack deep groove along midline. Adults sometimes found at base of tree trunks. Most common in sandy areas. Also come to lights.

## EASTERN HERCULES BEETLE *Dynastes tityus*

**Sp S F W**  Very large yellowish to olive-green beetle with black spotting on elytra. Male with long horn on head, two small ones and one long one on pronotum extending over head. Female lacks horns. Humidity turns these beetles black. Larvae feed on damaged and dying hardwoods. Adults sometimes aggregate; attracted to lights.

## RHINOCEROS BEETLE *Xyloryctes jamaicensis*

**Sp S F W**  Dark reddish brown with thick red hair underneath. Male with long, single horn projecting from head. Female with only a small knob. Pronotum of male deeply concave anteriorly. Elytra of both sexes deeply grooved with numerous punctures. Larvae feed on rotting wood and leaf litter. Adults readily come to lights.

## SUGARCANE BEETLE *Euetheola rugiceps*

**Sp S F W**  Medium-sized dull black beetle with strongly punctate pronotum and elytra. Front of head with two blunt teeth. Elytra with punctated striations that often collect mud and dirt. Larvae feed on roots of grasses, adults on grasses, sedges, rushes, sugarcane, and sweet potato. Common at lights.

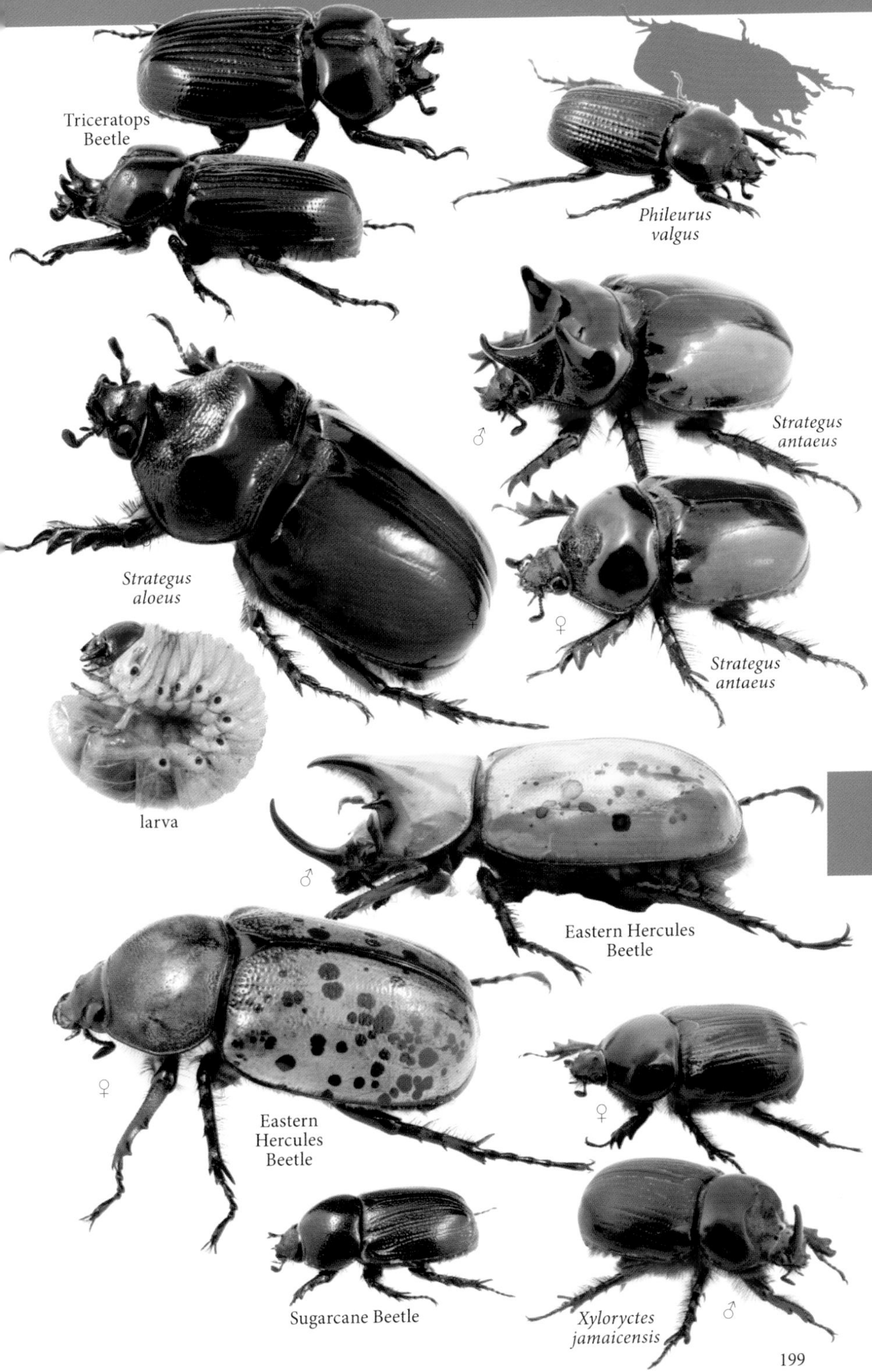

Triceratops
Beetle

*Phileurus
valgus*

*Strategus
antaeus*

♂

*Strategus
aloeus*

♀

*Strategus
antaeus*

larva

♂

Eastern Hercules
Beetle

♀

Eastern
Hercules
Beetle

♀

Sugarcane Beetle

*Xyloryctes
jamaicensis*

♂

199

### DUNG BEETLE (*Ateuchus histeroides*)

**Sp S F W** Small, black, shiny, and strongly convex with bronze sheen. Front of head with two teeth and it along with pronotum are coarsely punctate. Hind angle of pronotum extends below elytra. Scutellum not visible. Elytra each with eight coarse striations. Common in wooded areas where they feed on dung, fungus, and carrion. Adults readily attracted to lights.

### TUMBLEBUG (*Canthon imitator*)

**Sp S F W** Round, dull black beetle commonly seen rolling dung ball. Front of head with two small teeth. Eyes not unusually large, less than half as wide as long. Pronotum and elytra smooth.

### TUMBLEBUG (*Canthon vigilans*)

**Sp S F W** Round, dull black beetle. Front of head with two pronounced teeth. Eyes large, half as wide as long. Pronotum and elytra smooth. Nocturnal and attracted to lights.

### DUNG BEETLE (*Canthon viridis*)

**Sp S F W** Small, round, and metallic green. Front of head with two small teeth. Hind tibia with a single spur. Common in woodlands where adults can be seen perching on vegetation or fungi during the day. Multiple individuals will work together to roll dung of deer and other vertebrates. Also visits carrion.

### DUNG BEETLE (*Onthophagus striatulus*)

**Sp S F W** Small, round, black, bronzy beetle. Male with two thin horns on head. Female unarmed. Front of head without teeth. Pronotum coarsely punctate. Elytra with punctated striations. Found on fungi and vegetation during the day.

### SCOOPED SCARAB (*Onthophagus hecate*)

**Sp S F W** Small dull black or bronzy beetle with coarsely punctate and hairy pronotum. Males with long, flat, usually bifurcated hornlike projection extending from pronotum over head. Found on dung and carrion.

### GAZELLE SCARAB (*Digitonthophagus gazella*)

**Sp S F W** Round, bronze brown with a coppery or green luster. Elytra usually with light margins. Male with long, slender curving horns on head. Female with distinct transverse ridge on head. Femora with distinctive dark spot ventrally. Introduced from Africa to control cow dung. Attracted to lights.

### DUNG BEETLE (*Copris arizonensis*)

**Sp S F W** Black, shiny, oblong, and convex beetle. Male with prominent horn on head and a pair of large projections dorsally and laterally off of pronotum. Females without horns.

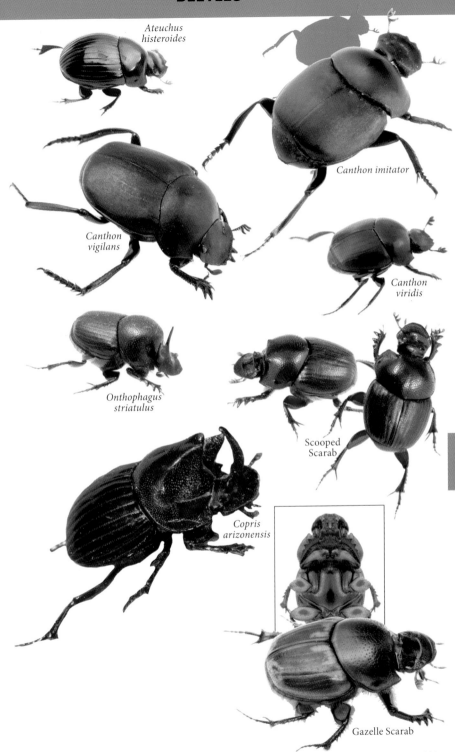

*Ateuchus histeroides*

*Canthon imitator*

*Canthon vigilans*

*Canthon viridis*

*Onthophagus striatulus*

Scooped Scarab

*Copris arizonensis*

Gazelle Scarab

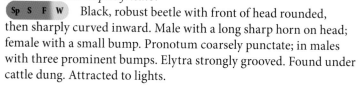

### DUNG BEETLE *Copris fricator*

**Sp S F W** Black, robust beetle with front of head rounded, then sharply curved inward. Male with a long sharp horn on head; female with a small bump. Pronotum coarsely punctate; in males with three prominent bumps. Elytra strongly grooved. Found under cattle dung. Attracted to lights.

### HUMPBACK DUNG BEETLE *Deltochilum gibbosum*

**Sp S F W** Large, round, long-legged, dull black beetle that looks tank-like. Male with large hump anteriorly on each elytron. Front of head with two sets of teeth. Lack tarsi on forelegs. Hind tibia long and curved. Found in wooded habitats where they are attracted to dung, carrion, and ripening fruit. Attracted to lights.

### DUNG BEETLE *Dichotomius carolinus*

**Sp S F W** Large, dull, black robust beetle with pronotum sloped upward. Head bears short tubercle between eyes (more prominent in male). Elytra strongly grooved. Hairs in these grooves posteriorly collect dirt. Found in open habitats feeding on dung of cattle and horses. Will come to lights as well.

### RAINBOW SCARAB *Phanaeus difformis*

**Sp S F W** Robust, brightly colored red, green, and/or blue with metallic reflections. Major male with prominent horn on head curving back over pronotum. Pronotum in male slanted backward forming a tight "U." Elytra green or blue. Feeds on cattle dung.

### MARSH BEETLE *Contacyphon* sp.

**Sp S F W** Small, tan or brown, strongly convex, with numerous yellow hairs over body. Larvae found in stagnant and flowing waters with abundant detritus. Adults are found on plants and detritus on land. Also attracted to lights.

### RIFFLE BEETLE *Stenelmis* sp.

**Sp S F W** Minute, elongated, brown or gray, with long legs. Pronotum longer than wide, often with sculpturing, including several elongated impressions. Elytra wider than pronotum, coarsely punctated with raised ridges. Adults and larvae found in clean streams and rivers. Attracted to lights.

### LONG-TOED WATER BEETLE *Helichus lithophilus*

**Sp S F W** Small, brown, oblong beetles covered in dense setae. Antennal segments 4–11 forming an expanded transverse club. Tarsi long. Adults found clinging to submerged rocks and logs in streams.

### TEXAS WATER PENNY *Psephenus texanus*

**Sp S F W** Dull, black, elongated beetle with pronotum tapered anteriorly. Tarsi paler than rest of leg. Adults found on emergent rocks in fast-flowing streams. Larvae aquatic and oval.

# BEETLES

*Copris fricator* ♀

♀

Humpback Dung Beetle ♂

♀

Rainbow Scarab ♂

♀

Rainbow Scarab ♀

*Dichotomius carolinus*

*Stenelmis* sp.

*Contacyphon* sp.

Long-toed Water Beetle

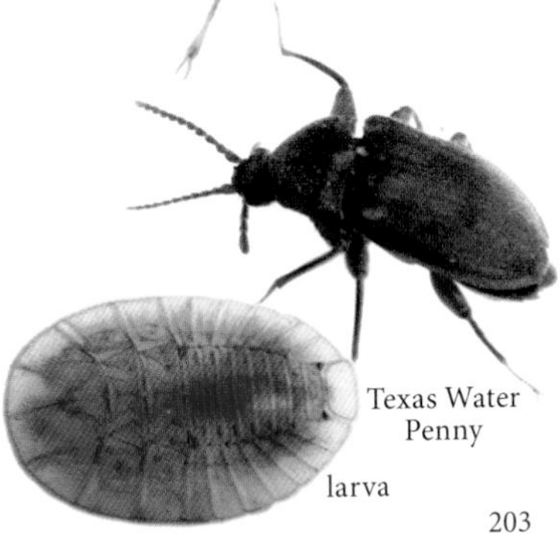

Texas Water Penny

larva

203

BUPRESTIDAE

### METALLIC WOOD-BORING BEETLE *Acmaeodera haemorrhoa*

Sp **S** **F** W   Elongated, bronze or black, with abdomen tapering rearward. Head and pronotum black. Elytra with numerous pale yellow spots. Anteromedially the spots are brown and around the tip of the elytra they are red. Found on composites.

### YELLOW-BORDERED FLOWER BUPRESTID

Sp **S** **F** W                                     *Acmaeodera flavomarginata*

Elongated, black, with abdomen tapering rearward. Pronotum black, sculptured, and with yellow stripe laterally continuing onto elytra. Tip of elytra with broad red stripe diffused over yellow and usually with central and lateral black spot. Common on composites.

### METALLIC WOOD-BORING BEETLE *Acmaeodera mixta*

Sp **S** **F** W   Common, but extremely variable species. Elongated tapering body. Head and pronotum reddish to black, often with yellow spot basolaterally. Elytra mostly yellow to mostly black with variable pattern of spots. Tip of elytra always with some yellow.

### METALLIC WOOD-BORING BEETLE *Acmaeodera ornatoides*

Sp **S** **F** W   Elongated, body tapering backward, with hairy black thorax and head. Elytra blue with variable pale spots; some crescent shaped. Larvae feed on oaks. Adults common in flowers of prickly pear, thistles, and poppy mallow.

### SCULPTURED PINE BORER *Chalcophora virginiensis*

Sp **S** **F** W   Large, brassy or gray color, with tapering abdomen. Elytra heavily sculptured with dark or shiny raised elevations and grayish or brassy depressions. Larvae feed on dead or dying pines. Adults are commonly encountered on sides of pines.

### METALLIC WOOD-BORING BEETLE *Chrysobothris femorata* Group

Sp **S** **F** W   Copper or bronze color, somewhat broad, but tapered toward tip. Elytra sculptured with numerous ridges and depressions. Several similar species in this group.

### METALLIC WOOD-BORING BEETLE *Lampetis drummondi*

Sp **S** **F** W   Large, purplish, and robust beetle with elytra tapering toward tip. Antennae and legs usually violet or purple. Thorax and elytra usually with clusters of yellow hairs, but these can be rubbed off. Feeds on acacia, pecan, oaks, mesquite, and many other trees.

### REDBUD BORER *Ptosima gibbicollis*

Sp **S** **F** W   Small, black, elongated beetle with contrasting yellow patches on elytra; broad sinuous stripe laterally on each side and two spots approaching, but not touching, middle near apex. Feeds on redbud.

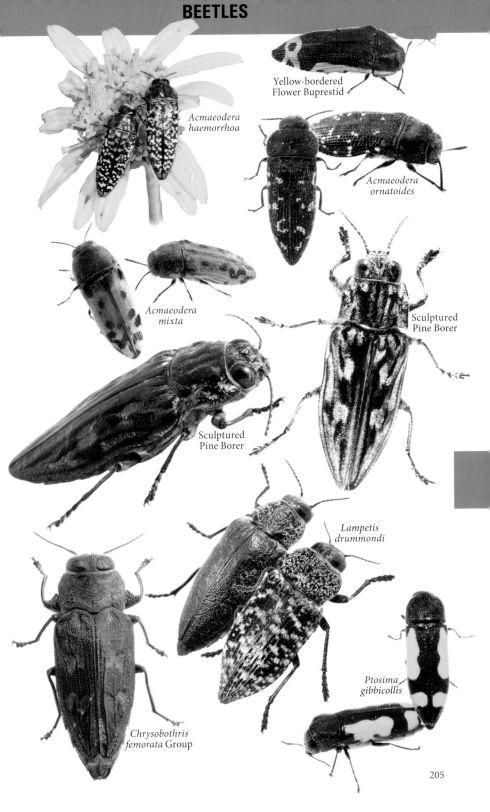

*Acmaeodera haemorrhoa*

Yellow-bordered Flower Buprestid

*Acmaeodera ornatoides*

*Acmaeodera mixta*

Sculptured Pine Borer

Sculptured Pine Borer

*Lampetis drummondi*

*Chrysobothris femorata* Group

*Ptosima gibbicollis*

## TURTLE BEETLE *Chelonarium lecontei*
CHELONARIIDAE

**Sp S F W** Small, reddish-black, convex, and oblong species with numerous patches of white setae on elytra. Can retract head and legs close to body to appear like a seed. Head concealed beneath extended pronotum. Antennal segments 1 and 4 small, 2–3 greatly enlarged and remainder serrate. Larvae found under bark. The adults are found on vegetation and are attracted to lights.

## TOE-WINGED BEETLE *Ptilodactyla* sp.
PTILODACTYLIDAE

**Sp S F W** Small, light to dark brown, oval species with pronotum narrowed and rounded anteriorly. Head concealed from above. Antennae of male pectinate, female filiform. Scutellum heart shaped. Pronotum and elytra covered in fine hairs. Adults feed on microfungi growing on foliage. Adults attracted to lights.

## CLICK BEETLE *Dicrepidius palmatus*
ELATERIDAE

**Sp S F W** Elongated, reddish brown to black, and clothed in fine hairs. Male antennae pectinate, female serrate. Pronotum longer than wide with sharp, ridged hind angles. Elytra has rows of deep punctures. Attracted to lights.

## FLAT WIREWORM *Aeolus mellillus*

**Sp S F W** Small, elongated, and orange with dark head and series of black spots on elytra. Pronotum with sharp, hind angle projections and an elongated black stripe of spot. Elytra with black stripe over scutellum, each side of midline anteriorly and an upside down "V" shape at apex. Encountered on soil and at lights.

## CLICK BEETLE *Agrypnus rectangularis*

**Sp S F W** Small, stocky, light to dark brown, with deep punctures with hairs in them on head, pronotum, and elytra. Antennae lighter than legs. Pronotum with hind angles rounded. Attracted to lights.

## TEXAS CLICK BEETLE *Alaus lusciosus*

**Sp S F W** Large, black or gray, covered with white or yellow scales, and two large black eye spots on pronotum. Antennae serrate. Eye spots more round than elliptical and usually with distinct margin of white scales. Found under loose bark and at lights.

## CLICK BEETLE *Diplostethus texanus*

**Sp S F W** Medium-sized, dark brown, with fine lighter brown small hairs covering body. Posterior angles of pronotum elongated and sharp. Antennae serrate. Attracted to lights.

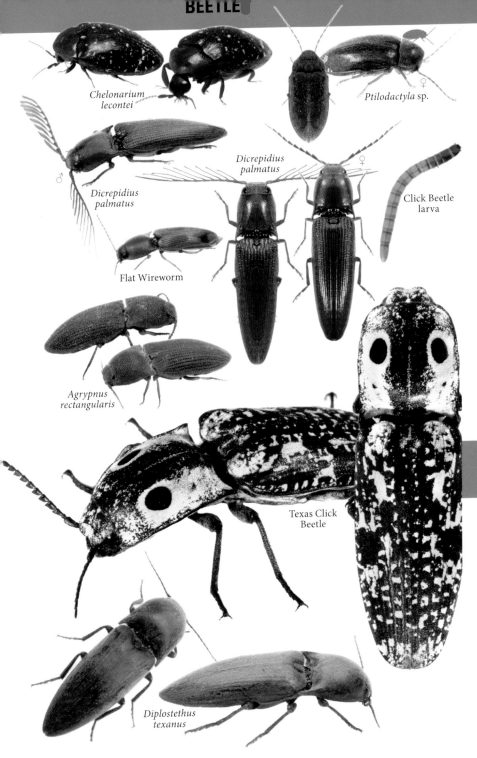

Chelonarium
lecontei

Ptilodactyla sp.

Dicrepidius
palmatus

♂

Dicrepidius
palmatus

Flat Wireworm

Click Beetle
larva

Agrypnus
rectangularis

Texas Click
Beetle

Diplostethus
texanus

### GULF WIREWORM *Heteroderes amplicollis*

ELATERIDAE

Sp **S** **F** **W**  Uniformly dark brown to black with pale tan antennae and legs. Pronotum with sharp, pronounced hind angles that are directed slightly outward and two sizes of punctures. Elytra with obvious rows of punctures. Fourth tarsal segment with membranous lobe underneath. Common at lights.

### CLICK BEETLE *Melanotus* sp.

Sp **S** **F** **W**  Dark to reddish- or yellowish-brown with comb like tarsal claws. Hind angles of pronotum somewhat blunt. Head with numerous hexagonal punctures. Antennae serrate. Elytra with nine punctate grooves. Body clothed in fine yellow hairs. Numerous species requiring genitalic dissection for ID. Attracted to lights.

### CLICK BEETLE *Orthostethus infuscatus*

Sp **S** **F** **W**  Large, reddish brown, clothed with short yellow setae, and strongly tapering rearward. Antennae reddish with second segment less than half length of third. Legs dark with simple claws. Hind angles of pronotum long and sharp. Elytra more finely and densely punctate than pronotum. Common at lights.

### CLICK BEETLE *Pherhimius fascicularis*

Sp **S** F **W**  Distinctive with reddish-brown head and pronotum clothed in swirls of yellow hairs and tan elytra with series of dark elongated stripes. Antennae pectinate. Hairs on elytra short. Legs and antennae dark. Attracted to lights.

### CLICK BEETLE *Selonodon* sp.

Sp **S** **F** W  Reddish- to dark brown prominent, sharp mandibles. Pronotum sometimes lighter than head and elytra; wider than long with sharp outward-projecting spines at hind angle. Female with last two abdominal segments exposed. Attracted to lights.

CANTHARIDAE

### SHORT-WINGED SOUTH TEXAS SOLDIER BEETLE *Belotus bicolor*

Sp **S** **F** **W**  Colorful, elongated beetle with reduced elytra. Head yellow anteriorly and black posteriorly. Pronotum yellowish orange. Elytra reduced and pointed towards tip; black anteriorly and yellow at apex. Wings exposed covering most of abdomen. Common on various composites and other flowers.

### GOLDENROD SOLDIER BEETLE *Chauliognathus pensylvanicus*

Sp **S** **F** **W**  Slender, soft-bodied with black head and yellow pronotum and elytra with variable amount of black. Common in open prairies and grasslands where adults visit flowers.

### SOLDIER BEETLE *Atalantycha bilineata*

**Sp** **S** F W  Soft-bodied orange beetle with dark gray elytra. Head with dark triangular mark and dark "equal" sign on pronotum. Found in hardwood and pine forests where adults visit flowers.

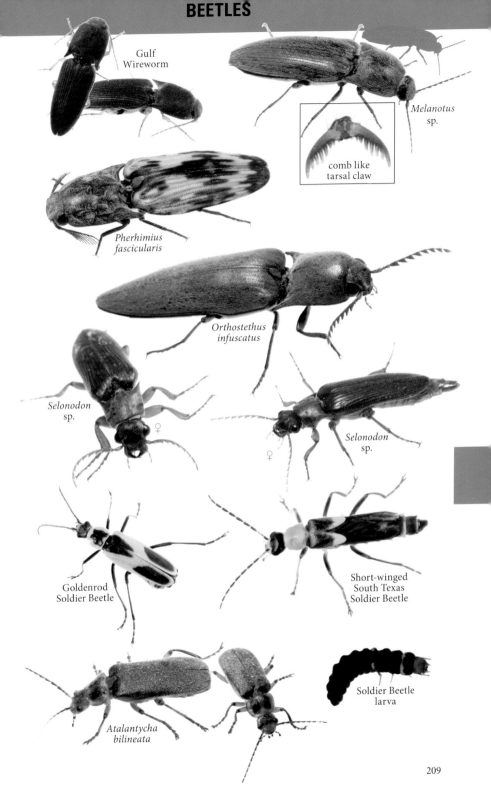

Gulf
Wireworm

*Melanotus*
sp.

comb like
tarsal claw

*Pherhimius
fascicularis*

*Orthostethus
infuscatus*

*Selonodon*
sp.
♀

*Selonodon*
sp.
♀

Goldenrod
Soldier Beetle

Short-winged
South Texas
Soldier Beetle

*Atalantycha
bilineata*

Soldier Beetle
larva

### BANDED NET-WING *Calopteron reticulatum*
LYCIDAE

**Sp S F W** Orange and black, teardrop-shaped, soft-bodied beetle. Antennae serrate. Pronotum orange with central black spot. Dark black band in upper third of elytra, usually tapering laterally, and broad band at apex. Larvae often found in groups where they may also pupate together. Found in wooded areas near water.

### END BAND NET-WING *Calopteron terminale*

**Sp S F W** Orange and black, teardrop-shaped, soft-bodied beetle. Antennae serrate. Pronotum orange with central black spot. Elytra with only terminal black band or if middle band present, not touching edges. Dark bands with a distinct blue metallic shimmer. Found in deciduous woodlands, especially near water.

### NET-WINGED BEETLE *Lycus sanguineus*

**Sp S F W** Soft-bodied, brilliant red, with terminal dark band on elytra. Tarsi and antennae black. Female has reduced wings. Larvae feed on fungi; adults on nectar and honeydew.

### NET-WINGED BEETLE *Plateros* sp.

**Sp S F W** Soft-bodied, dull black, nearly parallel-sided, with reddish to yellow pronotum bearing a large central black spot. Front of head short with downward projecting mouthparts. Pronotum lacking strong ridges. Elytra with ridges. Multiple species requiring examination of male genitalia to identify. Found in woodlands.

### BIG DIPPER FIREFLY *Photinus pyralis*
LAMPYRIDAE

**Sp S F W** Elongated, soft-bodied, largely black or brown, with finely wrinkled elytra. Large eyes and head concealed under pronotum. Pronotum yellowish with diffuse red central dot and a smaller black dot in middle of that. Elytra with narrow yellowish margins. Underside of terminal abdominal segments with light organ. Flashes at dusk over meadows, lawns, and woodland edges.

### FIREFLY *Photuris versicolor*

**Sp S F W** Elongated, soft-bodied, with banded antennae and legs. Pronotum yellow with red central dot and elongated black stripe. Elytra dark with yellow margins and central stripe.

### FIREFLY *Pleotomus pallens*

**Sp S F W** Smallish, pale species with large diffuse pink spot on posterior half of pronotum. Elytra pale to dark with yellowish margins. Larvae feed on snails.

### FIREFLY *Pyropyga minuta*

**Sp S F W** Small, black, soft-bodied, with large dark spot on pronotum with red and yellow margins. Diurnal firefly lacking a light organ. Common along wet roadside ditches.

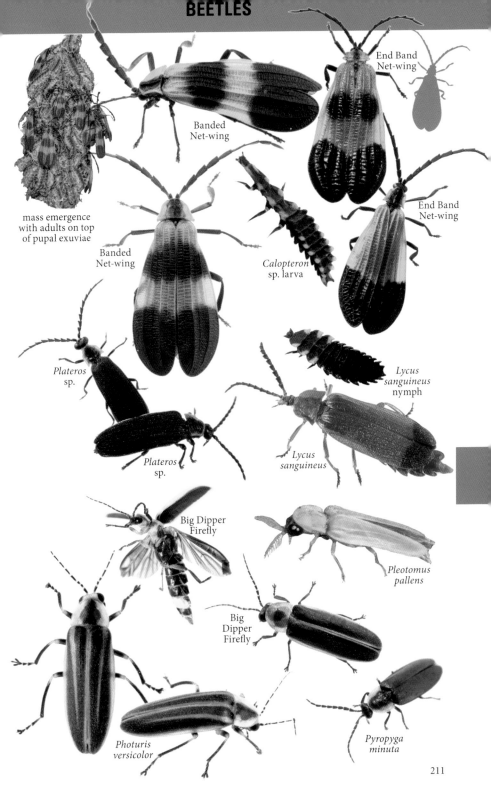

mass emergence
with adults on top
of pupal exuviae

Banded
Net-wing

End Band
Net-wing

Banded
Net-wing

*Calopteron*
sp. larva

End Band
Net-wing

*Plateros*
sp.

*Plateros*
sp.

*Lycus*
*sanguineus*
nymph

*Lycus*
*sanguineus*

Big Dipper
Firefly

*Pleotomus*
*pallens*

Big
Dipper
Firefly

*Photuris*
*versicolor*

*Pyropyga*
*minuta*

211

### LITTLE TEXAS GLOWWORM *Distremocephalus texanus* PHENGODIDAE

**Sp S F W** Small, soft-bodied, orange, with reduced elytra and dark abdomen. Antennae pectinate. Large dark eyes. Wings extend beyond elytra. Female wingless. Larvae eat snails. Comes to lights.

### GLOWWORM *Phengodes* sp.

**Sp S F W** Orange, soft-bodied, with orange head, pronotum, and abdomen. Wings extending beyond reduced elytra which can be dark at narrowed apex. Antennae pectinate. Female larviform. Larva feeds on millipedes. Adults attracted to lights.

### GLOWWORM *Phengodes fusciceps*

**Sp S F W** Orange, soft-bodied, with dark head, and dark wings extending beyond reduced elytra. Antennae pectinate. Pronotum and legs orange. Elytra reduced with dark, narrowed tips. Each abdominal segment with black anterior band. Female larviform. Larva feeds on millipedes. Adults attracted to lights.

### BLACK LARDER BEETLE *Dermestes ater* DERMESTIDAE

**Sp S F W** Small, black, and oblong with fine pale hairs covering entire body. Antennae and legs reddish brown. Introduced from Old World. Adults and larvae found on carrion.

### HORNED POWDER-POST BEETLES *Amphicerus cornutus* BOSTRICHIDAE

**Sp S F W** Small, uniformly brown to black beetle with large rounded and sculptured pronotum concealing head. Front of pronotum with lateral projection on each side. Tip of elytra sharply slanted downward and jagged on edges. Feeds on mesquite.

### APPLE TWIG BORER *Amphicerus bicaudatus*

**Sp S F W** Small, reddish to dark brown, elongated, and cylindrical, sparsely covered with short yellow hairs. Males with pair of forward-projecting horns off of pronotum and small tubercle at tip of elytra. Larvae feed on injured, diseased, or dead deciduous trees.

### HORNED POWDER-POST BEETLES *Lichenophanes bicornis*

**Sp S F W** Elongated, cylindrical, dark body with tufts of pale hair giving it a mottled look. Head much smaller than larger rounded pronotum which bears two forward-projecting hook-like horns. Larvae feed on hardwood twigs and branches. Attracted to lights.

### RED-SHOULDERED BOSTRICHID *Xylobiops basilaris*

**Sp S F W** Small, reddish brown to black, with rounded pronotum partially concealing head, and elytra with variable red patch anteriorly. Antennae and tarsi pale. Anterior portion of pronotum rougher than posterior. Tip of each elytron with three teeth. Larvae in sapwood and heartwood. Adults feed on deciduous hardwoods. Attracted to lights.

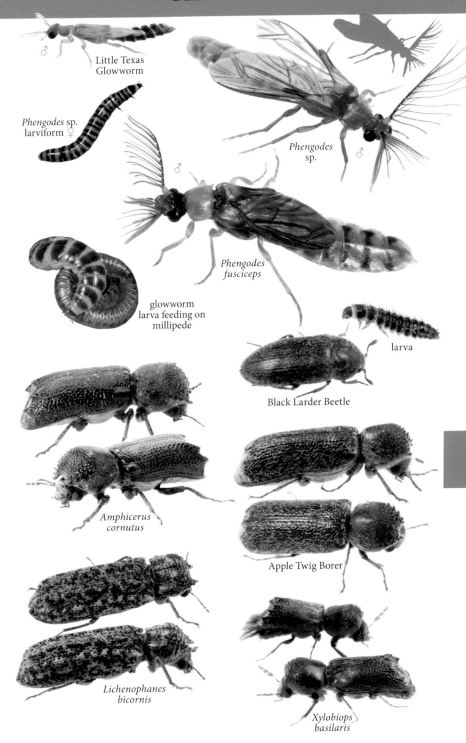

Little Texas Glowworm

♂

*Phengodes* sp. larviform ♀

♂

*Phengodes* sp. ♂

*Phengodes fusciceps*

glowworm larva feeding on millipede

larva

Black Larder Beetle

*Amphicerus cornutus*

Apple Twig Borer

*Lichenophanes bicornis*

*Xylobiops basilaris*

213

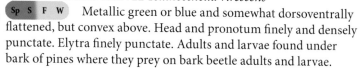

### BARK-GNAWING BEETLE *Temnoscheila virescens*
TROGOSSITIDAE

**Sp S F W** Metallic green or blue and somewhat dorsoventrally flattened, but convex above. Head and pronotum finely and densely punctate. Elytra finely punctate. Adults and larvae found under bark of pines where they prey on bark beetle adults and larvae.

### BARK-GNAWING BEETLE *Tenebroides laticollis*

**Sp S F W** Reddish brown to black, elongated, flattened, but with upper half slightly convex. Head and pronotum coarsely punctate. Elytra with punctated striations. Found under bark of hardwoods, in particular oaks. Occasionally come to lights.

### CHECKERED BEETLE *Cymatodera undulata*
CLERIDAE

**Sp S F W** Elongated with dark reddish head and pronotum, pale legs and antennae, and orange-striped elytra. Pronotum and head narrower than abdomen and pronotum noticeably longer than wide. Elytra with coarsely punctate striations that become faint posteriorly. Adults found on branches infested with wood-boring beetles. Attracted to lights.

### CHECKERED BEETLE *Pelonides quadripunctata*

**Sp S F W** Small, teardrop-shaped, with black head and pronotum and bright red elytra with four black spots. Antennae pectinate. Pronotum nearly as wide as long. Elytra finely and densely punctate. Adults found on various deciduous flowers.

### SOFT-WINGED FLOWER BEETLES *Attalus scincetus*
MELYRIDAE

**Sp S F W** Small, soft-bodied, brownish, with elytra expanded distally. Head yellow anteriorly and black posteriorly. Pronotum black with yellow lateral margins. Elytra brownish with dark medial stripe. Legs and antennae yellowish with some dark striping at base. Underside black. Found on flowers including cherry and dogwood.

### SOFT-WINGED FLOWER BEETLES *Collops vittatus*

**Sp S F W** Small, soft-bodied, somewhat oblong, red and bluish beetle. Antennae yellow basally, becoming dark; basal segments modified in males. Head bluish, pronotum red, sometimes with dark central spot. Elytra blue with red margins. Found on flowers.

### PARASITIC FLAT BARK BEETLES *Catogenus rufus*
PASSANDRIDAE

**Sp S F W** Reddish brown and flattened with bead-like antennae. Head with deep grooves. Pronotum longer than wide, tapered posteriorly with medial groove. Found under bark.

### SHINING FLOWER BEETLE *Acylomus* sp.
PHALACRIDAE

**Sp S F W** Tiny, shiny, brown to black, and hemispherical. Usually uniform in color with pale antennae and legs. Elytra sometimes with pale spots. Feeds on fungi growing on dead plants.

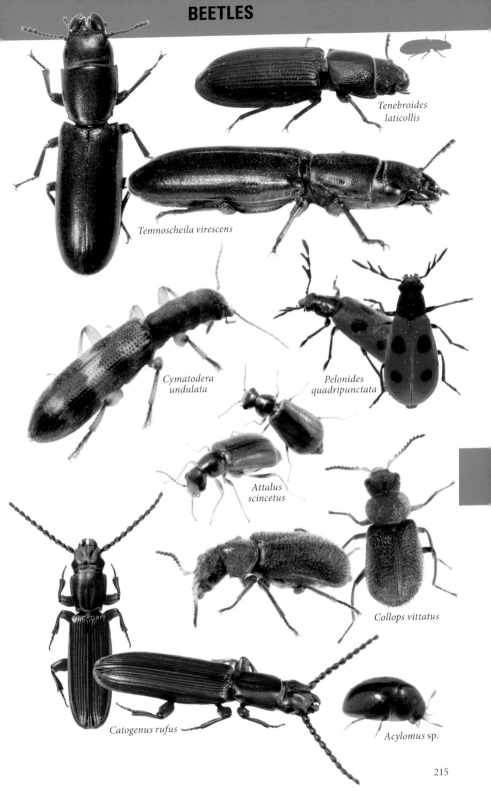

*Tenebroides
laticollis*

*Temnoscheila virescens*

*Cymatodera
undulata*

*Pelonides
quadripunctata*

*Attalus
scincetus*

*Collops vittatus*

*Catogenus rufus*

*Acylomus* sp.

### SMALL HIVE BEETLE *Aethina tumida* NITIDULIDAE

Sp S F W   Small, black, brown, or reddish-brown, ovoid beetle with clubbed antennae. Pronotum much wider than long; rounded laterally and narrowed anteriorly. Elytra truncate covering all but last abdominal segment. Adults found in beehives feeding on honey.

### SAP-FEEDING BEETLE *Epuraea* sp.

Sp S F W   Brown or reddish brown, elongated, and oval with clubbed antennae and covered in dense hairs. Pronotum twice as wide as long. Legs and antennae uniformly colored. Feeds on sap, fungi, and rotting fruit. Some species are found in beehives and leaf litter.

### SAP BEETLE *Lobiopa undulata*

Sp S F W   Variably colored, ovoid, flattened beetle. Antennae clubbed. Pronotum and elytra reddish brown to yellowish, usually with numerous dark markings. Lateral edges of both strongly flattened. Pronotum extends forward beyond eyes. Adults feed on sap and are found under bark. Attracted to lights.

### FOUR-SPOTTED FUNGUS BEETLE *Ischyrus quadripunctatus* EROTYLIDAE

Sp S F W   Elongated, convex, with black head and yellowish-tan to orange body with four black spots on pronotum. Antennae and legs largely black. Black pattern on elytra variable. Found on fungi and under bark. Attracted to lights.

### PLEASING FUNGUS BEETLE *Megalodacne heros*

Sp S F W   Elongated, oval, convexly rounded above, and shiny orange and black. Antennae, legs, pronotum, and head black. Elytra black with two orange stripes interrupted at middle. Elytra lack fine punctures. Found on shelf fungi.

### CLOVER STEM BORER *Languria mozardi*

Sp S F W   Slender, very elongated, and somewhat cylindrical, with reddish-orange head and thorax and metallic greenish-blue elytra. Antennal club made up of 5 segments. Two or more segments of abdomen red ventrally. Found on flowers and their stems.

### HANDSOME FUNGUS BEETLE *Endomychus biguttatus* ENDOMYCHIDAE

Sp S F W   Small, somewhat ovoid black beetle with reddish-orange elytra usually bearing four spots. Anterior spots on elytra can be small or absent. Found in deciduous forests often under bark where they feed on fungi.

### CONVERGENT LADY BEETLE *Hippodamia convergens* COCCINELLIDAE

Sp S F W   Shiny, oval ,and fairly elongated, with two white slanted stripes on black pronotum. Head black with sinuous white spot centrally. Pronotum with white margin. Elytra reddish orange, usually with twelve distinct spots. Abundant in agro-ecosystems.

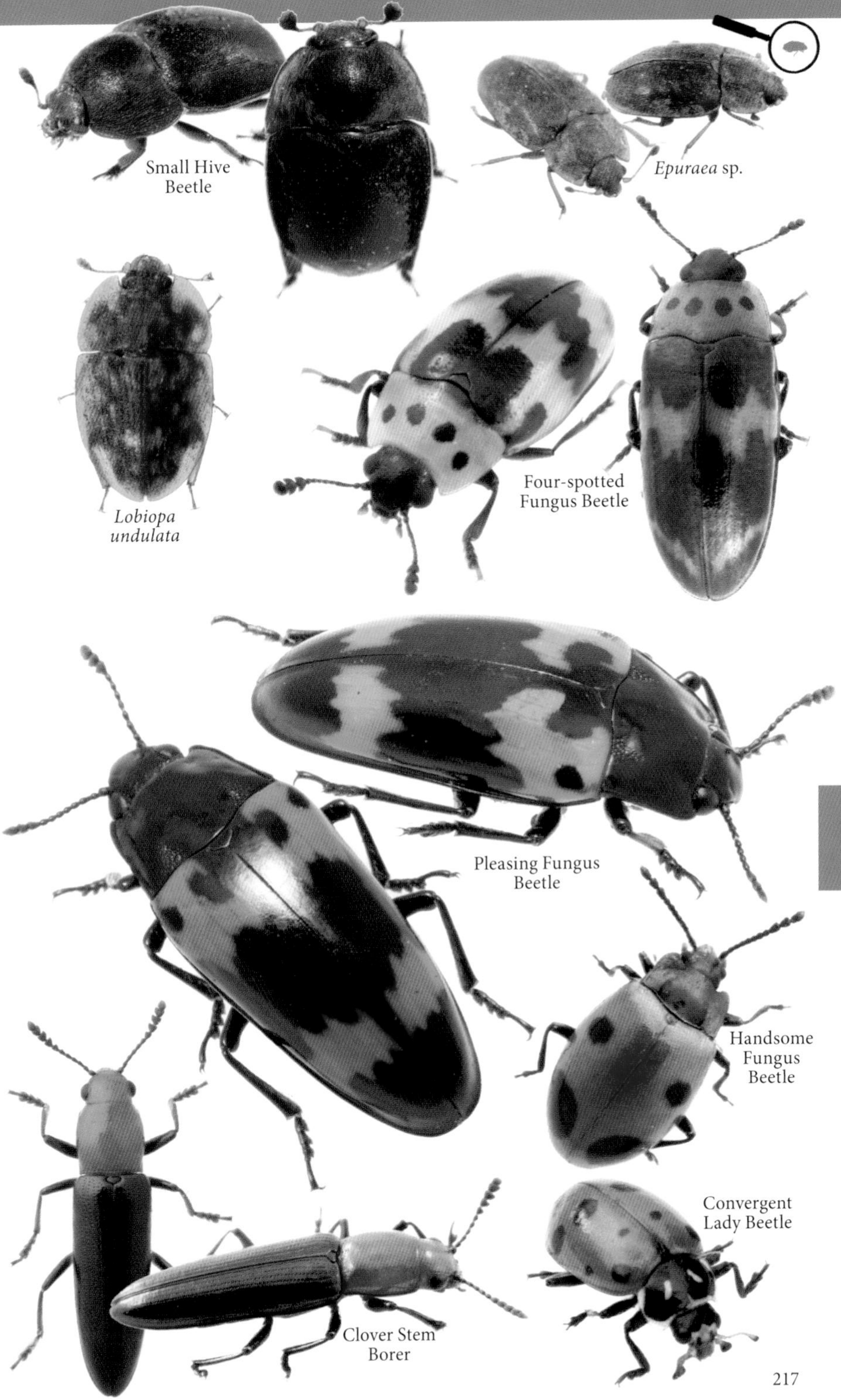

Small Hive Beetle

*Epuraea* sp.

*Lobiopa undulata*

Four-spotted Fungus Beetle

Pleasing Fungus Beetle

Handsome Fungus Beetle

Convergent Lady Beetle

Clover Stem Borer

**TWICE-STABBED LADY BEETLE** *Chilocorus stigma*

Sp **S F** W   Broadly oval, hemispherical black body with a red spot on each elytron. Elytral margins strongly reflexed. Thorax below dark. Common in trees with mealybugs and scales.

**SEVEN-SPOTTED LADY BEETLE** *Coccinella septempunctata*

Sp **S F** W   Oval, slightly elongated, hemispherical, orange or red elytra with 7 black spots. Head black with two white spots. Pronotum black, two white spots anterolaterally. A white spot anterior to scutellum on each elytron. Introduced from Europe.

**SPOTTED LADY BEETLE** *Coleomegilla maculata*

Sp **S F** W   Elongated, reddish orange to pink with large black spots. Head black with red triangle medially. Pronotum red with two large black spots. Each elytron with four black spots plus a spot over the scutellum and at the apex. Prefers moist habitats.

**POLISHED LADY BEETLE** *Cycloneda munda*

Sp **S F** W   Shiny, hemispherical, with spotless orange elytra. Head black with square white spot anteriorly. Pronotum black with white "W" in middle and nearly isolated black spot on each side. Elytra sometimes with wash of white across scutellum. Mid and hind tibia with pair of apical spurs. Feeds on aphids.

**ASHY GRAY LADY BEETLE** *Olla v-nigrum*

Sp **S F** W   Shiny, hemispherical, gray with numerous black spots on pronotum and elytra. Can be variably colored with black form that bears a red spot on each elytron. Note pattern on pronotum to distinguish from Twice-stabbed Lady Beetle. Can also be gray with single large posterior spot on each elytron.

**MULTICOLORED ASIAN LADY BEETLE** *Harmonia axyridis*

Sp **S F** W   Shiny, hemispherical, and incredibly variable in color and spotting. Pronotum white with up to five spots, sometimes conjoined, but best way to separate from other species. Can be very common, sometimes considered a nuisance. Attracted to lights.

**TWENTY-SPOTTED LADY BEETLE** *Psyllobora vigintimaculata*

Sp **S F** W   Tiny, shiny, oval, and pale. Head mostly white. Pronotum white, usually with five black spots. Elytra variable, but usually each with nine dark spots on a pale background, often over diffuse yellowish orange. Adults feed on powdery mildew.

**V-MARKED LADY BEETLE** *Neoharmonia venusta*

Sp **S F** W   Shiny, hemispherical, and incredibly variable in color. Can be pink or red with black spots to black with pale or red "C" spot on elytra. Sometimes pale "A" shape present in middle of elytra. Feeds on psyllids, scales, and beetle larvae.

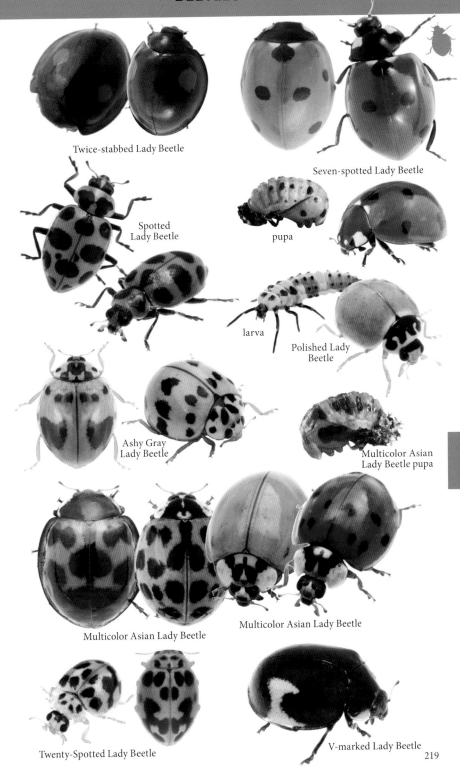

Twice-stabbed Lady Beetle

Seven-spotted Lady Beetle

Spotted
Lady Beetle

pupa

larva

Polished Lady
Beetle

Ashy Gray
Lady Beetle

Multicolor Asian
Lady Beetle pupa

Multicolor Asian Lady Beetle

Multicolor Asian Lady Beetle

Twenty-Spotted Lady Beetle

V-marked Lady Beetle

219

### MEALYBUG DESTROYER *Cryptolaemus montrouzieri* COCCINELLIDAE

**Sp** **S** **F** **W**  Small, hemispherical, with dark elytra and reddish-orange head and pronotum. Pronotum with dark medial spot posteriorly. Apex of elytra reddish brown. Body covered in fine hairs. Adults and larvae feed on scale insects.

### STREAKED LADY BEETLE *Myzia pullata*

**Sp** **S** **F** **W**  Shiny, hemispherical, reddish brown with black streaks on elytra. Head black. Pronotum reddish brown centrally, pale laterally with dark spot. Common on catalpa and persimmon.

### BARBER'S LADY BEETLE *Brachiacantha barberi*

**Sp** **S** **F** **W**  Tiny, oval, and strongly convex black beetle with aquamarine eyes and orange spots. Top of head orange. Pronotum with large lateral orange spots. Middle and apex of elytra with large orange spot that does not connect in middle.

### SPURLEG LADY BEETLE *Brachiacantha felina*

**Sp** **S** **F** **W**  Tiny, oval, and strongly convex black beetle with aquamarine eyes and reddish-orange spots. Top of head orange. Pronotum black with only anterolateral corners pale orange. Elytra each with four large orange spots.

### FALSE DARKLING BEETLE *Osphya varians* MELANDRYIDAE

**Sp** **S** **F** **W**  Elongated and soft-bodied, much like a soldier beetle. Head and elytra black with iridescent shimmer. Pronotum reddish orange either with paired black spots or not. Legs dark or pale. Male with lobe at apex of hind tibia. Penultimate tarsal segment lobed in both sexes. Adults found on flowers and trees.

### TUMBLING FLOWER BEETLE *Hoshihananomia octopunctata* MORDELIDAE

**Sp** **S** **F** **W**  Elongated, wedge shaped, with distinctive yellow or orange spots on black elytra. Head truncated posteriorly. Pronotum black with yellow or orange hairs. Abdomen with pale hairs underneath and on each segment dorsally. Larvae develop in dead or dying oak and beech. Adults found on flowers.

### TUMBLING FLOWER BEETLE *Mordella* sp.

**Sp** **S** **F** **W**  Elongated, wedge shaped, and generally uniformly black or gray. Head truncated posteriorly. Antennae serrate and somewhat clubbed. Long, sharp projection extending beyond elytra.

### TUMBLING FLOWER BEETLE *Mordellistena cervicalis*

**Sp** **S** **F** **W**  Elongated, wedge shaped, with reddish-orange head and pronotum. Head truncated posteriorly. First four antennal segments pale, remainder dark. Front and middle femur pale in male; female with all legs black.

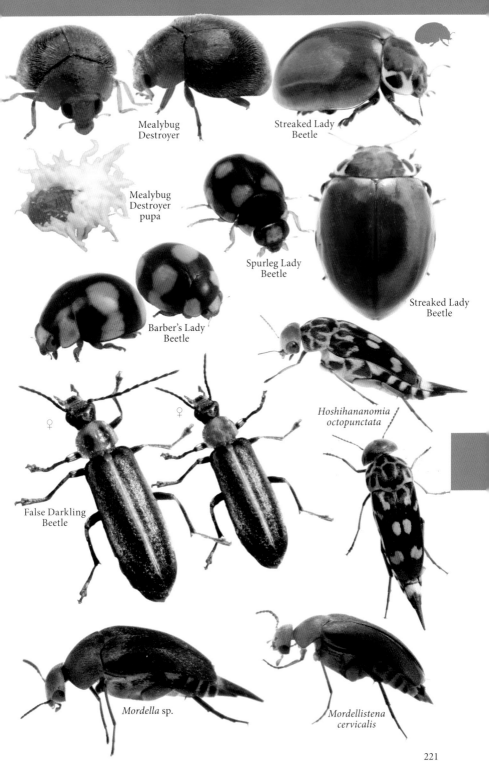

Mealybug
Destroyer

Streaked Lady
Beetle

Mealybug
Destroyer
pupa

Spurleg Lady
Beetle

Streaked Lady
Beetle

Barber's Lady
Beetle

*Hoshihananomia
octopunctata*

♀

♀

False Darkling
Beetle

*Mordella* sp.

*Mordellistena
cervicalis*

### IRONCLAD BEETLE *Zopherus nodulosus*

**Sp S F W** Unmistakable with round pronotum and body white above with black raised bumps and black below. Very hard with fused elytra. Antennae, legs, large eyes, and front of head black. Fringes of gold hair on head. Found on dead or dying oak, pecan, and elm trees. Feeds on lichen.

### IRONCLAD BEETLE *Zopherus xestus*

**Sp S F W** All black, with round convex head and fused elytra. Raised bumps on elytra. Golden hairs on face, tibia edge, and at base of each tarsal segment. Tip of abdomen with trilobed raised area on underside. Presumably feeds on lichen.

### FALSE MEALWORM BEETLE *Alobates pensylvanica*

**Sp S F W** Black, smooth, somewhat convexed, elongated, beetle with pronotum nearly as long as wide. Elytra with rows of fine punctures. Underside of head lacking tuft of golden hairs. Found under bark or decaying logs. Attracted to lights.

### DARKLING BEETLE *Blapstinus fortis*

**Sp S F W** Dark gray to black, ovoid, with squarish head that can be somewhat retracted beneath pronotum. Anterior and posterior angles of pronotum elongated into sharp points. Fine punctures on head and pronotum. Elytra with rows of punctures. Comes to lights.

### FORKED FUNGUS BEETLE *Bolitotherus cornutus*

**Sp S F W** Gray to reddish brown and roughly sculptured. Males with pair of anterior projecting, fringed horns on pronotum. Larvae and adults feed on shelf fungi. Adults active at night, coming to lights.

### DARKLING BEETLE *Bothrotes canaliculatus*

**Sp S F W** Oval, convex, reddish brown to black, and covered with fine golden hairs, often giving it a metallic look. Head longer than wide. Pronotum of female with large central depression and a smaller one on each side; male smoothly convex. Found on vegetation, but also attracted to lights.

### DARKLING BEETLE *Cryptoglossa infausta*

**Sp S F W** Elongated, black or gray, with rough legs and elytra. Pronotum smoothly convex with lateral margins somewhat "S" shaped. Elytra with rough bumps. Body can be covered with gray, waxy pruinescence. Leg surfaces with fine sculpturing. Often covered in dirt collected around sculpturing. Hides under rocks.

### DARKLING BEETLE *Cymatothes tristis*

**Sp S F W** Black, elongated, with smoothly rounded, convex pronotum and elytra narrowing toward tip with finely punctured striations. Femora swollen. Found under logs and rocks.

*Zopherus nodulosus*

*Zopherus xestus*

False Mealworm Beetle

*Blapstinus forti*

Forked Fungus Beetle ♂

♀

*Bothrotes canaliculatus* ♂

*Cryptoglossa infausta*

*Cymatothes tristis*

**DARKLING BEETLE** *Diaperis maculata*

Sp **S** **F** W  Shiny, round, smoothly convex, with black spots on reddish-orange elytra. Head black anteriorly and orange posteriorly (sometimes concealed by black pronotum). Elytra with one or two basal black spots and two larger blotches posteriorly that sometimes coalesce to form single band. Middle of elytra also striped in black. Adults and larvae feed on shelf fungi; also found under bark.

**DARKLING BEETLE** *Diaperis nigronotata*

Sp **S** **F** W  Shiny, round, smoothly convex, with black spots on reddish-orange elytra. Head black anteriorly and orange posteriorly. Elytra with five basal black spots across middle; sometimes coalescing into interrupted stripe. Large, diffuse black band posteriorly. Adults and larvae feed on shelf fungi.

**DARKLING BEETLE** *Eleodes goryi*

Sp **S** **F** W  Smooth, dull, elongated black beetle with long hind legs. Pronotum wider than long and smoothly convex. Abdomen teardrop-shaped with fine rows of punctures. Found under rocks and logs and on paths. Stands with abdomen directed upward.

**DARKLING BEETLE** *Embaphion muricatum*

Sp **S** **F** W  Black, somewhat dull, and with distinctive upward-turned flanges on pronotum and elytra appearing scoop shaped. Thin flanges may appear reddish. Fine row of setose punctures on elytra. Found under and often nearby rocks and in caves.

**DARKLING BEETLE** *Gondwanocrypticus obsoletus*

Sp **S** **F** W  Black to reddish brown, smoothly convex, and elongated. Basal antennal segments reddish. Legs often more reddish distally. Found in leaf litter, often associated with fire ants.

**DARKLING BEETLE** *Neomida bicornis*

Sp **S** **F** W  Small, strongly convex, and reflective green, blue, or red. Head dark, male with two prominent horns. Pronotum dull greenish blue or red with fine punctures. Elytra green or blue with rows of punctures. Found on fungi including under bark.

**LONG-JOINTED BEETLE** *Statira basalis*

Sp **S** **F** W  Shiny, elongated, with pronotum narrower than elytra, rounded anteriorly with ridge posteriorly. Variable color, but femora banded. Last antennal segment of male longer than preceding three. Found on deciduous trees and shrubs. Attracted to lights.

**YELLOW MEALWORM** *Tenebrio molitor*

Sp **S** **F** W  Dull black to reddish brown, elongated, with smooth, slightly convex pronotum. Elytra with shallow striations. Common food item in pet trade. Feeds on grains and mill products.

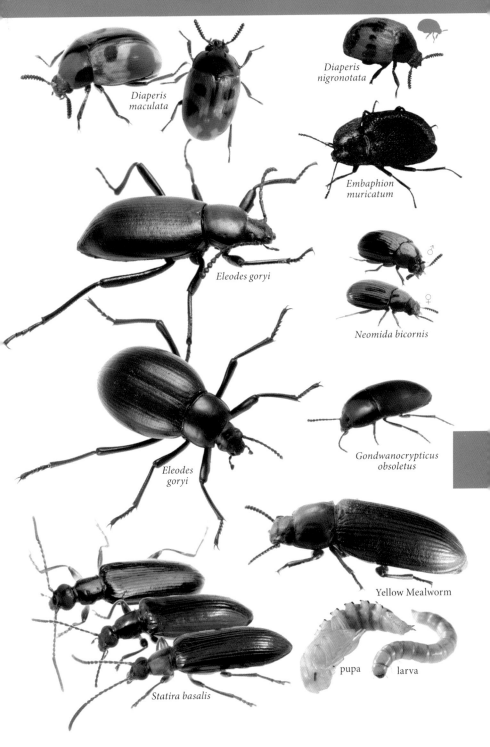

*Diaperis maculata*

*Diaperis nigronotata*

*Embaphion muricatum*

*Eleodes goryi*

*Neomida bicornis* ♂ ♀

*Gondwanocrypticus obsoletus*

*Eleodes goryi*

Yellow Mealworm

pupa  larva

*Statira basalis*

225

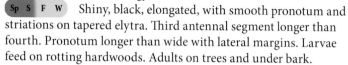

## DARKLING BEETLE *Strongylium tenicolle*
TENEBRIONIDAE

**Sp S F W** Shiny, black, elongated, with smooth pronotum and striations on tapered elytra. Third antennal segment longer than fourth. Pronotum longer than wide with lateral margins. Larvae feed on rotting hardwoods. Adults on trees and under bark.

## DARKLING BEETLE *Stenomorpha opaca*

**Sp S F W** Dull, grayish, with long legs, and elytra usually outlined in gray. Body slightly convex, but low lateral ridge on pronotum and elytra. Pronotum strongly incised behind head and with strongly angled posterior projections. Found under rocks.

## VELVETY BARK BEETLE *Penthe pimelia*
TETRATOMIDAE

**Sp S F W** Dull, black, with pronotum and elytra densely punctated and covered with velvety pubescence. Third antennal segment as long as previous two and last segment pale. Palps often held out in front of head. Scutellum prominent and black. Elytra tapered rearward. Found under loose bark and attracted to lights.

## POLYPORE FUNGUS BEETLE *Eustrophopsis bicolor*

**Sp S F W** Black, oval, elongated, nearly hemispherical, with tricolored antennae (pale, dark, last segment pale). Pronotum with fine punctures. Elytra with rows of coarse punctures. Middle and hind tibia with numerous transverse ridges. Found under bark of pines and hardwoods feeding on fungus.

## BUTTERCUP OIL BEETLE *Meloe americanus*
MELOIDAE

**Sp S F W** Large, black, soft-bodied, with reduced elytra and expanded abdomen. Male antennae modified in middle to have C-shaped kink used to grab female during premating display. Active, running around on ground. Larvae are bee parasitoids.

## BLACK BLADDER-BODIED MELOID *Cysteodemus wislizeni*

**Sp S F W** Distinctive shape with very large, round, iridescent, sculptured elytra. Body iridescent green, blue, or violet. Pronotum angulate laterally, lacking spines. Head with coarse dense punctures. Found walking along sand and rocky ground.

## BLISTER BEETLE *Zonitis dunniana*

**Sp S F W** Soft-bodied, bright yellow or greenish. Antennae black except for basal segment. Legs yellow except for distal tarsi. Long palps. Found on flowers, especially composites.

## BLISTER BEETLE *Nemognatha* sp.

**Sp S F W** Soft-bodied, usually orange, with extremely long mouthparts used to suck nectar. Antennae and legs usually black. Numerous species difficult to separate from photos. Larvae are parasitoids on solitary bees. Adults found on flowers.

# BEETLES

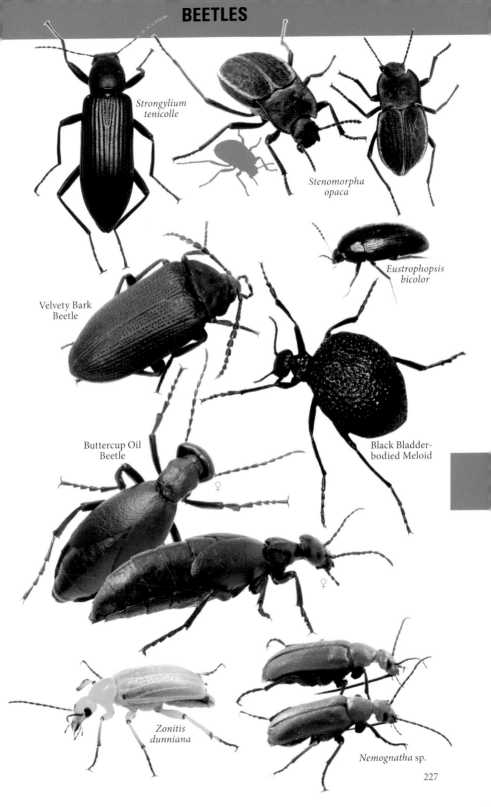

*Strongylium tenicolle*

*Stenomorpha opaca*

*Eustrophopsis bicolor*

Velvety Bark Beetle

Buttercup Oil Beetle

Black Bladder-bodied Meloid

♀

♀

*Zonitis dunniana*

*Nemognatha* sp.

227

**BLISTER BEETLE** *Cissites auriculata*

Sp **S** F **W** Unmistakable large orange beetle with big head and prominent mandibles and elytra with numerous black spots. Despite the mandibles, adults of this blister beetle do not feed. Larvae are parasitoids on carpenter bees.

 **BLISTER BEETLE** *Epicauta atrivittata*

Sp **S** F **W** Soft bodied, black with white stripes on elytra. Head and pronotum diffusely white, the former usually with two large black spots. Abdomen transversely striped. Legs and antennae black. Feeds on nightshades and mesquite. Attracted to lights.

 **BLISTER BEETLE** *Epicauta polingi*

Sp **S** F **W** Soft-bodied, cylindrical, with head and thorax light gray and elytra pinkish gray to gray brown. Eyes strongly notched around antennae. Males with enlarged, elongated basal antennal segment. Commonly come to lights.

 **BLISTER BEETLE** *Pyrota bilineata*

Sp **S** F **W** Cylindrical, soft-bodied, with orange head and pronotum, and dark striped elytra. Antennae dark. "Knees" and tarsi dark on otherwise orange legs. Two small dark spots on pronotum. Elytra tan or yellowish with longitudinal dark stripes.

 **BLISTER BEETLE** *Pyrota deceptiva*

Sp **S** F **W** Soft-bodied, elongated, yellowish orange, with six large black blotches on elytra. Head often darker than pronotum. Pronotum with variably sized black spots. Feeds on composites.

 **YELLOW-CRESCENT BLISTER BEETLE** *Pyrota insulata*

Sp **S** F **W** Soft-bodied, elongated, with black elytra margined in yellow or orange. Head with central pale spot. Pronotum orange with diffuse dark spot centrally and generally smaller, more defined spots laterally. Pale spots anteriorly and posteriorly on elytra may be fused with elytral margin. Adults found on honey mesquite. Readily comes to lights.

 **BLISTER BEETLE** *Pleurospasta reticulata*

Sp **S** F **W** Soft-bodied, reddish, with pale white or yellow elytra with reticulated pattern in form of two broad bands across tip. Usually two small dark spots basally on elytra. Legs and antennae red.

**BLISTER BEETLE** *Pseudozonitis longicornis*

Sp **S** F **W** Soft-bodied, elongated, with pale spot in center of head and red spot on pronotum. Elytra dark with yellow margins. Eyes slightly notched around antennae. Legs and antennae banded. Found on vegetation and attracted to lights.

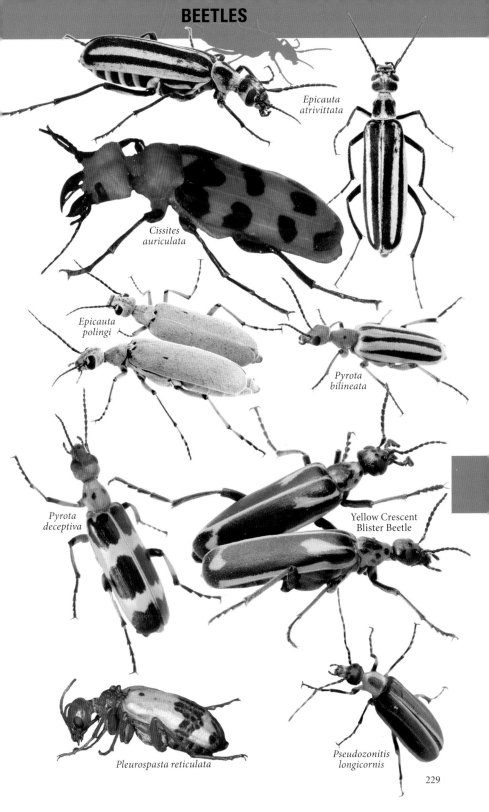

*Epicauta
atrivittata*

*Cissites
auriculata*

*Epicauta
polingi*

*Pyrota
bilineata*

*Pyrota
deceptiva*

Yellow Crescent
Blister Beetle

*Pleurospasta reticulata*

*Pseudozonitis
longicornis*

229

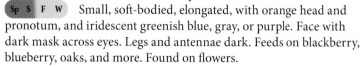

## FALSE BLISTER BEETLE *Heliocis repanda*

OEDEMERIDAE

**Sp S F W** Small, soft-bodied, elongated, with orange head and pronotum, and iridescent greenish blue, gray, or purple. Face with dark mask across eyes. Legs and antennae dark. Feeds on blackberry, blueberry, oaks, and more. Found on flowers.

## FALSE BLISTER BEETLE *Oxycopis thoracica*

**Sp S F W** Small, soft-bodied, elongated, and slender with dark head, orange pronotum, and grayish-black elytra. Antennae and legs black. Pronotum widest in anterior two-thirds. Adults on flowers of palmetto and asters. Attracted to lights.

## ANTLIKE FLOWER BEETLE *Acanthinus argentinus*

ANTHICIDAE

**Sp S F W** Minute, very ant-like, reddish brown to yellowish brown with sparse setae on sides. Pronotum humped in middle. Tarsi paler than rest of leg. Fast moving. Attracted to lights.

## ANTLIKE FLOWER BEETLE *Notoxus monodon*

**Sp S F W** Tiny, yellowish or reddish brown, dark brown stripe on elytra, and pronotum extended over head like a pointed hood. Antennae and legs yellowish-brown. Common at lights.

## ANTLIKE LEAF BEETLE *Elonus basalis*

ADERIDAE

**Sp S F W** Small, reddish brown to dark brown, with prominent orange spot on each shoulder. Eyes notched. Antennae pale basally. Femora darker than rest of legs. Elytra clothed in fine golden hairs. Adults found on leaves of deciduous shrubs. Attracted to lights.

## PALO VERDE ROOT BORER *Derobrachus hovorei*

CERAMBYCIDAE

**Sp S F W** Very large, reddish brown, with prominent mandibles, long antennae, and four strong lateral spines on pronotum. Antennae with only faint striations. Larvae feed on roots of poplar, cottonwood, oaks, mesquite, elm, and more. Attracted to lights.

## HARDWOOD STUMP BORER *Mallodon dasystomus*

**Sp S F W** Very large, somewhat flattened, reddish to dark brown, with prominent mandibles and rectangular pronotum usually with fine teeth laterally. Male pronotum rough, raised in middle, with two smooth areas; female smooth in middle. Lateral teeth on pronotum can be longer and irregular. Larvae feed in live heartwood of oak, elm, sycamore, pecan, and more. Attracted to lights.

## LONG-HORNED BEETLE *Prionus pocularis*

**Sp S F W** Large, reddish brown to black, with large mandibles. Pronotum smooth, but with raised edges. Large eyes. Elytra punctate. Antennae somewhat serrate. Found in pine forests. Attracted to lights.

# BEETLES

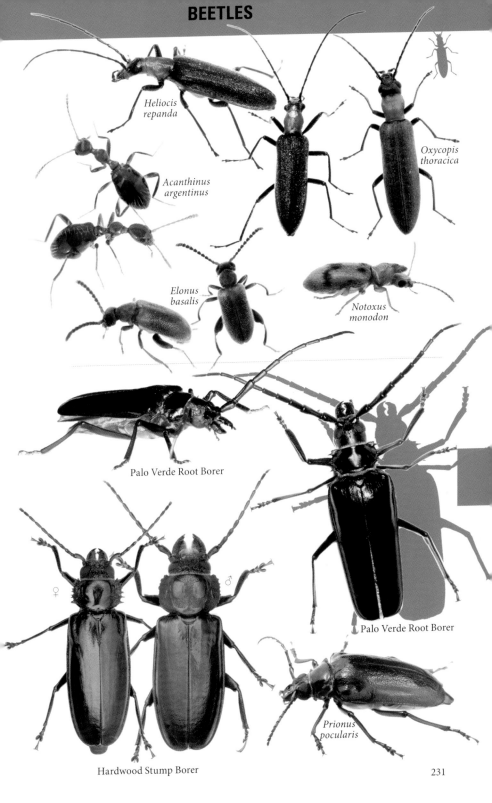

*Heliocis repanda*

*Acanthinus argentinus*

*Oxycopis thoracica*

*Elonus basalis*

*Notoxus monodon*

Palo Verde Root Borer

Palo Verde Root Borer

♀ ♂

Hardwood Stump Borer

*Prionus pocularis*

231

### LONG-HORNED BEETLE *Stenelytrana gigas*          CERAMBYCIDAE

**Sp S F W** Large, iridescent bluish-black body with orange tapering elytra. Antennae and legs dark. Mimics tarantula hawks. Adults attracted to tree sap and sugary baits. Occasionally will come to lights.

### SIX-SPOTTED FLOWER STRANGALIA *Strangalia sexnotata*

**Sp S F W** Elongated, strongly tapering rearward, with six black spots on elytra. Red head and pronotum. Black spots may be variously fused. Visits flowers including composites and *Opuntia*.

### STRANGE VIRILE BYCID *Strangalia virilis*

**Sp S F W** Elongated, strongly tapering rearward. Variably colored, but often with two longitudinal dark stripes on pronotum. Antennae can be reddish or black. Spots on elytra reddish or black and variously fused. Larger than similar *Strangalia* and male has terminal abdominal segment inflated. Visits flowers.

### BANDED LONGHORN *Typocerus velutinus*

**Sp S F W** Elongated, tapering rearward. Pronotum covered with fine yellow hairs, densest along anterior and posterior margins. Elytra reddish brown with variable yellow spots/bands. Larvae develop in deciduous hardwoods. Adults found on flowers.

### ZEBRA LONGHORN *Typocerus zebra*

**Sp S F W** Elongated, black beetle, tapering rearward, with distinctive yellow pattern on elytra. Pronotum with narrow margin of yellow hairs. Yellow on elytra variable, but with a yellow triangular mark always at the base. Legs all black or reddish brown basally. Larvae feed on decaying pine. Adults visit flowers.

### LONG-HORNED BEETLE *Cyrtinus pygmaeus*

**Sp S F W** Tiny, robust, elongated, bicolored body. Head, pronotum, and base of elytra reddish brown. Elytra with white transverse stripe at half its length, then black. Sharp spine present at base of each elytra. Femora swollen. Larvae feed in dry branches of hardwoods, especially oaks.

### OAK TWIG PRUNER *Anelaphus parallelus*

**Sp S F W** Elongated with long antennae. Reddish or dark brown with fine yellow hairs over body. Antennal segments 3 and 4 with short spines. Pronotum weakly rounded on sides. Elytra with two short spines at tip. Larvae develop in hardwoods. Attracted to lights.

### LONG-HORNED BEETLE *Cyrtophorus verrucosus*

**Sp S F W** Small, ant-mimicking bycid. Black with varying amounts of red. Elytral pattern distinct with pair of oblique white lines. Base of elytra with raised knobs. Larvae develop in hardwoods and pines. Adults attracted to lights.

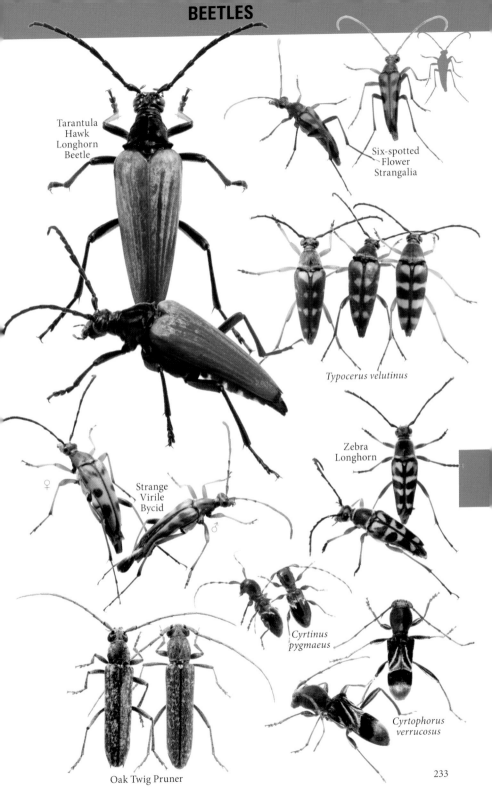

Tarantula Hawk Longhorn Beetle

Six-spotted Flower Strangalia

*Typocerus velutinus*

Zebra Longhorn

Strange Virile Bycid

♀

♂

*Cyrtinus pygmaeus*

Oak Twig Pruner

*Cyrtophorus verrucosus*

233

## OAK BORER *Enaphalodes atomarius* CERAMBYCIDAE

**Sp S F W** Large, elongated, and somewhat rounded dark body clothed in patches of yellow hairs. Antennal segments 3–5 each have a single spine. Male antennae twice as long as body; female length of body. Pronotum broadly rounded. Elytra each with two spines at tip. Larvae feed under bark of hardwoods.

## IVORY-MARKED BEETLE *Eburia quadrigeminata*

**Sp S F W** Large, elongated, brown body covered in fine pubescence and each elytra with four short elongated spots. Male antennae extend beyond body. Pronotum coarsely punctate with two dark raised bumps. White spots on elytra raised. Larvae feed on heartwood of oak, hickory, maple, and others. Attracted to lights.

## LONG-HORNED BEETLE *Euderces reichei*

**Sp S F W** Small, bicolored, elongated, ant-mimicking beetle. Head, pronotum, and base of elytra red. Thin white line separating dark apical portion. Narrow collar between pronotum and abdomen. Larvae feed on hackberry, acacia, soapberry, and others.

## BANDED HICKORY BORER *Knulliana cincta*

**Sp S F W** Large, somewhat slender species with long antennae. Usually gray with a pair of pale marks basally on elytra, but may be absent. A reddish form also exists in east Texas. Pronotum, femora, and elytra with distinct spines. Larvae feed on dead or dying hardwoods including oak and hickory. Commonly encountered at lights.

## LONG-HORNED BEETLE *Mannophorus laetus*

**Sp S F W** Elongated with black head, red pronotum, and black elytra with two yellow longitudinal stripes. Found in Tamaulipan brushlands where it visits flowers, especially composites.

## LONG-HORNED BEETLE *Megacyllene antennata*

**Sp S F W** Elongated, black beetle with yellow pronotum and distinct elytral markings. Yellow markings can be pale, approaching white. Larvae feed on mesquite. Adults attracted to lights.

## HICKORY BORER *Megacyllene caryae*

**Sp S F W** Black and yellow beetle with reddish antennae and legs. Transverse yellow bands on head and pronotum. Numerous yellow bands across elytra; second one from base interrupted on side. Larvae feed on dead hickory. Adults attracted to lights.

## LONG-HORNED BEETLE *Stenaspis solitaria*

**Sp S F W** Large, uniformly black beetle with prominent mandibles and long antennae. Larvae feed on mesquite and acacia. Adults active on hot days, often seen flying about.

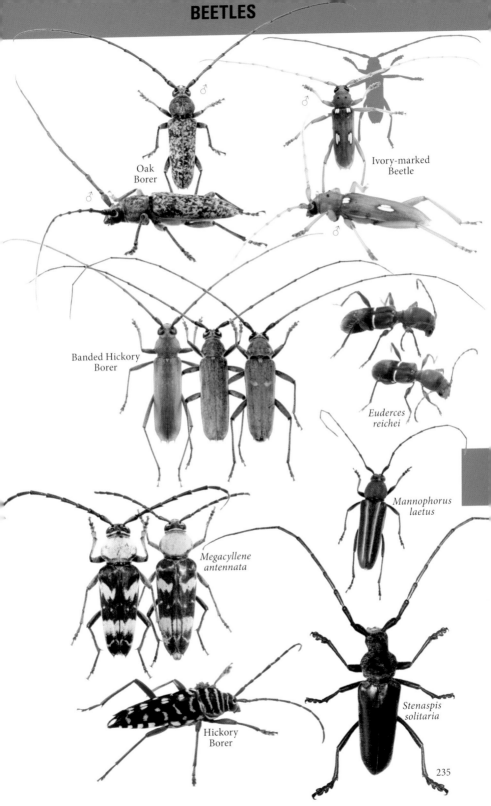

Oak Borer ♂

Ivory-marked Beetle

Banded Hickory Borer

*Euderces reichei*

*Mannophorus laetus*

*Megacyllene antennata*

Hickory Borer

*Stenaspis solitaria*

235

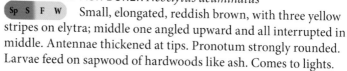

### RED-HEADED ASH BORER *Neoclytus acuminatus*
**Sp S F W**   Small, elongated, reddish brown, with three yellow stripes on elytra; middle one angled upward and all interrupted in middle. Antennae thickened at tips. Pronotum strongly rounded. Larvae feed on sapwood of hardwoods like ash. Comes to lights.

### COLORFUL BEETLE *Neoclytus mucronatus*
**Sp S F W**   Reddish brown with yellow bands on head, pronotum, and elytra. Scutellum yellow. Elytral pattern distinctive. Dark band across middle of elytra. Femora, especially hind legs, swollen and black. Larvae feed on dead or dying hackberry, persimmon, and hickory. Attracted to lights.

### LONG-HORNED BEETLE *Obrium maculatum*
**Sp S F W**   Small, shiny brown and tan beetle with long antennae. Pair of dark longitudinal stripes on narrowly constricted pronotum. Antennae banded. Femora swollen. Larvae feed on hardwoods including pecan and oak. Attracted to lights.

### RUSTIC BORER *Xylotrechus colonus*
**Sp S F W**   Reddish brown with broad pale stripes on elytra and basal dark spots somewhat encircled by yellow. Pronotum reddish brown, usually with yellow in corners. Hind femora swollen. Larvae feed on a variety of hardwoods including pine. Attracted to lights.

### ARROWHEAD BORER *Xylotrechus sagittatus*
**Sp S F W**   Dark reddish brown with pale markings down middle of elytra forming two arrowheads. Pronotum covered in fine pubescence. Femora dark and swollen. Feeds primarily on pine as well as other conifers. Attracted to lights.

### LONG-HORNED BEETLE *Stenaspis verticalis*
**Sp S F W**   Large with red head and pronotum, and shiny metallic green or blue elytra. Antennae and legs red with black bands at apices. Two black spots on pronotum. Adults commonly found at sap on various trees.

### LONG-HORNED BEETLE *Tylosis maculatus*
**Sp S F W**   Red, usually with five black spots on pronotum. Red elytra variously marked black; from six separate spots to one confluent area down midline. Feeds on various mallows.

### LONG-HORNED BEETLE *Tylosis oculatus*
**Sp S F W**   Bright red, elongated, with black head and two small dark spots on pronotum. Legs and antennae black. Feeds on various mallows.

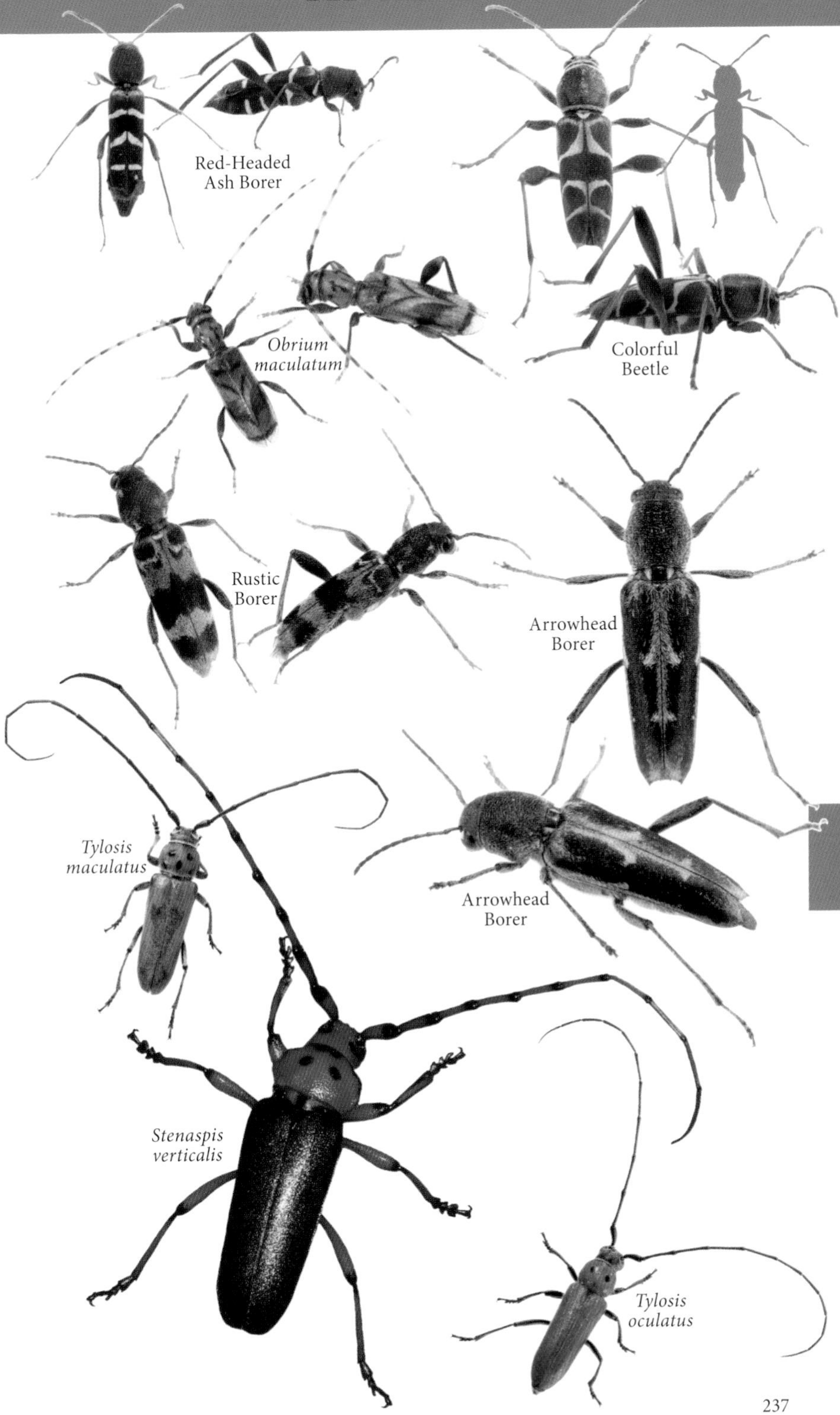

Red-Headed
Ash Borer

*Obrium
maculatum*

Colorful
Beetle

Rustic
Borer

Arrowhead
Borer

*Tylosis
maculatus*

Arrowhead
Borer

*Stenaspis
verticalis*

*Tylosis
oculatus*

237

### BUMELIA BORER *Plinthocoelium suaveolens*

CERAMBYCIDAE

**Sp S F W** Large, metallic green, blue, or bronze body with reddish-orange femora. Antennae and distal leg segments black. Pronotum with lateral spine. Larvae feed on tupelo, mulberry, and brumelia. Adults attracted to lights.

### FLAT OAK BORER *Smodicum cucujiforme*

**Sp S F W** Uniformly orange brown, shiny, and flat with strongly notched eyes. Antennae only slightly longer than abdomen. Larvae feed on oak, hickory, maple, and other hardwoods. Adults are found under loose bark and are attracted to lights.

### HUISACHE GIRDLER *Oncideres pustulata*

**Sp S F W** Elongated, robust, tan with broad pale stripe across elytra. Pronotum and elytra with numerous small black raised bumps. Female with large mandibles elongated for girdling tree branches. Larvae feed on huisache, mesquite, retama, and citrus.

### FLAT-FACED LONGHORN BEETLE *Ataxia crypta*

**Sp S F W** Elongated, reddish to dark brown, covered in gray, brown, and white pubescence. Pronotum wider than long. Antennae in male slightly longer than body; female shorter. First antennal segment with deep excavation. Elytra obliquely truncated at apices.

### LONG-HORNED BEETLE *Dorcasta cinerea*

**Sp S F W** Elongated, somewhat cylindrical, gray with orange, salmon, or tan longitudinal stripes. Antennae held out straight in front when at rest. Pronotum longer than wide and along with elytra, covered with raised black bumps. Larvae feed in herbaceous stems.

### LONG-HORNED BEETLE *Ecyrus dasycerus*

**Sp S F W** Small, robust, with long antennae and knobby pronotum and elytra. Variably colored gray, tan, and brown with washes of white, but always with a dark downward-arching stripe across base of elytra. Feeds on hardwoods including oaks.

### LESSER PINE BORER *Acanthocinus nodosus*

**Sp S F W** Elongated, gray, with distinctive pattern of black on elytra and very long antennae. Male with tuft of hair on fourth antennal segment. Female with tip of abdomen modified into a tube for ovipositing. Found in pine forests. Attracted to lights.

### LONG-HORNED BEETLE *Leptostylus transversus*

**Sp S F W** Small, robust, variably colored, with highly sculptured elytra. Usually blackish brown to gray, sometimes with reflections of green. Often with broad white stripe across lower third of elytra. Feeds on many hardwoods and conifers. Attracted to lights.

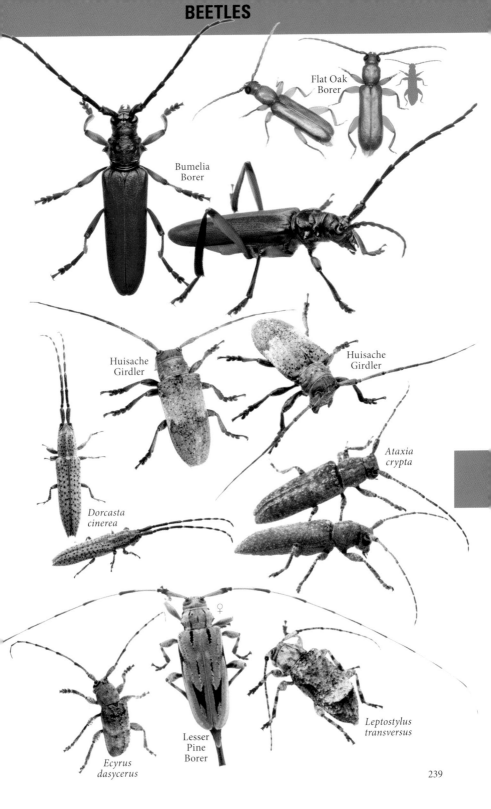

Flat Oak
Borer

Bumelia
Borer

Huisache
Girdler

Huisache
Girdler

*Ataxia
crypta*

*Dorcasta
cinerea*

♀

*Leptostylus
transversus*

Lesser
Pine
Borer

*Ecyrus
dasycerus*

239

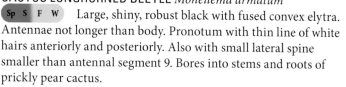

## CACTUS LONGHORNED BEETLE *Moneilema armatum* CERAMBYCIDAE

**Sp S F W** Large, shiny, robust black with fused convex elytra. Antennae not longer than body. Pronotum with thin line of white hairs anteriorly and posteriorly. Also with small lateral spine smaller than antennal segment 9. Bores into stems and roots of prickly pear cactus.

## LONG-HORNED BEETLE *Goes pulverulentus*

**Sp S F W** Elongated, brown to reddish brown, with fine white pubescence over pronotum and elytra. Pubescence absent from base and middle of elytra forming two dark bands. First antennal segment dark, remainder very pale. Pronotum with sharp spine laterally on each side. Larvae feed on heartwood from oaks, beech, sycamore, pine, and other hardwoods. Comes to lights.

## COTTONWOOD BORER *Plectrodera scalator*

**Sp S F W** Large, robust, and unmistakable black and white beetle. Long antennae, prominent spines on side of pronotum. Raised black bumps on elytra. Larvae feed on cottonwood, poplar, and willow. Adults can be found around base of trees.

## LONG-HORNED BEETLE *Sternidius mimeticus*

**Sp S F W** Small, robust, long banded antennae, brown with grayish pubescence. Dark patch laterally at middle of elytra. Larvae feed on numerous hardwoods and shrubs. Attracted to lights.

## RED MILKWEED BEETLE *Tetraopes tetrophthalmus*

**Sp S F W** Bright red species with black spots on pronotum and elytra. Antennae and legs all black. Eyes completely divided by antennae. Pronotum with central area raised. Elytral spots somewhat variable. Found on *Asclepias syriaca* milkweed, which is not common in Texas, but beetle is usually present when plant is found.

## TEXAS MILKWEED BEETLE *Tetraopes texanus*

**Sp S F W** Various shades of red with variable black spots. Usually four spots on pronotum and four spots centrally on elytra. First antennal segment and femora red. Raised area of pronotum sharply defined. Feeds on many species of milkweed.

## LEAF BEETLE *Myochrous* sp. CHRYSOMELIDAE

**Sp S F W** Small, gray, brown to black, often metallic colored and densely covered in setae. Antennae often bicolored. Lateral margins of pronotum often with sculpturing. Elytra with rows of coarse punctures. Some species active on plants at night and will also come to lights.

## LEAF BEETLE *Xanthonia* sp.

**Sp S F W** Small, brownish, oblong with pale antennae and legs. Numerous species associated with oaks and some come to lights.

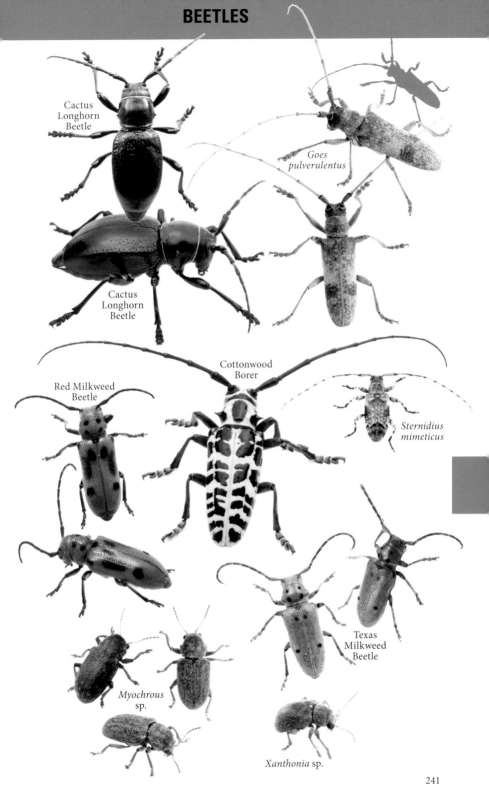

Cactus Longhorn Beetle

Cactus Longhorn Beetle

*Goes pulverulentus*

Red Milkweed Beetle

Cottonwood Borer

*Sternidius mimeticus*

Texas Milkweed Beetle

*Myochrous* sp.

*Xanthonia* sp.

## MOTTLED TORTOISE BEETLE *Deloyala guttata* CHRYSOMELIDAE

**Sp S F W** Broadly oval, convex in middle, with flanges around edges. Pronotal margins clear or golden. Elytra variable from black with golden-green markings to completely orange yellow, to completely black. Larva covers itself with branching masses of excrement and feeds on morning glory and its relatives.

## ANACUA TORTOISE BEETLE *Coptocycla texana*

**Sp S F W** Nearly circular, convex in middle, with broad, usually clear, flanges on pronotum and elytra. Elytral pattern variable with greens, coppery golds, and black, but usually with a fair extent of metallic green. Larva feeds on anacua and can be quite destructive.

## WILD OLIVE TORTOISE BEETLE *Physonota alutacea*

**Sp S F W** Broadly oval and strongly convex. Pronotum with clear flanged margins. Head concealed beneath pronotum. Elytra golden green with dark spots when disturbed (photo to right) and silver when undisturbed. Feeds on wild olive.

## AQUATIC LEAF BEETLE *Donacia* sp.

**Sp S F W** Elongated with pronotum narrower than tapering elytra that are often greenish gold. Elytra appears somewhat truncated. Antennae as long as body. Feeds on aquatic plants, including water lilies, where adults are often seen sitting.

## ROBED LEMA *Lema trabeata*

**Sp S F W** Small, orange and black, with pronotum and head much narrower than elytra. Head, antennae, pronotum, and legs all black. Elytra black with orange "C" along the outside margin. In some individuals, the orange in the middle and posteriorly can be nearly replaced by black. Feeds on ground cherries and daturas.

## SHINY FLEA BEETLE *Asphaera lustrans*

**Sp S F W** Small, oblong, convex, shiny red or orange and blue beetle. Body entirely orange or red except for metallic blue to black elytra and black antennae and distal leg segments. Feeds on skullcap. Jumps readily when disturbed.

## GLOBEMALLOW LEAF BEETLE *Calligrapha serpentina*

**Sp S F W** Oblong, convex, with pattern of black lines, curves, and dots. This pattern fairly consistent, but base color varies from red or orange to yellow green. Head and pronotum black. Base of antennae and legs reddish orange. Feeds on mallows.

## COTTONWOOD LEAF BEETLE *Chrysomela scripta*

**Sp S F W** Small, oblong, slightly convex, with red or orange margins and pattern of black spots and lines on elytra. Head and center of pronotum black with metallic reflections. First antennal segment black, middle pale, remainder black. Base color varies from pale tan to yellowish orange. Feeds on poplars and willows.

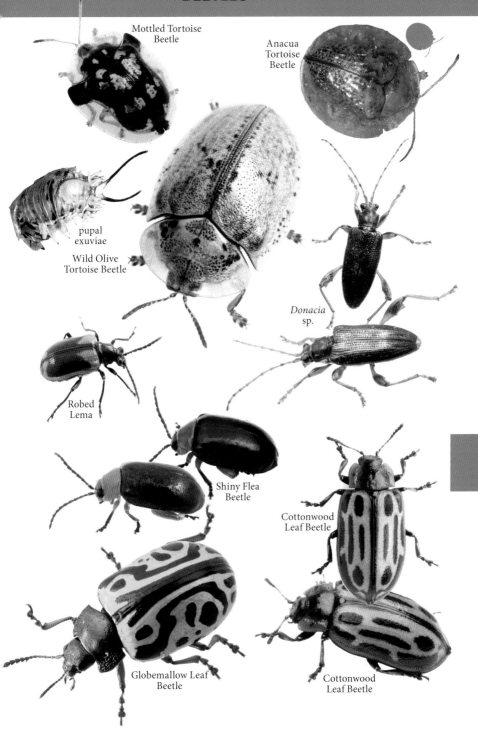

Mottled Tortoise
Beetle

Anacua
Tortoise
Beetle

pupal
exuviae

Wild Olive
Tortoise Beetle

*Donacia*
sp.

Robed
Lema

Shiny Flea
Beetle

Cottonwood
Leaf Beetle

Globemallow Leaf
Beetle

Cottonwood
Leaf Beetle

243

CHRYSOMELIDAE

### SWAMP MILKWEED LEAF BEETLE *Labidomera clivicollis*
**Sp S F W** Somewhat elongated and strongly convex with variable black pattern on yellow, orange, or red. Pronotum and head usually black, sometimes bluish. Tarsi noticeably expanded. Feeds on various milkweeds, including Talayote, in meadows, especially near wetlands.

### HALDEMAN'S GREEN POTATO BEETLE *Leptinotarsa haldemani*
**Sp S F W** Round, strongly convex, with black head and either iridescent green, purple, or blue elytra. Legs and antennae all black; tarsi noticeably expanded. Feeds on various nightshades.

### YELLOW-MARGINED LEAF BEETLE *Microtheca ochroloma*
**Sp S F W** Small, oval, shiny bronze brown or black with yellowish to orange elytral margins. Each elytra with 4 rows of coarse punctures. Distal half of tibia and all of tarsi yellow. Feeds on various members of the mustard family.

### CLAY-COLORED LEAF BEETLE *Anomoea laticlavia*
**Sp S F W** Robust, somewhat cylindrical, red, orange, or yellow with black elytral margins, variable black stripe down middle. Underside variably black or orange. Found in fields with shrubs and forbs including honey locust, beggar's lice, and mimosa.

### FLEA BEETLE *Capraita* sp.
**Sp S F W** Oval, variously patterned with light and dark browns, often bicolored antennae (distal segments darker), and enlarged hind femur. Metatarsal claw swollen. Some species attracted to lights.

### LEAF BEETLE *Derospidea brevicollis*
**Sp S F W** Elongated, pale yellowish, with two pale longitudinal stripes running down elytra. Head pale with dark posterior spot. Pronotum with two to three dark spots. Antennae uniformly dark. Femora pale; rest of leg dark. Feeds on prickly ash and citrus.

### BANDED CUCUMBER BEETLE *Diabrotica balteata*
**Sp S F W** Green, oblong, with red head and yellow spots on elytra. Pronotum sometimes lighter green than elytra. Basal antennal segments lighter. Femora all light green. Feeds on many different plants. Attracted to lights.

### SPOTTED CUCUMBER BEETLE *Diabrotica undecimpunctata*
**Sp S F W** Oblong, green or yellowish, with black head and 11–12 dark spots. Legs and antennae uniformly black or legs sometimes variously green. Larvae feed on roots of many different plants, including crops, making this a pest species in many areas.

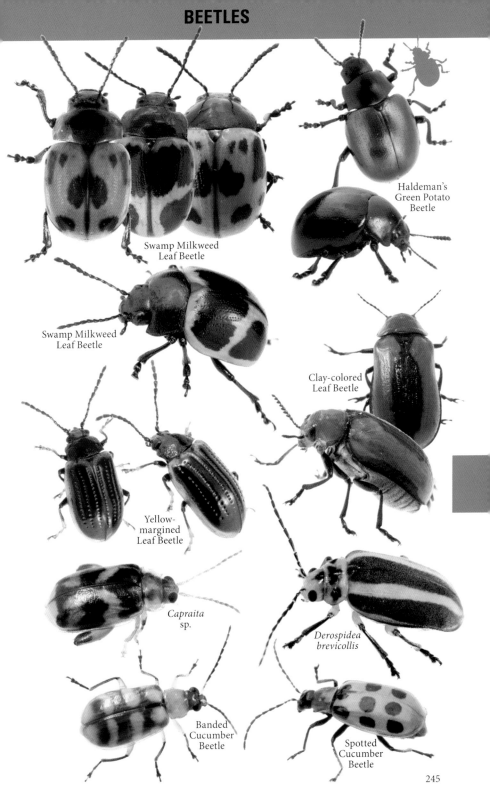

# BEETLES

Swamp Milkweed
Leaf Beetle

Haldeman's
Green Potato
Beetle

Swamp Milkweed
Leaf Beetle

Clay-colored
Leaf Beetle

Yellow-
margined
Leaf Beetle

*Capraita*
sp.

*Derospidea
brevicollis*

Banded
Cucumber
Beetle

Spotted
Cucumber
Beetle

245

### EIGHT-SPOTTED FLEA BEETLE *Omophoita cyanipennis*

**Sp S F W** Elongated, shiny, with red pronotum, and bluish-black elytra with eight white spots. Front of head with white spot. Hind femur dark reddish brown. Feeds on many different plants.

### LEAF BEETLE *Ophraella communa*

**Sp S F W** Small, elongated, pale yellow with three dark spots or stripes on pronotum and six variable dark lines on elytra. Overall color can be yellowish, brown, or gray. Distal antennal segments darker than basal. Feeds on ragweed.

### ELM LEAF BEETLE *Xanthogaleruca luteola*

**Sp S F W** Elongated, oblong, yellow to olive green, with dark spot between eyes and pronotum with three dark spots. Head often with additional smaller anterior dark spot. Middle spot on pronotum somewhat narrowed in middle. Broad dark stripe along outer margin of each elytron and sometimes a shorter medial stripe. Feeds on elms for which it is considered a pest.

### CASE-BEARING LEAF BEETLE *Cryptocephalus leucomelas*

**Sp S F W** Small, short, compact, with pale pronotum and elytra marked with red, brown, or black stripes. Head and legs reddish. Antennae uniformly colored. Pronotum with four longitudinal dark stripes. Elytra typically with two broad, irregular, transverse stripes and four small apical spots. Feeds on poplar and willow.

### WARTY LEAF BEETLE *Neochlamisus* sp.

**Sp S F W** Small, compact, dark brown to black, and very warty. Head, antennae, and legs can all be retracted close to body giving the appearance of caterpillar frass. Feeds on various plants.

### OAK TIMBERWORM *Arrhenodes minutus*

**Sp S F W** Elongated, slender, reddish brown, with short yellow stripes on elytra. Pronotum longer than wide and wider than elytra at base. Male with broad snout; female slender. Found on dead and dying trees. Attracted to lights.

### MARBLED FUNGUS WEEVIL *Euparius marmoreus*

**Sp S F W** Compact, brownish, gray, or black, with white pubescence and rounded snout. Elytra with pair of small dark spots anteriorly and larger spots at middle. Tibia and tarsi banded. Found under bark feeding on fungi. Attracted to lights.

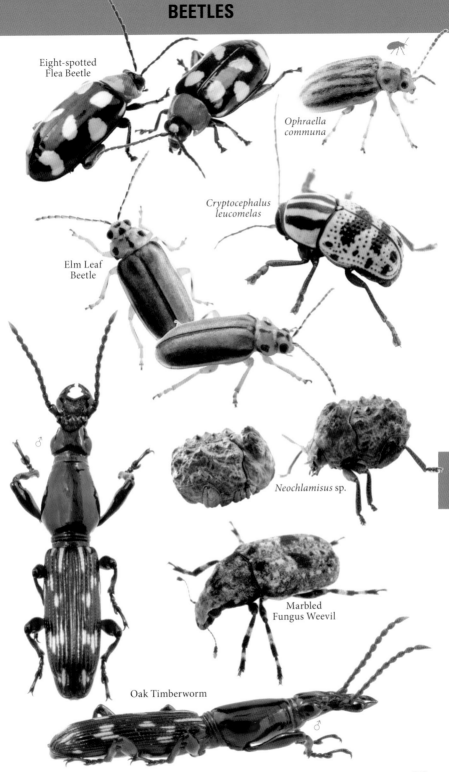

Eight-spotted
Flea Beetle

*Ophraella
communa*

*Cryptocephalus
leucomelas*

Elm Leaf
Beetle

♂

*Neochlamisus* sp.

Marbled
Fungus Weevil

Oak Timberworm

♂

**IRONWEED CURCULIO** *Rhodobaenus tredecimpunctatus*
**Sp S F W** Bright red, elongated, with distinct snout and black spots on pronotum and elytra. Head, antennae, and legs black. Central spot on pronotum similar in size to others, though usually elongated. Larvae develop inside stems of composites where adults are found on the flowers.

**GRANARY WEEVIL** *Sitophilus* sp.
**Sp S F W** Small, elongated, reddish brown, with orange spot or stripes on elytra. Pronotum and elytra densely and coarsely punctated. Antennae and legs reddish brown. Pale elytral spots, sometimes joined to form broad, diffuse stripe. Found in grains.

**WEEVIL** *Epicaerus* sp.
**Sp S F W** Compact, pear-shaped with truncated elytra when viewed laterally, and clothed in gray and white scales. Elytral pattern somewhat variable even within species. Found on a variety of vegetation. Some species attracted to lights.

**GOLDEN-HEADED WEEVIL** *Compsus auricephalus*
**Sp S F W** Robust, pastel colored, with head darker than rest of body. Head usually with at least some pink, brown, or gray coloration. Pronotum and elytra gray, white, or more often pastel green or blue with iridescence. Pronotum with two lateral raised smooth ridges. Elytra with several raised ridges. Feeds on numerous plants; sometimes considered a pest of citrus.

**WHITE-FRINGED WEEVIL** *Naupactus leucoloma*
**Sp S F W** Compact, elongated, and somewhat cylindrical, with pale stripe laterally on pronotum and elytra. Gray, brown, or black with pale scales. Rostrum short and broad with a distinct ridge on sides. Pronotum slightly longer than wide. Introduced from South America, only females known in the U.S.

**ACORN WEEVIL** *Curculio* sp.
**Sp S F W** Variously colored reddish, yellow, brown, and gray; oval and robust body with proboscis at least twice as long as pronotum. Elytra variously patterned with pale scales on dark background. Feeds on various nuts and acorns.

**ANT-LIKE WEEVIL** *Myrmex* sp.
**Sp S F W** Tiny, shiny, black, ant-like with sparse, short, erect white hairs on elytra. Scutellum white. White band of setae on sides below elytra. Femora slightly swollen. Found on various plants.

**RAGWEED WEEVIL** *Lixus scrobicollis*
**Sp S F W** Elongated, nearly cylindrical, dark, clothed with pale scales, and short, stout rostrum. Pronotum slightly longer than wide with a pale stripe along each side. Feeds on ragweed.

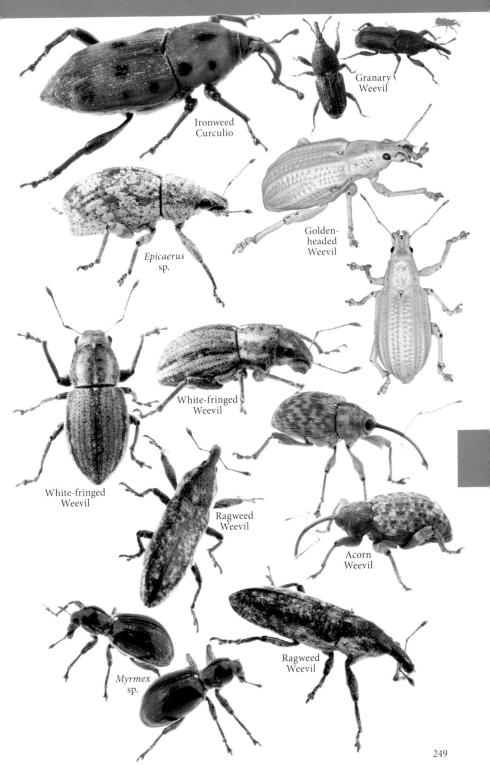

Ironweed
Curculio

Granary
Weevil

*Epicaerus*
sp.

Golden-
headed
Weevil

White-fringed
Weevil

White-fringed
Weevil

Ragweed
Weevil

Acorn
Weevil

*Myrmex*
sp.

Ragweed
Weevil

# Flies
# Order Diptera

Waved Light Fly
(*Pyrgota undata*)

**NATURAL HISTORY**  Flies are one of the most ubiquitous groups of insects occurring in nearly every habitat imaginable, including many having a close association with humans. True flies have only two (*di*) wings (*ptera*) with the hind wings reduced to a pair of stalks called halteres that act as gyroscopic or equilibrium organs when in flight. As a group, they arguably have more impact on man than any other insect order. This is because a number of species, particularly those with aquatic larvae, are major vectors of disease. It is estimated that a sixth of the world's population is infected with a fly-borne illness transmitted by mosquitos, black flies, sand flies, and others.

The mouthparts of flies are the sucking type and are variously modified to include piercing, lapping, and sponging functions. They have complete development and their larvae, often referred to as maggots, typically have no visible legs and appear wormlike. They occur in a dazzling array of habitats from freshwater, to various decaying organic material, to plants where they can be miners within the leaves, feeding on the plant itself, or predators.

The flies can be broken up into two main groups. The more primitive "nematocera" have many-segmented, relatively long antennae, and generally appear midge-mosquito-or gnat-like with dainty bodies and long legs. The more derived Brachycera contains the majority of our flies. They are generally stout-bodied flies with shorter, three-segmented antennae that can be variously modified bearing a style or arista (stout bristle).

250

# Identifying Characters

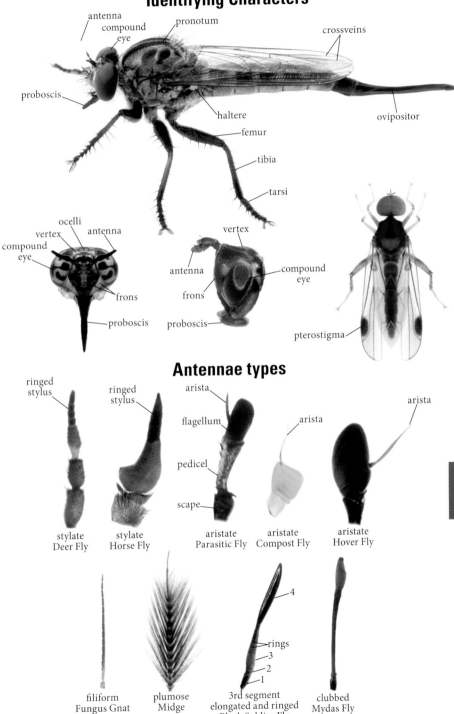

antenna
compound eye
pronotum
crossveins
proboscis
haltere
ovipositor
femur
tibia
tarsi

ocelli
vertex
antenna
compound eye
frons
proboscis

vertex
antenna
frons
proboscis
compound eye

pterostigma

# Antennae types

ringed stylus
stylate
Deer Fly

ringed stylus
stylate
Horse Fly

arista
flagellum
pedicel
scape
aristate
Parasitic Fly

arista
aristate
Compost Fly

arista
aristate
Hover Fly

filiform
Fungus Gnat

plumose
Midge

4
rings
3
2
1
3rd segment
elongated and ringed
Black Soldier Fly

clubbed
Mydas Fly

251

### PHANTOM CRANE FLY *Bittacomorpha clavipes*
**PTYCHOPTERIDAE**

**Sp S F W** Thin, elongated, wispy, with short wings, long thin antennae, and black and white–banded legs. The base of the tarsi are swollen and black. Thorax swollen, humpbacked, with white stripe down middle. Found in swamps and wetland environments.

### MARCH FLY *Dilophus orbatus*
**BIBIONIDAE**

**Sp S F W** Black body and wings with elongated head, stout antennae shorter than head, and thorax convex with two transverse rows of spines anteriorly. Front tibia with two rings of stout spines. Found on flowers in meadows and fields.

### LOVEBUG *Plecia nearctica*

**Sp S F W** Black body and wings with antennae no longer than head, and reddish-orange, humpbacked, convex thorax. Thorax black laterally and ventrally. Males with large, contiguous eyes. Often seen in copula and have mass swarms in the spring and fall, making them a nuisance pest, especially along the coast.

### CREOSOTE GALL MIDGE *Asphondylia auripila*
**CECIDOMYIIDAE**

**Sp S F W** Larvae of this fly make distinctive brown galls in creosote bush branches. The larvae have symbiotic fungi. The fly itself is somewhat nondescript.

### GRAPE TUBE GALLMAKER *Schizomyia viticola*

**Sp S F W** Larvae of this fly make bright red, upward-pointing tubes on the leaves of grape. There can be hundreds of these galls on a single leaf. The adult fly is nondescript.

### FUNGUS GNAT *Mycomya* sp.
**MYCETOPHILIDAE**

**Sp S F W** This is a group of diverse, long-legged dainty flies whose larvae feed on mycelia, spores, or fruiting bodies of fungi. The adults have antennae about half the length of the body and sometimes darker distally. The abdomen is elongated, thin, and often with dark banding. Some species are attracted to lights.

### BITING MIDGE *Culicoides* sp.
**CERATOPOGONIDAE**

**Sp S F W** Minute, biting flies with antennae extending back to thorax and many species with patterned wings. Sometimes called "no-see-ums," these can be abundant, but difficult to see. Only females bite and usually do so in the evening or at night. They can be a serious pest that vector diseases to both humans and livestock.

### DARK-WINGED FUNGUS GNATS
**SCIARIDAE**

**Sp S F W** These are small, generally dark, long-legged gnats with eyes that meet on top of their head forming a narrow bridge between the ocelli and antennae. They most often occur around swamps and forests, but some are found in caves or breed in flowerpots.

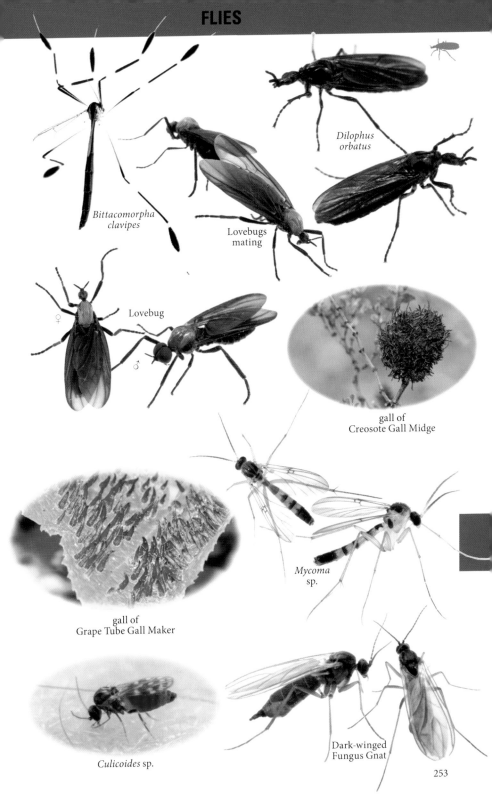

*Bittacomorpha clavipes*

Lovebugs mating

*Dilophus orbatus*

Lovebug

♀

♂

gall of Creosote Gall Midge

gall of Grape Tube Gall Maker

*Mycoma* sp.

*Culicoides* sp.

Dark-winged Fungus Gnat

253

### BITING MIDGES *Forcipomyia* sp.      CERATOPOGONIDAE
**Sp S F W** These are tiny ectoparasites of other insects, often seen sucking the blood from the wing veins of insects such as dragonflies, lacewings, and moths. Males have longer hairs on the antennae than females. Eggs are laid in decaying organic matter including dung.

### MIDGE *Chironomus* sp.      CHIRONOMIDAE
**Sp S F W** Elongated, cylindrical, gray, tan, or greenish bodies. Males with plumose antennae and usually a pair of small tubercles between and above the basal segment in both sexes. Pronotum wide in the middle with a notch. Larvae of many species are "blood worms" possessing hemoglobin and found in fresh water that may be highly polluted or clean. Adults do not bite.

### MOSQUITO *Aedes* spp.      CULICIDAE
**Sp S F W** This is a large and diverse genus. Many species have dark legs strongly banded with white. Most also have the dark thorax and abdomen with contrasting white stripes and spots.

### MOSQUITO *Anopheles crucians*
**Sp S F W** Wings with distinctive dark spots giving veins a banded appearance. Long palps dark, with pale bands. When at rest and feeding, usually holds body at a 45 degree angle or greater to the substrate. Larvae occur in a variety of habitats including swamps.

### GALLINIPPER *Psorophora ciliata*
**Sp S F W** Very large yellowish-brown mosquito with thick black tufts of setae on legs giving them a banded appearance. Pronotum with golden-brown stripe medially. Larvae are found in both temporary and permanent pools with weedy or woody edges where larvae are predaceous on other mosquitoes. Females feed on blood.

### MOSQUITO *Psorophora howardii*
**Sp S F W** Very large mosquito without banded legs, but lacking tufts of setae and without gold stripe down center of pronotum. Female with dark wings. Larvae predaceous. Females feed on blood.

### ELEPHANT MOSQUITO *Toxorhynchites rutilus*
**Sp S F W** Very large mosquito covered with metallic blue scales. Proboscis large and curved downward. Larvae breed in tree holes and artificial containers in deciduous forests. Adults feed on nectar.

### BLACK FLY *Simulium* sp.      SIMULIIDAE
**Sp S F W** Small, black, or gray, strongly humpbacked fly with variously marked pronotum. Antennae multi-segmented and relatively thick. Legs often banded. Larvae found in various freshwater habitats. Males have large, contiguous eyes. Females feed on blood.

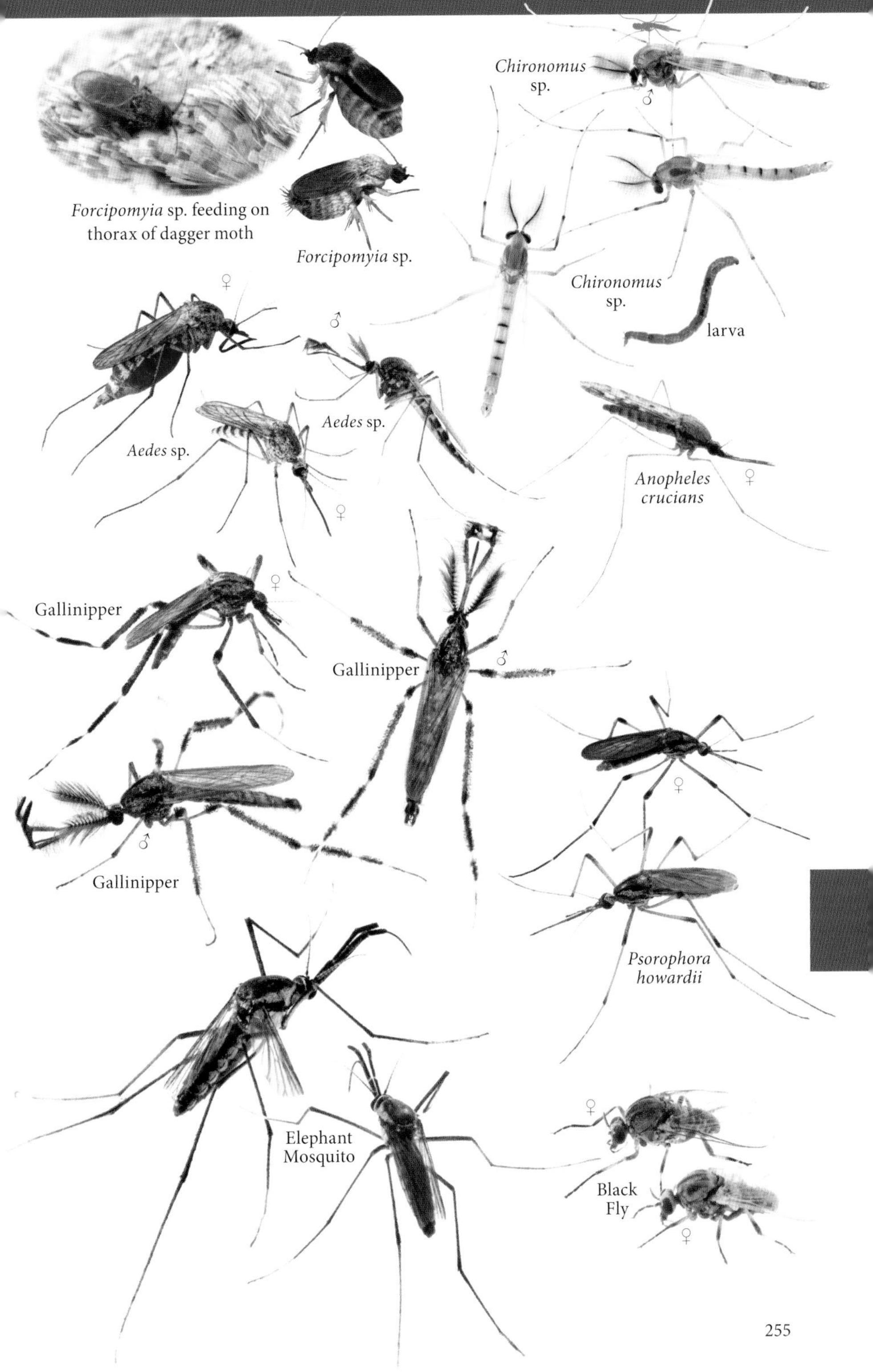

Forcipomyia sp. feeding on thorax of dagger moth

Forcipomyia sp.

Chironomus sp. ♂

Chironomus sp.

larva

Aedes sp. ♀

Aedes sp. ♂

Aedes sp. ♀

Anopheles crucians ♀

Gallinipper ♀

Gallinipper ♂

Gallinipper ♂

♀

Psorophora howardii

Elephant Mosquito

Black Fly ♀

♀

255

**FILTER FLY** *Clogmia albipunctata*          PSYCHODIDAE

**Sp S F W**   Small, mothlike fly with pale, hairy antennae, white spots on edges of wings, dark spots in middle, and white basally on leg segments. This cosmopolitan fly is found in buildings where larvae live on organic matter in drains. Also found in stagnant ponds.

**LIMONIID CRANE FLY** *Eugnophomyia luctuosa*          LIMONIIDAE

**Sp S F W**   Small black crane fly. Wings sometimes with iridescent sheen. Antennae long, 14–16 segments (13 in Tipulidae). Legs long. Larvae are aquatic and are found in various aquatic habitats. Adults visit flowers and are attracted to lights.

**CRANE FLY** *Tipula texanus*          TIPULIDAE

**Sp S F W**   Medium sized, grayish tan, with unmarked wings and abdomen. Eyes green. Common and ubiquitous early spring species in central Texas.

**CRANE FLY** *Brachypremna dispellens*

**Sp S F W**   Grayish tan, with very long, thin, white legs that it uses to hang vertically. Most commonly found along margins, especially undercut banks, of streams and creeks where it may aggregate in large numbers. Larvae are aquatic.

**TIGER CRANE FLY** *Nephrotoma* sp.

**Sp S F W**   Orangish-brown body with distinct darker markings on somewhat shiny thorax, usually tinted wings, and long legs. Distal leg segments often with a dark band. Attracted to lights.

**GIANT CRANE FLY** *Tipula* sp.

**Sp S F W**   Extremely large crane flies, with pale, darkly marked thorax, orange abdomen with black stripes, and wings with some maculation. Legs with distal dark bands. Attracted to lights.

**BLACK SOLDIER FLY** *Hermetia illucens*          STRATIOMYIDAE

**Sp S F W**   Black, greenish eyes with dark reticulated markings, antennae somewhat clubbed and V-shaped, and base of abdomen with pair of clear spots. Tibia white basally, dark distally; tarsi all white. Wings dark, with purplish sheen. Larvae breed in compost, outdoor toilets, and poultry manure.

**COMPOST FLY** *Ptecticus trivittatus*

**Sp S F W**   Elongated, large bright green eyes, lime green–yellowish body. Pronotum brownish above, yellowish green below. Legs pale with hind tibia and tarsi darker. Wings slightly amber. Larvae breed in compost. Adults occasionally come to lights.

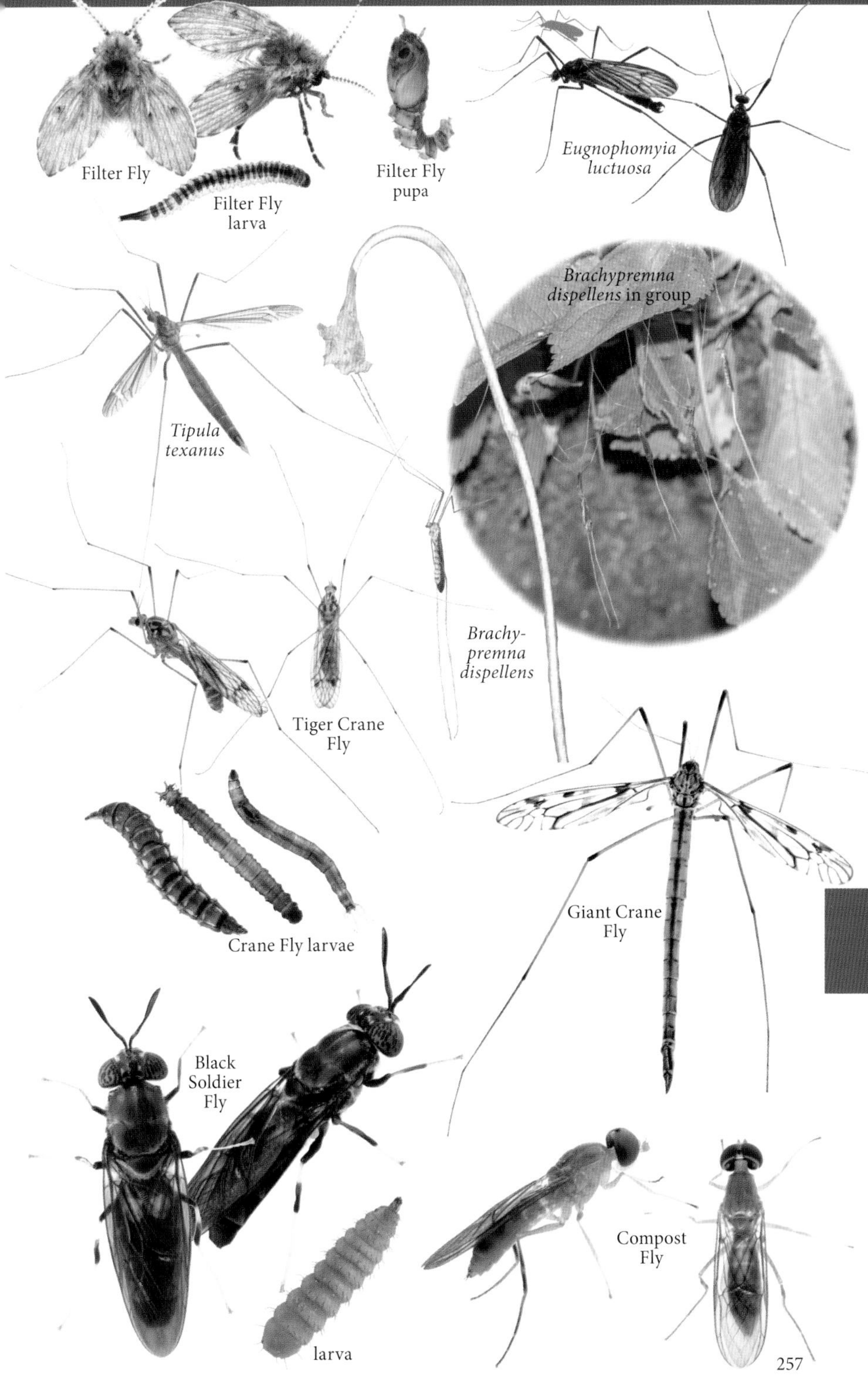

Filter Fly

Filter Fly larva

Filter Fly pupa

*Eugnophomyia luctuosa*

*Tipula texanus*

*Brachypremna dispellens* in group

*Brachy-premna dispellens*

Tiger Crane Fly

Crane Fly larvae

Giant Crane Fly

Black Soldier Fly

larva

Compost Fly

## GOLDEN-BACKED SNIPE FLY *Chrysopilus thoracicus*

**Sp S F W** Black with bright golden thorax, dark wings, and white legs. Abdomen with interrupted white or silvery band of hairs on each segment.

## SNIPE FLY *Rhagio* sp.

**Sp S F W** Pale to dark, sometimes with patterned wings, and abdomen often with dark transverse stripes. Pronotum sometimes with longitudinal stripes. Legs variably colored, but with two spurs on hind tibia. Attracted to lights.

## DEER FLY *Chrysops geminatus*

**Sp S F W** Yellow, with three dark longitudinal stripes on thorax. Base of antennae pale, tips dark. Eyes with green and red reticulated pattern. Wings with two distal dark bands. Abdomen yellow with series of interrupted transverse black bars. Second segment with dark inverted "V." Larvae live in spring-fed drainages.

## DEER FLY *Chrysops brunneus*

**Sp S F W** Reddish brown species with three narrow dark stripes on pronotum. Eyes with reticulated green, red, and black pattern. Wings diffusely dark with tan pterostigma (distal cell along leading edge of wing) often visible.

## HORSE FLY *Chlorotabanus crepuscularis*

**Sp S F W** Robust, hairy, yellowish green with reddish or yellow eyes. Active at dusk and dawn. Larvae predaceous in moist soil and floating vegetation near or in water. Adults occasionally visit lights.

## HORSE FLY *Leucotabanus annulatus*

**Sp S F W** Tan-brown above, grayish white below. Eyes green with low transverse lines. Thorax hairy and relatively unmarked. Abdomen dark with pale medial and transverse stripes and a pair of pale spots. Tarsi darker than rest of legs. Larvae are predators in rotting wood and tree holes. Adults attracted to lights.

## HORSE FLY *Tabanus americanus*

**Sp S F W** Largest horse fly, with bluish-green eyes and dark body and huge mouth parts. Underside dark with white bands of setae laterally. Legs reddish brown. Size alone makes this species unmistakable. Found in wooded habitats. Females have painful bite.

## BLACK HORSE FLY *Tabanus atratus*

**Sp S F W** Large, all black, including wings, with large mouth parts. Male with large contiguous eyes; females have them divided. Larvae live along wetland, pond, and stream margins. Females feed on mammalian blood and can be a pest to livestock. They have a painful bite and are capable of transmitting diseases, including anthrax, mechanically, but is not known to be a biological vector.

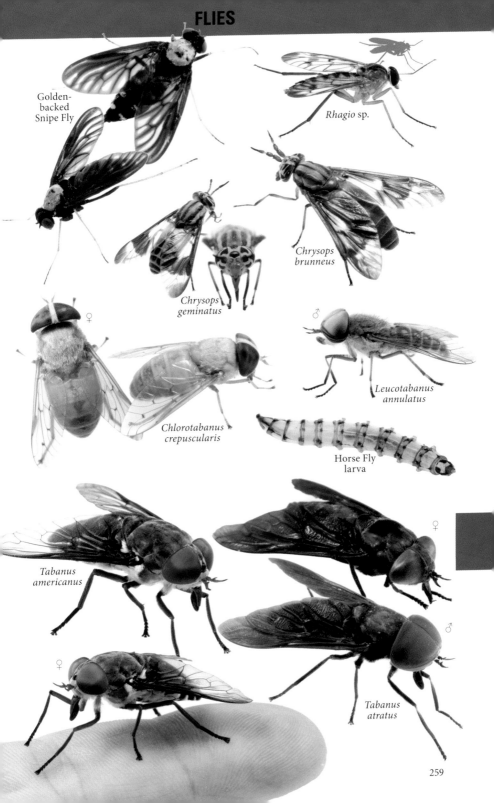

Golden-backed Snipe Fly

*Rhagio* sp.

*Chrysops geminatus*

*Chrysops brunneus*

♀

*Chlorotabanus crepuscularis*

♂

*Leucotabanus annulatus*

Horse Fly larva

*Tabanus americanus*

♀

♂

*Tabanus atratus*

♀

259

**ROBBER FLY** *Asilius sericeus*                    ASILIDAE

**Sp S F W**  Stout, reddish brown with dark stripe running down middle of tan pronotum. Wings reddish brown. Legs fairly uniform in color. Hunts insects visiting flowers, especially butterflies in open meadows and fields.

**ROBBER FLY** *Atomosia puella*

**Sp S F W**  Small, with greenish-red eyes and black, cylindrical abdomen with narrow white rings. Legs black except for basal half of tibia. Found in open fields where it feeds on small flying insects.

**ROBBER FLY** *Diogmites* sp.

**Sp S F W**  Greenish-red eyes with tan to reddish-brown body. Thorax usually with darker brown longitudinal stripes. Abdomen often with dark lateral stripes. Common in both woodland and open meadows where they hunt bees and similar flying insects. They typically hang from vegetation with their forelegs while eating prey. Sometimes referred to as the Green-eyed Monster.

**ROBBER FLY** *Efferia albibarbis*

**Sp S F W**  Gray with elongated abdomen terminating in broad white band and black tip. Femora gray, tibia mostly orange, tarsi gray or black. Widespread, found in open habitats including roadsides and fields.

**ROBBER FLY** *Holopogon* sp.

**Sp S F W**  Small, but robust robber fly, usually with white bands on dark abdomen. Legs uniformly black with hind tibiae swollen; twice as wide as front tibia. Commonly seen perching at the tip of twigs and stems where it hunts small insect prey.

**BEE-LIKE ROBBER FLY** *Laphria saffrana*

**Sp S F W**  Distinctive yellow, black, and orange robber fly. Black head and thorax covered with numerous yellows hairs; the latter mostly black in the middle. Abdomen orange and black and legs orange. A good mimic of yellow jackets. Adults often sit on tree stumps.

**BEE-LIKE ROBBER FLY** *Laphria macquarti*

**Sp S F W**  Large, hairy, yellow and black robber fly that mimics the American Bumble Bee (*Bombus pennsylvancius*). It is mostly black with a yellow thorax and basal abdominal segments and some yellow on legs. Prefers small beetles, but will take a wide range of prey.

**ROBBER FLY** *Leptogaster* sp.

**Sp S F W**  Very long, somewhat delicate, with thin banded abdomen and banded legs. Distal portion of hind tibia swollen. Found in meadows hanging from or perched on branch tips with the abdomen directed obliquely from the body. Some species attracted to lights.

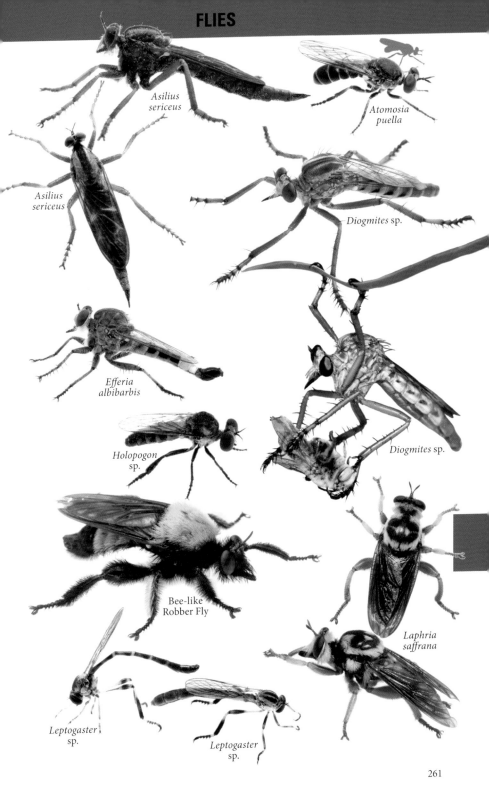

*Asilius sericeus*

*Atomosia puella*

*Asilius sericeus*

*Diogmites* sp.

*Efferia albibarbis*

*Diogmites* sp.

*Holopogon sp.*

Bee-like Robber Fly

*Laphria saffrana*

*Leptogaster sp.*

*Leptogaster sp.*

261

## ROBBER FLY *Machimus* sp.

**Sp S F W** Gray to reddish brown. Thorax usually with smooth, dark, irregular spots laterally and central longitudinal stripe. Legs may be banded and base of femur darker than remainder of leg.

## BEELZEBUB BEE-KILLER *Mallophora leschenaulti*

**Sp S F W** Very large, robust, mostly black; hairy head, thorax, abdomen, and legs. Back of head and base of abdomen yellow. Hind tibia with thick cluster of hairs. Mimics bumblebees. Takes a variety of prey, even occasionally hummingbirds!

## BEE KILLER *Mallophora fautrix*

**Sp S F W** Hairy, yellow and black bee mimic. Head and abdomen yellow. Top of thorax black except for posterior margin. Base of hind femur yellow, rest of legs hairy and black. Tarsal pads broad and yellow. Perches on grass and vegetation in open fields and wooded habitats.

## ROBBER FLY *Ospriocerus* sp.

**Sp S F W** Species in this genus are quite variable. Some reddish brown, others black with red abdomen. Often uniformly colored. Antennae longer than head.

## ROBBER FLY *Polacantha* sp.

**Sp S F W** Tan, gray, or reddish brown, with long, thin abdomen. Legs usually paler than rest of body. Perches on grass blades or twigs in open areas.

## ROBBER FLY *Promachus bastardii*

**Sp S F W** Dark brown to black with white rings on abdomen and white tip. Face with yellow setae. Dark eyes sometimes with greenish cast. Tarsal pads broad and yellow. Found in a variety of habitats, often seems to specialize on hunting wasps and bees. Perches on ground and vegetation.

## ROBBER FLY *Stenopogon rufibarbis*

**Sp S F W** Grayish brown with white hairs on face; mostly bare, black thorax and abdomen. Femora mostly black, distal apices tibia and tarsi reddish brown. Perches on ground and on vegetation.

## ROBBER FLY *Triorla interrupta*

**Sp S F W** Large, gray thorax and abdomen with distinctive dark bands on middle abdominal segments. Legs with prominent spines and reddish tinge distally. Top of thorax darker than sides. Hunts in open grasslands and meadows.

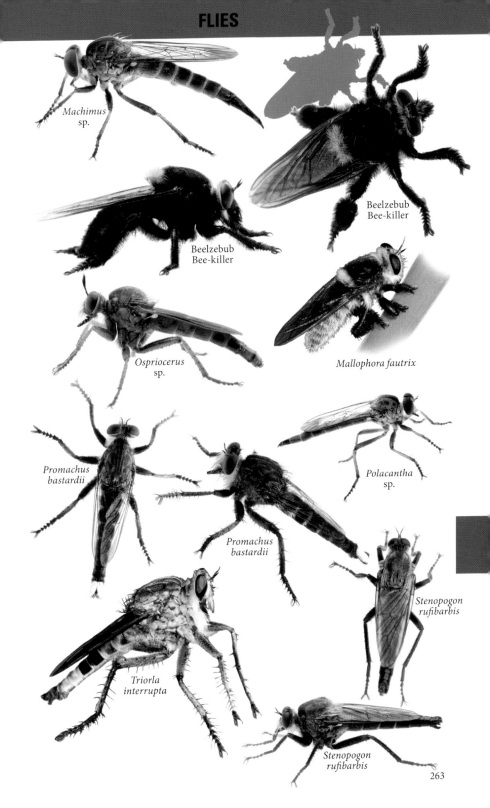

*Machimus* sp.

Beelzebub Bee-killer

Beelzebub Bee-killer

*Ospriocerus* sp.

*Mallophora fautrix*

*Promachus bastardii*

*Polacantha* sp.

*Promachus bastardii*

*Stenopogon rufibarbis*

*Triorla interrupta*

*Stenopogon rufibarbis*

263

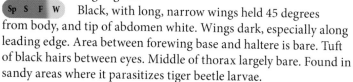

### BEE FLY *Anthrax georgicus*

Sp **S** F **W**   Black, with long, narrow wings held 45 degrees from body, and tip of abdomen white. Wings dark, especially along leading edge. Area between forewing base and haltere is bare. Tuft of black hairs between eyes. Middle of thorax largely bare. Found in sandy areas where it parasitizes tiger beetle larvae.

### BEE FLY *Chrysanthrax cypris*

Sp **S** F **W**   Black, densely clothed in golden-orange hairs. Wings long, narrow, and held 45 degrees from body and with basal two-thirds brown ending at an oblique angle posteriorly. Thought to be an external parasitoid of tiphiid and anthophorid pupae.

### BEE FLY *Exoprosopa* sp.

Sp **S** F **W**   Dark brown, thorax clothed with tan-brown hairs. Abdomen mostly black, with two white bands of hairs. Wings long, narrow, and held 45 degrees or greater from body. They are diffusely brown along leading edge and along the veins. Parasitoid of thread-waisted wasp, tiphiid, and spider wasp pupae.

### BEE FLY *Neodiplocampta miranda*

Sp **S** F **W**   Black thorax clothed with golden hairs and abdomen orange with some black areas in the middle of some anterior segments. Wings long, narrow, and held 45 degrees from body with variable color pattern, but diffusely dark along leading edge with dark brown over crossveins. Found on low-growing flowers.

### BEE FLY *Poecilanthrax lucifer*

Sp **S** F **W**   Dark body clothed in yellowish-golden hairs, including front of face. Abdomen with narrow and dark transverse bands. Wings diffusely brown; darkest along anterior edge. Found in ubiquitous habitats where it parasitizes larvae of noctuid moths. Adults frequently visit flowers to feed on nectar and pollen.

### BEE FLY *Villa* sp.

Sp **S** F **W**   Dark body, variously marked, but often with pale bands on abdomen. Wings long, narrow, relatively clear, and held 45 degrees from body. Endoparasites on moth, fly, and beetle larvae.

### TIGER BEE FLY *Xenox tigrinus*

Sp **S** F **W**   Large, black, with long, narrow wings distinctively patterned and held 45 degrees from body. Larvae are parasitoids of carpenter bees. Readily perches on man-made structures.

### MYDAS FLY *Mydas clavatus*

Sp **S** F **W**   Large, black, elongated, with prominent eyes and top of abdominal segment 2 bright reddish orange. Antennae as long as front tibia and clubbed. Found in meadows and forests.

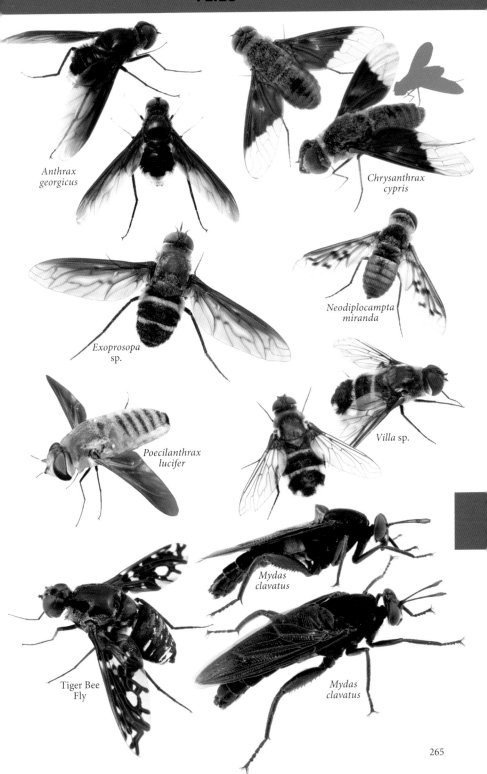

*Anthrax georgicus*

*Chrysanthrax cypris*

*Exoprosopa* sp.

*Neodiplocampta miranda*

*Poecilanthrax lucifer*

*Villa* sp.

*Mydas clavatus*

Tiger Bee Fly

*Mydas clavatus*

### STILETTO FLY *Ozodiceromyia* sp.        THEREVIDAE

**Sp S F W**   Grayish with tapering black and white abdomen. Eyes not separated on top. Top of thorax usually dark gray or black, bottom with thick mat of white hairs. Found in both open areas and woodlands. Visits flowers and attracted to lights.

### LONGLEGGED FLY *Condylostylus* sp.      DOLICHOPODIDAE

**Sp S F W**   Small, metallic green, gold, or red with long legs. Stiff vertical bristles present on head. Found in woodlands near water. Larvae develop in wet or dry soil. Adults have elaborate courtship behavior and are commonly seen moving around tops of leaves.

### LONGLEGGED FLY *Condylostylus sipho*

**Sp S F W**   Coppery, greenish gold, with black band distally in wings that partially or entirely closes a clear spot. Femora and tibia pale, tarsi dark. Antennae black. Found in woodlands near water.

### DANCE FLY *Empis* sp.          EMPIDIDAE

**Sp S F W**   Gray or tan with small round head, long stout proboscis, red eyes, somewhat tapering abdomen, and long legs. Commonly visits flowers, especially around water. Attracted to lights.

### BALLOON FLY *Hilara* sp.

**Sp S F W**   Small, stout, with round head bearing short, stout, downward-projecting proboscis. Eyes usually dull red. Male with first front tarsal segment swollen. May be seen resting on leaves. Some species attracted to lights.

### HYBOTID DANCE FLY *Syneches thoracicus*     HYBOTIDAE

**Sp S F W**   Small, stout, with extremely swollen thorax raised well above height of head and large, bright red eyes. Stout proboscis obliquely forward. Wings with dark pterostigma. Females have contiguous eyes. May be common on broad-leaved foliage in woodlands. Sometimes will come to lights.

### MEXICAN CACTUS FLY *Copestylum mexicanum*    SYRPHIDAE

**Sp S F W**   Robust, black thorax, bluish or black abdomen, and apical portion of wing black. Leading edge of wings amber beyond basal black area. Proboscis wedge shaped and directed downward below head. Visits different flowers.

### HOVER FLY *Eristalis stipator*

**Sp S F W**   White face, shiny, dark thorax clothed with pale pubescence, and white-banded black abdomen. Base of abdomen with pair of median projecting tan or brown triangles. Leading edge of wings with diffuse amber basally. Common visitor to flowers. Larvae are aquatic and called rat-tailed maggots.

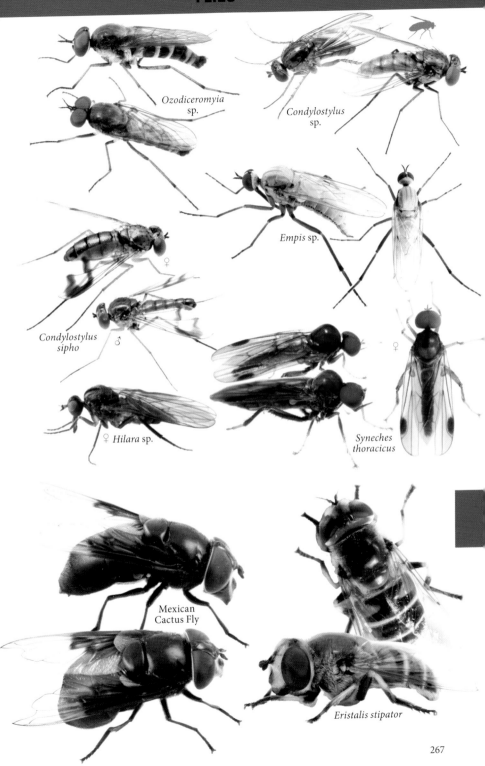

*Ozodiceromyia* sp.

*Condylostylus* sp.

*Empis* sp.

*Condylostylus sipho* ♂

♀

♀ *Hilara* sp.

*Syneches thoracicus*

Mexican Cactus Fly

*Eristalis stipator*

267

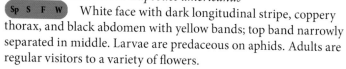

### AMERICAN HOVER FLY *Eupeodes americanus*  SYRPHIDAE

**Sp S F W**  White face with dark longitudinal stripe, coppery thorax, and black abdomen with yellow bands; top band narrowly separated in middle. Larvae are predaceous on aphids. Adults are regular visitors to a variety of flowers.

### YELLOWJACKET HOVER FLY *Milesia virginiensis*

**Sp S F W**  Large, distinctively patterned yellow, orange, and black, mimicking a yellow jacket. Abdomen somewhat flattened and covered with short hairs distally and below. Perches on fallen logs and on the ground. Flies with loud buzzing sound and somewhat aggressively, sometimes investigating people.

### HOVER FLY *Ocyptamus fuscipennis*

**Sp S F W**  Dark thorax with elongated, cylindrical, reddish-brown to almost black, somewhat banded abdomen. Wings diffusely dark with clear spot at wing tips. Abdomen somewhat narrowed basally when viewed from above. Larvae predaceous on aphids. Adults visit flowers.

### HOVER FLY *Ornidia obesa*

**Sp S F W**  Robust, metallic green or purplish blue with large green eyes. Wings with dark spot midway along leading edge and tiny dark spot at pterostigma. Maggots feed in outdoor toilets and similar situations and adults are known to carry *Salmonella*.

### HOVER FLY *Spilomyia longicornis*

**Sp S F W**  Yellow and black with distinctively patterned eyes. Black thorax with yellow upside down "V" posteriorly. Abdomen black with narrow yellow bands. Front tibia and tarsi black. Mimics yellow jackets and paper wasps. Visits flowers.

### THICK-LEGGED HOVER FLY *Syritta pipiens*

**Sp S F W**  Elongated, with large round head of nearly all eyes, cylindrical banded abdomen, and swollen hind femora. Apical third of hind femur with row of fine spines along bottom edge. Side of thorax with large pale spot. Larvae found in compost, manure, and other decaying organic matter.

### HOVER FLY *Toxomerus geminatus*

**Sp S F W**  Bronzy-black thorax outlined in yellow posteriorly; abdomen elongated with dark basal bands, followed by yellow, then diffuse reddish orange. Adults are common visitors to flowers.

### HOVER FLY *Xylota* sp.

**Sp S F W**  Dark, coppery-green, black abdomen with large pale spots or bands, and white tibia. Femora black; hind femora slightly swollen. Distal tarsi black. Visits flowers.

American
Hover Fly

Yellowjacket
Hover Fly

*Ocyptamus
fuscipennis*

*Ornidia
obesa*

Hover Fly
larva

*Spilomyia
longicornis*

Thick-
legged
Hover Fly

*Xylota* sp.

*Xylota* sp.

*Toxomerus geminatus*

### SCUTTLE FLY *Pseudacteon tricuspis*

Sp **S F W**  Minute, brown fly with a humped back and dark eyes. Introduced from Argentina to control the Red Imported Fire Ant. Adults parasitize ant workers, laying an egg in the thorax. The larva hatches and migrates to the head, eating out the head capsule.

### SCUTTLE FLY *Megaselia scalaris*

Sp **S F W**  Small, tan, robust fly with small head, dark, eyes and dark sclerites down an otherwise pale abdomen. Common species in homes where the larvae scavenge in moist decaying plant and animal matter. Adults have a characteristic zig-zag walking habit.

### HOUSE FLY *Musca domestica*
MUSCIDAE

Sp **S F W**  Grayish-tan, bristly thorax with faint dark longitudinal stripes, white face, reddish eyes, and usually a hint of amber at base of wings. Found in many cosmopolitan situations including homes, farms, stables, and garbage dumps.

### BLACK BLOW FLY *Phormia regina*
CALLIPHORIDAE

Sp **S F W**  Dark metallic blue or green with dull red eyes, bristly thorax, and first spiracle orange. Attracted to dung and carrion. Maggots are sometimes used to clean wounds in serious injuries and to forensically determine how long a corpse has been exposed to the environment.

### COMMON GREEN BOTTLE FLY *Lucilia sericata*

Sp **S F W**  Robust, bright metallic green, yellow green, or golden bronze, red eyes, white face, and bristly thorax. Larvae feed on carrion. Common in urban areas where adults visit carrion and flowers. Used in forensics to estimate time of death.

### FLESH FLY *Sarcophaga* sp.
SARCOPHAGIDAE

Sp **S F W**  Large, gray, with three dark longitudinal stripes on thorax, red eyes, and well-developed tarsal pads. Face is white and abdomen is black with gray quadrate spots. Abdomen with numerous stiff bristles. Females deposit live larvae on carrion and rotting organic matter.

### TACHINID FLY *Archytas apicifer*
TACHINIDAE

Sp **S F W**  Yellowish-brown thorax, white face, antennae orange with dark tips, and short bristle. Abdomen bluish black with numerous stiff bristles in posterior third. Base of wings amber. Commonly visits flowers. Larvae are parasitoids of noctuid moth caterpillars.

### PARASITIC FLY *Cylindromyia intermedia*

Sp **S F W**  Dark thorax with elongated, cylindrical, orange and black abdomen. Face white. Base of wings with amber patch. Abdomen orange laterally with dark medial spots and black tip. Parasitoids of stink bugs.

*Pseudacteon tricuspis*

*Megaselia scalaris*

emerging from pupa

House Fly

Black Blow Fly

Common Green Bottle Fly

*Sarcophaga* sp.

*Archytas apicifer*

*Sarcophaga* sp.

*Cylindromyia intermedia*

### PARASITIC FLY *Epalpus signifer*   TACHINIDAE

**Sp S F W**   Robust, bristly fly with white face, reddish eyes, dark thorax, and reddish-brown abdomen. Base of wings with amber patch. Larvae parasitize caterpillars of noctuid moths. Adults visit flowers, especially composites.

### PARASITIC FLY *Oestrophasia calva*

**Sp S F W**   Orange body with black-striped abdomen and dark markings in wings. Eyes a little darker than general body color. Posterior margin of thorax outlined in black. Abdomen with dark abdominal stripes widest at middle. Tip of abdomen with a few stout bristles. Legs darkest at tips. Parasitizes beetle larvae.

### FEATHER-LEGGED FLY *Trichopoda lanipes*

**Sp S F W**   Grayish eyes and thorax, dark wings, red or orange abdomen, and hind tibia with plumage of hairs. Abdomen orange in males, dark red in females. Parasitoids of true bugs including leaf-footed bugs and stink bugs. Adults visit flowers.

### NEOTROPICAL DEER KED *Lipoptena mazamae*   HIPPOBOSCIDAE

**Sp S F W**   Small, dorsoventrally flattened, winged or wingless, dark brown flies with a spider or tick-like appearance. Round head and short, black proboscis. Obligate ectoparasites of white-tailed deer. Individuals winged until they find a host at which time the wings are lost. Can feed in chains where one individual feeds on another that is feeding on White-tailed Deer. Mature larva "born alive" after feeding from internal "milk" glands within mother.

### VINEGAR FLY *Drosophila* sp.   DROSOPHILIDAE

**Sp S F W**   Small yellowish-bodied flies with large red eyes. Variably marked wings. Abdomen often with dark bands. Common in houses. Feeds on rotting fruit and other organic matter.

### LAUXANIID FLY *Homoneura* sp.   LAUXANIIDAE

**Sp S F W**   Yellow to brown with dark reddish-purple, iridescent eyes, numerous dark bristles on thorax and dark spots at crossveins in wings. Found in woodlands. Some species attracted to lights.

### STILT-LEGGED FLY *Calobatina geometra*   MICROPEZIDAE

**Sp S F W**   Elongated, cylindrically bodied fly with round head, long orange-and-black banded legs, and basal tarsal segments white. Middle and hind legs orange-black-orange-black. Often perches and walks around on deciduous foliage holding the forelegs in front.

### STILT-LEGGED FLY *Taeniaptera trivittata*

**Sp S F W**   Elongated, cylindrical, dark-bodied fly with round head and long orange legs with basal tarsal segments white. Middle and hind legs orange-black-orange-black. Perches and walks around on deciduous foliage holding the forelegs in front.

*Epalpus signifer*

*Oestrophasia calva*

Neotropical
Deer Ked

*Trichopoda
lanipes*

*Drosophila* sp.

*Homoneura*
sp.

*Calobatina
geometra*

*Taeniaptera
trivittata*

**MARSH FLY** *Euthycera arcuata* SCIOMYZIDAE

**Sp S F W** Reddish-orange eyes with two dark red transverse bands and reticulated wings that only slightly overlap when at rest. Face is white and sloped downward and forward. Legs orangish with basal tarsal segments white. Adults found on edges of different types of aquatic habitats and attracted to lights.

**PYRGOTID FLY** *Boreothrinax maculipennis* PYRGOTIDAE

**Sp S F W** Head round when viewed from above. Femora and tibia banded with basal third of hind tibia constricted. Wings with dense reticulated pattern. Larvae are parasitoids of scarab adults. Comes to lights.

**WAVED LIGHT FLY** *Pyrgota undata*

**Sp S F W** Large, distinctive reddish-brown to dark brown fly with dark, waved stripe along leading edge of wing. Adult female lands on feeding May Beetle (*Phyllophaga* sp.) causing it to fly and revealing the unprotected abdomen where it then deposits an egg while in flight. Common at lights.

**PYRGOTID FLY** *Sphecomyiella valida*

**Sp S F W** Head wider than long when viewed from above. Femora and tibia not strongly banded. Wings with dense reticulated pattern. Parasitoid of scarab adults. Attracted to lights.

**SUNFLOWER SEED MAGGOT** *Neotephritis finalis* TEPHRITIDAE

**Sp S F W** Reddish-gold to green eyes, tan body, and dark wings with numerous white spots. Along leading edge of wing in distal third, six pale spots form an inward-pointing triangle. Larvae feed on various composites. Adults occasionally visit lights.

**PICTURE-WINGED FLY** *Delphinia picta* ULIDIIDAE

**Sp S F W** Reddish-brown head and thorax, black abdomen, and dark wings with two white inward-pointing triangles at middle of the trailing edge. Moves wings in a distinctive rowing motion when walking. Larvae feed in compost and other decaying organic matter. Adults found on various plants and flowers.

**LESSER DUNG FLIES** *Copromyza equina* SPHAEROCERIDAE

**Sp S F W** Tiny dark flies with white wings that can aggregate in large numbers on dung and vegetation. Breed in decaying organic matter, especially dung of horses and cattle. Are fairly cold tolerant and can be active during winter.

**LESSER DUNG FLIES** *Norrbomia frigipennis*

**Sp S F W** Tiny dark flies with white wings that ride on the backs of dung beetles. They can be numerous, walking on a single beetle. They breed in dung that the beetle is also attracted to.

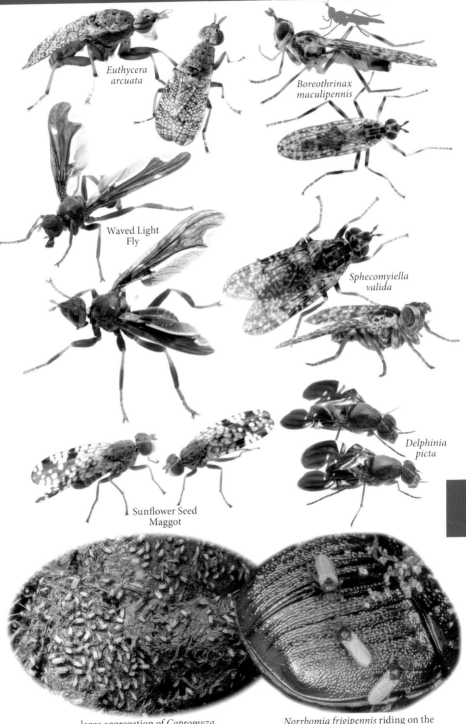

Euthycera
arcuata

Boreothrinax
maculipennis

Waved Light
Fly

Sphecomyiella
valida

Delphinia
picta

Sunflower Seed
Maggot

large aggregation of *Copromyza*
*equina* on horse dung

*Norrbomia frigipennis* riding on the
back of a Rainbow Scarab

275

# Butterflies and Moths
# Order Lepidoptera

Polyphemus Moth
(*Antheraea polyphemus*)

**NATURAL HISTORY**   Butterflies and moths are among the most familiar of insects. They belong to the order Lepidoptera, meaning scale (*lepido*) wing (*ptera*), referring to the numerous modified, flattened hairs that give them their distinctive colors and patterns. These scales come off easily when handled. The group has long been popular amongst collectors and watchers and often acted as the gateway to an appreciation of insects.

Butterflies and moths have complete development and the larval stage, called a caterpillar, has five or fewer prolegs in addition to three pairs of true legs. Caterpillars have well-developed silk glands modified from the salivary glands. In butterflies the pupa is often referred to as a chrysalis (plural, chrysalids) and in some moths the pupa is enclosed in a silken cocoon. Some caterpillars also use silk to sew leaves together and form retreats. Caterpillars of most species are herbivores. Species that feed on cultivated plants, grains, or fabrics are of considerable economic importance. Many species are important food resources for songbirds. Larvae have chewing mouthparts while most adults use a long, coiled siphoning tube, or proboscis, to take up nectar from flowers or fluids from fruit and sap.

Some species of moths (erebids and noctuids) have thoracic tympanic organs (akin to ears) that are capable of detecting bat sonar and thus aid in undertaking evasive maneuvers in flight to avoid being eaten. Parasitic mites live in these tympana and will destroy the organ, but interestingly they nearly always feed on a single tympana, leaving the moth with one to avoid bats.

# Identifying Characters

## Antennal Types

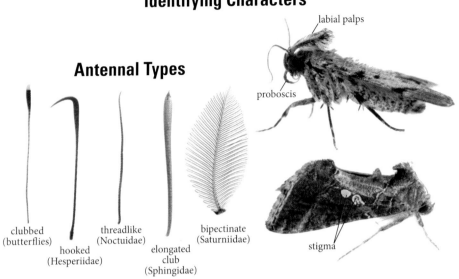

clubbed
(butterflies)

hooked
(Hesperiidae)

threadlike
(Noctuidae)

elongated
club
(Sphingidae)

bipectinate
(Saturniidae)

labial palps

proboscis

stigma

## Moth Markings

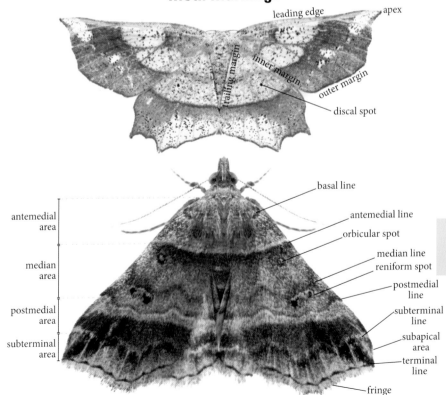

leading edge

apex

trailing margin

inner margin

outer margin

discal spot

basal line

antemedial
area

antemedial line

orbicular spot

median
area

median line

reniform spot

postmedial
area

postmedial
line

subterminal
area

subterminal
line

subapical
area

terminal
line

fringe

### GREAT PURPLE HAIRSTREAK *Atlides halesus*

LYCAENIDAE

**Sp S F W** Dark hind wing with one short and one long tail. With wings folded, three large reddish-orange spots at base of wings. Wings iridescent blue above. Top of abdomen blue, reddish orange below. Colors resemble a wasp. Larvae feed on mistletoe.

### WESTERN PYGMY BLUE *Brephidium exile*

**Sp S F W** Upperside of wings coppery brown. Underside of hind wing brown with white; three dark spots basally and row of larger black spots with reflective dashes along outer margin. Larvae feed on pigweed and saltbushes. Found in alkaline areas.

### JUNIPER HAIRSTREAK *Callophrys gryneus*

**Sp S F W** Upperside of wings reddish to dark brown. Underside of hind wing dull to bright green with irregular white line edged in reddish brown. Larvae feed on juniper. Found in open fields and juniper brakes where males perch on juniper looking for females.

### RED-BANDED HAIRSTREAK *Calycopis cecrops*

**Sp S F W** Two long tails on each hind wing. Upperside of wings brown with hind wing blue. Underside of wings grayish brown with broad red line edged in white. Outer margin of hind wing with black spots and blue patch. Larvae feed on fallen leaves of wax myrtle, sumacs, and oaks. Found in overgrown fields and forest edges. Similar Dusky-blue Groundstreak replaces this species south and west.

### SILVER-BANDED HAIRSTREAK *Chlorostrymon simaethis*

**Sp S F W** Upperside of wings brown or gray; male with purple irridescence. Underside of both wings green with silver-white band. Hind wing with one tail and red along outer margin. Larvae feed on balloon vine, eating into the "balloons." Forest edges and openings.

### EASTERN TAILED-BLUE *Cupido comyntas*

**Sp S F W** Upperside of male wings iridescent blue; females brown with some blue. Underside of wings pale gray with black spots and outer margin of hind wing with orange toward apex. Larvae feed on clover and vetch. Visits flowers close to ground.

### REAKIRT'S BLUE *Echinargus isola*

**Sp S F W** Upperside of wings light blue with dark veins. Underside of forewing with black dots encircled in white. Larvae feed on clover, rattleweed, mesquite, and indigo bush.

### CERAUNUS BLUE *Hemiargus ceraunus*

**Sp S F W** Upperside of wings light blue or brown with dark border. Similar to Reakirt's Blue except lacks row of dark spots on forewing. Larvae feed on woody legumes including partridge pea and mesquite.

# BUTTERFLIES AND MOTHS

Great Purple
Hairstreak

Western Pygmy
Blue

top
side of
wings

Red-banded
Hairstreak

top
side of
wings

Juniper
Hairstreak

Silver-banded
Hairstreak

Eastern
Tailed-blue

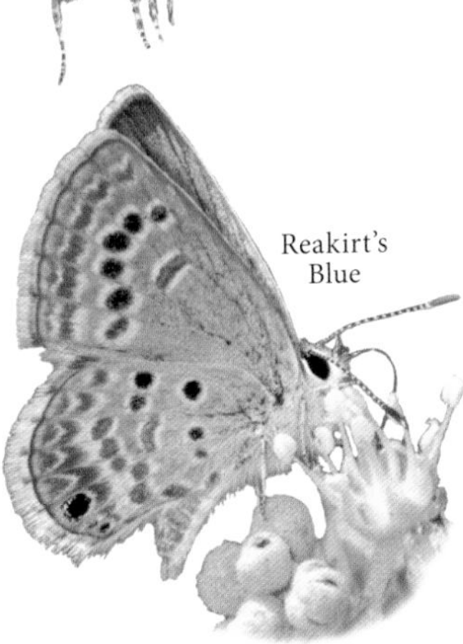

Reakirt's
Blue

Ceraunus Blue

279

### MARINE BLUE *Leptotes marina* LYCAENIDAE

**Sp** S F W   Upperside of wings blue, male with purple tinge. Underside with dark bands outlined in white and two dark submarginal spots. Larvae feed on flowers and seedpods of leadwort, alfalfa, mesquite, and other legumes. Found in a variety of habitats.

### OAK HAIRSTREAK *Satyrium favonius*

**Sp** S F W   Two tails on each hind wing. Upperside of wings grayish brown. Underside of wings with dark dashes edged in white creating a pair of irregular lines. Outermost line in hind wing also edged in red. Inner line of hind wing terminating in sideways "W." Larvae feed on leaves, buds, and male catkins of oaks.

### GRAY HAIRSTREAK *Strymon melinus*

**Sp** S F W   Upperside of wings dark to pale gray. Underside with dark dashes forming two irregular lines. Innermost line strongly edged in white and reddish orange. Outer edge of hind wing with two black spots surrounded by red orange. Most common hairstreak encountered in gardens. Larvae feed on a variety of flowers and fruits, but are often found on mallows and legumes.

### SOLDIER *Danaus eresimus* NYMPHALIDAE

Sp S **F** W   Like Monarch, but forewing tips have white spots and lack black crossband. Underside of hind wing with diffuse white shading in middle. Larvae feed on milkweeds.

### QUEEN *Danaus gilippus*

**Sp** S F W   Darker red-brown than Monarch, lacking black along veins on upperside. More white dots in middle of forewing than Soldier. Black veins on hind wing underside have white edging. Larvae feed on milkweeds.

### MONARCH *Danaus plexippus*

**Sp** S F W   Upperside of wings bright orange with dark veins and broad outer margin with white spots. Larvae feed on milkweeds. Adults take part in large migration northward from Mexico in the spring and south north of Texas in the fall and may occur in large numbers along route. Warming and planting of milkweed may be altering their movements as they can be found in summer and winter.

### VICEROY *Limenitis archippus*

**Sp** S F W   Orange and black, resembling monarch, but smaller and with rounded dark band in hind wing and veins more heavily outlined in black. Larvae feed on willows, poplars, and cottonwood.

### JULIA HELICONIAN *Dryas iulia*

**Sp** S F W   Elongated forewings. Bright orange above and below with thin black border around each wing. Larvae feed on passiflora. Found in woodland edges, openings, and nearby fields.

Marine
Blue

Gray
Hairstreak

top
side of
wings

Oak
Hairstreak

Soldier

Queen

Soldier

Queen

Monarch

Viceroy

Monarch
Caterpillar

Viceroy

Julia Heliconian

281

### ZEBRA LONGWING *Heliconius charitonia*
NYMPHALIDAE

**Sp S F W** Large, black, elongated wings with narrow yellow stripes. Larvae feed on passiflora. Males patrol for adult females and female chrysalids pupae. He will mate with her as she emerges. Found along forest edges and open fields.

### AMERICAN SNOUT *Libytheana carinenta*

**Sp S F W** Orange brown above, gray below, with labial palps elongated and extended forward. Tip of forewing somewhat squared off. Larvae feed on hackberry. Adults sit on branches where they look like dead leaves. Found in forest clearings, fields, and roadsides and known for phenominal population outbreaks in south Texas correlated with intensity and duration of dry periods immediately preceding drought-terminating rains.

### WHITE PEACOCK *Anartia jatrophae*

**Sp S F W** Upperside of wings white with light to dark brown markings and a double row of pale crescent shapes at margins. Forewing with single dark spot, hind wing with two. Larvae feed on water hyssop and ruellias. Found in open areas, especially near water.

### GULF FRITILLARY *Agraulis vanillae*

**Sp S F W** Elongated forewings; upperside bright orange with dark markings. Underside of both wings with elongated iridescent silvery-white spots. Larvae feed on passiflora. Found in pastures, open fields, woodland edges, and city gardens.

### VARIEGATED FRITILLARY *Euptoieta claudia*

**Sp S F W** Upperside of wings tawny orange with dark veins and black spots along wing margin. Underside of hind wing with mottled pattern; lacking silver spots. Hind wing margin slightly scalloped. Larvae feed on various plants including passiflora, may apple, violets, and flax species. Found in open sunny prairies, fields, and pastures.

### HACKBERRY EMPEROR *Asterocampa celtis*

**Sp S F W** Upperside light to dark orange brown with one or two dark eyespots on outer margin. Innermost dark bar on forewing margin is broken. Underside of hind wing with series of marginal eyespots. Larvae feed on hackberry. Abundant in edge habitats.

### TAWNY EMPEROR *Asterocampa clyton*

**Sp S F W** Forewing lacks eyespots, but has two complete dark bars along anterior margin. Underside of hind wing with row of small eyespots. Larvae feed on hackberry trees.

### EMPRESS LEILIA *Asterocampa leilia*

**Sp S F W** Upperside of wings chestnut brown with two solid bars along forewing margin, median white spots, and two black eyespots. Underside of both wings with large, obvious eyespots. Larvae feed on desert hackberry. Adults found drinking from tree sap and dung.

# BUTTERFLIES AND MOTHS

Zebra
Longwing

American
Snout

White
Peacock

Gulf
Fritillary
Chrysalis

Gulf
Fritillary

Variegated
Fritillary

Variegated
Fritillary

Gulf
Fritillary

Hackberry
Emperor

top
side of
wings

Tawny
Emperor

Hackberry
Emperor
chrysalis

Tawny
Emperor

Hackberry Emperor
caterpillar

Empress
Leilia

283

### CRIMSON PATCH *Chlosyne janais*

NYMPHALIDAE

**Sp** S F W  Upper and lower sides of forewings black with small white spots. Upperside of hind wing with large orange-red patch basally. Larvae feed on flame acanthus and related species.

### BORDERED PATCH *Chlosyne lacinia*

**Sp** S F W  Variable, with upperside all black with spots and with broad orange band, often margined in white, running through both wings. Larvae feed on ragweed and various composites and are gregarious when young. Found in open fields to oak woodlands.

### SILVERY CHECKERSPOT *Chlosyne nycteis*

**Sp S** F W  Upperside of wings orangish yellow with dark borders and markings. Hind wing with dark submarginal spots with white centers. Larvae feed on Frostweed, composites like Black-eyed Susan and sunflowers. Found in meadows, forest openings, and streamsides.

### THEONA CHECKERSPOT *Chlosyne theona*

**Sp S F** W  Upperside of wings with dark checkered pattern and median black stripe separating two yellowish-orange bands. Larvae feed on Cenizo Blanca and paintbrush. Found along limestone edges, open oak woodlands, and desert foothills.

### TEXAN CRESCENT *Anthanassa texana*

**Sp S F W**  Upperside dark brown with small white spots distally and irregular reddish spots basally. Outer edge of forewing indented below tip. Larvae feed on low plants such as ruellias, jacobina and Mexican shrimp plant. Found in deserts, dry gullies, open areas, road side parks, streamside and city parks.

### PEARL CRESCENT *Phyciodes tharos*

**Sp S F W**  Variable. Usually upperside of wings orange with dark edges, veins thinly outlined in black, and row of submarginal black spots in hind wing. Underside of hind wing with dark marginal patch containing pale crescent-shaped mark. Larvae feed on several species of composites. Generally found in open pastures and roadsides.

### PHAON CRESCENT *Phyciodes phaon*

**Sp S F W**  Upperside of forewing dark orange and black with pale cream-colored median band. Hind wing with submarginal rows of black spots. Underside of hind wing cream-colored to yellowish with dark markings. Larvae feed on frogfruit and mat grass. Found in open areas, roadsides, and pastures.

### VESTA CRESCENT *Phyciodes graphica*

**Sp S F W**  Upperside of wings orange with black lines and row of submarginal black spots on hind wing. Larvae feed on hairy tubetongue. Adults found in thorn and mesquite woodlands, deserts, prairies, roadsides, and streambeds.

# BUTTERFLIES AND MOTHS

Crimson Patch

Bordered Patch

Crimson Patch Caterpillar

Bordered Patch Caterpillar

Theona Checkerspot

Silvery Checkerspot

Pearl Crescent

Texas Crescent

Phaon Crescent

Vesta Crescent

### MALACHITE *Siporeta stelenes*
NYMPHALIDAE

Sp **S** **F** **W**  Large, with upperside of wings dark brown to black with translucent yellowish-green patches. Underside of wings orange brown with greenish-white patches. Larvae feed on cafetin and yerba maravilla. Adults feed on flower nectar and bird droppings.

### MEXICAN BLUEWING *Myscelia ethusa*

Sp **S** **F** **W**  Upperside of both wings black with iridescent blue bands and white spots on outer half of forewing. Larvae feed on Vasey's Adelia. Adults come to rotting fruit. They perch on tree trunks with wings closed to blend in with the bark.

### MOURNING CLOAK *Nymphalis antiopa*

Sp **S** F **W**  Upperside of both wings dark, with yellow margins and row of iridescent blue spots along inner edge. Short projections on both wings. Larval plants include willows, poplars, and hackberry. Adults feed on sap from oak trees and will readily land on the ground.

### RED-SPOTTED PURPLE  *Limenitis arthemis*

Sp **S** **F** W  Upper wings blackish with blue iridescence and reddish-orange spots near forewing tips. Underside of both wings iridescent blue with orange spots. Larvae feed on willows, cottonwoods, and poplars. Found in open and forested edges.

### GOATWEED LEAFWING *Anaea andria*

Sp **S** **F** **W**  Upperside of wings reddish with margins variably marked dark. Forewings with hooked anterior tips; hind wings each with a tail. Underside of wings brown, appearing like a dead leaf. Larvae feed on goatweed, other crotons, and various euphorbs.

### QUESTION MARK  *Polygonia interrogationis*

Sp **S** **F** **W**  Forewing strongly hooked at tip. Upperside of wings reddish orange with black spots. Hind wing with tail. Underside of wings brown with "?" white mark in center of hind wing. Larvae feed on elm, hackberry, nettles, and more. Found in open wooded areas.

### COMMON BUCKEYE *Junonia coenia*

Sp **S** **F** **W**  Upperside of wings brown. Forewing with two orange bars along forewing margin and one large eyespot within a band of white. Each hind wing with two eyespots and orange band along margin. Larvae feed on snapdragon, toadflax, plaintain, and others.

### RED ADMIRAL *Vanessa atalanta*

Sp **S** **F** **W**  Upperside of wings black with white spots near apex in forewing. Red band medially in forewing and along margin in hind wing. Larvae feed on nettle. Adults will feed from sap in trees.

Malachite

Mexican Bluewing

Mourning Cloak

Red-Spotted Purple

Goatweed Leafwing

Question Mark

Common Buckeye Caterpillar

Common Buckeye

Red Admiral

287

### AMERICAN LADY *Vanessa virginiensis*  NYMPHALIDAE

**Sp S F W** Upperside of forewing with white bar and several white spots at apex including single white spot in the orange area. Underside of hind wing with two large eyespots. Larvae feed on various sunflowers. Found in open areas with low vegetation.

### PAINTED LADY *Vanessa cardui*

**Sp S F W** Similar to American Painted Lady, but no white spot in the orange area below apex on forewing. Underside of hind wing with four small eyespots. Larvae feed on various sunflowers and thistles where caterpillars will make a "dirty" nest in the leaves. Found in a wide variety of habitats.

### LITTLE WOOD SATYR *Megisto cymela*

**Sp S F W** Light grayish brown. Underside of forewing with two yellow-rimmed black eyespots; hind wing with three. Two dark bands running across both wings on underside. Larvae feed on various grasses. Found in grassy woods and openings.

### COMMON WOOD NYMPH *Cercyonis pegala*

**Sp S F W** Upperside of forewing brown with two large eyespots in a field of yellow; also visible below. Underside of hind wing with several smaller eyespots rimmed in yellow. Larvae feed on grasses. Found in open sunny grassy areas as well as woodland edges.

### GEMMED SATYR *Cyllopsis gemma*

**Sp S F W** Wings lack eyespots. Underside of hind wing with silvery patch along outer margin containing four black reflective spots may appear as two from a distance. Larvae feed on grasses. Found in open areas and along woodland edges near streams and ponds.

### CAROLINA SATYR *Hermeuptychia sosybius*

**Sp S F W** Underside of both wings with small, submarginal eyespots rimmed in yellow. Two irregular narrow dark bands cross both wings. Larvae feed on grasses. Found in grassy meadows to woodlands. A similar, cryptic species, Intricate Satyr *H. intricata*, was recently described. It can not be reliably differentiated from Carolina, without examining the dorsal forewing of the male for androconia lacking in Intricate and through genitalic differences.

### SOUTHERN PEARLY-EYE *Lethe portlandia*

**Sp S F W** Both wings with a submarginal row of four eyespots encircled in yellow. Hind wing with additional smaller eyespots. Antennae with orange clubs. Larvae feed on giant cane. Found in shady, damp woodlands near streams.

### ZEBRA SWALLOWTAIL *Eurytides marcellus*  PAPILIONIDAE

**Sp S F W** Large, white and black, with long tails. Underside of hind wing with irregular red stripe and two red spots. Larvae feed on pawpaw. Found in meadows and moist low woodlands.

# BUTTERFLIES AND MOTHS

American Lady

op
e of
ngs

American Lady
Caterpillar

top
side of
wings

Painted Lady

Little Wood
Satyr

Common
Wood
Nymph

Common Wood
Nymph

Gemmed
Satyr

Carolina
Satyr

Southern
Pearly-eye

Zebra
Swallowtail

Zebra Swallowtail

## WESTERN GIANT SWALLOWTAIL *Papilio rumiko*

PAPILIONIDAE

**Sp S F W**  Large, black and yellow, with single tail off of hind wing. Very similar to Eastern Giant, but with larger black dot in third yellow cell from forewing apex and yellow stripes on thorax extending further back to forewing base. The split of this species from the Eastern Giant Swallowtail is recent and its validity as a distinct species is questionable.

## EASTERN GIANT SWALLOWTAIL *Papilio cresphontes*

**Sp S F W**  Large, black and yellow, with single tail off of hind wing. Very similar to Western Giant, but with smaller black dot in third yellow cell from forewing apex and yellow "stripes" on thorax broken into a series of dots that don't extend back to forewing base. Larvae feed on the citrus family.

## EASTERN TIGER SWALLOWTAIL *Papilio glaucus*

**Sp S F W**  Large, yellow, with long tail off hind wing and dark "tiger stripes." Female either like male with blue along posterior hind wing margin or with yellow replaced by black. Larval food plants include cottonwood, tuliptree, sweet bay, and cherry.

## TWO-TAILED SWALLOWTAIL *Papilio multicaudata*

**Sp S F W**  Like Eastern Tiger, but with two tails on each hind wing beware of broken tails and narrower black stripes on yellow wings. Larvae feed on chokeberry and hoptree.

## PALAMEDES SWALLOWTAIL *Papilio palamedes*

**Sp S F W**  Upperside of wings with broad pale yellow band. Underside of hind wing with orange and blue submarginal cells and pale basal band. Larvae feed on redbay.

## BLACK SWALLOWTAIL *Papilio polyxenes*

**Sp S F W**  Black wings have yellow spot bands in postmedian area and margin Spots are reduced on male which has blue spot band on hind wing. Both sexes have orange spot with dark center on inner edge of hind wing. Larvae feed on many plants including parsley.

## PIPEVINE SWALLOWTAIL *Battus philenor*

**Sp S F W**  Upperside black with iridescent blue to blue-green on hind wing less on female. Underside of hind wing with single row of orange spots in iridescent blue field. Larvae feed on pipevines. Found in a variety of habitats.

## SPICEBUSH SWALLOWTAIL *Papilio troilus*

**Sp S F W**  Upperside of wings black with pale blue or ivory spots along margin. Underside of hind wing with two rows of orange spots in iridescent blue field. Larvae feed on spicebush, sassafras, and other laurels. Found in deciduous woodlands, open fields, and roadsides.

# BUTTERFLIES AND MOTHS

Western Giant Swallowtail

Eastern Giant Swallowtail caterpillar

Eastern Giant Swallowtail

black form ♀

Eastern Tiger Swallowtail

♀

♂

Eastern Tiger Swallowtail

Two-tailed Swallowtail

♂

Black Swallowtail

♀

Palamedes Swallowtail

Palamedes Swallowtail

Black Swallowtail Caterpillar

caterpillar

top side of wings

Pipevine Swallowtail

top side of wings

Spicebush Swallowtail

291

## SLEEPY ORANGE *Abaeis nicippe*

PIERIDAE

**Sp S F W** Upperside of both sexes orange edged in black; forewing with small black spot. Underside of wings reddish brown in winter; yellowish orange in summer. Larvae feed on sennas.

## ORANGE SULPHUR *Colias eurytheme*

**Sp S F W** Upperside of wings orangish yellow with dark margin, black spot in forewing and orange spot in hind wing. Underside of hind wing with silver spot surrounded by two concentric dark rings and a smaller spot above it. Larvae feed on alfalfa, clovers, and other legumes. Found in meadows and roadsides.

## BOISDUVAL'S YELLOW *Eurema boisduvaliana*

**Sp S F W** Upperside of wings bright yellow with black borders. In male, weak "dog's head" pattern on upperside of forewing. Hind wings slightly pointed. Larvae feed on sennas. Found more often in undergrowth and forest edges.

## LYSIDE SULPHUR *Kricogonia lyside*

**Sp S F W** Upperside of wings white to yellow, often with dark vertical bar along front edge of hind wing. Underside of wings with raised veins and a satin white or greenish sheen. Larvae feed on Texas guaiacum. Found in scrub lowlands to seasonally dry forests.

## LARGE ORANGE SULPHUR *Phoebis agarithe*

**Sp S F W** Large, upperside of wings pale to bright orange without markings. Underside of wings with faint, straight, submarginal line and usually with at least two small silver spots on hind wing. Some individuals mostly white. Larvae feed on Texas ebony.

## CABBAGE WHITE *Pieris rapae*

**Sp S F W** Upperside of wings white; forewing with black tip and two submarginal spots in female, one in male. Upperside of hind wing in both sexes with single marginal dark spot. Underside of wings in both sexes yellowish or gray green. Larvae feed on mustards. Common in a variety of open spaces and gardens.

## DAINTY SULPHUR *Nathalis iole*

**Sp S F W** Small, with elongated forewings, variable on underside. Upperside of wings yellow with black markings. Underside of forewing with basal orange streak and two black spots distally. Larvae feed on asters such as dogweed.

## CLOUDLESS SULPHUR *Phoebis sennae*

**Sp S F W** Large, with upperside of wings lemon yellow and unmarked except for dark spot in females. Underside of wings with two pink-edged silver spots. Larvae feed on senna. Often found in open disturbed areas, including parks and yards.

# BUTTERFLIES AND MOTHS

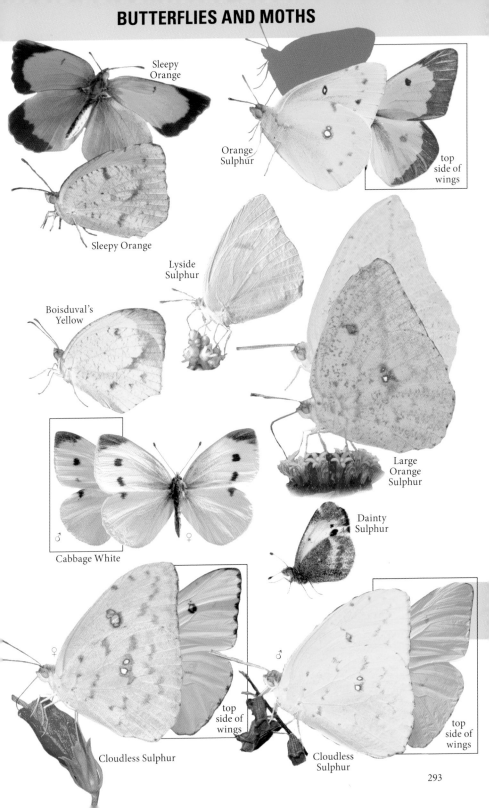

Sleepy Orange

Orange Sulphur

top side of wings

Sleepy Orange

Lyside Sulphur

Boisduval's Yellow

Large Orange Sulphur

♂ Cabbage White ♀

Dainty Sulphur

♀ Cloudless Sulphur

top side of wings

♂ Cloudless Sulphur

top side of wings

### CHECKERED WHITE *Pontia protodice* PIERIDAE

**Sp S F W** Upperside of female forewing heavily checkered; male with dark markings on outer half. Underside of wings with pale checkered pattern. Larvae feed on different mustards. Found in a variety of habitats including vacant lots, fields, pastures, and roadsides.

### LITTLE YELLOW *Pyrisitia lisa*

**Sp S F W** Upperside of wings with dark, wide apices. Underside of wings variable, but hind wing usually with small scattered dark spots including two basally, and a round pink spot at upper apex. Larvae feed on senna. Found in fields and roadsides.

### TAILED ORANGE *Pyrisitia proterpia*

**Sp S F W** Hind wing with pointed tail later in the year, absent in summer form. Upperside of wings orange with black apex in forewing. Underside of wings may be uniformly orangish yellow summer or yellow with fine brownish lines and blotching fall. Larvae feed on mesquite and senna. Found in open and disturbed areas.

### SOUTHERN DOGFACE *Zerene cesonia*

**Sp S F W** Upperside of wings with yellow "dog's head" encompassed by black and distinct "eye" not touching black border. Underside of forewing with silver dot surrounded by black; hind wing with two silver dots, often edged in pink. Larvae feed on indigo bush, kidneywood, and clovers. Found in short-grass prairies and roadsides.

### FATAL METALMARK *Calephelis nemesis* RIODINIDAE

**Sp S F W** Variable with upperside of wings orange to brown, sometimes with median area darker. Somewhat checkered pattern with silver bands may be visible. Larvae feed on old man's beard. Found in brushy and weedy roadsides, washes, and ditches.

### RED-BORDERED METALMARK *Caria ino*

**Sp S F W** Upperside of wings reddish brown with outer edge orange and metallic submarginal line and black dots. Leading edge of forewing in both sexes wavy. Underside of male wings reddish, female orange. Larvae feed on spiny hackberry.

### BLUE METALMARK *Lasaia sula*

**Sp S F W** Upperside of male wings metallic blue; female gray. Both checkered with dark markings. Underside of wings brown and checkered. Larvae feed on screwbean mesquite.

### RED-BORDERED PIXIE *Melanis pixe*

**Sp S F W** Unmistakable; upperside of wings black with yellow apices in forewing, four red dots basally and marginal row of red or orange dots in hind wing. Larvae feed on guamuchil. Found in woodland edges near water and city parks.

Checkered White

♀ ♂

top side of wings

Little Yellow

Tailed Orange

Southern Dogface

top side of wings

Southern Dogface Caterpillar

Fatal Metalmark

♀ ♂

Red-bordered Metalmark

Blue Metalmark

♀ ♂

Blue Metalmark

Red-bordered Pixie

### HOARY EDGE *Achalarus lyciades*

Sp S F W    Upperside of wings dark brown with transparent gold band in middle. Fringes checkered. Underside of hind wing dark brown with wide silvery white band along outer margin. Larvae feed on beggar's ticks and false indigo. Found in clearings and edges of open sandy woodlands.

### WHITE-STRIPED LONGTAIL *Chioides albofasciatus*

Sp S F W    Wings dark brown; upperside of forewing with pale spots at apex. Hind wing with tail as long as rest of wing and underside with silver-white band across middle of wing. Larvae feed on legume vines including snoutbean. Males perch on plants darting out at rival males.

### SILVER-SPOTTED SKIPPER *Epargyreus clarus*

Sp S F W    Wings brown with transparent gold band in forewing. Underside of hind wing with silver-white band across middle. Larvae feed on various legumes including locusts and wisteria. Common in disturbed and open woodlands, forest edges, fields, and gardens.

### NORTHERN CLOUDYWING *Thorybes pylades*

Sp S F W    Wings brown with clear, small, triangular spots in forewing. Two dark irregular bands on underside of hind wing. Larvae feed on tick treefoils, wild beans, beggar's ticks, and other legumes. Found in open or scrubby woodlands and forest edges.

### BROWN LONGTAIL *Urbanus procne*

Sp S F W    Wings brown gray with long tails on hind wing. Forewing with or without pair of narrow white bands visible on both sides. Larvae feed on Bermuda, Johnson, and other grasses. Found in grassy openings and forested edges.

### LONG-TAILED SKIPPER *Urbanus proteus*

Sp S F W    Wings dark brown with bases and body iridescent blue green and long tails off hind wing. Forewings with pale spots above and below. Underside of hind wing with dark spots. Larvae feed on various legumes. Fly in brushy fields, disturbed habitats, gardens, and forest edges.

### GUAVA SKIPPER *Phocides polybius*

Sp S F W    Large, wings iridescent blue. Upperside of forewing with greenish rays extending from base and short red bars medially along leading edge. Head yellow, thorax black with blue stripes. Larvae feed on guava. Found in subtropical woods as well as city parks where the planting of guava trees has encouraged their spread.

Hoary Edge

White-striped Longtail

Hoary Edge

Northern Cloudywing

top side of wings

Northern Cloudywing

Silver-spotted Skipper

Long-tailed Skipper

Brown Longtail

Guava Skipper

Long-tailed Skipper

### BRAZILIAN SKIPPER *Calpodes ethlius*

**Sp S F W** Large, robust, with long, pointed forewings. Upperside of both wings brown with large translucent spots. Underside of wings reddish brown; hind wing with three or four cream spots. Body often with blue iridescence above. Larvae feed on cannas. Fast and powerful flier that is most active at dawn and dusk.

### DUN SKIPPER *Euphyes vestris*

**Sp S F W** Widespread, plain brown skipper. Upperside of wings brownish black. Male with dark spot basally and female with several white spots. Underside of wings grayish brown. Larvae feed on sedges. Common in meadows, swamps, and stream edges near deciduous woods.

### FIERY SKIPPER *Hylephila phyleus*

**Sp S F W** Antennae short. Upperside of wings yellowish orange; male with a dark elongated basal spot and dark jagged margin. Underside of hind wing with small black spots. Female with more orange-brown wings above and below. Larvae feed on Bermuda grass. Found in sunny open fields, lawns, gardens, and roadsides.

### SOUTHERN BROKEN-DASH *Wallengrenia otho*

**Sp S F W** Upperside of wings brown with some orange patches; male with dark interrupted black basal patch and female with several translucent pale spots. Underside of hind wing in both sexes with band of pale spots. Larvae feed on grasses. Found in openings near wooded streams and swamps.

### CLOUDED SKIPPER *Lerema accius*

**Sp S F W** Wings dark brown. Upperside of male forewing with dark basal area. Female forewing with transparent white spots. Underside of hind wing variously marked, but usually with violet sheen. Larvae feed on grasses.

### DELAWARE SKIPPER *Anatrytone logan*

**Sp S F W** Wings yellowish orange with black borders and veins on upperside. Forewing with narrow black bar toward apex. Underside of wings unmarked. Larvae feed on grasses. Common in a variety of grassy and disturbed areas.

### SACHEM *Atalopedes campestris*

**Sp S F W** Upperside of wings yellowish orange with broad, dark border and often dark square spot basally in male. Female wings variably colored, but with transparent white spot medially in forewing. Larvae feed on grasses including Bermuda.

# BUTTERFLIES AND MOTHS

Brazilian
Skipper

Dun
Skipper

top
side of
wings

Dun Skipper

top
side of
wings

Fiery Skipper

Southern
Broken-dash

Clouded Skipper

Clouded
Skipper

Delaware Skipper

top
side of
wings

Sachem

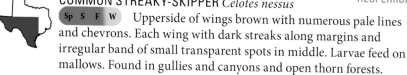

## COMMON STREAKY-SKIPPER *Celotes nessus*

**Sp S F W** Upperside of wings brown with numerous pale lines and chevrons. Each wing with dark streaks along margins and irregular band of small transparent spots in middle. Larvae feed on mallows. Found in gullies and canyons and open thorn forests.

## WHITE-PATCHED SKIPPER *Chiomara georgina*

**Sp S F W** Upperside of wings variable, mottled, with black, brown, gray, and white. Hind wings with large white central patch. Underside of wings white with brown along the outer margins. Females with less extensive white. Larvae feed on Barbados cherry.

## FUNEREAL DUSKYWING *Erynnis funeralis*

**Sp S F W** Dark brown to black with forewings long, narrow, and pointed. Hind wing somewhat square with prominent white fringe. Larvae feed on legumes. Common in open habitats including gardens.

## JUVENAL'S DUSKYWING *Erynnis juvenalis*

**Sp S F W** Dark brown to black with forewings long, narrow, and pointed. Hind wing with brown fringe. Upperside of wing in male brown, with clear spots and scattered dark and white marks. Underside of hind wing with two pale apical spots. Larvae feed on oaks. Found in oak woodlands and associated fields.

## HORACE'S DUSKYWING *Erynnis horatius*

**Sp S F W** Dark brown to black with forewings long, narrow, and pointed. Hind wing with brown fringe. Upperside of male uniform with little contrast; female more contrasty and grayer. Larvae feed on oaks. Found in oak woodlands and forest edges.

## COMMON CHECKERED-SKIPPER *Pyrgus communis*

**Sp S F W** Upperside of wings checkered black and white. Females with more black and males often with blue hairs basally. Fringe in males checkered; females white. Underside of wings white with tan and olive spots. Essentially identical to White-checkered Skipper, and where they overlap in range they can't be separated from photos. Larvae feed on mallows. Common in open sunny habitats including prairies, pastures, yards, and trails.

## WHITE CHECKERED-SKIPPER *Pyrgus albascens*

**Sp S F W** Essentially, identical to Common Checkered-skipper and can only be separated by dissection where the ranges overlap. White Checkered-skipper has more of a coastal distribution and is generally paler than Common Checkered-skipper.

# BUTTERFLIES AND MOTHS

Common Streaky-skipper

White-patched Skipper

Funereal Duskywing

underside of wings

Juvenal's Duskywing

Horace's Duskywing

underside of wings

Common Checkered-skipper or White-Checkered Skipper

Common Checkered-skipper or White-Checkered Skipper

301

### SPOTTED APATELODES *Apatelodes torrefacta*

**Sp S F W** Forewings broaden considerably toward tips; gray with dark curved lines widening toward body and large dark brown patch basally. Larvae feed on ashes, maples, oaks, and other deciduous trees.

### LUNA MOTH *Actias luna*

**Sp S F W** Unmistakable, large, bright green with long tails. Each wing has a transparent eyespot and the outer margins are pink or yellow. Larvae feed on sweetgum, walnuts, birch, alder, sumacs, and other deciduous trees. Found in deciduous hardwood forests.

### SPINY OAKWORM MOTH *Anisota stigma*

**Sp S F W** Reddish or orange brown with dark spots scattered across wings. Forewing with small white spot and posterior third with dark transverse line. Males smaller than females. Larvae feed on oaks and are found in deciduous forests.

### POLYPHEMUS MOTH *Antheraea polyphemus*

**Sp S F W** Large, upperside of wings yellowish brown with a translucent spot in each forewing and a large dark eyespot with translucent spot in the hind wing. Both wings with submarginal dark line outlined in pink. Larvae feed on oaks, willows, maple, grape, and birch. Found both in deciduous forests and urban areas.

### PINK-STRIPED OAKWORM *Anisota virginiensis*

**Sp S F W** Forewing orange brown with purplish posterior margin and white spot in center of wing. Males smaller with large translucent patch in middle. Larvae feed on various oaks.

### REGAL MOTH *Citheronia regalis*

**Sp S F W** Large, elongated, gray forewings with reddish-orange veins and creamy yellow spots. Head and thorax red with yellow stripes. Larvae feed on hickory, pecan, black walnut, sweetgum, sumac, sycamore, and others.

### IO MOTH *Automeris io*

**Sp S F W** Male forewings bright yellow with scattered dark markings; female reddish brown to purplish red. Hind wing in both sexes with large dark eyespot with white dash in the middle and a reddish and black submarginal line. Larvae feed on hackberry, willow, mesquite, redbud, clover, oak, and more. Larvae have stinging spines.

### IMPERIAL MOTH *Eacles imperialis*

**Sp S F W** Large, yellow wings with purplish-brown spots, bands, and patches. Each wing with pale white spot in center encircled by purplish brown. Larvae feed on oaks, sweetgum, maples, sassafras, and other deciduous trees.

# BUTTERFLIES AND MOTHS

Spotted Apatelodes

Luna Moth

Spotted Apatelodes

Spiny Oakworm Moth

Luna Moth caterpillar

♂ ♀

Pink-striped Oakworm

Polyphemus Moth

♂ Io Moth

Regal Moth

Io Moth ♀

Imperial Moth

## ROSY MAPLE MOTH *Dryocampa rubicunda*

SATURNIIDAE

**Sp S F W** Wings pale to bright yellow with variable amount of pink along margins and bases. Thorax heavily covered with yellow hairs. Larvae feed on maples and oaks. Adults emerge in the late afternoon into early evening.

## CECROPIA MOTH *Hyalophora cecropia*

**Sp S F W** Very large, dark brown wings with forewings red at base. Each wing with crescent-shaped white spot outlined in red and black and submarginal reddish and white line. Thorax abdomen densely clothed in red hairs. Larvae feed on various trees including maples, wild cherries, oaks, ash, beech, and willow.

## HUBBARD'S SMALL SILKMOTH *Syssphinx hubbardi*

**Sp S F W** Forewings dark gray with small, central white spot. Upperside of hind wings diffusely red or pinkish out to gray margin and with single black dot in middle of each. Larvae feed on acacia and honey mesquite.

## PINK-SPOTTED HAWKMOTH *Agrius cingulata*

SPHINGIDAE

**Sp S F W** Large, robust body with gray tapering abdomen and pink bands. Forewing mottled grayish brown with dark wavy lines. Hind wing gray with black bands and pink basally. Larvae feed on sweet potato, jimsonweed, and related plants.

## WAVED SPHINX *Ceratomia undulosa*

**Sp S F W** Forewing gray or brown with wavy black and pale lines and a white spot outlined in black. Hind wing gray or brown with diffuse black bands. Larvae feed on ash, privet, oak, and hawthorn.

## WALNUT SPHINX *Amorpha juglandis*

**Sp S F W** Variable, gray to pink with broad dark stripe widening to leading edge in forewing. Posterior margin of hind wing scalloped and usually protruding beyond forewing when at rest. Abdomen with ridges of hairs around segments. Larvae feed on walnut, hickory, alder, beech, and related trees.

## NESSUS SPHINX *Amphion floridensis*

**Sp S F W** Stout body with brown wings. Forewing with dark bands. Abdomen with two yellow bands; posterior one may be hidden at rest. Larvae feed on grape, peppervine, and cayenne pepper.

## VIRGINIA CREEPER SPHINX *Darapsa myron*

**Sp S F W** Forewings brown to yellowish gray with dark, often olive-tinted bands. Outermost edge of forewings undulate. Upperside of hind wing orange. Larvae feed on Virginia creeper and grape. Common in woodlands and brushy areas.

# BUTTERFLIES AND MOTHS

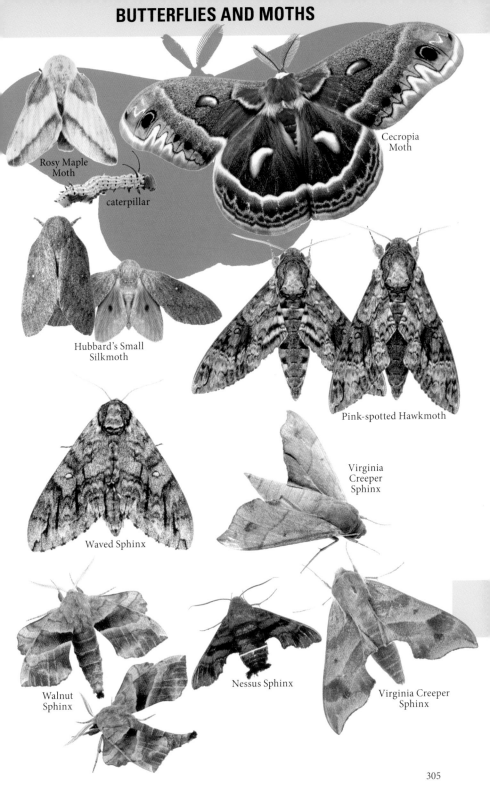

Rosy Maple
Moth

caterpillar

Cecropia
Moth

Hubbard's Small
Silkmoth

Pink-spotted Hawkmoth

Waved Sphinx

Virginia
Creeper
Sphinx

Walnut
Sphinx

Nessus Sphinx

Virginia Creeper
Sphinx

305

SPHINGIDAE

### LETTERED SPHINX *Deidamia inscriptum*
**Sp S F W** Forewing light brown to gray with dark markings and a small white spot near tip; outer margin deeply scalloped. Hind wing is orange-brown with a dark margin. Perches with abdomen raised. Larvae feed on grape and Virginia creeper.

### PAWPAW SPHINX *Dolba hyloeus*
**Sp S F W** Wings dark brown to black with scattered white scales. Pattern on wings somewhat diffuse, not strongly contrasting. Larvae feed on pawpaw, littleleaf sweetfern, and possum haw.

### MOURNFUL SPHINX *Enyo lugubris*
**Sp S F W** Body and wings brown or red. Forewing with large dark patch in latter half and a small tan spot in middle of wing. Outer margin of forewing scalloped. Tip of male abdomen flanged to form a "T." Larvae feed on grape.

### ELLO SPHINX *Erinnyis ello*
**Sp S F W** Forewings grayish brown, with or without a dark streak running their length. Hind wings orange with dark margins. Larvae feed on papaya, euphorbs, poinsettia, and other woody plants.

### ACHEMON SPHINX *Eumorpha achemon*
**Sp S F W** Upperside of forewings pinkish-brown with dark square spot at tips and midway along inner margin. Hind wing pink with broken black submarginal line and brownish border. Thorax with dark, triangular, inward-pointing spots. Larvae feed on grape.

### VINE SPHINX *Eumorpha vitis*
**Sp S F W** Strikingly marked with dark rectangles and triangles in forewing. Thorax with pair of dark rounded spots. Hind wing with pinkish inner margin. Abdomen dark with pale median stripe and pale margins. Larvae feed on evening primrose and grape.

### PANDORUS SPHINX *Eumorpha pandorus*
**Sp S F W** Wings light gray with olive-green cast. Forewing with elongated dark spot on inner margin and dark spot on outer margin just before tip. Pale hind wing with two dark patches. Thorax with dark spots on either side. Larvae feed on grape, *Cissus*, and Virginia creeper.

### SMALL-EYED SPHINX *Paonias myops*
**Sp S F W** Forewing violet gray with orange spots along inner margin and at outer apex. Antemedial and postmedial lines are edged in violet. Hind wing with blue eyespot edged in black. Thorax with orange stripe down center edged in dark violet. Often rests with hind wing protruding beyond leading edge of forewing. Larvae feed on various deciduous trees including black cherry and serviceberry.

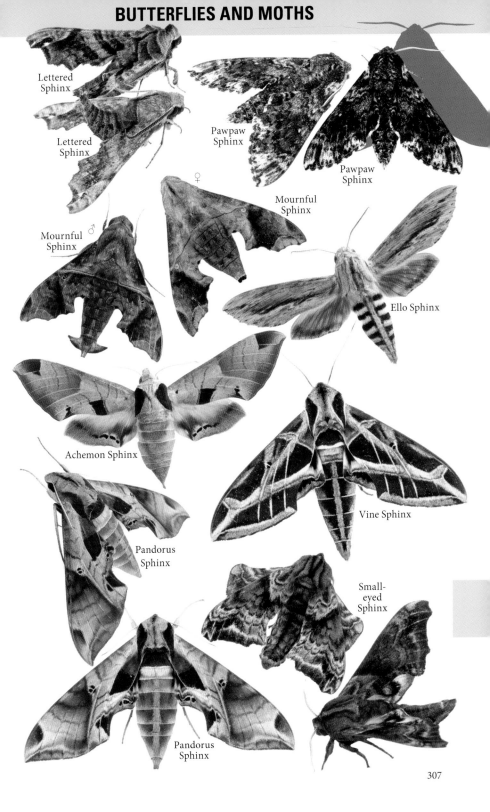

Lettered
Sphinx

Lettered
Sphinx

Pawpaw
Sphinx

Pawpaw
Sphinx

Mournful
Sphinx

♀

Mournful
Sphinx

Mournful ♂
Sphinx

Ello Sphinx

Achemon Sphinx

Vine Sphinx

Pandorus
Sphinx

Small-
eyed
Sphinx

Pandorus
Sphinx

307

## SNOWBERRY CLEARWING *Hemaris diffinis*

Sp **S** F W   Day-flying bumblebee mimic with largely clear wings, surrounded by dark border. Thorax with yellow hairs; abdomen black, some segments prior to tip are yellow. Blue occasionally visible on basally on abdomen. Larvae feed on snowberry and honeysuckle.

## WHITE-LINED SPHINX *Hyles lineata*

Sp **S** F W   Upperside of forewing dark olive brown with tan margins, cream-colored medial line, and thin white lines. Hind wing black with pink median patch and thin white border. Larvae feed on evening primrose, apple, elm, tomato, grape, and more.

## FIVE-SPOTTED HAWK MOTH *Manduca quinquemaculata*

Sp **S** F W   Large; forewing streaked with dark lines; thin black subterminal lines help distinguish it from Carolina Sphinx. Abdomen with five or six pairs of orange spots. Larvae feed on tomato, potato, tobacco, and other nightshades, caterpillar known as Tomato Hornworm.

## RUSTIC SPHINX *Manduca rustica*

Sp **S** F W   Large; forewing white with dark, jagged lines and large variably gray or brown patches in basal and median areas. Hind wing gray with dark bands and white spots. Abdomen usually with three pairs of yellow spots basally. Larvae feed on fringe tree and jasmine.

## CAROLINA SPHINX *Manduca sexta*

Sp **S** F W   Large; forewing light to dark brown with numerous white scales and wavy white lines. Discal spot small and white. Hind wing with wavy gray bands not as distinct as in Five-spotted Hawk Moth. Abdomen with six pairs of yellow spots. Larvae feed on tomato, potato, tobacco, and other nightshades.

## MODEST SPHINX *Pachysphinx modesta*

Sp **S** F W   Large, robust, with tan or gray wings. Forewings with dark medial band, sometimes extending to tip, and outer margin strongly scalloped. Upperside of hind wing with large purplish-red basal patch and smaller basal band outlined in black. Larvae feed on poplar and willow.

## PLEBIAN SPHINX *Paratrea plebeja*

Sp **S** F W   Forewing grayish with black and white streaks and a small white spot encircled by black. Hind wing largely black with outer white margin. Feed on common trumpet creeper and lilac.

## TERSA SPHINX *Xylophanes tersa*

Sp **S** F W   Forewings and abdomen elongated and strongly tapering. Upperside of forewings pale brown to lavender gray with thin dark lines running entire distance. Hind wing dark brown with row of submarginal white triangles. Larvae feed on starcluster, buttonweed, pentas, *Manettia*, and catalpa.

# BUTTERFLIES AND MOTHS

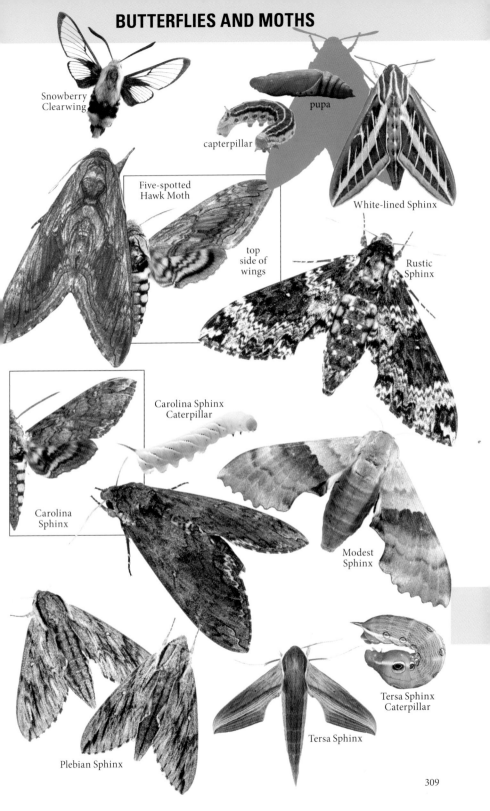

Snowberry Clearwing

pupa

capterpillar

White-lined Sphinx

Five-spotted Hawk Moth

top side of wings

Rustic Sphinx

Carolina Sphinx Caterpillar

Carolina Sphinx

Modest Sphinx

Plebian Sphinx

Tersa Sphinx Caterpillar

Tersa Sphinx

**PECAN CARPENTERWORM MOTH** *Cossula magnifica*  COSSIDAE
**Sp S F W** Forewings gray with tiny black dots and vertical dashes and tip of wings with large brownish patch, resembles broken branch. Distinctly paler basally and just before brown terminal patch. Larvae feed on hickory, pecan, oak, and persimmon.

**LITTLE CARPENTERWORM MOTH** *Prionoxystus macmurtrei*
**Sp S F W** Resembles Robin's Carpenterworm Moth but smaller and gray, with dense network of black lines in forewing. Hind wing gray and somewhat translucent. Larvae feed on oak, maple, and ash.

**CARPENTERWORM MOTH** *Prionoxystus robiniae*
**Sp S F W** Forewing whitish, somewhat translucent, with gray and black mottling; usually several darker patches. Hind wing yellowish orange in male with black border. Larvae feed on ash, chestnut, oaks, locusts, poplars, and others.

**PEACHTREE BORER** *Synanthedon exitiosa*  SESIIDAE
**Sp S F W** Female bluish black with black forewings and translucent hind wings. Abdomen with broad red band. Male bluish black with transparent, amber wings outlined in black and yellow scales between antennae. Tip of abdomen with lateral tufts. Larvae feed on cherry, peach, plum, and other fruit trees.

**MAPLE CALLUS BORER** *Synanthedon acerni*
**Sp S F W** Forewings transparent with black border and a black postmedial band. Head is orange, thorax reddish orange to black and abdomen tapering with fanned orange tufts at end. Larvae feed on maple. Very common at lights.

**GRAPE ROOT BORER** *Vitacea polistiformis*
**Sp S F W** Forewings dark with rusty base and veins. Thorax reddish brown with black bands. Abdomen reddish brown with yellow and black bands. Legs orangish. Larvae feed on grape.

**ROSE HOOKTIP** *Oreta rosea*  DREPANIDAE
**Sp S F W** Variably colored, yellow and pinkish-brown. Forewing with tip hooked and dark postmedial line. Larvae feed on birch and viburnum.

AUTOSTICHIDAE
**FIVE-SPOTTED GLYPHIDOCERA MOTH** *Glyphidocera lactiflosella*
**Sp S F W** White to light gray with peppering of dark scales forming spots. Submarginal dark stripe in forewing curved. Forewings curved inward medially. Base of antennae white and legs banded.

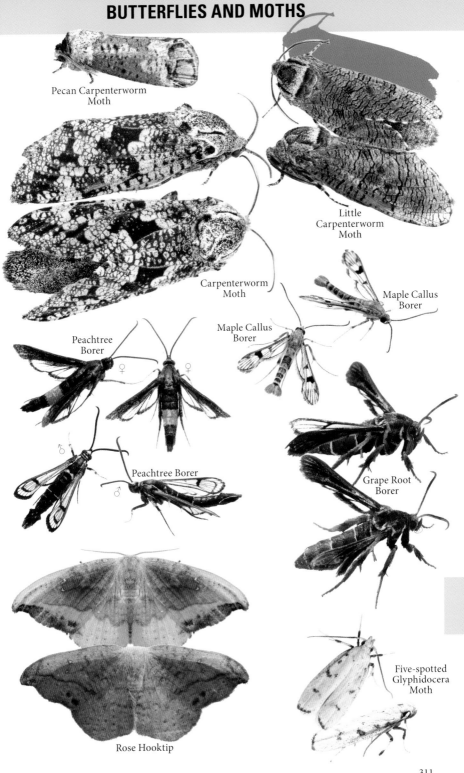

Pecan Carpenterworm
Moth

Little
Carpenterworm
Moth

Carpenterworm
Moth

Maple Callus
Borer

Maple Callus
Borer

Peachtree
Borer
♀ ♀

♂

Peachtree Borer
♂

Grape Root
Borer

Five-spotted
Glyphidocera
Moth

Rose Hooktip

311

### CREAM-BORDERED DICHOMERIS *Dichomeris flavocostella*

GELECHIIDAE

**Sp S F W** Black forewings with white or creamy outer edge creating the appearance of a large black medial diamond and two black spots apically. Long palps and antennae held back over body. Larvae feed on goldenrod and various composites.

### BLACK-SPOTTED TWIRLER *Deltophora sella*

**Sp S F W** Forewing white or gray with two larger black spots anteriorly and one smaller circular one posteriorly. Wings strongly pointed. Larval food plant unknown.

### PALMERWORM MOTH *Dichomeris ligulella*

**Sp S F W** Variable, female grayish to reddish brown with dark area medially and apically. Male with creamy-white lateral margins. Palps extend forward. Larvae skeletonize hackberry, apple, oak, cherry and more.

### RED-NECKED PEANUTWORM MOTH *Stegasta bosqueella*

**Sp S F W** Forewing black with cream-colored to orange, irregular, medial patch along inner margin and large white subapical spot. Larval food plant is the peanut.

### CONSTRICTED TWIRLER *Theisoa constrictella*

**Sp S F W** Forewings orangish-brown, strongly pointed at tips and with darker basal area of wing edged by black and white lines. Dark triangular mark edged in white midway on leading edge of wing. Larvae feed on elm.

### FLOWER MOTH multiple species

SCYTHRIDIDAE

**Sp S F W** Small, dark brown, gray, or black, sometimes with white streaks or patches in forewings. Numerous species that can't be identified from photos. Common on flowers, especially yellow composites, where there may be numerous individuals on a single flower. Some species may be associated with sandy areas.

### DIMORPHIC GRAY *Tornos scolopacinaria*

GEOMETRIDAE

**Sp S F W** Female pale yellow to pinkish; male gray. Both sexes with forewings bearing faint dark peppering and large black apical spot. Distal border of forewings with broad dark band. Larvae feed on various composites including coreopsis. Several other species of *Tornos* occur in the state and are problematic, especially in central Texas, so use caution when identifying.

### COMMON GRAY *Anavitrinella pampinaria*

**Sp S F W** Light tan to gray, peppered with dark spots and mottling. First abdominal segment forming white band, bordered anteriorly by black line that extends onto wings. Dark postmedial line wavy and toothed. Larvae feed on maple, poplar, ash, cotton, and more.

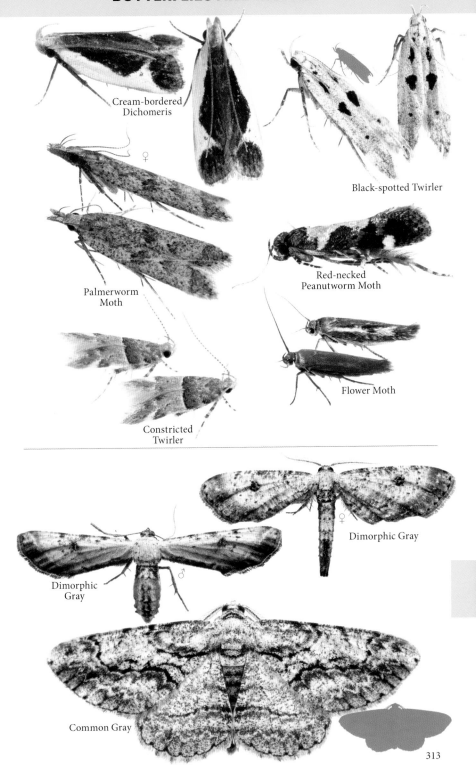

Cream-bordered Dichomeris

♀

Black-spotted Twirler

Palmerworm Moth

Red-necked Peanutworm Moth

Flower Moth

Constricted Twirler

Dimorphic Gray

♀

Dimorphic Gray

♂

Common Gray

# LEPIDOPTERA

**BENT-LINE CARPET** *Costaconvexa centrostrigaria*
Sp S F W Male forewing gray with grayish black antemedial line and outer edge of postmedial line. Female with the area between these darkened. Both sexes with small dark distal dot in the outer edge of the medial space. Larvae feed on knotweed, smartweed, and similar plants.

**PACKARD'S WAVE** *Cyclophora packardi*
Sp S F W Pale orange to reddish brown wings peppered with black spots. Antemedial and postmedial lines are visible as line of small dots. Both sets of wings with a small white discal spot outlined in black. Larvae possibly feed on sweet-fern and oak.

**SOUTHERN ANGLE** *Speranza varadaria*
Sp S F W Forewings tan, brown, or gray and finely peppered with pale median band edged by dark brown posteriorly. Forewing outer margin somewhat sinuate. Each wing with a small black discal dot. Larvae feed on groundsel tree.

**FAINT-SPOTTED ANGLE** *Digrammia ocellinata*
Sp S F W Wings pale and brownish gray, faintly mottled with brown shading posterior to postmedial line in forewing and extending on to hind wing. Postmedial line with diffuse pattern of dark spots. Subterminal line darker; often accented with short dark dashes along veins. Larvae feed on black locust.

**THE BEGGAR** *Eubaphe mendica*
Sp S F W Forewings ovoid, semi-translucent yellow, with purplish-gray antemedial and postmedial lines broken into large spots. Larvae feed on violet.

**ORANGE BEGGAR** *Eubaphe unicolor*
Sp S F W Body and wings uniformly orange. Forewings elongated and rounded. Antennae, legs, and eyes black. Larvae feed on violet.

**SOMBER CARPET** *Disclisioprocta stellata*
Sp S F W Wings light to dark or purplish brown and densely patterned with wavy dark and white lines. Median area of wings often darker. Postmedial line in forewing with two larger "teeth" at middle. Larvae feed on amaranth and devil's claw.

**LESSER GRAPEVINE LOOPER MOTH** *Eulithis diversilineata*
Sp S F W Wings orangish with fine brown lines and inner median area purplish brown. Posterior edge of postmedian line sharply pointed at middle. Typically perches with abdomen curved upward. Larvae feed on grape and Virginia creeper.

# BUTTERFLIES AND MOTHS

Bent-lined Carpet ♀

Packard's Wave

Bent-lined Carpet

Southern Angle

Southern Angle

Faint-spotted Angle

The Beggar

Orange Beggar

Somber Carpet

Lesser Grapevine Looper Moth

315

### CURVE-TOOTHED GEOMETER *Eutrapela clemataria*

GEOMETRIDAE

Sp S F W   Wings light brown to dark purplish brown with well-defined dark postmedial line. Tips of forewings with diffuse pale area. Subterminal region on both wings may be darker. Larvae feed on ash, basswood, birch, maple, poplar, and many other trees.

### COMMON EUPITHECIA *Eupithecia miserulata*

Sp S F W   Wings tan, gray, or brown marked with faint dark lines. Forewing with obvious black discal spot and subterminal area with faint white spot. Larvae feed on composites, grape, oaks, willow, and many other plants.

### FIVE-LINED GRAY *Glena quinquelinearia*

Sp S F W   Broad gray wings with nearly straight black medial lines. Subterminal area with fainter lines. Abdomen narrowly banded black. Small black discal spot on each wing. Larvae feed on maple, oak, willow, and others.

### TEXAS GRAY *Glenoides texanaria*

Sp S F W   Wings gray to brown with indistinct dark, wavy lines. Subterminal area darker, peppered, sometimes purplish red. When visible, subterminal pale line scalloped. Larval food plant unknown.

### GREEN BROOMWEED LOOPER *Fernaldella fimetaria*

Sp S F W   Rests with wings together over body. Underside of wings golden brown and boldly marked with white spots and bands margined in black. Abdomen golden brown with white bands. Larvae feed on prairie broomweed.

### MOSSY CARPET *Hammaptera parinotata*

Sp S F W   Light brown to gray forewings variably washed with olive green and indistinct dark bands. Subterminal white line zigzagged with two black teeth at middle. Fringe of wings checkered. Larval food plant unknown.

### CHICKWEED GEOMETER *Haematopis grataria*

Sp S F W   Yellow wings with bright pinkish postmedial line, subterminal line, and fringe. Each forewing with prominent pink discal spot. Larvae feed on chickweed, clover, and similar low plants.

### DOT-LINED WAVE *Idaea tacturata*

Sp S F W   Wings white with fine dark wavy lines and brown peppering. Small black discal spot in each wing, but somewhat lost amongst other spots. Abdomen white with black spots. Larvae likely feed on clover.

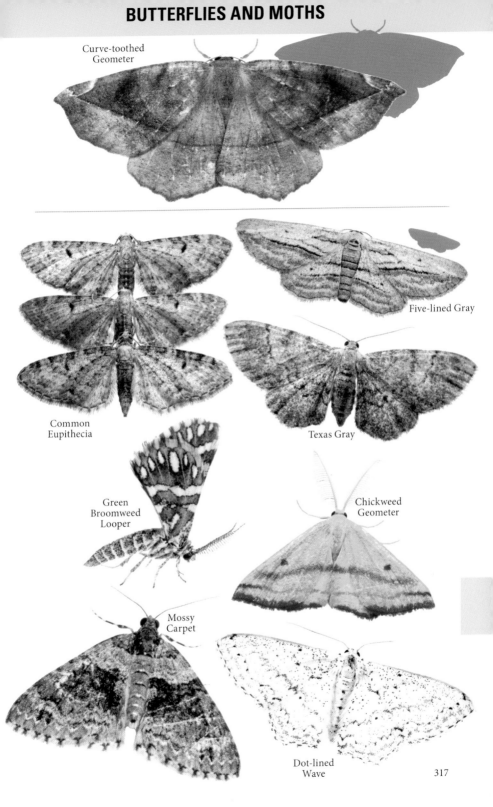

Curve-toothed Geometer

Common Eupithecia

Five-lined Gray

Texas Gray

Green Broomweed Looper

Chickweed Geometer

Mossy Carpet

Dot-lined Wave

### BLACK-DOTTED RUDDY *Ilexia intractata*                   GEOMETRIDAE

Sp **S** **F** W   Red to reddish-brown wings, variously mottled with three evenly spaced faint dark lines. Each wing with a small discal black spot. Larvae feed on holly.

### BROWN-SHADED GRAY *Iridopsis defectaria*

Sp **S** **F** W   Wings variable, tan, olive, or purplish. Forewing dark; wavy antemedial, medial, and postmedial lines usually edged in brown above or below. Abdomen with black bands. Larvae feed on alder, birch, poplar, willow, and other plants.

### PANNARIA WAVE *Leptostales pannaria*

Sp **S** **F** W   Grayish or more commonly reddish-brown wings peppered with small black spots and yellow-edged wavy lines. Leading edge of forewing yellow or reddish. Fringe reddish. Abdomen brown with yellow dorsal spots.

### MESQUITE/SIGNATE LOOPERS *Rindgea cyda* and *R. s-signata*

Sp **S** **F** W   Wings tan or brown with dark wavy postmedian line that does not extend to wing margin and with pale marginal stripe above. Antemedial and median lines are diffuse. Wing margin checkered. Larvae feed on mesquite. These two species overlap broadly in Texas and are mostly indistinguishable by pattern.

### JUNIPER-TWIG GEOMETER *Patalene olyzonaria*

Sp **S** **F** W   Wings tan, brown, or orange, faint antemedial line and bold, dark medial line. Small dark discal spot. Forewings hooked at tip, more so in female.

### SMALL PHIGALIA *Phigalia strigataria*

Sp **S** **F** W   Wings light gray, peppered with dark spotting similar to Toothed Phigalia. Dark postmedial line is straighter, less jagged on inner margin and often fragmented throughout. Female is flightless with tiny, reduced wings. Larvae feed on blueberry, elm, oak, willow, and other woody plants.

### TOOTHED PHIGALIA *Phigalia denticulata*

Sp **S** **F** W   Wings light gray, peppered with dark spotting. Dark wavy antemedial, median, and postmedial lines present. Forewing postmedial line more jagged than others and touching median line at inner margin. Female is flightless with tiny, reduced wings. Larvae likely feed on a variety of woody plants.

### OAK BEAUTY *Phaeoura quernaria*

Sp **S** **F** W   Charcoal gray or brown wings mottled with white and black jagged lines. Anterior basal area largely white or white with diffuse brown. Dark postmedial line broadly margined with white in some. Larvae feed on oaks, ash, cherry, elm, poplar, willow, and more.

# BUTTERFLIES AND MOTHS

Black-dotted Ruddy

Brown-shaded Gray

Pannaria Wave

Mesquite/Signate Looper

Juniper-twig Geometer

♀

♂

Small Phigalia

Toothed Phigalia

Oak Beauty

319

# LEPIDOPTERA

**COMMON TAN WAVE** *Pleuroprucha insulsaria*　　　GEOMETRIDAE
Sp **S** F W　　Uniformly tan or brownish wings with faint light peppering. Wings narrowly scalloped with yellowish margin. Faint median line is usually evident. Larvae feed on various composites, corn, goldenrod, oak, and a variety of other plants.

**LARGE MAPLE SPANWORM** *Prochoerodes lineola*
Sp **S** F W　　Wings variable from pale yellow to purplish brown. Dark postmedial line jags upward at wing margin. Both sets of wings with tiny dark discal spot. Area below postmedial line with diffuse dark markings. Forewing tip slightly hooked. Larvae feed on birch, blueberry, cherry, oak, poplar, willow, and many other plants.

**BIG BEND EMERALD** *Dichorda rectaria*
Sp **S** F W　　Similar to Showy Emerald *Dichorda iridaria*; not shown of eastern part of state. Wings pale green with well-delineated white antemedial line in forewing and postmedial line in fore- and hind wing. Leading edge of forewing speckled brown. Tiny discal spot present in each wing. Larvae feed on skunkbush.

**RED-BORDERED EMERALD** *Nemoria lixaria*
Sp **S** F W　　Green with pale antemedial and postmedial lines that sometimes have dark edge. Fringe of wings with red and white checkering. Abdomen with series of white spots edged in red. Small dark discal spot present in each wing. Larvae feed on oak.

**LARGE LACE-BORDER** *Scopula limboundata*
Sp **S** F W　　White or tawny wings marked with wavy light brown lines. Subterminal area often with dark mottling, sometimes resulting in lacy appearance. Small dark discal spot in each wing. Larvae feed on apple, bedstraw, blueberry, dandelion, and more.

**BLACKBERRY LOOPER** *Chlorochlamys chloroleucaria*
Sp **S** F W　　Dull green wings with broad white or cream-colored antemedial stripe absent in hind wing and postmedial line. Wings with white leading edge and fringe. Larvae feed on blackberry, strawberry, and composites.

**SOUTHERN EMERALD** *Synchlora frondaria*
Sp **S** F W　　Green wings with wavy, white antemedial and postmedial lines. Small faint white veins present along subterminal area. Abdomen with medial white stripe. Larvae feed on blackberry, chrysanthemum, Spanish needle, and other low-growing plants.

**AMERICAN LAPPET MOTH** *Phyllodesma americana*　　LASIOCAMPIDAE
Sp **S** F W　　Reddish brown, sometimes with bluish-gray diffusion and strongly scalloped wings. At rest, scalloped leading edge of hind wing extends below forewing. Larvae feed on oak, poplar, and rose.

# BUTTERFLIES AND MOTHS

Common Tan Wave

Large maple Spanworm

Big Bend Emerald

Red-bordered Emerald

Large Lace-Border

Blackberry Looper

Southern Emerald

American Lappet Moth

American Lappet Moth

LASIOCAMPIDAE

## EASTERN TENT CATERPILLAR MOTH *Malacosoma americana*
**Sp S F W** Wings brown with cream-colored antemedial and postmedial stripe, usually encompassing paler medial area. Thorax and abdomen hairy. Larvae feed on numerous deciduous trees including apple, crab apple, and cherry.

## FOREST TENT CATERPILLAR MOTH *Malacosoma disstria*
**Sp S F W** Yellowish, tan, or brown with distinct antemedial and postmedial lines; area between these lines sometimes darkened. Fringe unevenly checkered. Larvae feed on alder, birch, cherry, maple, oak, and many other deciduous trees.

## DOT-LINED WHITE *Artace cribrarius*
**Sp S F W** White to gray wings with white veins and dotted black lines. Thorax, abdomen, and legs all thickly covered with hairs. Larvae feed on oak, cherry, and rose.

## SOUTHWESTERN APOTOLYPE *Apotolype brevicrista*
**Sp S F W** Gray forewing with dark patterning and small crest of bluish-black scales on top of thorax. Forewing antemedial stripe and postmedial stripes wavy. Larvae feed on mesquite. Two similar species in the genus *Tolype* occur in east Texas.

EREBIDAE

## YELLOW SCALLOP MOTH *Anomis erosa*
**Sp S F W** Yellowish, tan, to brown with wings peppered with light color. Forewing with rusty-red antemedial lines forming a loop at middle and encompassing small white orbicular dot encircled by brown. Tip of forewings heavily scalloped. Larvae feed on mallow.

## VELVETBEAN CATERPILLAR MOTH *Anticarsia gemmatalis*
**Sp S F W** Variable yellowish, tan, or gray with somewhat pointed wings and strong dark median line, sometimes edged in cream and rusty red. Some individuals with heavy mottling across wings. Apex of forewing with small semicircular buff patch. Larvae feed on numerous crops including alfalfa, soybean, and velvetbean.

## GROTE'S BERTHOLDIA *Bertholdia trigona*
**Sp S F W** Forewing long, narrow, and somewhat pointed at apex with large yellowish translucent patch along leading edge. Several small black dots in yellow patch and numerous others peppered across wings. Hind wing short and white with pink along inner margin. Larvae feed on algae and moss early on, switching to herbaceous plants in later instars.

## BLACK WITCH *Ascalapha odorata*
**Sp S F W** Unmistakable, very large; mottled dark gray with iridescent patches. Females with pale median band. Larvae feed on mesquite and cassia. Highly migratory and liable to show up almost anywhere; suggests a bat in flight.

# BUTTERFLIES AND MOTHS

Eastern Tent Caterpillar Moth

Forest Tent Caterpillar Moth

Forest Tent Caterpillar Moth

Eastern Tent Caterpillar

Forest Tent Caterpillar

Dot-lined White

Southwestern Apotolype

Grote's Bertholdia

Velvetbean Caterpillar Moth

Yellow Scallop Moth

♂ Black Witch

# LEPIDOPTERA

**BENT-WINGED OWLET** *Bleptina caradrinalis* EREBIDAE

Sp S F W  Forewing light to purplish gray. Antemedial and postmedial lines wavy and faint; dark medial line usually more prominent. Subterminal line pale, usually darkly bordered and somewhat indistinct. Larvae feed on dead leaves.

**VETCH LOOPER MOTH** *Caenurgia chloropha*

Sp S F W  Pale tan, brown, or reddish brown. Forewing usually with small dark patch at middle of postmedial line. Subterminal line is row of tiny dark spots. Larvae feed on vetch and other legumes.

**GIRLFRIEND UNDERWING** *Catocala amica*

Sp S F W  Forewing grayish, somewhat peppered, and often with wash of yellow or orange. Nondescript antemedial, median, and postmedial lines with blotch of black along leading edge of wing. Hind wing yellowish orange with broad black subterminal band interrupted at anal angle. Larvae feed on oak.

**ULTRONIA UNDERWING** *Catocala ultronia*

Sp S F W  Tan, gray, or brown forewing with wide diffuse black area along trailing edge. Wing tips usually pale. Hind wing reddish orange with black median and subterminal bands and grayish fringe. Larvae feed on apple, cherry, hawthorn, and plum.

**ILIA UNDERWING** *Catocala ilia*

Sp S F W  Large and quite variable with forewings gray, brown, blackish, or olive green. Antemedial line in forewing usually well defined and wavy. White reniform spot generally present. Hind wing reddish orange with median and subterminal black bands and checkered pale fringe. Larvae feed on oak.

**SAD UNDERWING** *Catocala maestosa*

Sp S F W  Large, forewing grayish with long, dark, crescent-shaped band at apex. Reniform spot, pale rusty orange. Hind wing black with white checkered fringe. Larvae feed on pecan and walnut.

**LITTLE NYMPH UNDERWING** *Catocala micronympha*

Sp S F W  Variable, but forewings usually gray, brown, and black with apex of wing somewhat delineated by dark crescent band and white streak within. Subterminal band white, but may be faint. Antemedial and postmedial stripes, when present, bordered by brown. Larvae feed on oak.

**YELLOW-COLLARED SCAPE MOTH** *Cisseps fulvicollis*

Sp S F W  Dark brown to black with yellowish-orange collar behind head. Forewing with yellowish leading edge, especially basally. Hind wing with large translucent patch. Rests with wings closed over abdomen; compare to Grapeleaf Skeletonizer. Larvae feed on grasses and sedges.

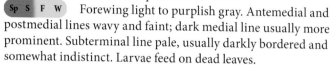

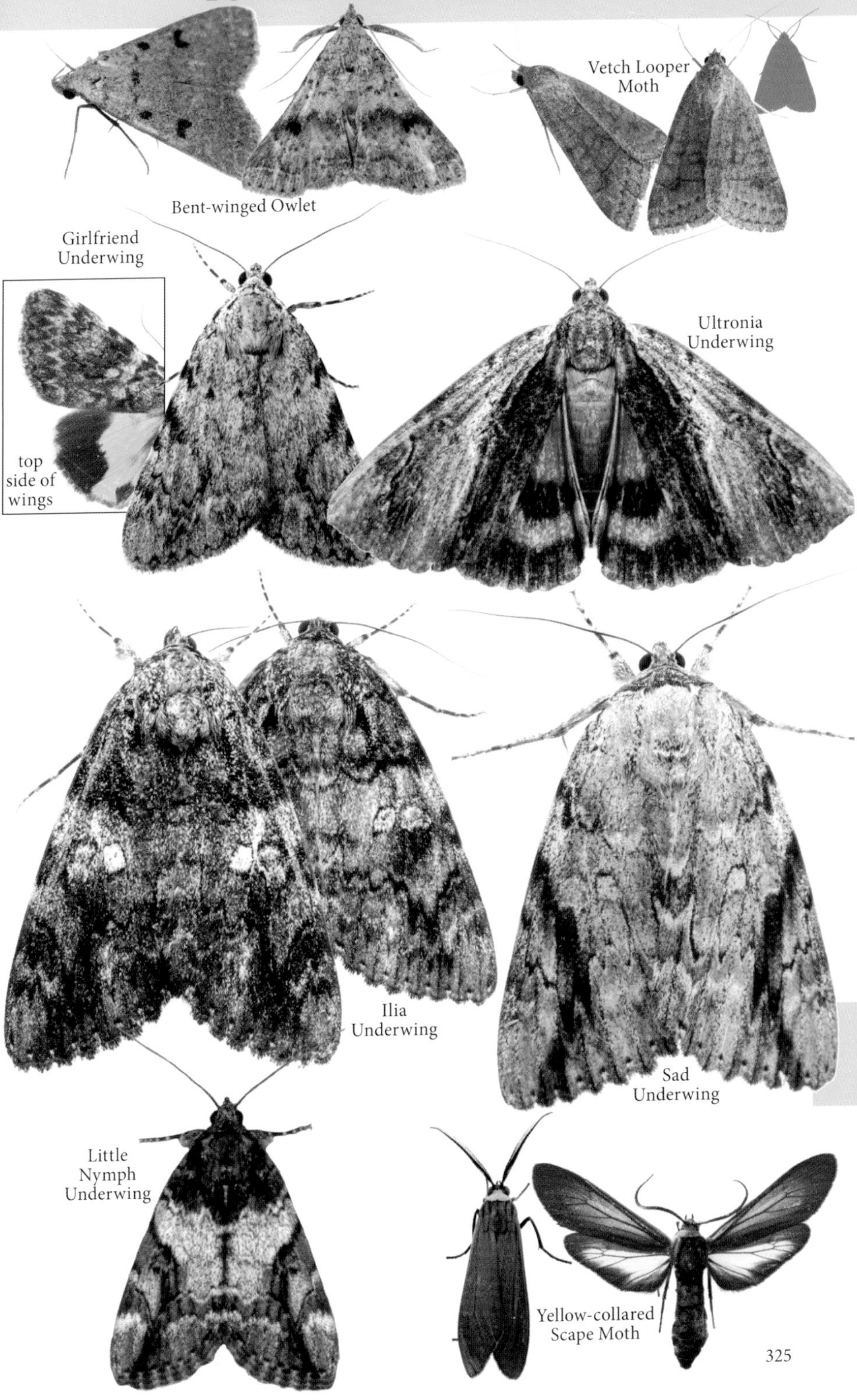

# BUTTERFLIES AND MOTHS

Vetch Looper
Moth

Bent-winged Owlet

Girlfriend
Underwing

top
side of
wings

Ultronia
Underwing

Ilia
Underwing

Sad
Underwing

Little
Nymph
Underwing

Yellow-collared
Scape Moth

325

## ONE-BANDED LICHEN MOTH *Cisthene unifascia* — EREBIDAE

Sp **S** F **W** Forewing dark gray with pale yellowish streak along leading edge and medial band that narrows considerably at middle and may or may not be interrupted. Hind wing pink with small black apical patch. Thorax pinkish orange with gray dorsal patch. Larvae feed on lichens.

## THIN-BANDED LICHEN MOTH *Cisthene tenuifascia*

Sp **S** F **W** Forewing dark gray with pale yellowish streak along leading edge and median band that narrows slightly at middle. Hind wing reddish with narrow black border. Thorax yellowish orange with gray dorsal patch. Larvae feed on lichens.

## LEAD-COLORED LICHEN MOTH *Cisthene plumbea*

Sp **S** F **W** Forewing dark gray with pale yellowish streak along leading edge and semicircular spot extending downward at middle. Hind wing pink with narrow black border. Thorax pinkish orange with gray dorsal patch. Larvae feed on lichens.

## EVERLASTING BUD MOTH *Eublemma minima*

Sp **S** F **W** Forewings white with broad, diffuse, brownish bands in median and subterminal areas. In profile, median band with tuft of scales along trailing edge. Larvae feed on cudweed.

## NORTHERN GIANT FLAG MOTH *Dysschema howardi*

Sp **S** F **W** Forewing black with bold, contrasting white lines. Hind wing pale cream colored male or orange female with reddish-orange subterminal band sometimes bluish black with blue triangles edged in black. Larvae feed on composites.

## SOUTHERN TUSSOCK MOTH *Dasychira meridionalis*

Sp **S** F **W** Forewing gray to brown with lighter tan area basally. Area surrounding reniform spot usually white, often extending to median band. Postmedial band dark, well defined, and darker posteriorly. Larvae feed on oak.

## SALT MARSH MOTH *Estigmene acrea*

Sp **S** F **W** Forewing white with black spots, usually boldest along leading edge. Upperside of hind wing and underside of all wings orange in male, white in female with small black blotches. Abdomen orange with white tip and black medial spots. Larvae feed on apple, cabbage, corn, potato, tobacco , and other plants. Poorly named based on the original description as a pest of salt-grass hay; an anomaly.

## ARID EUDESMIA *Eudesmia arida*

Sp **S** F **W** Wings black with broad median orange band and narrower subterminal band. Body yellowish orange. Antennae and legs black. Larvae feed on lichens growing on rocks, walls, and cliffs.

One-banded
Lichen Moth

Thin-banded
Lichen Moth

One-banded
Lichen Moth

Lead-colored
Lichen Moth

Everlasting Bud Moth

♂

Northern Giant Flag
Moth

Northern
Giant Flag
Moth

Southern
Tussock
Moth

Salt Marsh Moth

Arid
Eudesmia

327

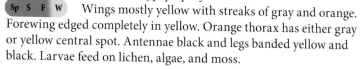

## PAINTED LICHEN MOTH *Hypoprepia fucosa*

EREBIDAE

**Sp S F W** Wings mostly yellow with streaks of gray and orange. Forewing edged completely in yellow. Orange thorax has either gray or yellow central spot. Antennae black and legs banded yellow and black. Larvae feed on lichen, algae, and moss.

## SMALL NECKLACE MOTH *Hypsoropha hormos*

**Sp S F W** Forewing pale gray to reddish brown with three to four white spots at middle, increasing in size toward midline. Pale gray spot subapically. Large tuft of scales rising high on head and thorax. Larvae feed on persimmon.

## COMMON IDIA *Idia aemula*

**Sp S F W** Forewing reddish brown to gray and peppered with dark scales. Reniform and larger orbicular spots yellowish orange. Antemedial and postmedial lines fairly uniform in width. Larvae feed on leaf litter.

## AMERICAN IDIA *Idia americalis*

**Sp S F W** Forewing reddish brown to gray and peppered with dark scales. Reniform and larger orbicular spots brownish orange. Antemedial, median, and postmedial lines widest at leading edge of wing. Larvae feed on leaf litter and lichen.

## AMBIGUOUS MOTH *Lascoria ambigualis*

**Sp S F W** Gray to purplish brown. Forewing with dark, broadly diffuse antemedial line. Postmedial line wavy. Subterminal line pale, edged with dark brown. Reniform spot is white crescent shape, often reduced to two small end points in female. Larvae feed on ragweed.

## DETRACTED OWLET *Lesmone detrahens*

**Sp S F W** Brown to violet gray with pale band across both wings. Forewing with dark median band and a small white reniform spot. Subterminal line bordered above by dark brown band. Larvae feed on cassia.

## BLACK-AND-YELLOW LICHEN MOTH *Lycomorpha pholus*

**Sp S F W** Forewing elongated with broadly rounded tips. Anterior half of forewing yellowish-orange, posterior bluish black. Head and thorax bluish black. Larvae feed on lichen.

## LIVE OAK METRIA *Metria amella*

**Sp S F W** Wings brownish gray. Forewing with dark double median line and pale stripe posterior to it. Thin antemedial line diffusely bordered by yellow. Individuals vary, but are often darkest in middle and posterior areas of wing. Feed on live oak.

# BUTTERFLIES AND MOTHS

Painted Lichen Moth

Small Necklace Moth

Small Necklace Moth

Ambiguous Moth ♀

Common Idia

American Idia

Detracted Owlet

Ambiguous Moth ♀

Black and Yellow Lichen Moth

Live-oak Metria

## WITHERED MOCIS *Mocis marcida*

EREBIDAE

**Sp S F W** Gray to reddish brown. Forewing with rusty brown antemedial and postmedial medial line; latter fading before reaching trailing margin of wing. Center of wings often with two short dark lines, sometimes with an additional transverse line through them. Black spot of variable size anteromedially. Larvae feed on grass.

## WHITE-MARKED TUSSOCK MOTH *Orgyia leucostigma*

**Sp S F W** Forewing somewhat uniformly gray or tan with no shading around faint white reniform spot. Postmedial line strongest at leading edge of wing and scalloped throughout. Female whitish and wingless. Larvae feed on apple, birch, elm, willow, and more.

## DARK-SPOTTED PALTHIS *Palthis angulalis*

**Sp S F W** Forewing pinkish tan to reddish brown and held creased downward when at rest. Dark brown median band fading toward leading edge of wing. Male with long, upturned labial palps. Larvae feed on many different coniferous and deciduous trees.

## FAINT-SPOTTED PALTHIS *Palthis asopialis*

**Sp S F W** Similar to Dark-spotted Palthis, but wings purplish gray and conspicuous dark patch near forewing apex. Antemedial line and dark border relatively straight, fading at leading edge of wing. Dark reniform spot bisected by thin white line. Male with long upturned palps. Larvae feed on composites, coralberry, corn, and more.

## RED-LINED PANOPODA *Panopoda rufimargo*

**Sp S F W** Wings grayish tan to yellowish tan. With rusty-red, nearly parallel, antemedial and postmedial lines edged in yellow. Reniform spot pale yellowish or black. Subterminal line sometimes visible as small white dots. Larvae feed on beech and oak.

## COMMON OAK MOTH *Phoberia atomaris*

**Sp S F W** Gray to tan wings. Forewing with wavy antemedial and postmedial lines edged in yellow. Subterminal line wavy and darker brown between it and postmedial line. Reniform spot dark brown generally edged in yellow. Larvae feed on oak.

## MOONSEED MOTH *Plusiodonta compressipalpis*

**Sp S F W** Yellowish, tan, or purplish-brown forewings with dark median band divided into three narrow lines terminating in tuft of scales. Several amorphous gold-edged spots. Larvae feed on moonseed and snailseed.

## DEAD-WOOD BORER MOTH *Scolecocampa liburna*

**Sp S F W** Forewing straw colored with large reniform spot either black or outlined by black. Postmedial and subterminal lines in the form of dark dots. Larvae bore into decaying logs and stumps.

# BUTTERFLIES AND MOTHS

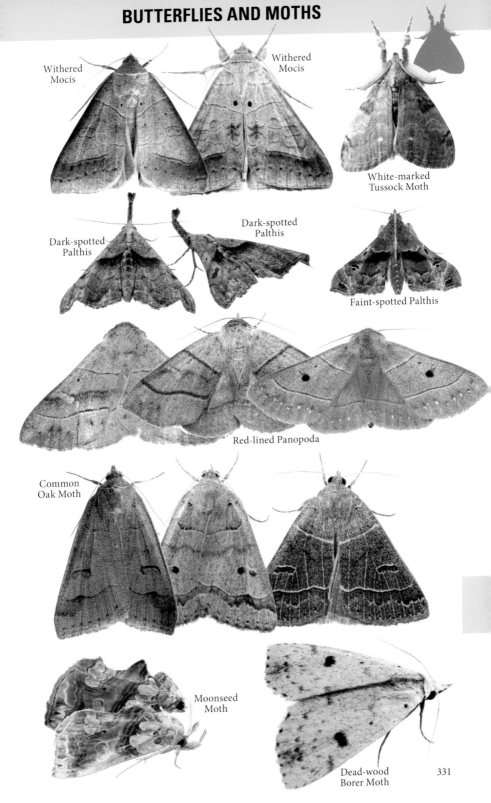

Withered Mocis

Withered Mocis

White-marked Tussock Moth

Dark-spotted Palthis

Dark-spotted Palthis

Faint-spotted Palthis

Red-lined Panopoda

Common Oak Moth

Moonseed Moth

Dead-wood Borer Moth

## TEXAS WASP MOTH *Horama panthalon*

EREBIDAE

**Sp S F W** Terrific wasp mimic with long, narrow, dark forewing. Thorax with four yellow-orange spots and a pair of lateral stripes. Male hind legs with black and yellowish-orange flange. Abdomen metallic purple or blue with orange bands. Larval food plant is Desert Yaupon. Adults regularly visit flowers especially *Eupatorium*.

## AGREEABLE TIGER MOTH *Spilosoma congrua*

**Sp S F W** Forewing white with variable brown spots along antemedial, postmedial, and subterminal lines. Hind wing and abdomen white and unmarked. Forelegs with coxae and femora yellowish orange. Larvae feed on dandelion, plantain, and pigweed.

## ORANGE VIRBIA *Virbia aurantiaca*

**Sp S F W** Forewing brownish orange, sometimes with dusky discal spot and diffuse brown shading along subterminal line. Hind wing orange with black subterminal band and discal spot. Larvae feed on corn, dandelion, pigweed, plantain, and other low vegetation.

## LUNATE ZALE *Zale lunata*

**Sp S F W** Wings various shades of brown and variably marked. Double antemedial and postmedial lines fade toward wing leading edge. Some individuals with white patches along subterminal line. Larvae feed on oak, cherry, plum, and willow.

## DARK MARATHYSSA *Marathyssa inficita*

**Sp S F W** Rests with wings tightly rolled and abdomen usually elevated. Grayish forewings with broad pale median area and reddish-orange patches in basal and terminal areas. Larvae feed on sumac.

## LARGE PAECTES *Paectes abrostoloides*

NOCTUIDAE

**Sp S F W** Wings gray to brown. Forewing with basal crescent-shaped patch. Postmedial line double and somewhat kinked at middle. Perches with abdomen raised. Larvae feed on sweetgum.

## IPSILON DART *Agrotis ipsilon*

**Sp S F W** Forewing dark gray with pale basal and subterminal areas or largely brown with gray leading edge. Two black darts from reniform spot and terminal area point toward each other. Reniform, orbicular, and claviform spots gray outlined in black. Larvae feed on various plants and crops.

## RASCAL DART *Agrotis malefida*

**Sp S F W** Gray forewing darker along leading edge and numerous veins thinly outlined in black. Head and collar blackish, epaulets on thorax contrasting gray. Claviform and reniform spots dark. Orbicular spot usually outlined by pale color. Larvae feed on low vegetation including clover, corn, and tomato.

# BUTTERFLIES AND MOTHS

Texas Wasp Moth ♂

Agreeable Tiger caterpillar

Agreeable Tiger Moth

Orange Virbia

Lunate Zale

Dark Marathyssa

Dark Marathyssa

Large Paectes

Large Paectes

Ipsilon Dart

Rascal Dart

Rascal Dart

# LEPIDOPTERA

### AFFLICTED DAGGER MOTH *Acronicta afflicta*
**Sp S F W**  Dark, reddish- or greenish-brown, and pale orbicular spot with gray center. Terminal and subterminal lines are a series of pale chevrons. Thorax is usually diffusely pale at middle. Larvae feed on oaks.

### AMERICAN DAGGER MOTH *Acronicta americana*
**Sp S F W**  Pale, uniformly gray. Postmedial line a series of white chevrons margined in black posteriorly. Reniform spot may or may not be obvious, but with gray center. Fringe a dark checkered pattern. Larvae feed on many trees and woody plants including alder, ash, basswood, elm, chestnut, and hickory.

### CLEAR DAGGER MOTH *Acronicta clarescens*
**Sp S F W**  Somewhat uniformly gray or tan. Basal dark, longitudinal stripe extends through antemedial line. Reniform spot often brownish. Postmedial line jagged and darkly outlined. Larvae feed on apple, cherry, hawthorn, plum, and more.

### RUDDY DAGGER MOTH *Acronicta rubricoma*
**Sp S F W**  Light gray with double postmedial and antemedial lines in forewing edged with dark gray. Orbicular spot outlined in black, reniform spot usually with gray center. Anal and basal dashes thin and indistinct. Larvae feed on hackberry and elm.

### EIGHT-SPOTTED FORESTER *Alypia octomaculata*
**Sp S F W**  Forewing black with two large cream-colored spots; hind wing with two large white spots. Thorax bordered laterally with pale yellow stripe. Legs with yellow or orange tufts of hair. Larvae feed on pepper vine, grape, and Virginia creeper.

### GREEN CUTWORM MOTH *Anicla infecta*
**Sp S F W**  Tan to light gray and peppered with fine small black spots. Forewing with rusty terminal line. Reniform spot black, fragmented, and outlined by pale yellow or rusty brown. Black collar behind head often visible. Larvae feed on grasses.

### GOLDEN LOOPER *Argyrogramma verruca*
**Sp S F W**  Forewing reddish or tan with gold wash. Antemedial and postmedial lines toothed and edged with shaded lilac-colored bands. Stigma golden, edged in white, and broken into a larger and smaller spot. Head and thorax with large tufts. Larvae feed on low-growing plants including Arrowhead, curled dock, and tobacco.

### SOYBEAN LOOPER *Chrysodeixis includens*
**Sp S F W**  Forewing bronzy brown or gray. Head and thorax with large tufts. Stigma silver, separated into two spots; the innermost one somewhat "U" shaped with gold center. Larvae feed on goldenrod, lettuce, soybean, and tobacco.

# BUTTERFLIES AND MOTHS

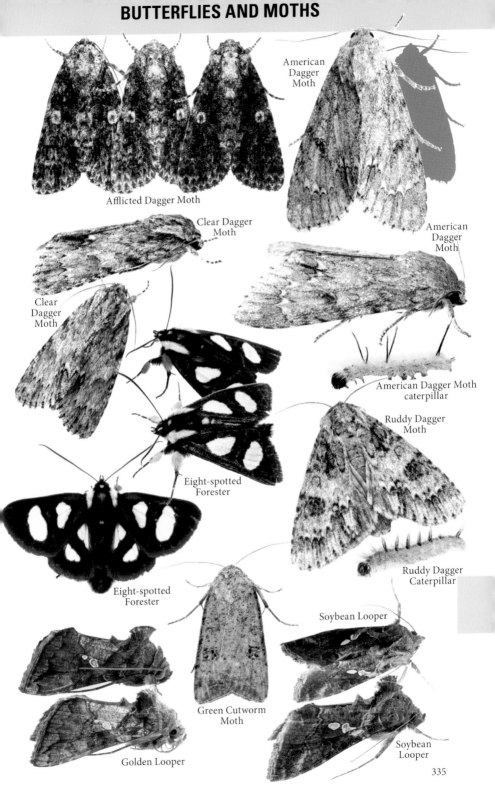

American Dagger Moth

Afflicted Dagger Moth

Clear Dagger Moth

American Dagger Moth

Clear Dagger Moth

American Dagger Moth caterpillar

Ruddy Dagger Moth

Eight-spotted Forester

Eight-spotted Forester

Ruddy Dagger Caterpillar

Soybean Looper

Green Cutworm Moth

Golden Looper

Soybean Looper

335

### DARK-BANDED COBUBATHA *Cobubatha lixiva*

NOCTUIDAE

**Sp S F W** Forewing pale gray anteriorly and orangish brown distally separated by broad dark band medially that is expanded in the middle. Leading edge of wing with dark patch at subterminal line. Larval food plant unknown.

### WHITE-DOTTED GROUNDLING *Condica videns*

**Sp S F W** Wings tawny brown. Forewing with diffuse dark stripe running through white reniform spot. Veins dark and peppered with small white specs. Tuft of hairs on head. Larvae feed on various composites including goldenrod.

### GROTE'S SALLOW *Copivaleria grotei*

**Sp S F W** Forewing dark gray with green accents. Orbicular and reniform spots white with dark centers; claviform spot and subterminal area grayish. Thorax with white band down middle. Larvae feed on ash.

### SHARP-STIGMA LOOPER *Ctenoplusia oxygramma*

**Sp S F W** Dark grayish brown with prominent tufts on head and thorax. Dark median patch bisected by oblique, silver-edged elongated stigma. Larvae feed on composites like goldenrod.

### STRAIGHT-LINED CYDOSIA *Cydosia aurivitta*

**Sp S F W** Sexually dimorphic with elongated narrow wings. Forewing bluish black with orangish-red antemedial and postmedial bands and orangish spot in central median area. Female with series of white spots in dark areas. Larval food plant unknown.

### GRATEFUL MIDGET *Elaphria grata*

**Sp S F W** Reddish or orange brown. Dark veins peppered with white. Antemedial and postmedial lines slightly curved and white. Orbicular spot small and black. Reniform spot hourglass shaped with two small black dots. Larvae likely feed on fungus.

### CHALCEDONY MIDGET *Elaphria chalcedonia*

**Sp S F W** Thorax with broad pale stripe that extends along leading edge of wing. Postmedial line forms white blotch at forewing leading edge. Larvae feed on snapdragon.

### FESTIVE MIDGET *Elaphria festivoides*

**Sp S F W** Wings gray to straw colored with brownish "saddle" in inner medial area. Reniform spot is curved or hook shaped and open on outer wing edge. Subterminal area is brown and contrasts with pale apical patch. Thorax with dark brown collar anteriorly. Larvae feed on box elder and possibly green algae.

# BUTTERFLIES AND MOTHS

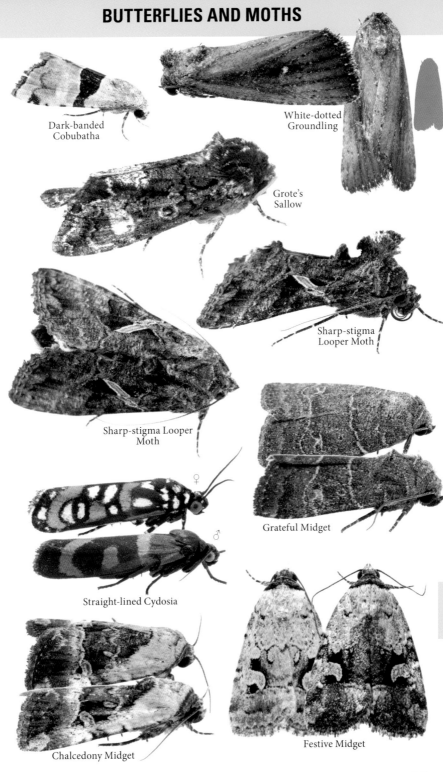

Dark-banded
Cobubatha

White-dotted
Groundling

Grote's
Sallow

Sharp-stigma
Looper Moth

Sharp-stigma Looper
Moth

♀

♂

Grateful Midget

Straight-lined Cydosia

Chalcedony Midget

Festive Midget

**LANTANA MOTH** *Diastema tigris*

**Sp S F W** Forewing brindled with parallel lines of rusty orange and white. Basal, antemedial, and median lines dark red and interrupted into irregular spots. Larvae feed on lantana.

**BELOVED EMARGINEA** *Emarginea percara*

**Sp S F W** Forewing greenish gray with black in outer median area and a large irregular pale patch extending to leading edge. Dark lines and band diffusely edged in white. A dark basal stripe extends back to posterior margin of thorax. Larvae feed on mistletoe.

**PINK-WASHED LOOPER MOTH** *Enigmogramma basigera*

**Sp S F W** Forewing pinkish brown with rusty-brown patch in middle of wing along trailing edge forming a "saddle." Stigma silver and interrupted into two oblong spots; anterior-most spot usually with dark center. Larvae feed on umbellate water pennywort.

**PEARLY WOOD-NYMPH** *Eudryas unio*

**Sp S F W** Forewing white. Subterminal area crimson with scalloped subterminal line edged in olive green anteriorly. Leading edge of wing dark red bleeding into bluish black at either end. Larvae feed on evening primrose, false loosestrife, grape, hibiscus, Virginia creeper, and more.

**THE WEDGLING** *Galgula partita*

**Sp S F W** Sexually dimorphic and variable. Male forewing yellowish tan to rusty brown with diffuse black patch midway along leading edge. Pale postmedial line edged by darker stripe anteriorly. Orbicular spot round, reniform spot hourglass shaped and both subtly outlined in white. Female similar, but wings darker, often reddish brown. Larvae feed on wood sorrel.

**ARMYWORM MOTH** *Mythimna unipuncta*

**Sp S F W** Forewing pale tan to orangish brown with tiny white spot at center and outlined in black. Orbicular and reniform spots orangish and often indistinct. Dark, slanted apical dash may be visible. Hind wing gray with dark veins. Larvae feed on grasses.

**BLACK-BORDERED LEMON** *Marimatha nigrofimbria*

**Sp S F W** Wings lemon yellow to pale yellow with black terminal line. Two black spots on each wing small and black. Fringe purplish gray. Larvae feed on grasses.

**SPOTTED PHOSPHILA** *Phosphila miselioides*

**Sp S F W** Forewing mottled dark green and black with large white or brownish reniform spot, but may be obscured. Orbicular spot generally indistinct, sometimes pale. Diffuse black stripe usually visible along inner median area. Larvae feed on greenbrier.

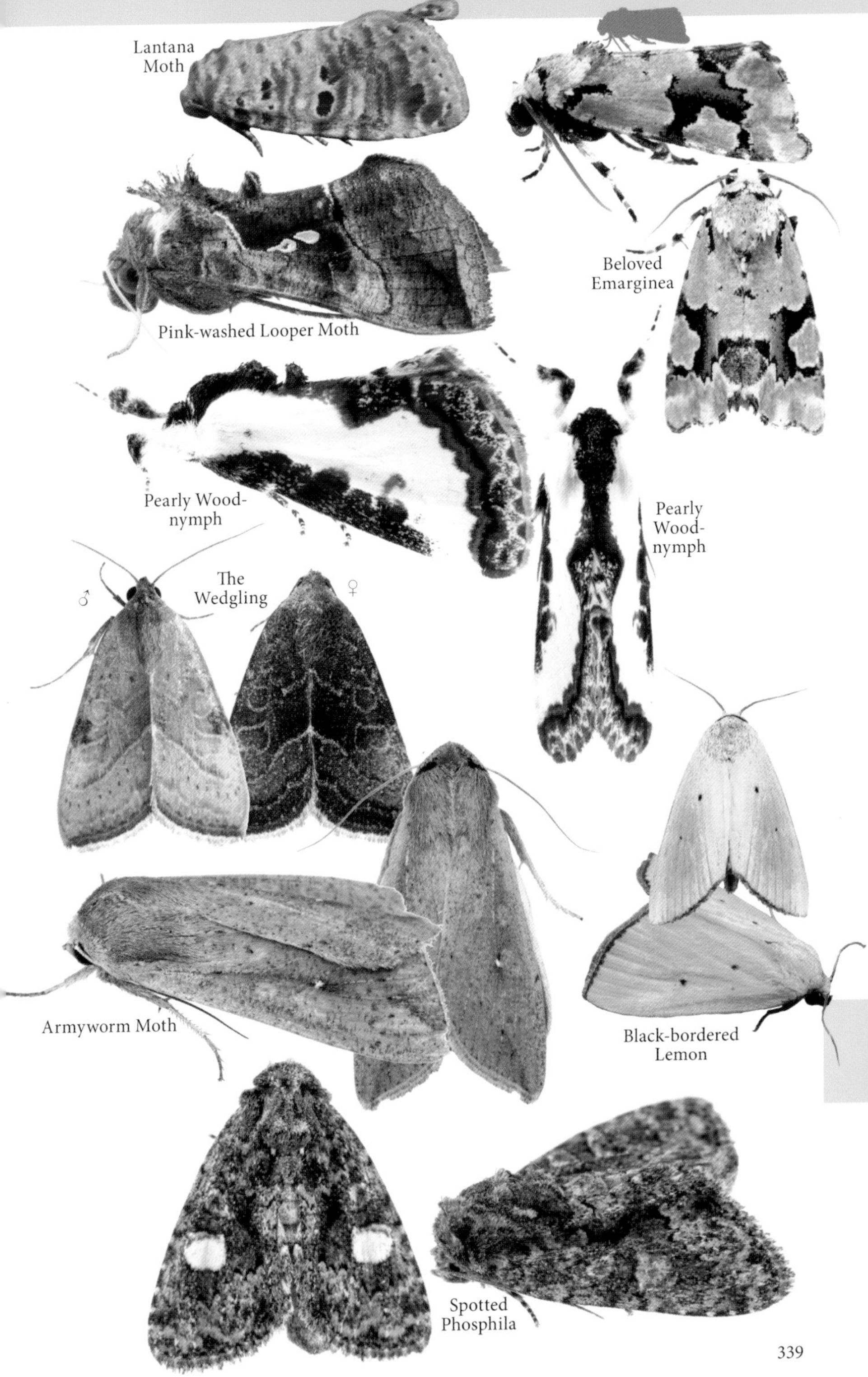

# BUTTERFLIES AND MOTHS

Lantana
Moth

Beloved
Emarginea

Pink-washed Looper Moth

Pearly Wood-
nymph

Pearly
Wood-
nymph

♂ The
Wedgling ♀

Armyworm Moth

Black-bordered
Lemon

Spotted
Phosphila

NOCTUIDAE

**OLIVE-SHADED BIRD DROPPING MOTH** *Ponometia candefacta*
Sp **S** F W  Forewing white with dark olive median band, often indistinguishable toward outer edge, creating a "saddle." Postmedial band slanted and yellowish olive, meeting median band at gray patch along inner margin. Gray reniform spot outlined in white. Subterminal area usually gray. Larvae feed on ragweed.

**THE HALF-YELLOW** *Ponometia semiflava*
Sp **S** F W  Forewing bicolored with lemon yellow to yellowish orange anteriorly and chocolate brown posteriorly. Larvae feed on various composites.

**ROLAND'S SALLOW** *Psaphida rolandi*
Sp S F W  Forewing brown or greenish gray. Orbicular and reniform spots circled in white, edged by black. Subterminal line speckled white. Larvae feed on oaks.

**THE BROTHER** *Raphia frater*
Sp **S** F W  Forewing gray with wavy antemedial and postmedial dark lines often connected by thin dark line parallel to trailing edge. Orbicular and reniform spots thinly outlined in black.

**ARCIGERA FLOWER MOTH** *Schinia arcigera*
Sp **S** F W  Forewing maroon to brown with pale median terminal areas. Antemedial line white and smoothly curved. Postmedial line nearly straight. Male hind wing yellow with black terminal line; female hind wing black with white fringe. Larvae feed on composites, camphorweed, horseweed, and sea lavender.

**THREE-LINED FLOWER MOTH** *Schinia trifascia*
Sp S F **W**  Forewing banded olive green and pale white. Pale antemedial line curves upward sharply before reaching outer margin. Hind wing white in male; white with olive subterminal band in female. Larvae feed on false boneset and joe-pye weed.

**YELLOW-STRIPED ARMYWORM** *Spodoptera ornithogalli*
Sp S F W  Forewing intricately patterned. Orbicular spot blends into oblique pale median streak. Veins are white in median area. Subterminal area gray. Male with rusty tan saddle along inner margin of medial area. Larvae feed on grasses and various crops.

**FALL ARMYWORM MOTH** *Spodoptera frugiperda*
Sp S F W  Sexually dimorphic. Male with rusty-red orbicular spot and darker reniform spot outlined in white and connected by pale teardrop. Subterminal area usually with dark patch. Forewing of female uniformly grayish brown with indistinct markings. Larvae feed on grasses and various crops.

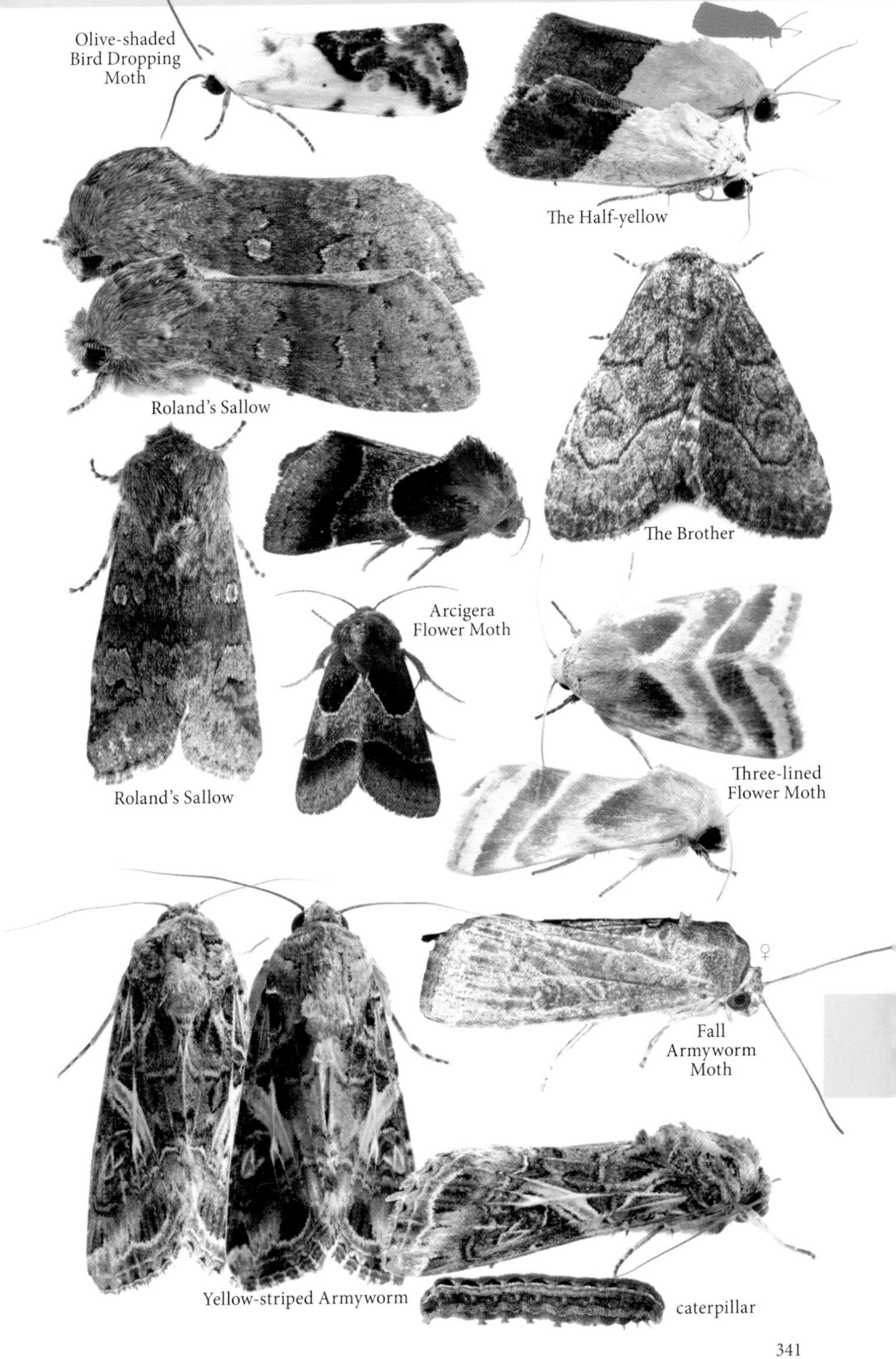

Olive-shaded
Bird Dropping
Moth

The Half-yellow

Roland's Sallow

The Brother

Roland's Sallow

Arcigera
Flower Moth

Three-lined
Flower Moth

♀

Fall
Armyworm
Moth

Yellow-striped Armyworm

caterpillar

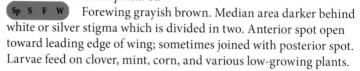

### GRAY LOOPER *Rachiplusia ou*

NOCTUIDAE

**Sp S F W** Forewing grayish brown. Median area darker behind white or silver stigma which is divided in two. Anterior spot open toward leading edge of wing; sometimes joined with posterior spot. Larvae feed on clover, mint, corn, and various low-growing plants.

### SOUTHERN SPRAGUEIA MOTH *Spragueia dama*

**Sp S F W** Boldly marked orange and black forewing with three cream-colored patches along leading edge; middle spot U shaped. Area between cream patches black in female, orange in male.

### EXPOSED BIRD-DROPPING MOTH *Tarache aprica*

**Sp S F W** Sexually dimorphic. Female forewing darkly mottled with white median and subapical cream-colored patch along leading edge; median patch with small dark orbicular spot. Male forewing mostly white with dark antemedial and postmedial patches along leading edge; tip of wings dark to medial area in an oblique line. Larvae feed on cultivated and probably native mallows.

### POLISHED BIRD-DROPPING MOTH *Tarache expolita*

**Sp S F W** Forewing grayish brown, somewhat shiny, with broad white band along leading edge. Large white patch medially in subterminal area, often washed with brown or olive green. Larval food plant unknown.

### EYED BAILEYA *Baileya ophthalmica*

NOLIDAE

**Sp S F W** Forewing gray to gray brown with narrow cream patch basally. Median area along leading edge diffusely gray. Reniform spot thinly outlined in black with small dark central spot. Jagged subterminal line white, heavily outlined in black. Male with entirely buff-colored thorax; female gray or brown. Larvae feed on ironwood, eastern hornbeam, and hazel.

### SORGHUM WEBWORM *Nola cereella*

**Sp S F W** Forewing creamy white with tan median band and postmedial line. Up to five tufts of scales along leading edge. Larvae feed on sorghum and grasses.

PTEROPHORIDAE

### MORNING-GLORY PLUME MOTH *Emmelina monodactyla*

**Sp S F W** Forewing light gray to pinkish brown and darkest at subterminal area along leading edge. Pale thorax triangular shaped when viewed dorsally. Abdomen with black, short, parallel dashes. Larvae feed on morning glory and relatives.

### BELFRAGE'S PLUME MOTH *Pselnophorus belfragei*

**Sp S F W** Forewing white with black dashes along leading edge at antemedial, postmedial, and subterminal areas. Abdomen with thin parallel white lines. Larvae feed on Carolina ponysfoot.

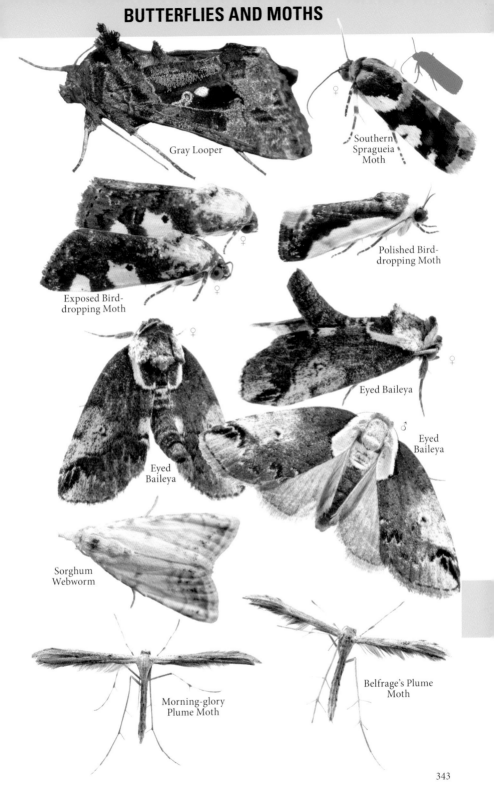

Gray Looper

Southern
Spragueia
Moth

♀

Exposed Bird-
dropping Moth

♀

♀

Polished Bird-
dropping Moth

♀

Eyed Baileya

♀

Eyed
Baileya

♂

Eyed
Baileya

Sorghum
Webworm

Morning-glory
Plume Moth

Belfrage's Plume
Moth

### SPOTTED DATANA *Datana perspicua*

NOTODONTIDAE

Sp **S F** W  Forewing straw colored with five reddish-brown transverse lines, though some may be faint. Brown reniform and smaller orbicular spot conspicuous. Apical dash, brown and distinct. Front of thorax brown. Larvae feed on sumac and smoke tree.

### WHITE-DOTTED PROMINENT *Nadata gibbosa*

Sp **S F** W  Forewing tawny with straight antemedial and postmedial lines. Two small white spots in median area. Outer margin often scalloped. Thorax with high tuft of hairs projecting anteriorly. Larvae feed on oak, birch, cherry, maple, and more.

### WHITE-BLOTCHED HETEROCAMPA *Heterocampa umbrata*

Sp **S F** W  Forewing mossy green with grayish-white patches. Curved black line extends from reniform crescent to inner subterminal line and usually borders a large pale patch. Outer subterminal line bordered by black chevrons. Leading edge of hind wing hairy, often projecting under forewing. Larvae feed on oak.

### ORANGE-BANDED PROMINENT *Litodonta hydromeli*

Sp **S F** W  Forewing grayish green and often peppered with small black spots. Antemedial and postmedial lines scalloped and doubled with white middle. Area below median line often grayish. Basal and terminal areas with orange shading. Larvae feed on gum bumelia.

### ANGULOSE PROMINENT *Peridea angulosa*

Sp **S F** W  Grayish forewing with double antemedial and postmedial lines with orangish middle. An incomplete white patch is often visible in outer margin of medial area. Subterminal area with thin black veins. Leading edge of hind wing hairy, often projecting under forewing. Larvae feed on oak.

### UNICORN PROMINENT *Schizura unicornis*

Sp **S F** W  Forewing multicolored with scalloped, double antemedial and postmedial lines. Subterminal area with large tan patch with black veins. Larvae feed on hickory, maple, oak, and more.

### YELLOW-SPOTTED WEBWORM *Anageshna primordialis*

CRAMBIDAE

Sp **S F** W  Brownish gray. Forewing with black-edged pale, often yellow, lines and spots. Dark reniform spot, somewhat figure-eight shaped. Larval food plant unknown.

### HOLLOW-SPOTTED BLEPHAROMASTIX *Blepharomastix ranalis*

Sp **S F** W  Wings shiny, tan to yellow, with sharp dark lines terminating along outer edges to spots. Postmedial line is sharply kinked. Leading edge of wing is brown along basal half. Larvae feed on goosefoot.

# BUTTERFLIES AND MOTHS

Spotted Datana

White-dotted Prominent

White-blotched Heterocampa

Orange-banded Prominent

Unicorn Prominent

Angulose Prominent

Yellow-spotted Webworm

Hollow-spotted Blepharomastix

345

### GRAPE LEAFFOLDER *Desmia funeralis*

CRAMBIDAE

**Sp S F W** Forewing black with two large white spots in median area. Hind wing with broad median white patch that extends across the thorax. Underside of abdomen with continuous white patch. Male with joint at midpoint of antennae. Larvae feed on evening primrose, grape, and redbud. Grape Leafroller (*Desmia maculalis*) identical from above, but differs in reduced amount of white on underside of abdomen.

### DARK DIACME *Diacme adipaloides*

**Sp S F W** Forewing variably pale yellow with square purplish orbicular and reniform spots along brown leading edge. All wings have broken antemedial and postmedial bands and broad purplish-brown subterminal line. Larval food plant unknown.

### MELONWORM MOTH *Diaphania hyalinata*

**Sp S F W** Forewing semi-translucent white, narrowly bordered by brown along all but inner margin. Hind wing with brown along trailing margin. Tip of abdomen with orangish-brown tuft of brushy hairs. Larvae feed on cucumber, melon, and squash.

### WATERLILY BORER *Elophila gyralis*

**Sp S F W** Variable with wings uniformly grayish brown to orange brown and forewing with faint pattern of lines and spots edged in white or boldly patterned with white spots and lines. Elongated medial dark patch when present extends across both forewings, often with a white spot in each. Larvae feed on water lily.

### WATERLILY LEAFCUTTER *Elophila obliteralis*

**Sp S F W** Forewing mottled brown with jagged median and subterminal lines edged in white. Broad black median band. Reniform spot white, connecting to white patch along leading edge. Larvae feed on aquatic plants including duckweed and pondweed.

### ORANGE EPIPAGIS *Epipagis fenestralis*

**Sp S F W** Forewing boldly patterned tan-orange and white. Postmedial line sinuous, widening toward leading edge. Hind wing white and crossed with narrow brownish bands.

### SPOTTED PEPPERGRASS MOTH *Eustixia pupula*

**Sp S F W** Forewing white with numerous evenly spaced black spots. Face and labial palps black. Feeds on peppergrass, field pennycress, and cabbage.

### DUSKY HERPETOGRAMMA *Herpetogramma phaeopteralis*

**Sp S F W** Wings dull, grayish brown, with weakly patterned dusky lines. Orbicular spot tiny and black; reniform spot larger and crescent shaped. Larvae feed on grass.

Grape
Leaffolder

♂

Dark Diacme

Grape
Leafroller

Melonworm
Moth

Waterlily
Borer

Waterlily
Leafcutter

Orange
Epipagis

Spotted
Peppergrass
Moth

Dusky Herpetogramma

### SPOTTED BEET WEBWORM *Hymenia perspectalis*   CRAMBIDAE

**Sp S F W**   Forewing brown with a broken white median band and an extended white patch along postmedial line at leading edge. Larvae feed on variety of plants including beet, chard, and potato.

### WHIP-MARKED SNOUT MOTH *Microtheoris vibicalis*

**Sp S F W**   Forewing pale yellowish white and boldly marked with oblique pink or red antemedial and postmedial bands that are generally connected medially. Larval food plant unknown.

### TWO-BANDED PETROPHILA *Petrophila bifascialis*

**Sp S F W**   Forewing white, lightly peppered with tan, with a double orangish-brown median band and three oblique apical dashes. Hind wing pale with row of black and silver spots posteriorly. Larvae aquatic, feeding on diatoms and algae on rocks. Adults mimic jumping spiders both in pattern on wings and in behavior.

### SCRAPED PILOCROCIS *Pilocrocis ramentalis*

**Sp S F W**   Wings brown with bronze sheen. Forewing with strongly curved white postmedial line edged in black. Reniform spot edged in black and crescent-shaped. Larvae feed on false nettle and cardinal's guard.

### SOUTHERN PURPLE MINT MOTH *Pyrausta laticlavia*

**Sp S F W**   When fresh, forewing golden yellow and boldly patterned with purplish-pink stripe along leading edge, median and subterminal bands. Older individuals often more brown than yellow and with diffuse purplish-pink bands. Larvae feed on mint.

### YELLOW-BANDED PYRAUSTA *Pyrausta pseuderosnealis*

**Sp S F W**   Forewing reddish pink with wavy yellow postmedial band. Antemedial band somewhat variable and faint yellow. Hind wing with yellow patch at inner margin of postmedial line. Larval food plant unknown.

### CELERY LEAFTIER *Udea rubigalis*

**Sp S F W**   Forewing tan, brown, or reddish with dusky lines and spots. Reniform spot is figure-eight shaped. Palps extend forward in front of head. Larvae feed on various low plants and crops, including beans, beet, celery and spinach.

### GENISTA BROOM MOTH *Uresiphita reversalis*

**Sp S F W**   Forewing tan to rusty brown with brown dotted lines. Reniform and orbicular spots blackish. Hind wing contrastingly bright orange when visible. Palps extend forward in front of head. Larvae feed on acacia, genista, bluebonnets, and Texas mountain laurel.

# BUTTERFLIES AND MOTHS

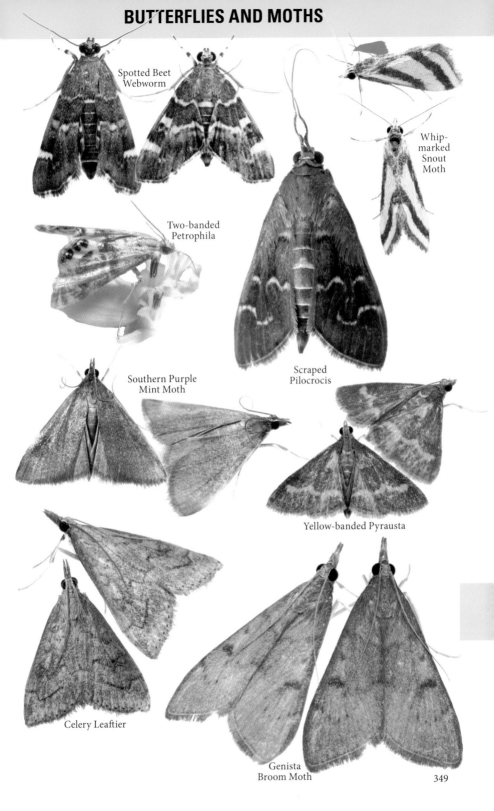

Spotted Beet
Webworm

Whip-
marked
Snout
Moth

Two-banded
Petrophila

Scraped
Pilocrocis

Southern Purple
Mint Moth

Yellow-banded Pyrausta

Celery Leaftier

Genista
Broom Moth

### TRUMPET VINE MOTH *Clydonopteron sacculana*

PYRALIDAE

**Sp S F W** Wings reddish- to purplish-brown. Forewing gray posterior to postmedial line. Antemedial band diffuse, but usually visibly orange. Postmedial line with white spot at leading edge. Leading edge of forewing also indented and somewhat scalloped at middle. Larvae feed on seedpods of trumpet creeper.

### BROAD-BANDED EULOGIA *Eulogia ochrifrontella*

**Sp S F W** Forewing is reddish brown anteriorly, dark brown posterior to median line, and grayish posteriorly, so as to appear somewhat tricolored. Median and postmedial lines wavy. Larvae feed on apple, oak, and pecan.

### BOXWOOD LEAFTIER *Galasa nigrinodis*

**Sp S F W** Forewing brick red with broad, variable, pale patch across median area that is most prominent along outer wing edge. Leading edge indented at middle. Rests with wings held straight back and body held up by long tufted legs. Larvae feed on boxwood.

### SUNFLOWER MOTH *Homoeosoma electella*

**Sp S F W** Wings tan gray, peppered with white band along leading edge of forewing. Short, black dashes at inner median and central postmedial areas. Wings often held somewhat rolled or folded under at rest. Larvae feed on various composites.

### PINK-FRINGED HYPSOPYGIA *Hypsopygia binodulalis*

**Sp S F W** Forewing olive, sometimes with purplish tinge with narrow pinkish stripe along leading edge and pinkish fringe; both of which fade with age. Antemedial and postmedial lines pale yellowish and widened at leading edge. Larval food plant unknown.

### YELLOW-FRINGED HYPSOPYGIA *Hypsopygia olinalis*

**Sp S F W** Forewings purplish red with narrow yellow stripe along leading edge and yellow fringe. Antemedial and postmedial lines yellow and widened at leading edge. Abdomen often held above wings when at rest. Larvae feed on oak.

### DARKER MOODNA *Moodna ostrinella*

**Sp S F W** Forewing bicolored, reddish anteriorly and grayish black posteriorly. Median band broadly edged white. Reniform area whitish; subterminal area reddish. Larvae feed on numerous trees and low plants including cotton, oak, pine, and sumac.

### MAPLE WEBWORM *Pococera asperatella*

**Sp S F W** Forewing reddish or gray with white median band fading toward leading edge. Antemedial and postmedial line black and doubled with light gray between each. Larvae feed on maple.

# BUTTERFLIES AND MOTHS

Trumpet Vine Moth

Broad-banded Eulogia

Trumpet Vine Moth

Boxwood Leaftier

Pink-fringed Hypsopygia

Sunflower Moth

Yellow-fringed Hypsopygia

Maple Webworm

Maple Webworm

Darker Moodna

351

**BAGWORM MOTH** *Cryptothelea* sp.

**Sp S F W** Male with uniform dark brown wings and body and bipectinate antennae. Eyes large on otherwise small head. Female wingless. Larvae likely feed on trees, shrubs, and low plants.

**EVERGREEN BAGWORM MOTH** *Thyridopteryx ephemeraeformis*

**Sp S F W** Male with robust body, translucent wings, and bipectinate antennae. Rings of hair around abdominal segments. Female wingless. Larvae feed on a variety of trees and shrubs.

**FRILLY GRASS-TUBEWORM MOTH** *Acrolophus mycetophagus*

**Sp S F W** Forewing whitish to pale yellow with scattered dark spots, most pronounced in median and subterminal areas. Middle legs with long frilly hair like scales. Larvae feed on bracket fungus.

**CLEMENS' GRASS TUBEWORM MOTH** *Acrolophus popeanella*

**Sp S F W** Variable with forewing tan to gray and brindled with dark lines and spots. Pale streaks usually along leading edge and middle of wing. Large, hairy labial palps extend back over head. Larvae feed on roots of red clover.

**TEXAS GRASS TUBEWORM MOTH** *Acrolophus texanella*

**Sp S F W** Forewing grayish brown, somewhat brindled and darker posterior to postmedial line. Dark patch along leading edge in medial area. Thorax with posterior projecting hair like scales and hairy labial palps extend back over head. Larvae feed on grass.

**DARK-COLLARED TINEA** *Tinea apicimaculella*

**Sp S F W** Forewing light brown to tan and shiny with dark brown patch at inner basal area. Central median areas of subterminal line peppered with dark scales, often resulting in a curved line or streak. Head yellowish. Lacks dark spot near upper margin of median area. Larval food plant unknown.

**WHITE-SPOTTED OAK LEAFROLLER** *Archips semiferana*

**Sp S F W** Forewing tannish brown with irregular white bands, most prevalent toward leading edge. Broad, brown oblique stripe in middle of wing. Larvae feed on oak, apple, and witch hazel.

**FILIGREED MOTH** *Chimoptesis pennsylvaniana*

**Sp S F W** Wings black with greenish-white strongly scalloped band down middle. Outer and inner edge of forewing and legs banded. Palps projecting anteriorly. Larval host plant unknown.

*Cryptothelea* sp.

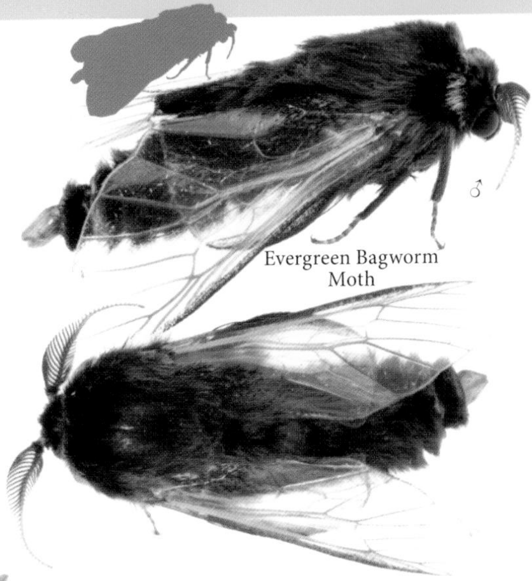

Evergreen Bagworm
Moth

Bagworm
Moth Case

Clemens' Grass
Tubeworm

Frilly Grass
Tubeworm Moth

Dark-collard Tinea

Texas Grass
Tubeworm Moth

White-spotted Oak
Leafroller

Filigreed Moth

353

# LEPIDOPTERA

**OBLIQUE-BANDED LEAFROLLER** *Choristoneura rosaceana*
**Sp S F W** Forewings bell-shaped, yellow, tan, or reddish-brown brindled with fine dark lines. Antemedial line more or less straight. Male with basal fold along leading edge of forewing. Larvae feed on a variety of woody plants including blueberry, oak, and pine.

**GARDEN TORTRIX** *Clepsis peritana*
**Sp S F W** Forewing tan to pinkish brown with brown oblique median band. Wings lightly speckled. Dark subapical patch along leading edge and often dark patch at middle of outer edge. Larvae feed on various low plants including strawberry.

**FILBERTWORM MOTH** *Cydia latiferreana*
**Sp S F W** Tan to reddish forewing has broad metallic silver to gold median and postmedial bands. Leading edge with oblique metallic dashes. Larvae feed on beech, filbert, hazelnut, and oak.

**SCULPTURED MOTH** *Eumarozia malachitana*
**Sp S F W** Forewing grayish anteriorly, rosy red posteriorly with large round, white-edged olive green median patch. Eyes green. Larvae feed on persimmon.

**PECAN BUD MOTH** *Gretchena bolliana*
**Sp S F W** Forewing grayish brown, irregularly mottled with dark lines. Black, irregular band usually running from subterminal area through central median area. Larvae feed on pecan.

**BLACK-SHADED PLATYNOTA MOTH** *Platynota flavedana*
**Sp S F W** Forewing pale white to reddish brown with median area broad, shaded in black or dark gray. Terminal line pale. Some individuals pale with dark, oblique antemedial band. Palps extend forward in front of head. Larvae feed on various low plants including composites, blueberry, and clover.

**TUFTED APPLE BUD MOTH** *Platynota idaeusalis*
**Sp S F W** Forewing variably gray to light brown. Basal area pale and rounded posteriorly. Median area with three lines of raised scales. Palps extend forward in front of head. Larvae feed on a variety of trees and plants including apple, black walnut, box elder, clover, and pine.

**LENTIGINOS MOTH** *Sparganothoides lentiginosana*
**Sp S F W** Forewing orangish to light brown, lightly peppered with darker scales. Often a black patch visible at inner postmedial area, but can be reduced or absent. Palps extend forward in front of head. Larval food plant unknown.

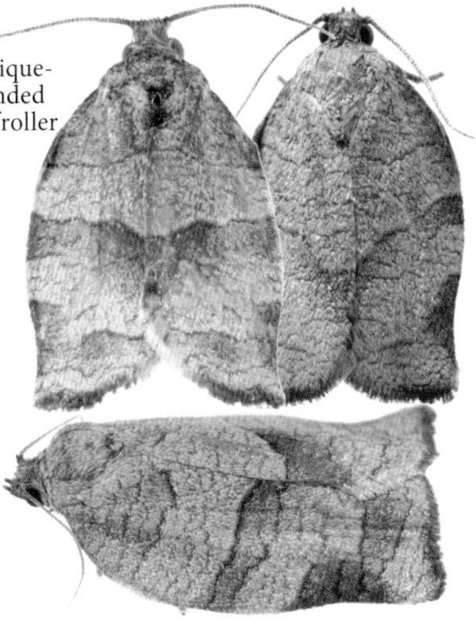

# BUTTERFLIES AND MOTHS

Oblique-
banded
Leafroller

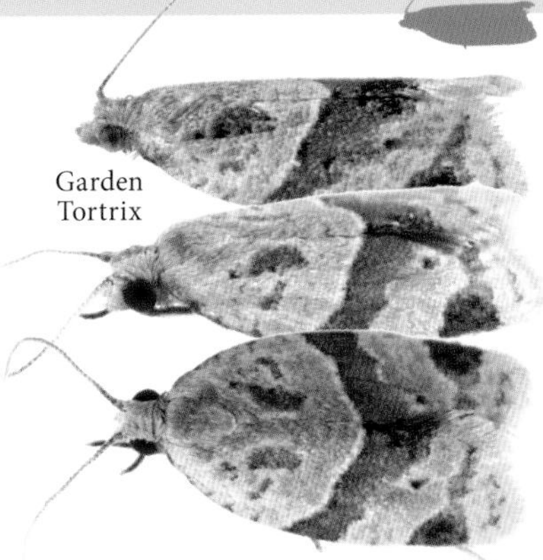

Garden
Tortrix

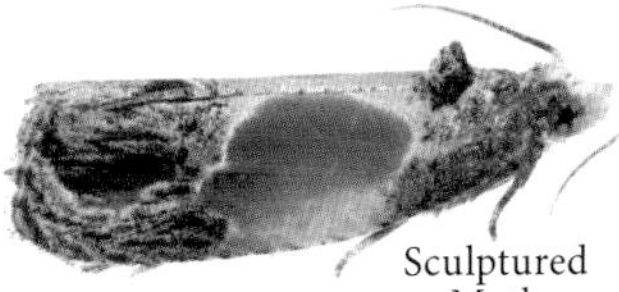

Oblique-banded Leafroller

Sculptured
Moth

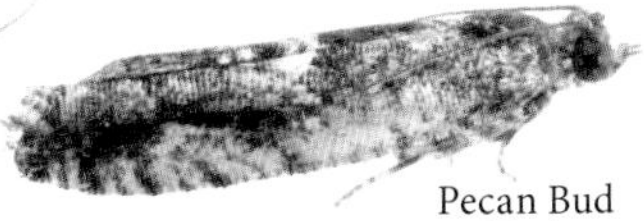

Pecan Bud
Moth

Filbertworm Moth

Black-shaded
Platynota Moth

Lentiginos
Moth

Tufted Apple Bud Moth

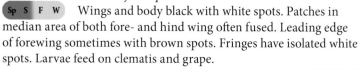

## MOURNFUL THYRIS *Thyris sepulchralis*
THYRIDIDAE

**Sp S F W** Wings and body black with white spots. Patches in median area of both fore- and hind wing often fused. Leading edge of forewing sometimes with brown spots. Fringes have isolated white spots. Larvae feed on clematis and grape.

## AILANTHUS WEBWORM MOTH *Atteva aurea*
ATTEVIDAE

**Sp S F W** Forewing reddish orange with clusters of white to pale yellow spots edged in black. Wings somewhat rolled around body. Hind wing black. Head with white spot above. Legs black with white bands. Larvae feed on Ailanthus and other various trees and shrubs.

## DIAMONDBACK MOTH *Plutella xylostella*
PLUTELLIDAE

**Sp S F W** Forewings in male brown with jagged pale stripe down middle. Female with less contrast. Wings curved upward distally with prominent fringe. Larvae feed on members of the mustard family.

## YELLOW-COLLARED SLUG MOTH *Apoda y-inversum*
LIMACODIDAE

**Sp S F W** Forewing pale yellow to orangish with dark median and subterminal lines that converge towards leading edge. Two faint brown stripes form an "X" near anal angle. Larvae feed on beech, hickory, ironwood, and oak.

## SPINY OAK-SLUG MOTH *Euclea delphinii*

**Sp S F W** Forewing dark brown marked with variably-sized green patches in inner median and outer postmedial areas; sometimes these patches are extensive and fused, in others they are nearly absent. Green areas bordered by chestnut-colored patches posteriorly. Reniform spot black and usually large. Larvae feed on trees and woody plants, including beech, maple, and oak.

## SPUN GLASS SLUG MOTH *Isochaetes beutenmuelleri*

**Sp S F W** Forewing orange brown or yellow brown with marbled pattern of indistinct brown lines and silver-gray patches. Thorax with large tuft of hair like scales. Legs heavily tufted and splayed out when at rest. Larvae feed on swamp oak.

## SOUTHERN FLANNEL MOTH *Megalopyge crispata*
MEGALOPYGIDAE

**Sp S F W** Forewing yellowish to cream colored with chestnut coloring basally. Leading edge of wing with stripe and white veins in median area. Thorax chestnut with pale yellow collar. Tip of legs black. Larvae feed on hackberry, pecan, and others. Larvae, often called "asps," have hairs that are stinging spines.

## GRAPELEAF SKELETONIZER *Harrisina americana*
ZYGAENIDAE

**Sp S F W** Wings semi-translucent black. Thorax with reddish-orange collar. Antennae black and pectinate. Abdomen black and with broad tuft distally. Larvae feed on grape, redbud, and Virginia creeper.

# BUTTERFLIES AND MOTHS

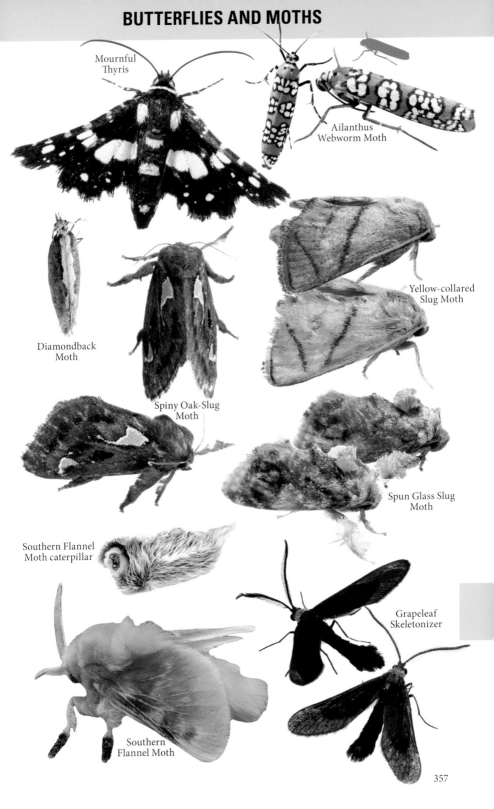

Mournful Thyris

Ailanthus Webworm Moth

Diamondback Moth

Spiny Oak-Slug Moth

Yellow-collared Slug Moth

Spun Glass Slug Moth

Southern Flannel Moth caterpillar

Grapeleaf Skeletonizer

Southern Flannel Moth

# Ants, Bees, Wasps, and Sawflies
# Order Hymenoptera

Paper Wasp
(*Polistes exclamans*)

**NATURAL HISTORY**   This is a large, diverse, and beneficial group of insects. It includes many familiar species groups. They are characterized by hooks (hamuli) on the anterior margin of the smaller hind wing that hook onto the posterior margin of the forewing so that they function as a single unit. This may be responsible for their ordinal name with *Hymeno* referring to the god of marriage and *ptera*, wings, describing the married or joined wings. *Hymen* may also refer to membrane, but the actual origin is unclear. Many species are parasites of pest species (especially caterpillars) and as a group they are major pollinators of numerous plants, including many crop species. They have complete development and chewing mouthparts. Many have tonguelike structures for lapping up fluids and others have suctorial mouthparts.

Many species are social, with different castes and cooperative parental care. The sex of the individual is determined by fertilization with unfertilized eggs becoming males and fertilized eggs females. Some, most notably social species, can sting. The stinger is a modification of the egg-laying structure, so only females (all workers in social species) can sting. In most species the sting is used to paralyze prey, but it can also be used for defense. There are two distinct groups within the order, the first known as "Symphyta" include the sawflies, horntails, and wood wasps. The larvae of these species are free-living and look like hairless caterpillars with sawfly larvae being gregarious foliage feeders that can denude a plant quickly. The second, larger group, the Apocrita, include most recognizable species that have a narrow waist. Many are parasitoids of other insects and have legless maggots dependent on their mother to locate food.

# Identifying Characters

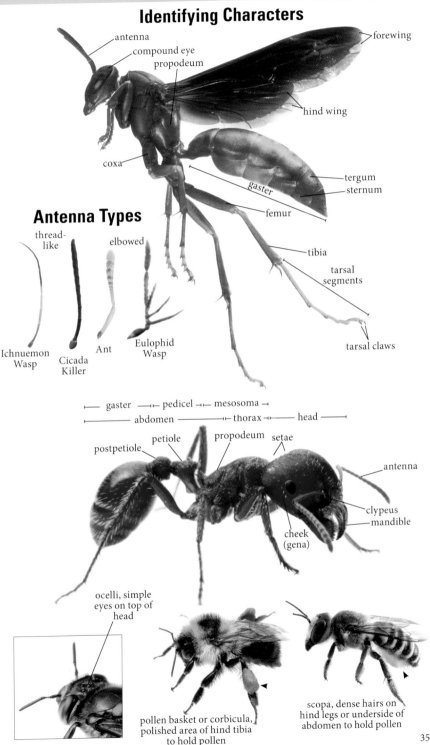

antenna

compound eye

propodeum

forewing

hind wing

coxa

tergum

sternum

gaster

femur

## Antenna Types

thread-
like

elbowed

tibia

tarsal
segments

tarsal claws

Ichnuemon
Wasp

Cicada
Killer

Ant

Eulophid
Wasp

gaster — pedicel — mesosoma

abdomen — thorax — head

postpetiole

petiole

propodeum

setae

antenna

clypeus

mandible

cheek
(gena)

ocelli, simple
eyes on top of
head

pollen basket or corbicula,
polished area of hind tibia
to hold pollen

scopa, dense hairs on
hind legs or underside of
abdomen to hold pollen

359

### ARGID SAWFLY *Arge* sp.

Sp **S** F W  Robust, typically with reddish-orange thorax; black or iridescent blue head, abdomen, and wings; and three-segmented antennae with the third segment much longer than the others. Larvae are caterpillar-like but with more than five prolegs, and feed on leaves of various trees and shrubs.

### CONIFER SAWFLY *Neodiprion* sp.

Sp **S** **F** W  Small, robust, variably colored group from greenish-brown to black or red without a narrow waist. Antennae with 13 or more segments and serrate in females, pectinate or bipectinate in males. Larvae feed externally on conifers and can be quite destructive.

### PIGEON TREMEX *Tremex columba*

Sp **S** F W  Large, elongated, nearly cylindrical, and unmistakable. Can have various amounts of black. Female with stout, posteriorly projecting ovipositor. Eggs laid in diseased, dying, and cut wood of many deciduous trees where larvae chew tunnels.

### COMMON SAWFLY *Strongylogaster tuberculiceps*

Sp **S** F W  Elongated, black head, red thorax and abdomen without a narrow waist. Antennae nine segmented; first two segments shorter and broader than next two. Wings black or iridescent blue. Larvae feed on ferns.

### COMMON SAWFLY *Aneugmenus flavipes*

Sp **S** F W  Robust, black with dark wings, yellow legs, and abdomen lacking a waist. Antennae nine segmented; first two segments shorter and broader than next two. Broad yellow stripe laterally behind head running on thorax. Larvae feed on ferns.

### STEM SAWFLY *Cephus* sp.

Sp **S** F W  Elongated, nearly cylindrical, with black head and broad yellow bands on black abdomen. Legs yellow, sometimes dark distally. Pronotum elongated. Larvae feed in grass stems and are major pests of wheat. Only two species in the US: *C. cinctus* and the very similar introduced *C. pygmaeus*.

### XYELID SAWFLY *Xyela* sp.

Sp **S** F W  Small, yellow and black, with thin terminal filament off of antennal segment three. Abdomen without waist. Female with upward, oblique projecting ovipositor. Larvae feed on buds and pollen of conifers.

### CHALCIDID WASP *Brachymeria tegularis*

Sp **S** F W  Small, robust, black with enlarged yellow hind femora. Antennae expanded in last two-thirds. Hyperparasitoid of flies which are parasitoids of grasshoppers.

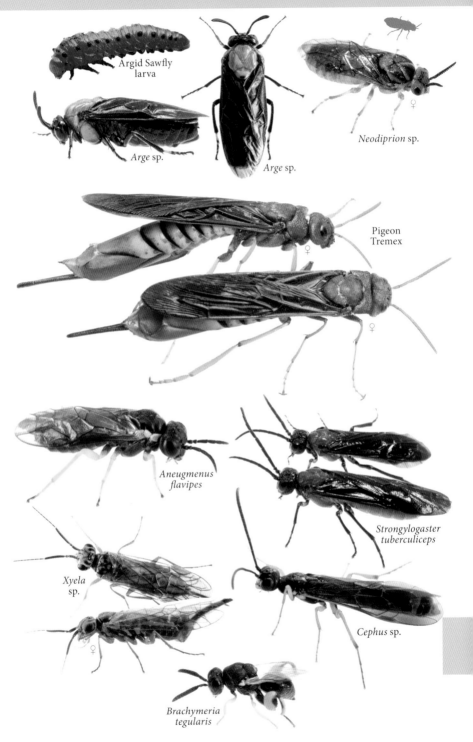

Argid Sawfly
larva

*Arge* sp.

*Arge* sp.

*Neodiprion* sp.
♀

Pigeon
Tremex
♀

♀

*Aneugmenus
flavipes*

*Strongylogaster
tuberculiceps*

*Xyela*
sp.

♀

*Cephus* sp.

*Brachymeria
tegularis*

### EULOPHID WASP *Elasmus polistis*

**Sp S F W** Small, sexually dimorphic parasitoids of paper wasps. Male black with pectinate antennae and pale legs. Female tan with small head, filiform antennae, thorax with small black dots, red abdomen and white legs. Can be abundant around paper wasp nests.

### EULOPHID WASP *Melittobia* sp.

**Sp S F W** Minute dark wasps with yellow and black bicolored antennae and legs with black bands basally. Gregarious ectoparasitoids of bee and wasp pupae.

### ORMYRID WASP *Ormyrus* sp.

**Sp S F W** Minute, robust, metallic blue wasp with elbowed antennae and abdomen narrowing to a point. Forewing with long marginal vein. Parasitoids of various gall-forming insects including cynipids, chalcids and some flies, beetles and thrips.

### EUPELMID WASP *Eupelmus* sp.

**Sp S F W** Robust, elongate, sometimes wingless and ant-like. Female with long oblique, posterior projecting ovipositor. Can be reddish-brown, black or metallic blue. Most are ectoparasitoids of the immature stages of a variety of insects and spiders.

### GALL WASPS

**Sp S F W** Numerous species that are difficult to identify from photos. Small often with short, large, round abdomen and humpbacked appearance. Some with reduced wings. Induce galls on plants for larval development. Most are species specific to the plants the larvae feed on and are more easily recognized by the gall.

### LARGER EMPTY OAK APPLE WASP *Amphibolips quercusinanis*

**Sp S F W** These large green "apple" galls are a common sight on red oak leaves. They form on the underside of the leaf and have reddish spots that become yellowish-brown and slightly raised.

### COCKROACH EGG PARASITOID WASP *Evania appendigaster*

**Sp S F W** Black, somewhat iridescent blue, laterally compressed with long legs and very short abdomen. Solitary endoparasitoid of American Cockroach and Oriental Cockroach egg cases. Found indoors in homes and other buildings.

### BRACONID WASPS *Cotesia empretiae*

**Sp S F W** Small black parasitoids of Saddleback Caterpillar with orange legs and long antennae. Distal half of hind tibia and anterior half of hind tarsi dark. Parasitizes caterpillars in summer. Larvae feed internally on the caterpillar and then construct cocoons in later winter, emerging in spring of the following year. A single caterpillar can have dozens of larvae. Emergence is synchronized happening over just a few minutes.

# ANTS, BEES, WASPS, AND SAWFLIES

*Elasmus polistis*
♂
♀

*Melittobia* sp.

*Eupelmus* spp.

*Orymyrus* sp.

Gall Wasps

Larger Empty Oak Apple Wasp gall

*Evania appendigaster*

*Cotesia empretiae*

*Cotesia empretiae*
Saddleback Caterpillar
Moth parasite

### BRACONID WASP *Atanycolus* sp.
**Sp S F W** Black, elongated, round head, long antennae, red abdomen and long ovipositor in females. Hard to see, but first antennal segment sharply excavated at both basal and apical ends. Parasitoids of wood boring beetle larvae. Will come to lights.

### BRACONID WASP *Yelicones delicatus*
**Sp S F W** Small, elongate, robust yellowish-orange with black eyes, tarsi and wing veins. Front tarsus with segments 2–4 wider than long. Femora and hind tibia somewhat swollen. Occurs in wooded areas and occasionally comes to lights.

### ICHNEUMON WASP *Acrotaphus wiltii*
**Sp S F W** Elongated, nearly cylindrical body, black head, reddish-brown thorax, legs and abdomen with black tip. Wings yellowish-orange with banded wings. The larva is an external parasitoids of the Arabesque Orb Weaver *Neoscona arabesca*. Attracted to lights.

### ICHNEUMON WASP *Coelichneumon* sp.
**Sp S F W** Elongated, black with white marked face, thorax, legs, and antennae. Antennae with long white band at middle segments. Outer edge of black legs with white stripe. Parasitoid of notodontid and noctuid moth caterpillars.

### ICHNEUMON WASP *Compsocryptus* sp.
**Sp S F W** Reddish-orange with banded wings and long, up-turned ovipositor in female. Eyes dull reddish-brown. Antennae darker in apical half. Two dark transverse stripes and apical margin of wings black. Apical half of hind tibia black.

### ICHNEUMON WASP *Cratichneumon* sp.
**Sp S F W** Elongated, bicolored white and black antennae and reddish-brown abdomen. Head and thorax black or reddish with white or yellow spots. Antennae with middle segments pale.

### ICHNEUMON WASP *Trogomorpha arrogans*
**Sp S F W** Red body, dark eyes, tricolored antennae, dark wings with broad orange transverse band, most of hind femora and tibia black. Antennae somewhat variable, usually with reddish-orange base, dark tips and some middle segments yellow.

### ICHNEUMON WASP *Metopius* sp.
**Sp S F W** Elongated body with cylindrical black abdomen banded with yellow. Fore and middle tibia usually yellow, hind tibia with at least some black. Endoparasitoids of various moth caterpillars, particularly those concealed in rolled leaves.

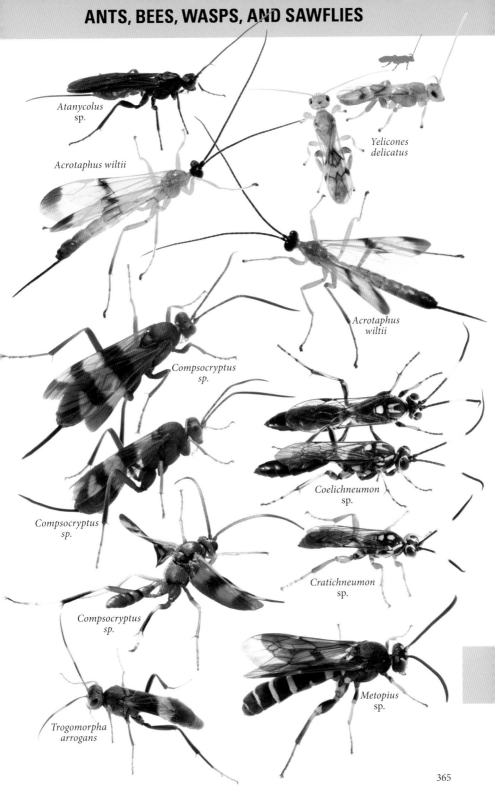

*Atanycolus*
sp.

*Yelicones*
*delicatus*

*Acrotaphus wiltii*

*Acrotaphus*
*wiltii*

*Compsocryptus*
*sp.*

*Coelichneumon*
sp.

*Compsocryptus*
*sp.*

*Cratichneumon*
sp.

*Compsocryptus*
*sp.*

*Metopius*
sp.

*Trogomorpha*
*arrogans*

365

### ICHNEUMON WASP *Odontocolon* sp.

**Sp S F W** Elongated black wasp with cylindrical abdomen and reddish-brown legs. Antennae as long as body. Hind femora with spine midway down its length. Head somewhat quadrate, wider than long, from above. Black pterostigma evident in wings.

### SHORT-TAILED ICHNEUMON WASPS *Ophion* sp.

**Sp S F W** Yellow to reddish-brown, laterally compressed abdomen with greenish eyes. Antennae longer than abdomen. Ovipositor short, barely projecting beyond tip of abdomen. Parasitoids of moth caterpillars. Common at lights.

### ICHNEUMON WASP *Phytodietus* sp.

**Sp S F W** Elongated, black abdomen with white rings around each segment. Mid and hind tibia and tarsi banded black and white. Antennae not longer than body. Female with stout, straight, relatively long ovipositor. Parasitizes micromoths including tortricids.

### GIANT ICHNEUMON WASP *Megarhyssa macrurus*

**Sp S F W** Both sexes large, reddish-brown. Female with laterally compressed abdomen with narrow yellow transverse stripes and black vertical stripe on face below each antenna. Female with ovipositor three times as long as forewing used to bore through wood to reach Pigeon Tremex larvae that they parasitize. Male with cylindrical abdomen and two yellow longitudinal stripes on thorax. Found in forested areas.

### PLATYGASTRID WASP *Idris* sp.

**Sp S F W** Minute golden yellow and black with terminal antenna segment greatly expanded. Large transversely elongated head with big eyes. Wings often reduced. Found walking around in leaf litter. Parasites of spider egg sacs.

### TEXAS MACROTERA *Macrotera texana*

**Sp S F W** Small, black head and thorax, reddish-orange abdomen. Males can often have disproportionately large, broad, heads. Strict cactus specialist.

### MINING BEE *Andrena* sp.

**Sp S F W** Highly variable, but generally black and moderately hairy. Face, when viewed head on, wider than long with facial fovea or dense patches of setae in indentions running along side the inner margin of each eye. Common visitors to flowers in a variety of habitats, but many are host specific.

### MINING BEE *Perdita* sp.

**Sp S F W** Small to minute, black or yellow. Face round when viewed head on with all females and most males having hairless fovea. Common visitors to flowers in a variety of habitats, but most species restrict their pollen collection to a single plant family.

*Odontocolon* sp.

*Ophion* sp. ♂

*Phytodietus* sp.

*Idris* sp.

Texas Macrotera

*Perdita* sp.

*Andrena* sp.

Giant Ichneumon Wasp ♂

♀

### WESTERN HONEY BEE *Apis mellifera*

APIDAE

Sp S F W    Orange-brown to dark brown, elbowed antennae and hair on eyes. Domesticated and wild populations are highly social with hives of a single queen and more than 20,000 workers. Wild colonies typically occur in tree cavities. Common visitors to flowers where they collect pollen and drink nectar. Regularly used to pollinate food crops such as almonds, apples and alfalfa.

### SOUTHERN PLAINS BUMBLE BEE *Bombus fraternus*

Sp S F W    Large, yellow and black, hairy, thorax yellow with broad black spot, head noticeably short. Nests underground and is a common visitor to grasslands and urban gardens.

### AMERICAN BUMBLE BEE *Bombus pensylvanicus*

Sp S F W    Large with front of thorax yellow, back black. First three abdominal segments yellow. Lacks yellow hairs on face. Common in large fields and open farmlands across the state where it frequents various flowers. Nests on ground among long grass.

### BLUEBERRY DIGGER *Habropoda laboriosa*

Sp S F W    Black and yellow, hairy, thorax all yellow, abdomen black with single yellow band in anterior third. Males have white face. Common spring visitor to blueberries.

### TEPANEC LONG-HORNED BEE *Melissodes tepaneca*

Sp S F W    Head and thorax covered with dark, golden hairs, abdomen black with thin bands of golden or pale hairs. Antennae not elbowed and as long as body. Eyes turquoise to greenish. Generalist, but common on sunflowers.

### SOUTHERN CARPENTER BEE *Xylocopa micans*

Sp S F W    Large, shiny bluish-black bee with nearly circular face. Female thorax with sparse golden hairs. Male with white face, greenish eyes and thorax covered with thick golden hairs. Visits many different flowers in open fields. Nests in wood.

### HORSEFLY-LIKE CARPENTER BEE *Xylocopa tabaniformis*

Sp S F W    Large, hairy, black with white stripes laterally on abdomen. Eyes black to blue. Male with white face. Visits flowers and nests in wood.

### EASTERN CARPENTER BEE *Xylocopa virginica*

Sp S F W    Large, bluish-black with covering of golden hairs on thorax and hairless abdomen. Hair in center of thorax usually absent resulting in a dark spot. Males have white face. Often found near woodlands and adjacent meadows where it will visit flowers for nectar. Nests in wood, including man-made structures and can be quite destructive.

Western
Honey
Bee

Western Honey Bee

Southern
Plains
Bumble
Bee

American
Bumble Bee

♀

Blueberry
Digger

♂

Southern
Carpenter ♀
Bee

♂

Tepanec
Long-
horned Bee

♂

Eastern Carpenter
Bee

♂

Horsefly-
like
Carpenter
Bee

♂

♀

369

# HYMENOPTERA

 **DARK-WINGED STRIPED-SWEAT BEE** *Agapostemon splendens*
HALICTIDAE
**Sp S F W** Brilliant metallic green head and thorax with green abdomen in females and black and plae yellow banded gaster in males. Wings dark. Legs with golden hairs. Common visitor to many different flowers.

 **LIGATED FURROW BEE** *Halictus ligatus*
**Sp S F W** Small, social black bee thinly covered with white hairs on head and thorax. Abdomen black with thin white bands. Antenna dark basally and pale for most of its length. Lower part of face yellow or white and hairless in male. Distal part of each leg yellow. Common visitor to many different flowers.

 **LEAF CUTTER BEE** *Megachile* sp.
MEGACHILIDAE
**Sp S F W** Stout-bodied, dull grayish-black, covered with pale hairs and thin white stripes on abdomen. Tip of male abdomen turns downward quickly; female with scopa for collecting pollen beneath abdomen. Common visitors to a variety of flowers.

 **BLUEBERRY BEE** *Osmia ribifloris*
**Sp S F W** Robust, metallic blue or bluish-green, covered in short hairs. Eyes large and narrow. Face obliquely sloped. Uses a variety of preexisting cavities, including abandoned mud dauber nests, in early spring for their nest. Good pollinators of blueberries and other spring flowers.

 **SQUARE-HEADED WASP** *Tachytes distinctus*
CRABRONIDAE
**Sp S F W** Elongated, black with reddish wings and dark tips. Eyes large and greenish-yellow. Hind femora red female or black male. Pronotum with margin of gold or silver hairs. Females with three pale abdominal bands; male with four. Found in sandy areas.

 **SQUARE-HEADED WASP** *Liris* sp.
**Sp S F W** Black, somewhat robust, with clear to dark wings. Head transversely elongate when viewed from above. Visit flowers and provision nests in sandy areas with crickets.

 **WESTERN CICADA KILLER** *Sphecius grandis*
**Sp S F W** Large, robust, hairless red thorax with black lateral stripes, red abdomen with pale yellow bands and amber wings. Females hunt and sting cicadas, dragging them back to burrow dug in sand. Adults visit flowers.

 **EASTERN CICADA KILLER** *Sphecius speciosus*
**Sp S F W** Large, robust reddish-brown thorax covered in short hairs, amber wings and black and yellow abdomen. Females hunt and sting cicadas. She will then drag the paralyzed prey back to a burrow excavated in the soil. A single egg is laid on one to four cicadas for the larva to eat. Adults will visit flowers.

Dark-winged
Striped-Sweat
Bee
♀

Ligated
Furrow
Bee
♂

Ligated
Furrow
Bee
♂

*Megachile*
sp.

Blueberry Bee

*Tachytes
distinctus*
♀

*Liris* sp.

Western
Cicada
Killer

Eastern Cicada
Killer

### HORSE GUARD WASP *Stictia carolina* CRABRONIDAE

Sp **S F** W  Large, robust, mostly black, with three interrupted yellow stripes basally on abdomen male or five down length of abdomen female. Legs mostly yellow. Captures horse flies to provision nests excavated in sandy soils.

### SAND WASP *Stizoides renicinctus*

Sp **S F** W  Black, robust, with broad orange band on abdomen anterior to the midpoint. Wings black or iridescent blue with pale tips. "Cuckoos," laying their eggs in the nests of sphecids like *Prionyx*.

### SQUARE-HEADED WASP *Astata* sp.

Sp **S F** W  Compact, black with large eyes and reddish, rather short pointed abdomen. Male's eyes contiguous above and with white patch on face. Makes burrows in soil where it provisions nest with stink bug nymphs.

### THREAD-WAISTED WASP *Ammophila* sp. SPHECIDAE

Sp **S F** W  Black, elongated, abdomen with a narrow waist and orange and black "clubbed" tip. Side of thorax often with pair of short white stripes. Larvae feed on paralyzed caterpillars, sawflies and spiders, which female mass provisions in burrow she digs out. Commonly visits flowers.

### BLUE MUD WASP *Chalybion californicum*

Sp **S F** W  Large, iridescent bluish-black, with short thin waist, pronounced club and bluish-black iridescent wings. Builds mud nests on side of buildings and various structures. Provisions nest with spiders and visits flowers for nectar.

### BLACK AND YELLOW MUD DAUBER *Sceliphron caementarium*

Sp **S F** W  Elongate, black and yellow with very long, thin waist and yellow-orange and black clubbed tip. Amount of yellow is variable. Wings amber. Makes mud nests provisioned with spiders. Adults are common visitors to flowers.

### THREAD-WAISTED WASP *Sphex lucae*

Sp **S F** W  Large, black, short narrow waist and reddish-orange abdomen. Wings amber; darkest towards tip and sometimes with iridescence. Males all black. Females provision earthen burrows with katydids. May have gregarious nesting sites.

### GREAT BLACK WASP *Sphex pensylvanicus*

Sp **S F** W  Large, bluish-black with iridescent blue wings. Waist shorter than elongated tip of abdomen. Females provision earthen burrows with katydids and grasshoppers. May have gregarious nesting sites. Visits flowers in open meadows and fields.

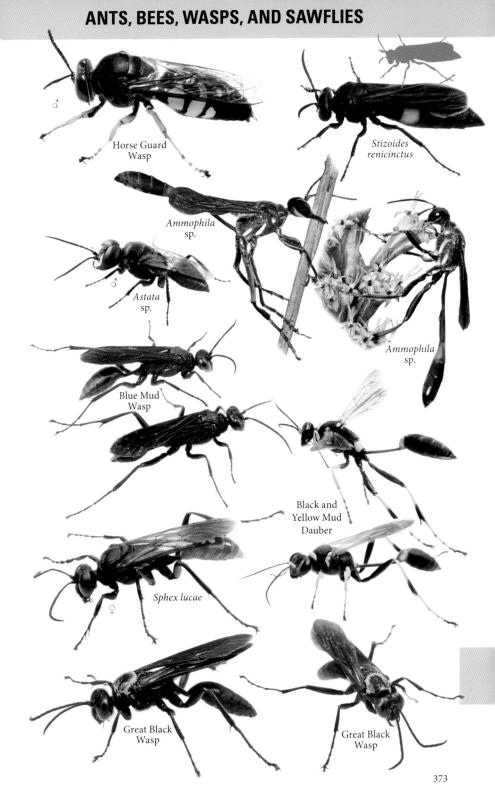

Horse Guard
Wasp

*Stizoides
renicinctus*

*Ammophila*
sp.

*Astata*
sp.

*Ammophila*
sp.

Blue Mud
Wasp

Black and
Yellow Mud
Dauber

*Sphex lucae*

Great Black
Wasp

Great Black
Wasp

### ORGAN-PIPE MUD DAUBER *Trypoxylon politum*

SPHECIDAE

**Sp S F W** Large, black, with iridescent bluish-black wings, abdomen distinctly ribbed and hind tarsi pale. Builds distinct "organ pipe" nests on protected vertical surfaces, including walls. Female provisions nest with as many as 18 spiders per cell.

### CUCKOO WASP *Hedychrum* sp.

CHRYSIDIDAE

**Sp S F W** Small, robust, metallic green or blue and heavily sculptured body. Abdomen distinctly concave below, allowing individuals to curl up into a ball when disturbed. Eggs are laid in the open nest cells of their hosts. Early instar larvae kill the host egg crabronids and sphecids and consume the remaining provisions.

### TEXAS LEAF CUTTING ANT *Atta texana*

FORMICIDAE

**Sp S F W** Reddish-brown, size variable, but generally large ants with very big heads and a spiky thorax and propodeum in workers and soldiers. Easily recognizable because of their large mound colonies containing up to 2 million individuals in sandy soils and the trails of workers carrying pieces of cut vegetation.

### CARPENTER ANT *Camponotus castaneus*

**Sp S F W** Reddish-brown, elongated, large, shiny, clypeus with transverse ridge with rounded head. Workers look similar to reproductives, just without wings and larger heads. Nest in decaying wood, soil and under rocks. Reproductives attracted to lights.

### EASTERN BLACK CARPENTER ANT *Camponotus pennsylvanicus*

**Sp S F W** Large, black, shiny with long erect golden hairs along margins of gaster segments. Nests in rotting wood, but commonly associated with man-made structures where they are destructive. Mating swarms occur on the first warm humid afternoon in the spring.

### HAIRY PANTHER ANT *Neoponera villosa*

**Sp S F W** Large, black, with patches of grayish hairs on head, thorax and gaster. Predatory feeding on insects, especially in the forest canopy. Nests in cavities, hollow logs and bases of epiphytes. Workers commonly seen foraging low to the ground. Has a painful sting.

### ANT *Colobopsis impressa*

**Sp S F W** Yellowish-brown and black distinctive ants with truncated looking heads that are used to plug holes in the nest entrances of galls, twigs and hollow stems of the woody plants in which they live. They feed on the nutrients scavenged from vertebrate excrement and dead insects.

### ARMY ANT *Labidus coecus*

**Sp S F W** Male reproductives, also known as "sausage flies" are most commonly encountered at lights. They are large, winged and have an elongated gaster. Workers are nearly always subterranean. They raid other ant nests, but are also somewhat opportunistic.

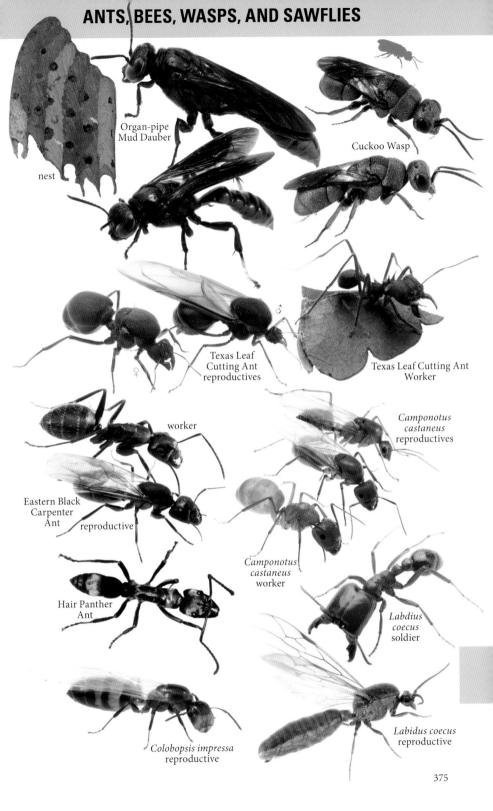

Organ-pipe
Mud Dauber

nest

Cuckoo Wasp

♂

Texas Leaf
Cutting Ant
reproductives

♀

Texas Leaf Cutting Ant
Worker

worker

*Camponotus
castaneus*
reproductives

Eastern Black
Carpenter
Ant

reproductive

*Camponotus
castaneus*
worker

Hair Panther
Ant

*Labdius
coecus*
soldier

*Colobopsis impressa*
reproductive

*Labidus coecus*
reproductive

### ANT *Leptogenys elongata*
FORMICIDAE

Sp **S F W** Elongated, reddish-brown with large, anteriorly projecting mandibles and squared petiole. Found under rocks and logs where they feed on isopods and other small invertebrates.

### HONEYPOT ANT *Myrmecocystus* sp.

Sp **S F W** Slender, bicolored, with red head and thorax and black gaster. Long legs. Nest in soil where some workers hang from the ceiling in underground chambers and store nectar and honeydew in their greatly swollen gasters.

### RED HARVESTER ANT *Pogonomyrmex barbatus*

Sp **S F W** Large, robust, red, large square-headed ants. Head heavily sculptured. Propodeum with stout spines. Nest usually a plant-free gravelly area, three to four feet in diameter. Feeds on seeds and scavenges for insects. Not aggressive, but has a painful sting.

### SEED HARVESTER ANT *Pogonomyrmex rugosus*

Sp **S F W** Large, robust, dark, large square-headed ants, bicolored ants with a reddish gaster. Head heavily sculptured. Propodeum with stout spines. Nest usually a plant-free gravelly area, three to four feet in diameter. Feeds on seeds and scavenges for insects and vegetation. Not aggressive, but has a painful sting.

### GRACEFUL TWIG ANT *Pseudomyrmex gracilis*

Sp **S F W** Long, slender, orange and black, large eyes that bulge from head laterally, and two-segmented petiole. Variable in degree of brownish-black and orange colors. Wasp-like with small colonies in twigs. Has a potent sting. Feeds on live insects, fungal spores and tends aphids feeding for honeydew.

### RED IMPORTED FIRE ANT *Solenopsis invicta*

Sp **S F W** Ubiquitous and feared ant. Usually somewhat bicolored with reddish-brown head and thorax and a darker brown gaster. Petiole with two humps. Found in open, disturbed areas where it is omnivorous and aggressive. Introduced from Brazil.

### NATIVE RED FIRE ANT *Solenopsis geminata*

Sp **S F W** Similar to the Red Imported Fire Ant, but usually more uniform reddish-brown in color and on average larger in size. Usually found in non-disturbed areas.

### ACROBAT ANT *Crematogaster laeviuscula*

Sp **S F W** Small, distinctively shaped ants with reddish-brown head, thorax and propodeum with a shiny black heart-shaped gaster. They are commonly found foraging on branches and in trees, especially in riparian areas.

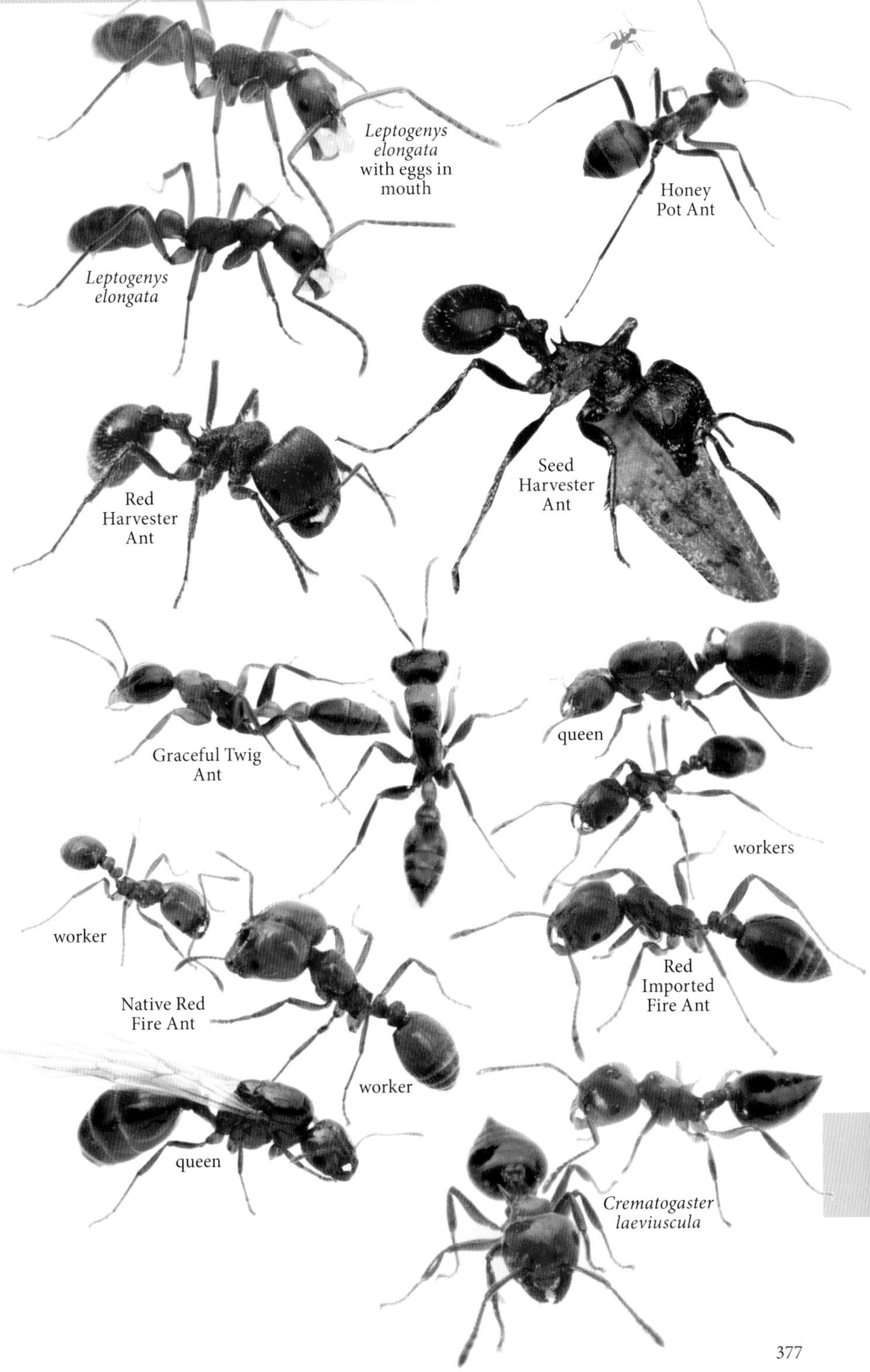

*Leptogenys elongata* with eggs in mouth

Honey Pot Ant

*Leptogenys elongata*

Red Harvester Ant

Seed Harvester Ant

Graceful Twig Ant

queen

workers

worker

Native Red Fire Ant

Red Imported Fire Ant

worker

queen

*Crematogaster laeviuscula*

MUTILLIDAE

### THISTLEDOWN VELVET ANT *Dasymutilla gloriosa*

**Sp S F W** Black body with female wingless and covered in long white hair. Male winged, with long orange hairs on thorax and distal two-thirds of abdomen. Female resembles creosote seed. Found walking on ground or in creosote, willow and other trees. Lays eggs in cocoons of bembecine wasps where the larvae consume the prey.

### VELVET ANT *Dasymutilla bioculata*

**Sp S F W** Female wingless, variable in color, but often red or orange with basal dark spot on abdomen and posterior half of abdomen dark. Male winged, black, variable, but generally two orange spots basally on abdomen. Ectoparasitoids of bembecine wasps.

### COW KILLER *Dasymutilla occidentalis*

**Sp S F W** Female wingless, large strikingly marked with orange, yellow or red on black. Base of abdomen with two large circular colored spots, separated from colored tip by black band. Lower half of body black. Males with dark brown wings and only the head, thorax and distal half of abdomen are pale colored. Found in open fields and forest edges. Ectoparasitoids of large crabronids.

### VELVET ANT *Dasymutilla quadriguttata*

**Sp S F W** Female wingless, orange with black abdomen bearing four pale spots. Basal antennal segment orange, remaining segments dark. Male with dark wings and black with two basal red or orange spots on middle abdominal segments.

### VELVET ANT *Myrmilloides grandiceps*

**Sp S F W** Female small, wingless, reddish-orange with head distinctly wider than long, sharply angled posterolaterally, thorax narrow and abdomen black with two narrow pale spots and tip of abdomen pale. Pale spots on abdomen can be gray or white. Some individuals with basal half of abdomen reddish-orange.

### VELVET ANT *Pseudomethoca frigida*

**Sp S F W** Female small, wingless, red or orange with head wider than long and sharply angled posterolaterally. Abdomen with two small to large grayish, white or light orange round spots basally. Distal segments of abdomen typically dark. Ectoparasitoid of *Lasioglossum*.

### NOCTURNAL VELVET ANT *Sphaeropthalma* sp.

**Sp S F W** Males winged, reddish-brown, narrowly elongate and often with dark spot over ocelli. Lay eggs in cells of a variety of bees and wasps. Nocturnal; attracted to lights.

### VELVET ANT *Timulla vagans*

**Sp S F W** Male with dark wings, head and thorax black, abdomen reddish-orange with black bands of hair distally on each segment. Female wingless, similar to male, but with addition of white bands on abdomen.

# ANTS, BEES, WASPS, AND SAWFLIES

Thistledown
Velvet Ant

♂

♀

Dasymutilla
bioculata

Cow Killer

Dasymutilla
quadriguttata

Pseudomethoca
frigida

Myrmilloides
grandiceps

Sphaerophthalma
sp.

Timulla
vagans

### TARANTULA HAWK *Pepsis* sp.

**Sp S F W** Very large, bluish-black body with orange wings. Females are seen hunting for tarantulas and other large spiders that they then paralyze with a sting and then drag back to a burrow where they lay a single egg. The larva hatches and feeds on the spider.

### SPIDER WASP *Tachypompilus ferrugineus*

**Sp S F W** Reddish-brown with dark wings and sides of thorax dark above legs and below wings. Distal segments of each abdominal segment margined in black. Two prominent spines distally on hind tibia not the same length. Visit flowers. Ectoparasitoid of spiders.

### SCOLIID WASP *Campsomeris plumipes*

**Sp S F W** Black, hairy, elongated with yellow banding on abdomen and prominent mandibles. Thorax black with yellow band anteriorly and posteriorly. Male with antennae extending beyond thorax, female to back of thorax or less. Ectoparasitoid on scarab larvae in soil. Common visitors to flowers in meadows.

### SCOLIID WASP *Trielis octomaculata*

**Sp S F W** Black or reddish-brown, hairy, with eight dorsal abdominal spots on abdomen thinly connected at middle. Pale spots bright to pale yellow. Male with longer antennae and more elongated abdomen. Prominent mandibles. Common visitors to flowers.

### FIVE-BANDED THYNNID WASP *Myzinum quinquecinctum*

**Sp S F W** Elongated, black with yellow banding on abdomen and yellow "=" on posterior half of thorax. Wings uniformly dark. Female with shorter, reddish antennae, and broader abdomen. Male with longer black antennae, elongated abdomen with ventral hook.

### FOUR-TOOTHED MASON WASP *Monobia quadridens*

**Sp S F W** Black, robust with white band basally on pointed abdomen and iridescent blue wings. White band anteriorly on thorax. Including mandibles, head looks triangular from front. Adults common at flowers. Nests in wood, including abandoned carpenter bee nests, where larvae feed on moth caterpillars.

### BALD-FACED AERIAL YELLOWJACKET *Dolichovespula maculata*

**Sp S F W** Robust, black with white markings on head, thorax and distally on abdomen. Wings dark. Nests are large oval paper nests in trees and bushes with entrance low on side. Frequent visitor to flowers where adults take nectar and are generalist predators.

### MEXICAN HONEY WASP *Brachygastra mellifica*

**Sp S F W** Small, compact, black, with terminal abdominal segments yellow and distinctly wider than long head, when viewed above. Nests low to mid way up in trees and shrubs. Produce and store honey in paper carton nests.

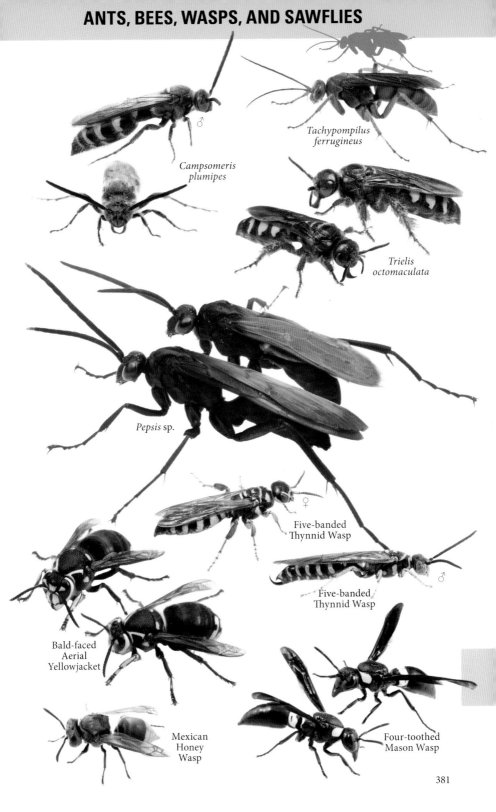

*Tachypompilus ferrugineus*

*Campsomeris plumipes*

♂

*Trielis octomaculata*

*Pepsis* sp.

♀

Five-banded Thynnid Wasp

♂

Five-banded Thynnid Wasp

Bald-faced Aerial Yellowjacket

Mexican Honey Wasp

Four-toothed Mason Wasp

### POTTER WASP *Eumenes fraternus*

Sp S F W  Black, with elongated, distally swollen waist and large tapering abdomen tip bearing two pale spots. Wings dark. Anterior and posterior margins of thorax with white stripe. Female creates a mud nest on vegetation and provisions it with small caterpillars or sawfly larvae.

### POTTER AND MASON WASP *Euodynerus hidalgo*

Sp S F W  Black, heavily punctured, with yellow face, dark wings and yellow stripes on thorax and abdomen. Base of antennae yellowish. Variable amount of red. Nests in preexisting cavities, including old bee nests in banks.

### RED PAPER WASP *Polistes carolina* or *rubiginosus*

Sp S F W  Two common, red species with black wings that can only be told apart with microscopic examination of the side of face. Together they constitute the well known "red wasp" that commonly makes nests under the eves of houses and in shrubs.

### PAPER WASP *Polistes dorsalis*

Sp S F W  Reddish-brown, with variable black and yellow. Antennae orange basally, dark for posterior half. Legs dark basally with dark band on apex of hind tibia. Sides of thorax often very dark. Build nests in shrubbery and under eaves of buildings.

### PAPER WASP *Polistes exclamans*

Sp S F W  Brightly colored, red and yellow species. Antennae dark with orange tips. Thorax often with pair of longitudinal pale stripes. Abdomen with a lot of yellow distally.  Build nests under eaves of structures and in trees and shrubs.

### PAPER WASP *Polistes metricus*

Sp S F W  Dark red with brownish-black abdomen, pale tibia and tarsi, and dark wings. Top of thorax variable in amount of red, but generally darker than rest of thorax. Antennae dark. Build nests under eaves of structures and in trees and shrubs.

### EASTERN YELLOWJACKET *Vespula maculifrons*

Sp S F W  Robust, black and yellow. Workers with top of thorax black. First abdominal tergite has anchor-shaped black mark with tapered base. Queen with black spots on abdomen. Found in forests, meadows and urban areas where colonies, numbering in the thousands, are underground or in stumps and fallen logs. Adults visit flowers where they take nectar. Very aggressive.

### SOUTHERN YELLOWJACKET *Vespula squamosa*

Sp S F W  Robust, black and yellow or black and orange with pair of yellow stripes on black thorax. Workers and males lack black spots on abdomen. Mainly social parasites with nests established in the nests of other yellowjacket species after killing the queen.

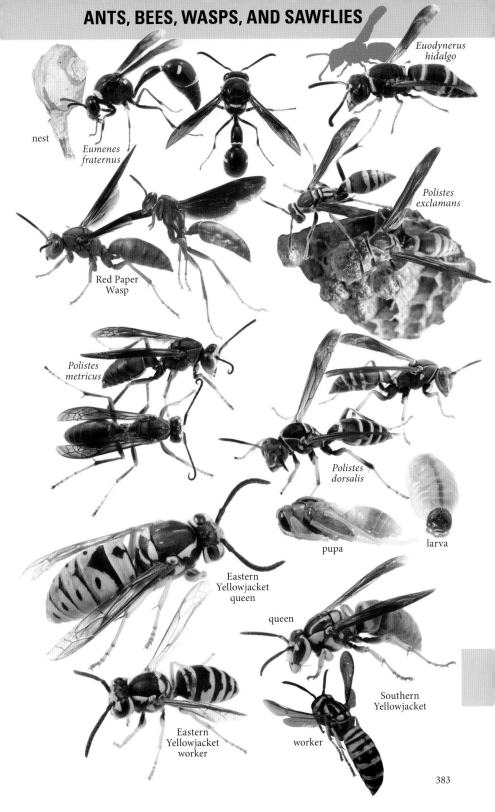

nest

*Eumenes fraternus*

*Euodynerus hidalgo*

Red Paper Wasp

*Polistes exclamans*

*Polistes metricus*

*Polistes dorsalis*

pupa

larva

Eastern Yellowjacket queen

queen

Eastern Yellowjacket worker

Southern Yellowjacket

worker

383

As with most insect groups, there are no comprehensive catalogs or species lists for non-insect arthropods occurring in Texas. We, however, can extrapolate that if there are nearly 30,000 insect species, there are likely over 3,000 non-insect arthropod species found in Texas. The major terrestrial groups that your average observer will encounter include the isopods, centipedes, millipedes, and arachnids. Many of these are closely associated with insects, either occurring in the same habitat as many insects or as predators of insects. The following pages are meant to represent just some of the more common or distinctive species that you may encounter and provide a small guide to the taxonomic placement of others. The higher-level taxonomy for the non-insect arthropod groups that follow and their close relatives is provided below.

subphylum Chelicerata
    class Arachnida
        subclass Acari—ticks and mites
        order Amblypygi—tailless whipscorpions
        order Araneae—spiders
        order Uropygi—whipscorpions
        order Opiliones—harvestmen
        order Palpigradi—microscorpions
        order Pseudoscorpiones—pseudoscorpions
        order Schizomida—short-tailed whipscorpions
        order Scorpiones—scorpions
        order Solifugae—windscorpions
        order Ricinulei—hooded tickspiders
    class Merostomata—horseshoe crabs
    class Pycnogonida—sea spiders
subphylum Crustacea
    class Malacostraca
        order Decapoda—crabs, crayfishes, lobsters, and shrimp
        order Amphipoda—amphipods
        order Isopoda—isopods
subphylum Myriapoda
    class Chilopoda—centipedes
    class Diplopoda—millipedes
    class Symphyla—symphylans
    class Pauropoda—paurpods

Golden Silk
Orbweaver
(*Nephila clavipes*)

## Crustaceans

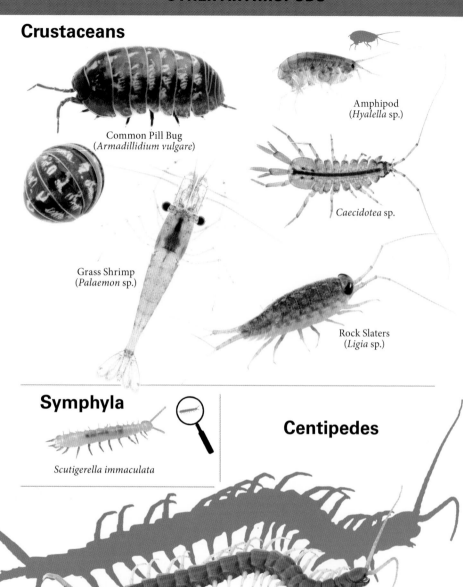

Common Pill Bug
(*Armadillidium vulgare*)

Amphipod
(*Hyalella* sp.)

*Caecidotea* sp.

Grass Shrimp
(*Palaemon* sp.)

Rock Slaters
(*Ligia* sp.)

## Symphyla

*Scutigerella immaculata*

## Centipedes

Giant Redheaded Centipede
(*Scolopendra heros*)

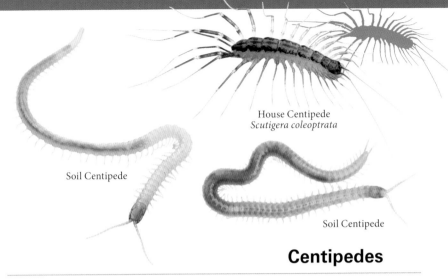

House Centipede
*Scutigera coleoptrata*

Soil Centipede

Soil Centipede

## Centipedes

## Millipedes

Desert Millipede
(*Orthoporus ornatus*)

*Narceus americanus*

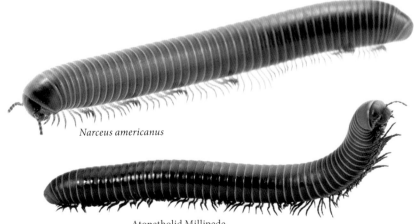

*Narceus americanus*

Atopetholid Millipede

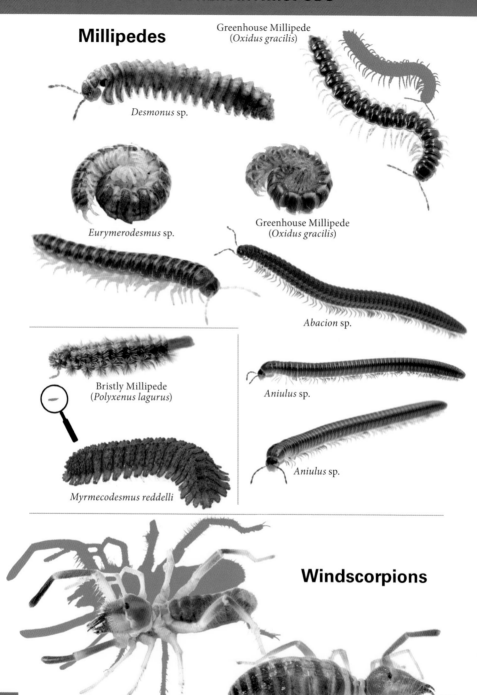

## Millipedes

Greenhouse Millipede
(*Oxidus gracilis*)

*Desmonus* sp.

*Eurymerodesmus* sp.

Greenhouse Millipede
(*Oxidus gracilis*)

*Abacion* sp.

Bristly Millipede
(*Polyxenus lagurus*)

*Aniulus* sp.

*Myrmecodesmus reddelli*

*Aniulus* sp.

## Windscorpions

Straight-faced
Windscorpion

Straight-faced
Windscorpion

## Scorpions

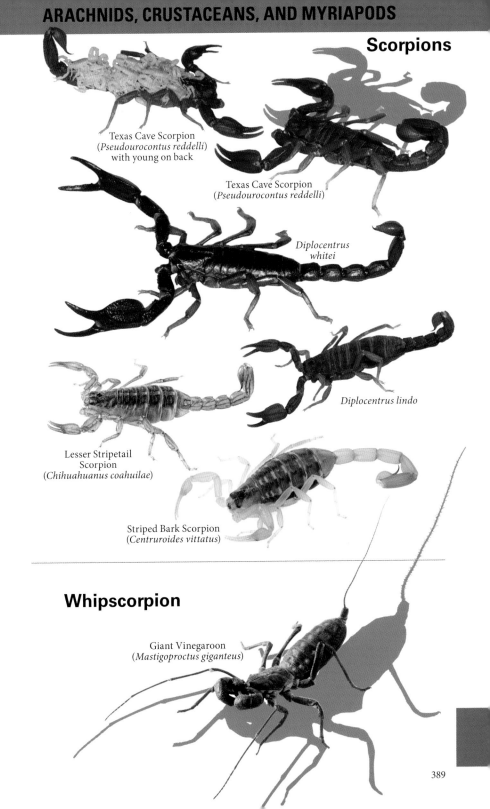

Texas Cave Scorpion
(*Pseudouroctonus reddelli*)
with young on back

Texas Cave Scorpion
(*Pseudouroctonus reddelli*)

*Diplocentrus
whitei*

*Diplocentrus lindo*

Lesser Stripetail
Scorpion
(*Chihuahuanus coahuilae*)

Striped Bark Scorpion
(*Centruroides vittatus*)

## Whipscorpion

Giant Vinegaroon
(*Mastigoproctus giganteus*)

389

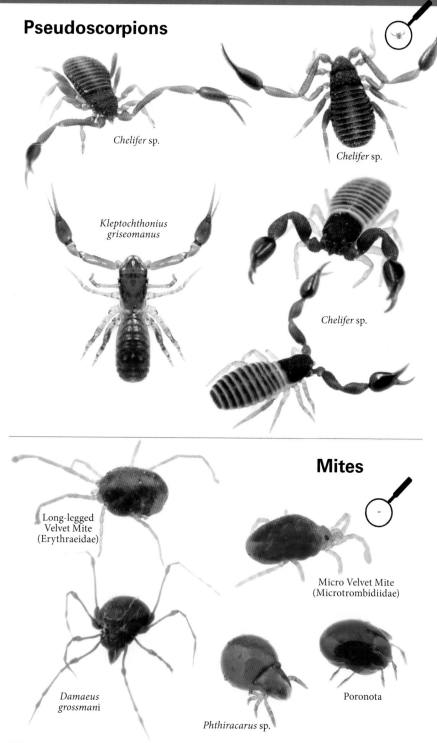

## Pseudoscorpions

*Chelifer* sp.

*Chelifer* sp.

*Kleptochthonius
griseomanus*

*Chelifer* sp.

## Mites

Long-legged
Velvet Mite
(Erythraeidae)

Micro Velvet Mite
(Microtrombidiidae)

*Damaeus
grossman*i

Poronota

*Phthiracarus* sp.

## Ticks

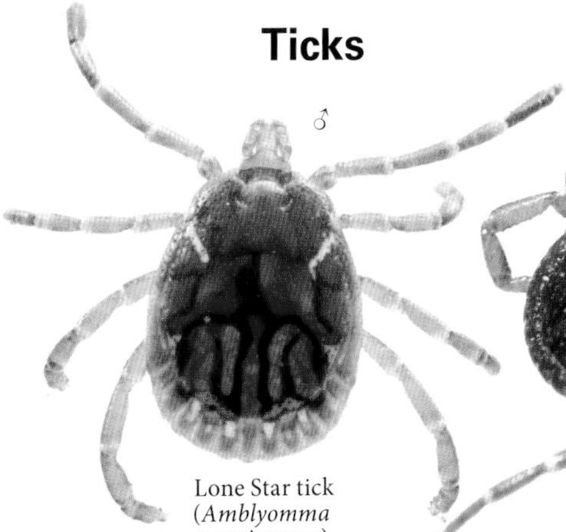

Lone Star tick
(*Amblyomma americanum*)

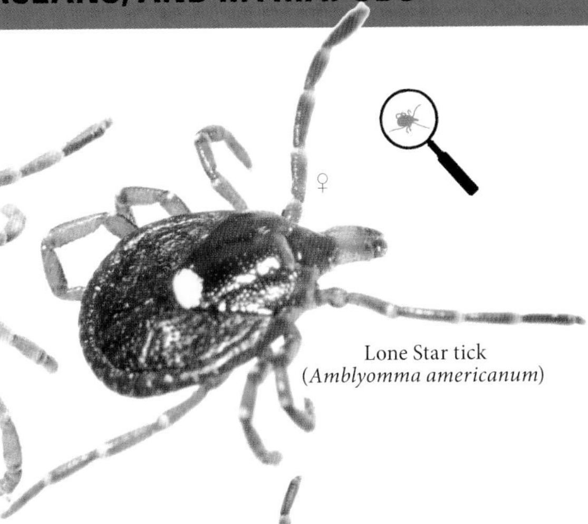

Lone Star tick
(*Amblyomma americanum*)

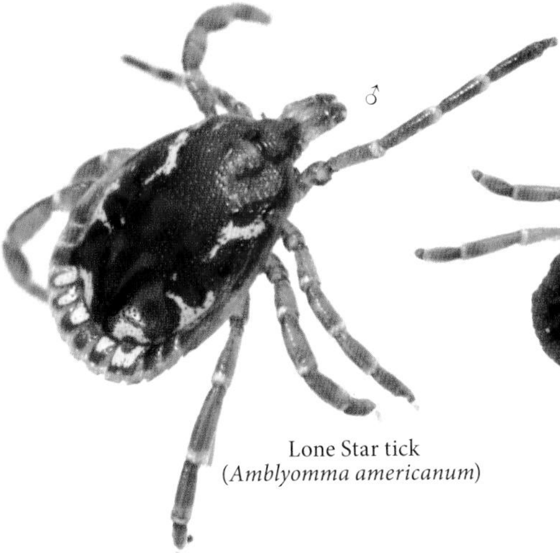

Lone Star tick
(*Amblyomma americanum*)

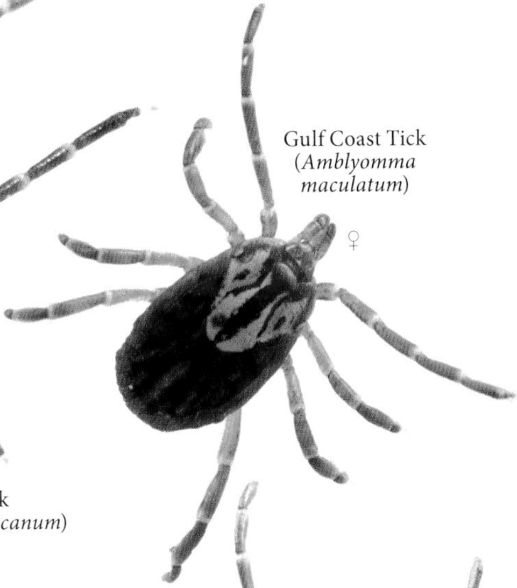

Gulf Coast Tick
(*Amblyomma maculatum*)

Gulf Coast Tick
(*Amblyomma maculatum*)

American Dog Tick
(*Dermacentor variabilis*)

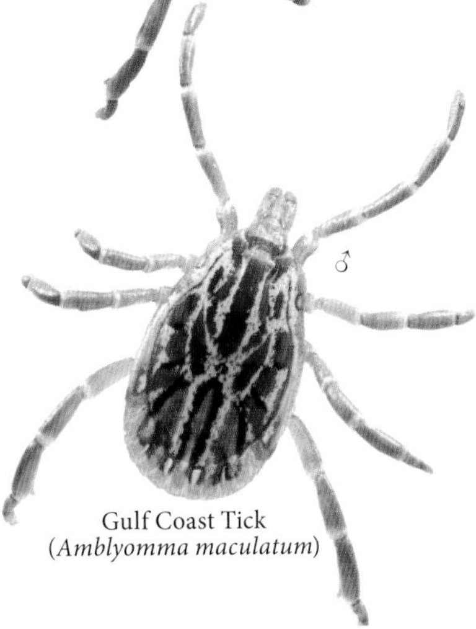

391

# Harvestmen

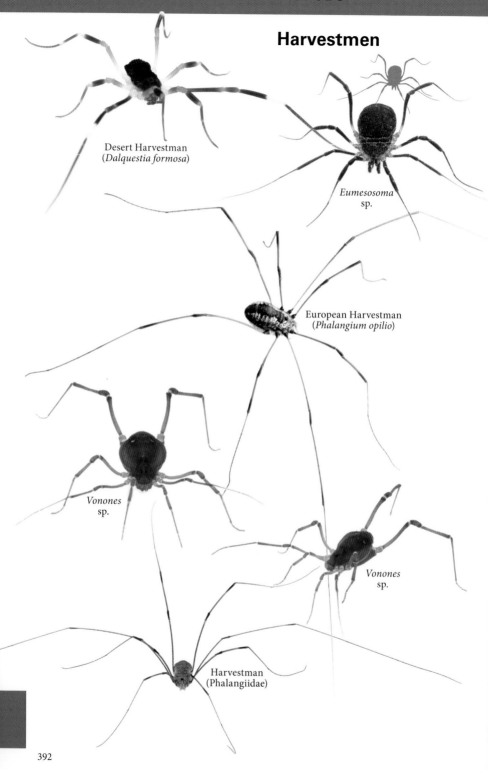

Desert Harvestman
(*Dalquestia formosa*)

*Eumesosoma*
sp.

European Harvestman
(*Phalangium opilio*)

*Vonones*
sp.

*Vonones*
sp.

Harvestman
(Phalangiidae)

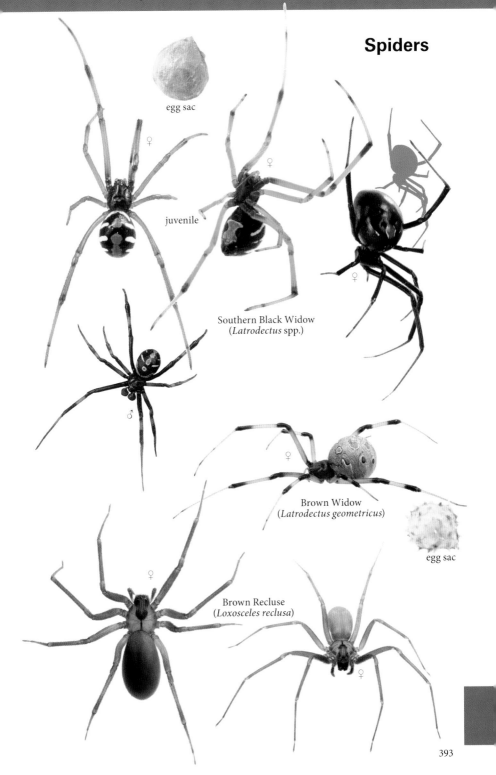

# Spiders

egg sac

♀

juvenile

♀

Southern Black Widow
(*Latrodectus* spp.)

♂

♀

Brown Widow
(*Latrodectus geometricus*)

egg sac

♀

Brown Recluse
(*Loxosceles reclusa*)

♀

## Spiders

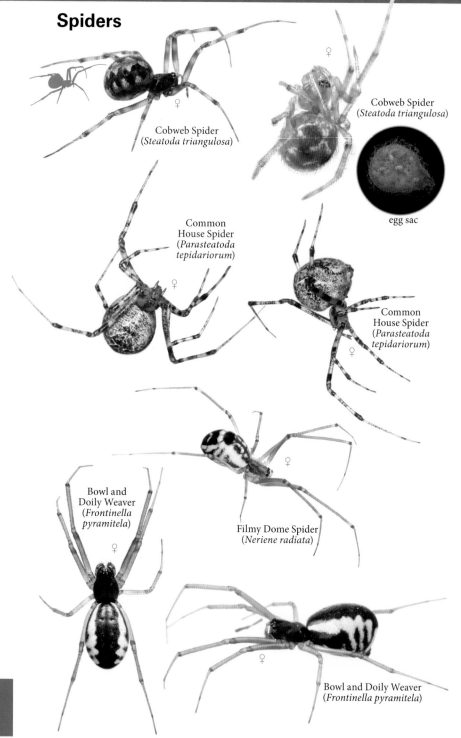

Cobweb Spider
(*Steatoda triangulosa*) ♀

Cobweb Spider
(*Steatoda triangulosa*) ♀

egg sac

Common
House Spider
(*Parasteatoda
tepidariorum*) ♀

Common
House Spider
(*Parasteatoda
tepidariorum*) ♀

Bowl and
Doily Weaver
(*Frontinella
pyramitela*) ♀

Filmy Dome Spider
(*Neriene radiata*) ♀

Bowl and Doily Weaver
(*Frontinella pyramitela*) ♀

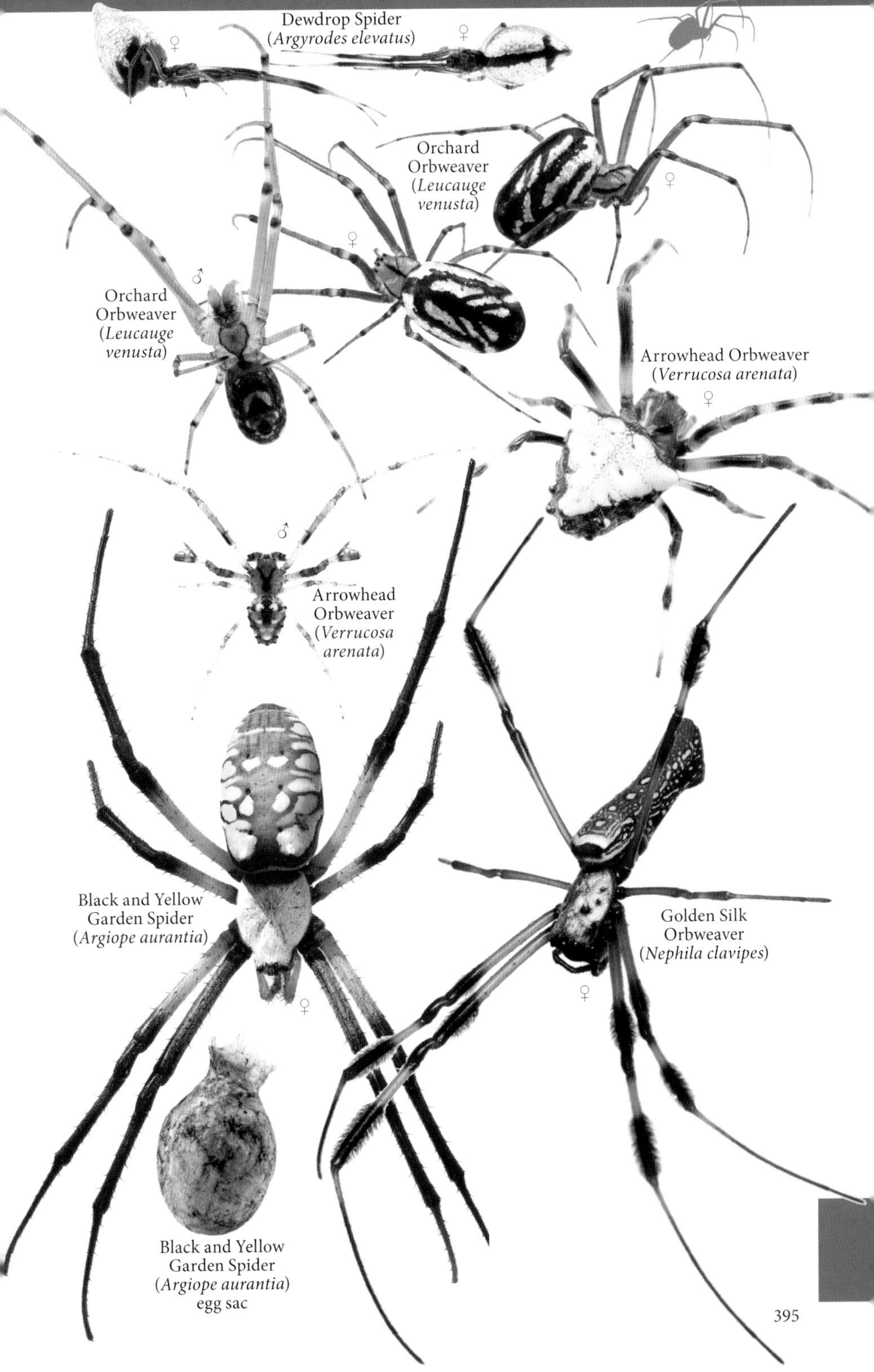

Dewdrop Spider
(*Argyrodes elevatus*) ♀

Orchard
Orbweaver
(*Leucauge
venusta*) ♀

Orchard
Orbweaver
(*Leucauge
venusta*) ♂

Orchard
Orbweaver
(*Leucauge
venusta*) ♀

Arrowhead Orbweaver
(*Verrucosa arenata*) ♀

Arrowhead
Orbweaver
(*Verrucosa
arenata*) ♂

Black and Yellow
Garden Spider
(*Argiope aurantia*) ♀

Golden Silk
Orbweaver
(*Nephila clavipes*) ♀

Black and Yellow
Garden Spider
(*Argiope aurantia*)
egg sac

395

# Spiders

Furrow Orbweaver
(*Larinioides cornutus*)
♀

Furrow Orbweaver
(*Larinioides cornutus*)
♀

Furrow Orbweaver
(*Larinioides* sp.)
♀

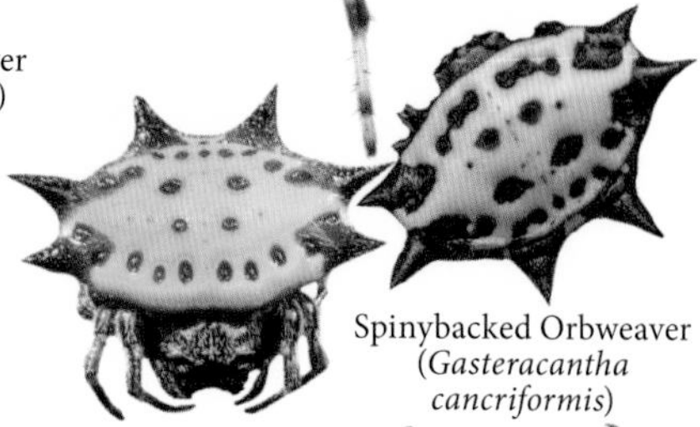

Spinybacked Orbweaver
(*Gasteracantha
cancriformis*)

Cat-faced Spider
(*Araneus gemmoides*)
♀

Spotted Orbweaver
(*Neoscona crucifera*)
♀

♂

Starbellied Orbweaver
(*Acanthepeira stellata*)
♀

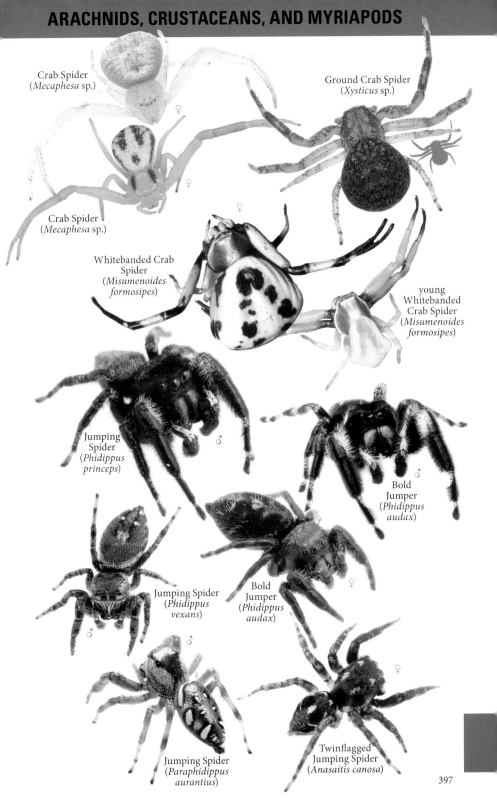

Crab Spider
(*Mecaphesa* sp.)
♀

Ground Crab Spider
(*Xysticus* sp.)
♀

Crab Spider
(*Mecaphesa* sp.)
♀

Whitebanded Crab
Spider
(*Misumenoides
formosipes*)

young
Whitebanded
Crab Spider
(*Misumenoides
formosipes*)

Jumping
Spider
(*Phidippus
princeps*)
♂

Bold
Jumper
(*Phidippus
audax*)
♂

Jumping Spider
(*Phidippus
vexans*)
♂

Bold
Jumper
(*Phidippus
audax*)
♀

Jumping Spider
(*Paraphidippus
aurantius*)
♂

Twinflagged
Jumping Spider
(*Anasaitis canosa*)
♀

397

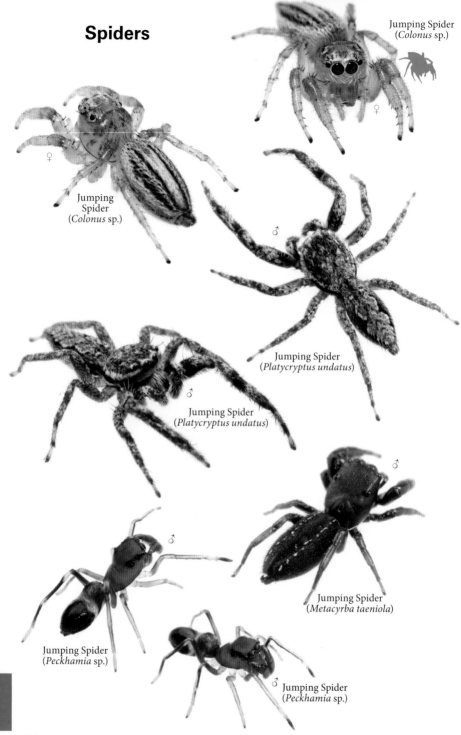

## Spiders

Jumping Spider
(*Colonus* sp.)

♀

Jumping
Spider
(*Colonus* sp.)

♂

Jumping Spider
(*Platycryptus undatus*)

♂

Jumping Spider
(*Platycryptus undatus*)

♂

Jumping Spider
(*Metacyrba taeniola*)

♂

Jumping Spider
(*Peckhamia* sp.)

♂ Jumping Spider
(*Peckhamia* sp.)

Pantropical Jumper
(*Plexippus paykulli*) ♀

Peppered Jumper
(*Pelegrina galathea*) ♀

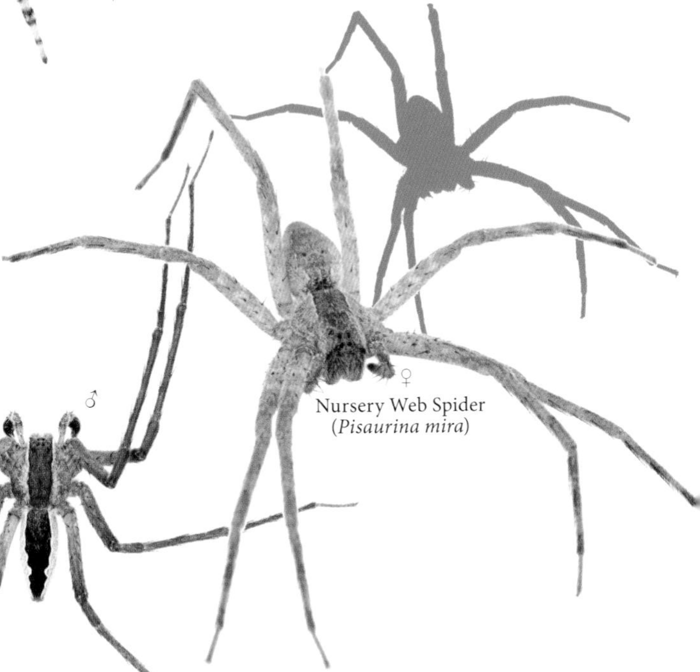

Nursery Web Spider
(*Pisaurina mira*) ♀

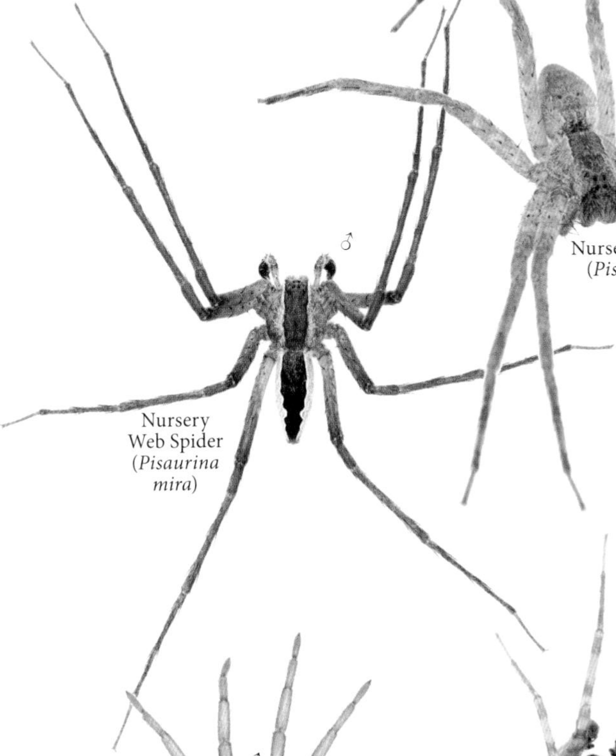

Nursery
Web Spider
(*Pisaurina
mira*) ♂

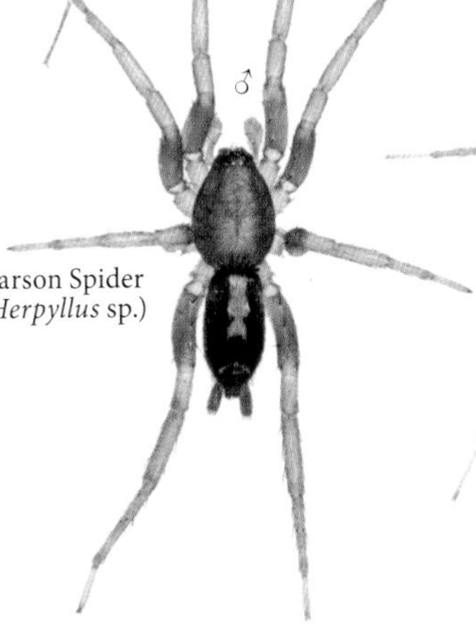

Parson Spider
(*Herpyllus* sp.) ♂

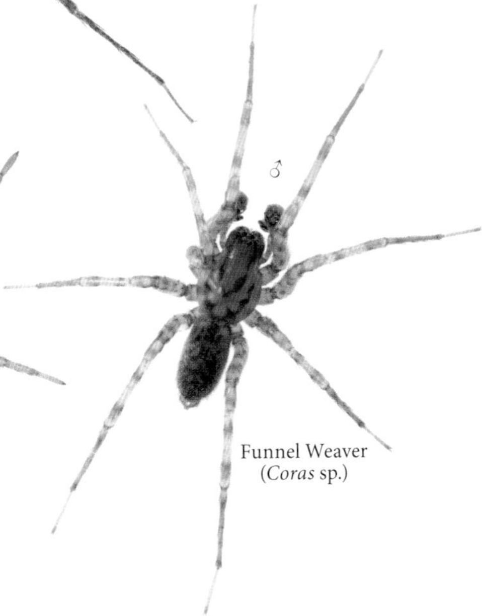

Funnel Weaver
(*Coras* sp.) ♂

## Spiders

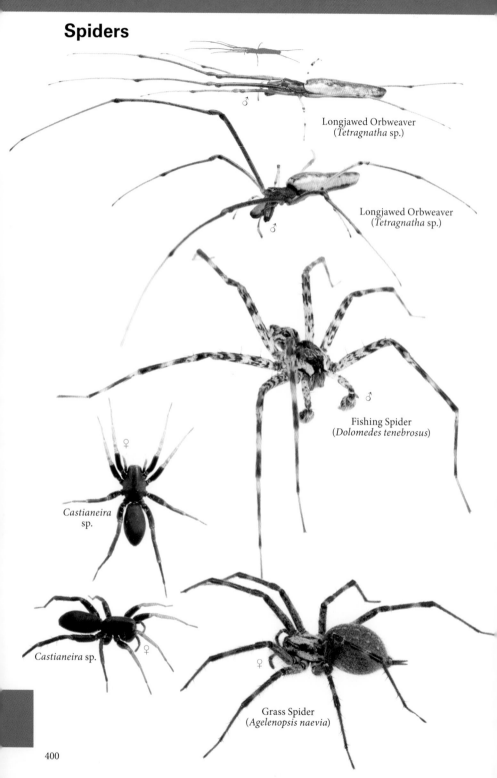

Longjawed Orbweaver
(*Tetragnatha* sp.)

Longjawed Orbweaver
(*Tetragnatha* sp.)

Fishing Spider
(*Dolomedes tenebrosus*)

*Castianeira*
sp.

*Castianeira* sp.

Grass Spider
(*Agelenopsis naevia*)

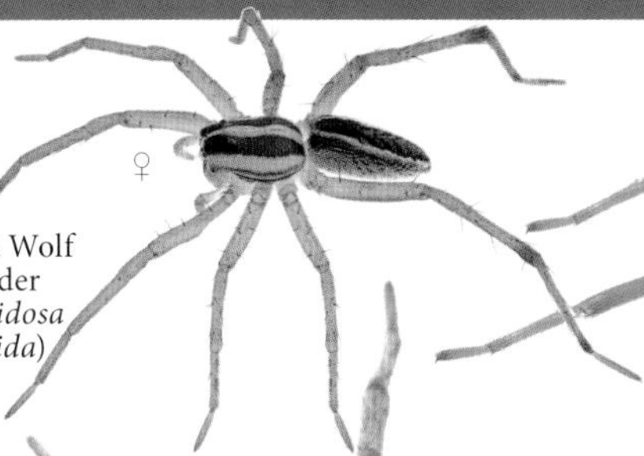

Rabid Wolf
Spider
(*Rabidosa
rabida*)
♀

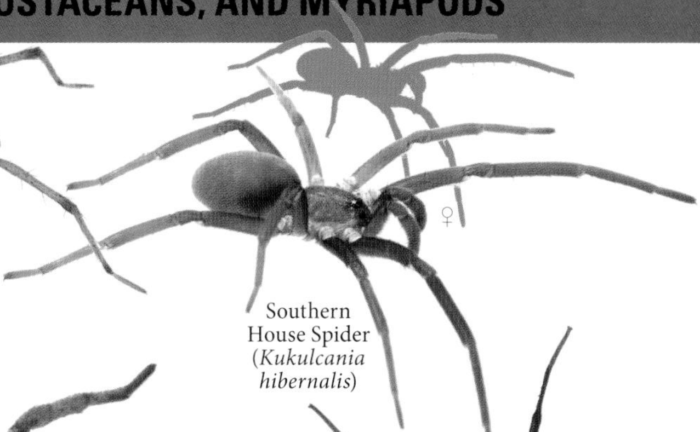

Southern
House Spider
(*Kukulcania
hibernalis*)
♀

♂

Burrowing
Wolf Spider
(*Geolycosa* sp.)
♀

♀

Tarantula
(*Aphonopelma armada*)

# Additional Resources

Dragonhunter
(*Hagenius brevistylus*)

There are many print and digital resources available today for the insect enthusiast and professional alike. Only a few years ago, resources for the identification of most groups were limited to the peer-reviewed literature. Especially with the advent of the Internet, and various citizen science initiatives in particular, there has been resurgence in the appreciation and study of insect natural history. We have tried to provide a thorough, though not exhaustive list of these resources here, organized by taxonomic groups.

## GENERAL INSECTS

*A Field Guide to Common Texas Insects* by Bastiaan M. Drees and John A. Jackman. Gulf Publishing Company, 1998.

*A Guide to Common Freshwater Invertebrates of North America* by J. Reese Voshell, Jr. The McDonald and Woodward Publishing Company, 2002.

*American Insects: A handbook of the Insects of America North of Mexico*, 2nd edition by Ross H. Arnett, Jr. CRC Press, 2000.

*Evolution of the Insects* by David Grimaldi and Michael S. Engel. Cambridge University Press, 2005.

*Field Guide to Insects and Spiders of North America* by Arthur V. Evans. National Wildlife Federation, 2007.

*Insects of Texas: A practical guide* by David H. Kattes. Texas A&M University Press, 2009.

*Insects of the Texas Lost Pines* by Stephen W. Taber and Scott B. Fleenor. Texas A&M University Press, 2003.

*Insects: Their natural history and diversity with a photographic guide to insects of eastern North America* by Stephen A. Marshall. A Firefly Book, 2006.

*Invertebrates of Central Texas Wetlands* by Stephen W. Taber and Scott B. Fleenor. Texas Tech University Press, 2005.

*Kaufman Field Guide to Insects of North America* by Eric R. Eaton and Kenn Kaufman. Houghton Mifflin Company, 2007.

*Peterson Field Guide to Insects* by Donald J. Borror and Richard E. White. Houghton Mifflin Company, 1970.

*Texas Bug Book: The good, the bad and the ugly* by C. Malcom Beck and John H. Garrett. University of Texas Press, 1999.

*Garden Insects of North America: The ultimate guide to backyard bugs* by Whitney Cranshaw. Princeton University Press, 2004.

BugGuide—BugGuide.net
iNaturalist—iNaturalist.org
Austin Bug Collection—AustinBug.com
Texas Entomology—TexasEnto.net

## ARACHNIDS AND RELATIVES

*A Field Guide to Spiders & Scorpions of Texas* by John A. Jackman. A Gulf Publishing Book. 1999.

*Common Spiders of North America* by Richard A. Bradley. University of California Press, 2013.

*How to Know the Spiders*, 3rd edition by B. J. Kaston. The Pictured Key Nature Series, 1972.

*Spiders of the Carolinas* by L. L. Gaddy. Kollath and Stensaas Publishing, 2009.

*Spiders of the Eastern United States: A photographic guide* by W. Mike Howell and Ronald L. Jenkins. Pearson Education, 2004.

*Spiders of the North Woods*, 2nd edition by Larry Weber. Kollath and Stensaas Publishing, 2013.

## MINOR AMETABOLOUS ORDERS

Collembola—www.collembola.org

Bristletails of North America—archaeognatha.myspecies.info

## AQUATIC ORDERS

*American Stoneflies: A photographic guide to the Plecoptera* by Bill P. Stark, Stanley W. Szczytko, and C. Riley Nelson. The Caddis Press, 1998.

*An Introduction to the Aquatic Insects of North America*, 4th edition, edited by Rich W. Merritt, Kenneth W. Cummins, and Martin B. Berg. Kendall Hunt Publishing Company, 2008.

*Aquatic Entomology: The fisherman's and ecologists' illustrated guide to insects and their relatives* by W. Patrick McCafferty. Jones and Bartlett, 1998.

*Damselflies of Texas: A field guide* by John C. Abbott. University of Texas Press, 2011.

*Dragonflies and Damselflies of Texas and the South-central United States* by John C. Abbott. Princeton University Press, 2005.

*Dragonflies and Damselflies of the West* by Dennis Paulson. Princeton University Press, 2009.

*Dragonflies of Texas: A field guide* by John C. Abbott. University of Texas Press, 2015.

*Larvae of the North American Caddisfly Genera (Trichoptera)*, 2nd edition by Glenn B. Wiggins. University of Toronto Press, 1996.

Mayfly Central—www.entm.purdue.edu/mayfly

OdonataCentral— www.OdonataCentral.org

Trichoptera Nearctica—www.trichoptera.org

## SMALL INSECT ORDERS

*How to Know the Grasshoppers, Crickets, Cockroaches, and their Allies* by Jacques R. Helfer. Dover Publications, 1987.

Psocoptera of Texas—sam-diane.com/psocopteraoftexas.html

## GRASSHOPPERS, KATYDIDS, AND RELATIVES

*Field Guide to Grasshoppers, Katydids, and Crickets of the United States* by John L. Capinera, Ralph D. Scott, and Thomas J. Walker. Cornell University Press, 2004.

*How to Know the Grasshoppers, Crickets, Cockroaches and their Allies* by Jacques R. Helfer. Dover Publications, 1987.

*Stick Insects of the Continental United States and Canada: Species and early studies* edited by Chard Arment. Coachwhip Publications, 2006.

## TRUE BUGS

*How to Know the True Bugs* by J. A. Slater and R. M. Baranowski. Pictured Key Nature Series, 1978.

## LACEWINGS, ANTLIONS, DOBSONFLIES, SCORPIONFLIES, AND ALLIES

Lacewing Digital Library—lacewing.tamu.edu

## BEETLES

*A Field Guide and Identification Manual for Florida and Eastern U.S. Tiger Beetles* by Paul M. Choate, Jr. University Press of Florida, 2003.

*A Field Guide to the Tiger Beetles of the United States and Canada: Identification, Natural History, and Distribution of the Cicindelidae* by David L. Pearson, C. Barry Knisley, and Charles J. Kazilek. Oxford University Press, 2006.

*American Beetles, Volume 1: Archostemata, Myxophaga, Adephaga, Polyphaga: Staphyliniformia* by Ross H. Arnett, Jr. and Michael C. Thomas. CRC Press, 2001.

*American Beetles, Volume 2: Polyphaga: Scarabaeoides through Curculionoidea* by Ross H. Arnett, Jr., Michael C. Thomas, Paul E. Skelley, and J. Howard Frank. CRC Press, 2002.

*Beetles of Eastern North America* by Arthur V. Evans. Princeton University Press, 2014.

*Beetles: The Natural History and Diversity of Coleoptera* by Stephen Marshall. A Firefly Book, 2018.

*Field Guide to the Jewel Beetles (Coleoptera: Buprestidae) of Northeastern North America* by Steven M. Paiero, Morgan D. Jackson, Adam Jewiss-Gaines, Troy Kimoto, Bruce D. Gill, and Stephen A. Marshall. University of Guelph, 2012.

*Fireflies, Glow-worms, and Lightning Bugs: Identification and natural history of the fireflies of the eastern and central United States and Canada* by Lynn Frierson Faust. The University of Georgia Press, 2017.

*Host Plants of Leaf Beetle Species Occurring in the United States and Canada* by Shawn M. Clark, Douglas, G. LeDoux, Terry N. Seeno, Edward G. Riley, Arthur J. Gilbert, and James M. Sullivan. Special Publication of the Coleopterists Society, 2004.

*Illustrated Key to the Longhorned Woodboring Beetles of the Eastern United States* by Steven W. Lingafelter. Special Publication of the Coleopterists Society, 2007.

*Peterson Field Guide to Beetles* by Richard E. White. Houghton Mifflin Company, 1983.

*The Dynastine Scarab Beetles of the United States and Canada (Coleoptera: Scarabaeoidea: Dynastinae)* by Brett C. Ratcliffe and Ronald D. Cave. Bulletin of the University of Nebraska State Museum, 2017.

*The Scarabaeoid Beetles of Nebraska* by Brett C. Ratcliffe and M. J. Paulsen. Bulletin of the University of Nebraska State Museum, 2008.

## ■ FLIES

*Flies: The natural history and diversity of Diptera* by Stephen A. Marshall. A Firefly Book, 2012.

*Mosquitoes of the Southeastern United States* by Nathan D. Burkett-Cadena. The University of Alabama Press, 2013.

The Diptera Site—diptera.myspecies.info/

## ▨ BUTTERFLIES AND MOTHS

*A Field Guide to Butterflies of Texas* by Raymond W. Neck. Gulf Publishing Company, 1996.

*A Swift Guide to Butterflies of North America* by Jeffrey Glassberg. A Sunstreak Book, 2012.

*Butterflies of Houston and Southeast Texas* by John Tveten and Gloria Tveten. University of Texas Press, 1996.

*Butterflies of Oklahoma, Kansas, and North Texas* by John M. Dole, Walter B. Gerard, and John M. Nelson. University of Oklahoma Press, 2004.

*Butterflies of the Lower Rio Grande Valley* by Roland H. Wauer. A Spring Creek Press Book, 2004.

*Caterpillars of Eastern North America* by David L. Wagner. Princeton University Press, 2005.

*Finding Butterflies in Texas: A guide to the best sites* by Roland H. Wauer. Spring Creek Press, 2006.

*Kaufman Guide to Butterflies of North America* by Jim P. Brock and Kenn Kaufman. Houghton Mifflin Company, 2003.

*Moths of Western North America* by Jerry A. Powell and Paul A. Opler. University of California Press, 2009.

*Peterson Field Guide to Moths of Northeastern North America* by David Beadle and Seabrooke Leckie. Houghton Mifflin Company, 2012.

*Peterson Field Guide to Moths of Southeastern North America* by Seabrooke Leckie and David Beadle. Houghton Mifflin Company, 2018.

Moth Photographers Group—mothphotographersgroup.msstate.edu
Butterflies and Moths of North America—www.butterfliesandmoths.org

## ANTS, BEES, WASPS, AND SAWFLIES

*Ants of North America: A guide to the genera* by Brian L. Fisher and Stefan P. Cover. University of California Press, 2007.

*Bumble Bees of North America* by Paul Williams, Robbin Thorp, Leif Richardson, and Sheila Colla. Princeton University Press, 2014.

*The Bees in Your Backyard: A guide to North America's bees* by Joseph S. Wilson and Olivia Messinger Carrill. Princeton University Press, 2016.

*Urban Ants of North America and Europe: Identification, biology, and management* by John Klotz, Laurel Hansen, Reiner Pospischil, and Michael Rust. Cornell University Press, 2008.

Phantom Crane Flies
(*Bittocomorpha clavipes*)
mating

# Photographic Credits

All the photos in this book were taken by John and Kendra Abbott with the exception of the following:

**Michael Battenberg**—*Megarhyssa macrurus,* p. 367
**Lee Hoy**—*Dactylotum bicolor,* p. 95
**Jena Johnson**—mantidfly larvae emerging from eggs, p. 161
**Barrett Klein**—illustrations of female *Calopteryx maculata,* p. 51; *Hetaerina titia,* p. 51; *Neoneura amelia,* p. 51; *Argia fumipennis,* p. 53; *Argia immunda,* p. 53; *Argia moesta,* p. 53; *Argia nahuana,* p. 53; *Argia plana,* p. 53; *Argia sedula,* p. 53; *Argia translata,* p. 53; *Argia tibialis,* p. 53; *Enallagma civile,* p. 55; *Enallagma signatum,* p. 55; *Enallagma exsulans,* p. 55; *Ischnura hastata,* p. 55; *Ischnura posita,* p. 55; *Ischnura ramburii,* p. 55; *Telebasis salva,* p. 55
**Greg Lasley**—*Dichromantispa interrupta,* p. 165; *Dryas iulia,* p. 281
**Mike Quinn**—*Anisembia texana,* p. 73; *Triozocera* sp., p. 87
**Seth Patterson**—*Sermyle mexicana,* p. 107
**Nolie Schneider**—*Lepisma saccharina,* p. 43

# Glossary

**abdomen**—third (posterior) division of the insect body that contains the reproductive system and most of the digestive and respiratory systems.

**ametabolous**—a simple type of metamorphosis with the immature stages lacking only genitalia and therefore no change in body form development to the adult other than size.

**anal loop**—foot-shaped or circular cluster of cells in hindwing base of dragonflies (Odonata).

**annulated**—comprised of rings.

**antemedial line**—line that separates the basal and median areas of the forewing in moths (Lepidoptera).

**antenna (*pl.* antennae)**—paired, segmented, sensory appendages, usually arising in front and above on the head.

**anterior**—at or toward the front.

**anterolateral**—at or toward the front and side.

**apex**—usually referring to the distal-most point.

**apical**—at or toward the apex.

**aristate**—type of antennae that bears a specialized bristle or hair-like process (Diptera).

**Auchenorrhyncha**—suborder of Hemiptera characterized by a beak that appears to arise from the lower part of the head; includes cicadas, leafhoppers, spittle bugs, and planthoppers.

**basal**—at or toward the base of the main body or closer to the point of attachment.

**basal line**—dark line cutting across basal section of wing (Lepidoptera).

**basal stalk**—narrowing of wing, where it attaches to thorax, in some damselflies (Odonata).

**bifurcated**—a structure that is divided or forked into two arms.

**bipectinate**—having comb-like teeth on both sides, as in some antennae.

**brochosomes**—intricately structured microscopic granules secreted by leafhoppers and typically found on their body surface and, more rarely, eggs (Hemiptera).

**buccula (*pl.* bucculae)**—small distended area consisting of elevated sclerites or ridges on the ventral part of the head and side of the rostrum in some Hemiptera.

**capitate**—type of antennae that have a distinctive club at tip.

**cercus (*pl.* cerci)**—one of a pair of appendages originating from abdominal segment 11, but usually visible as if on segment 10.

**claviform spot**—a round spot positioned between the orbicular spot and the inner margin on the forewing in some moths (Lepidoptera).

**clavus**—delineated area of the wing in Hemiptera, posterior and lateral to the scutellum.

**clubbed**—referring to antennae with a distinct club at their tip.

**clypeus**—part of the insect head below the frons where the labrum is attached.

**cocoon**—protective silk covering for the pupa in many holometabolous insects.

**collophore**—ventral tube in springtails (Collembola).

**complete metamorphosis**—see holometabolous.

**compound eye**—aggregation of ommatidia, each representing a single facet of the eye.

**convex**—outline or surface curved like the exterior of a circle.

**copula**—the act of mating.

**corium**—elongated, middle portion of heteropteran hemelytron that is usually leathery (Hemiptera).

**cornicle**—paired tubular structures on the abdomen of aphids that discharge defensive lipids and alarm pheromones.

**coxa (*pl.* coxae)**—the basal-part of the leg.

**crossveins**—transverse wing veins that connect the longitudinal veins.

**cubital loop**—area of cubitus formed by joining of $Cu_{1a}$ and $Cu_{1b}$ (Psocodea).

**cubitus (Cu)**—the sixth longitudinal vein in wings.

**cuneus**—distal section of the corium in the heteropteran forewing (Hemiptera).

**detritus**—organic matter produced by decomposition of organisms.

**discoidal cell**—median cell in wing (Psocodea).

**distal**—at or near the furthest end from the attachment of an appendage.

**dorsal**—upper surface.

**dorsoventrally**—referring to the axis joining the dorsal and ventral surfaces.

**ectoparasite**—a parasite that lives externally on and at the expense of another organism (host) which it does not kill.

**elytron (*pl.* elytra)**—modified, hardened, forewing of a beetle that serves to protect the hind wings and abdomen (Coleoptera).

**epaulet**—referring to shoulder area.

**exuviae (*pl.*)**—portion of the integument of a nymph or larva that is shed from the body during the process of molting.

**facet**—individual elements of the compound eye.

**fastigium**—extreme point or front of the vertex (Orthoptera).

**femur (*pl.* femora)**—third, and usually largest, segment (from body) of the leg.

**filament**—a thread-like slender process of uniform diameter.

**filamentous**—long, threadlike antennae.

**foretarsi**—referring to the tarsi on the front pair of legs.

**forewing**—the first pair of wings attaching to the second thoracic segment.

**fovea**—pit or depression.

**frons**—large sclerite, above the clypeus, representing front of head.

**furca (*pl.* furcula)**—springing organ of springtails found on ventral surface of abdomen (Collembola).

**gaster**—swollen part of the abdomen of some Hymenoptera that lies posterior to the petiole (wasp).

**genal comb**—row of strong spines on the lateroventral border of the head in fleas (Siphonaptera).

**geniculate**—strongly elbowed antennae.

**glabrous**—characterized by being smooth and without hair or punctures.

**globular**—spherical in shape.

**gregarious**—referring to insects that congregate or live in communities, but that are not social.

**haltere**—modified hind wing of flies used for balancing in flight (Diptera).

**hemelytron**—forewing of heteropteran true bugs (Hemiptera).

**hemimetabolous**—incomplete development in which the body gradually changes at each molt, with wing buds growing larger.

**Hexapoda**—subphylum of arthropods containing insects.

**holometabolous**—development in which there is a pupal stage between the larval and adult stages.

**humeral angle**—angle at the base of the anterior margin of the wing.

**humerus**—referring to the shoulder.

**hypermetamorphosis**—undergoing a major change in morphology between larval instars.

**hyperparasitoid**—a secondary parasitoid that develops upon another parasite or parasitoid.

**jugum**—paired lateral lobes of the head in heteropteran true bugs (Hemiptera).

**labial palp**—one-to-five segmented paired appendage of the labium.

**labium**—the floor of the mouth, also known as the "lower lip."

**labrum**—the roof of the mouth, also known as the "upper lip."

**lamellate**—antennae with the club formed of closely opposed leaf-like segments.

**larva (*pl.* larvae)**—immature insect after emerging from egg; usually restricted to holometabolous insects.

**leading edge**—anterior margin of wing when in flight.

**littoral zone**—region of a lake lying along the shore.

**mandible**—jaws in insects with biting-chewing mouthparts.

**mating hook**—genital structure in male angel insects (Zoraptera).

**maxilla (*pl.* maxillae)**—second pair of jaws, variously modified.

**maxillary palp**—one- to seven-segmented structure on the maxilla.

**median line**—line that passes through the median area of the forewing, usually between the orbicular and reniform spots, in some moths (Lepidoptera).

**median ridge**—elevated area along the midline.

**mesosoma**—middle of three major body divisions (thorax), but in some Hymenoptera includes the propodeum.

**mesothorax**—second or middle thoracic segment.

**metamorphosis**—change in body form between immature and adult stages in insects.

**metathorax**—third or last thoracic segments.

**metatibial flange**—expanded area of tibia on hind leg in some leaf-footed bugs (Hemiptera: Coreidae).

**middorsal**—middle of upper surface.

**molting**—formation of new cuticle followed by shedding of old cuticle.

**moniliform**—bead-like antennae.

**nodulus**—where $Cu_2$ connects with Anal vein in Psocodea.

**nodus**—indentation near the middle of the anterior margin of the wing in dragonflies and damselflies (Odonata).

**nymph**—an immature insect with gradual metamorphosis (Ametabolous or Hemimetabolous) after emerging from the egg.

**ocellus (*pl.* ocelli)**—a simple eye of adult and nymph insects. Typically three in number and located on the vertex.

**ommatidium (*pl.* ommatidia)**—a single facet of the compound eye.

**omnivorous**—describing organisms that feed on any plant or animal.

**ootheca**—a protective covering for eggs (Blattodea and Mantodea).

**orbicular spot**—a round spot or outline in the inner median part of the forewing of moths (Lepidoptera).

**outer margin**—referring to lateral-most edge.

**ovipositor**—female organ used for laying eggs.

**parasitoid**—a parasite that kills its host.

**parthenogenetic**—development from an unfertilized egg.

**pectinate**—referring to a structure, including antennae, that is comblike.

**pedicel**—second segment of the antenna.

**penultimate**—next to last.

**percussion**—drumming or tapping a structure on the substrate (Plecoptera).

**phytophagous**—organisms that eat plants.

**piercing-sucking**—mouthpart stylets used for piercing animal or plant tissue and sucking up the resultant fluids.

**posterolateral**—referring to the side of the rearmost portion of a structure.

**postmedial line**—line that separates the median area from the subterminal area of the forewing in some moths (Lepidoptera).

**postpetiole**—area of abdomen in aculeate Hymenoptera posterior to petiole.

**preapical claw**—claw anterior to the apex.

**proboscis**—elongated, tubelike, mouthparts.

**pronotum**—upper surface of prothorax.

**propodeum**—in aculeate Hymenoptera, first abdominal segment that is fused with the thorax.

**propupa**—stage in the nymphal development of some thrips and scale insects (Thysanoptera and Hemiptera).

**prosternum**—the anteriormost sternal sclerite between the forelegs.

**prothorax**—first thoracic segment.

**pruinescence**—waxy or powdery covering on some dragonflies and damselflies that exudes from the cuticle and turns the body light blue, gray, or white (Odonata).

**pruinose**—exhibiting pruinescence.

**pterostigma**—pigmented spot near the anterior margin of the fore- and sometimes hind wings.

**pubescence**—clothed in fine, short setae.

**punctate**—referring to a surface that is microscopically pitted.

**punctures**—having pits or small depressions.

**pupa**—the developmental stage between the larva and adult in insects with complete or holometabolous development.

**pupating**—becoming a pupa.

**raptorial**—adapted for capturing prey by grasping.

**reniform spot**—a spot, often kidney-shaped, in the outer median part of the forewing in some moths (Lepidoptera).

**reticulated**—referring to a surface that has a netlike or intermeshed appearance.

**rostrum**—tubelike mouthparts found in some insects.

**scale**—a flattened seta or hair.

**scalloped**—referring to a series of rounded, convex projections forming an ornamental edge.

**scape**—the first segment of the antenna.

**sclerite**—a plate on the body wall surrounded by membrane or sutures.

**scutellum**—posterior portion of the meso- or metanotum, behind the scutum.

**scutum**—middle third of the meso- or metanotum, in front of the scutellum

**secondary genitalia**—set of structures on male dragonflies and damselflies used as an intromittent organ to transfer sperm to the female (Odonata).

**seta (*pl.* setae)**—a hair arising from the cuticle.

**spatulate**—shaped as a spatula; typically rounded or broad at the apex and tapered at the base.

**spermatophore**—an encapsulated package of spermatozoa.

**spine**—an unjointed cuticular extension, often thornlike.

**Sternorrhyncha**—suborder of Hemiptera including psyllids, whiteflies, aphids, scales, and mealybugs.

**sternum**—ventral surface of a segment.

**stigmasac**—enlarged area where $R_1$ separates from R in winged Psocodea.

**striate**—descriptive of surface with numerous fine, parallel lines.

**stylate**—antenna type with a style, or short, cylindrical appendage (Diptera).

**subapical**—referring to the area below or just before the apex.

**subimago**—winged, penultimate instar; subadult (Ephemeroptera).

**submargin**—just within the margin.

**subterminal line**—line of scales often present between the postmedial and terminal lines in some moths (Lepidoptera).

**suture**—external groove that may indicate the fusion of two sclerites.

**tandem**—two individuals, usually male and female, connected, but not by reproductive structures.

**tarsus (*pl.* tarsi)**—last segment of the leg, distal to the tarsus.

**tegmen (*pl.* tegmina)**—leathery, hardened forewing (Orthoptera).

**tergite**—sclerotized, dorsal surface of a segment.

**tergum**—dorsal surface of a segment.

**terminal line**—outermost line on the wings before the fringe in some moths (Lepidoptera).

**thorax**—middle of the three major divisions of the insect body.

**tibia**—fourth leg segment (from the body), following the femur.

**tibiotarsi**—fused tibia and tarsus in some insects.

**transverse**—extending across the surface.

**tremulation**—act of trembling or moving up and down without contacting the substrate beyond the legs.

**truncate**—abruptly ending or cutting off.

**tubercle**—small, rounded protuberance.

**tylus**—distal part of the clypeus or anteclypeal region of the head in heteropteran Hemiptera.

**tympanum (*pl.* tympana)**—structure sensitive to vibration, comprising a membrane, air sac, and specialized sensory organ.

**ventrolateral**—referring to the outer margin of the underside.

**vertex**—top of the head.

**vestigial**—structure or process that is small or degenerate.

# Index

# About the Authors

John and Kendra Abbott are professional nature photographers, educators, and outdoor enthusiasts based in Tuscaloosa, AL. John grew up in Texas, spending most of his life learning about the insects in the state. He has focused on dragonflies and damselflies throughout much of his career and has written three books on these beautiful subjects that contain much of their photography. Kendra is an ecologist and focused on endangered species and conservation issues for much of her career. Both are currently at The University of Alabama where John is Chief Curator and Director of Research and Collections for the UA Museums. Kendra is a Research Associate in the Department of Biological Sciences where she actively conducts research and teaches. They feel lucky to be able to teach and excite others about the amazing biodiversity they have been able to observe through their travels and photography.

Photo by Greg W. Lasley.